W9-DHV-871

TILL

From the Library of

Eric Till

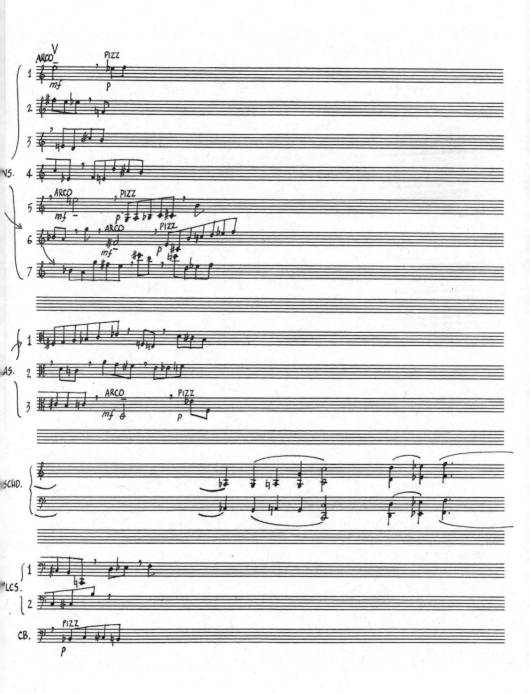

UNHEARD OF

LIFE WRITING SERIES

In the **Life Writing Series,** Wilfrid Laurier University Press publishes life writing and new life-writing criticism and theory in order to promote autobiographical accounts, diaries, letters, and testimonials written and/or told by women and men whose political, literary, or philosophical purposes are central to their lives. The Series features accounts written in English, or translated into English from French or the languages of the First Nations, or any of the languages of immigration to Canada.

From its inception, **Life Writing** has aimed to foreground the stories of those who may never have imagined themselves as writers or as people with lives worthy of being (re)told. Its readership has expanded to include scholars, youth, and avid general readers both in Canada and abroad. The Series hopes to continue its work as a leading publisher of life writing of all kinds, as an imprint that aims for both broad representation and scholarly excellence, and as a tool for both historical and autobiographical research.

As its mandate stipulates, the Series privileges those individuals and communities whose stories may not, under normal circumstances, find a welcoming home with a publisher. **Life Writing** also publishes original theoretical investigations about life writing, as long as they are not limited to one author or text.

Series Editor
Marlene Kadar
Humanities Division, York University

Manuscripts to be sent to
Lisa Quinn, Acquisitions Editor
Wilfrid Laurier University Press
75 University Avenue West
Waterloo, Ontario, Canada N2L 3C5

John Beckwith

UNHEARD OF
Memoirs of a Canadian Composer

WILFRID LAURIER
UNIVERSITY PRESS

We acknowledge the support of the Canada Council for the Arts for our publishing program. We acknowledge the financial support of the Government of Canada through the Canada Book Fund for our publishing activities.

Library and Archives Canada Cataloguing in Publication

Beckwith, John, 1927–
   Unheard of : memoirs of a Canadian composer / John Beckwith.

(Life writing series)
Includes a list of compositions.
Includes bibliographical references and index.
Issued also in electronic formats.
ISBN 978-1-55458-358-4

   1. Beckwith, John, 1927–. 2. Composers—Canada—Biography. I. Title. II. Series: Life writing series

ML410.B397A3 2012   780.92   C2011-905721-2

Electronic monograph.
Issued also in print format.
ISBN 978-1-55458-398-0 (PDF). —ISBN 978-1-55458-385-0 (EPUB)

   1. Beckwith, John, 1927–. 2. Composers—Canada—Biography. I. Title. II. Series: Life writing series (Online)

ML410.B397A3 2012a   780.92   C2011-905722-0

Cover design by Sandra Friesen. Cover photo, by André Leduc, shows John Beckwith in rehearsal, Walter Hall, Toronto, September 2010. Text design by Catharine Bonas-Taylor. Endpapers reproduce pages 47 and 48 from the manuscript score of *Circle, with Tangents*, for harpsichord and thirteen strings (1967).

This book is printed on FSC recycled paper and is certified Ecologo. It is made from 100% post-consumer fibre, processed chlorine free, and manufactured using biogas energy.

Printed in Canada

Every reasonable effort has been made to acquire permission for copyright material used in this text, and to acknowledge all such indebtedness accurately. Any errors and omissions called to the publisher's attention will be corrected in future printings.

Contents

List of Illustrations

List of Music Examples

LIFE, PART I

1

Father

The surname Beckwith is Anglo-Saxon, and it means "beechwood." My father's branch of the family traces back to the emigration of Samuel Beckwith from his birthplace, Pontefract in Yorkshire, to the area near New London, Connecticut, in 1638. His is the first of twenty-five alphabetically listed names of land grantees in the village of Lyme (now Old Lyme), Connecticut. After he died in 1680 or '81, his children and grandchildren continued to live and work in the area. There is a Beckwith Lane and a Beckwith Hill in Old Lyme, and the name was still to be seen on a few rural mailboxes when my son Lawrence and I visited in 1977. Samuel's *great*-grandson John, born at Lyme, seventh son of James Beckwith, emigrated in 1760 (at the mature age of forty-seven) with his wife Jane and their children to Cornwallis, Nova Scotia. He was among the New Englanders who benefited from the cheap settlement offers made by the British on the expulsion of the Acadians at that period. Thus, I may be described as a descendant of "Nova Scotia Yankees." An opportunist rather than a loyalist, this John may have been a prototypical Canadian "survivor": he died in Cornwallis in 1810, aged ninety-seven.

Other John Beckwiths in the family include his son, his great-great-grandson, and his great-great-great-grandson; the last two were respectively my great-grandfather, John Albert Beckwith, and my grandfather, John Leander Beckwith (1856–1934). A colleague of mine at the University of Toronto, the political economist Wilbur Grasham, once sent me a page from a parish minute book in Braintree, England, which he was researching; it contained the following entry dated 6 September 1619:

3

Notice is given us by William Stebbing of a wench intertained at John Beckwiths dwelling on Cursing greene that is supposed to have a greate belly, which the constables have warning to looke affter and to take order to remmove her if they find the report to be true.

A very distant cousin, no doubt. Other remotely or unrelated cognomens include John Christmas Beckwith, the late-eighteenth-century Norwich organist and composer, and the English art historian John Beckwith, with whom I have sometimes been confused in library catalogues. The British army officer Lieutenant Colonel (later Sir) Thomas Sydney Beckwith, one of four Beckwiths found in the *Dictionary of Canadian Biography* (two New Brunswick natives and two British émigrés), was described in a contemporary quotation as "certainly a very clever fellow, but a very odd fish." He served briefly during the War of 1812, but as his *DCB* biography remarks, "his talents do not seem to have been put to the best use in North America"; he died in India.[1]

The most illustrious of Dad's Nova Scotia forebears was named not John but Mayhew. Born in Cornwallis in 1798, great-grandson of the original Nova Scotia Yankee, he was a prosperous merchant, a pillar of the Baptist Church, one of the founders of Acadia University, and member for King's County of the Nova Scotia legislature for twenty-one years. In registering my birth and later at my baptism, my parents gave me the name John Mayhew Beckwith. This was a nice historical touch, but my growing egalitarian and socialist leanings in my early twenties led me to suppress the middle name, and with apparent success: at least, as far as I know, among the few researchers who have probed my career none has ever discovered it. Perhaps today I feel more relaxed and less of an inverse snob about all this; my paternal family background has become for me a matter of interest and curiosity, and not of either pride or shame.

Photos in the Middleton, Nova Scotia, museum show the grim faces of John Albert Beckwith and his wife Rebecca Barnaby. He was born in 1830, eldest of the eleven children born to Mayhew and his wife Eunice Rand, and operated as a farmer and fruit grower and packer in Nictaux. He died in 1900. According to an obituary (1898), Rebecca "engaged in every good work, beloved by all, and left an influence for good that will live while time lasts." No penetrating view of her personality emerges from this. In those days you had to clench your teeth in order to hold the pose during the long photo exposure, so the stern looks of the pair are similarly unenlightening: they may have been a fun-loving couple.[2]

My great-grandparents, John Albert Beckwith and Rebecca Barnaby.

They had seven sons (no daughters); of the six who survived to maturity, one remained in Nova Scotia while the others all "went west" around 1881—among them William (born 1853?), John Leander (born 1856), and Herbert (born 1858)—travelling across the continent on the then-new Great Northern Railroad to seek their fortunes in Oregon. John Leander, according to a memoir by his daughter, had left home at fifteen, apprenticed to a dry-goods dealer in Nictaux, and by the age of twenty-five was operating his own haberdashery business there. After a year or two in Portland, he and his brothers moved to Victoria, British Columbia, where, in the 1887 city directory, he is described as a "manufacturers' agent." The following year he returned to Nova Scotia to claim his bride, Agnes Smith McLeod. My grandparents were married in Berwick, Nova Scotia, on 20 September 1888, and immediately took the journey west to Victoria on another newly opened rail line, the Canadian Pacific Railway.

The McLeods were "planters" on Nova Scotia's south shore. A James McLeod settled in Liverpool, Nova Scotia, in 1760 (the same year that the first Beckwith came to Cornwallis). He emigrated from County Derry, Ireland, a descendant of the MacLeods of Skye. The last point is vital in view of the passionate interest in the Skye connection on the part of some family members, including Grace McLeod Rogers, my father's aunt, and

My great-grandfather, Arthur McLeod (note the barrister's satchel).

Grace McLeod Beckwith, my father's sister and therefore *my* aunt. The original planter is listed as "McLeod"; I remembered that the Rogers cousins spelled the name "MacLeod," and when I asked my aunt about this she said, "Oh, that was Aunt Grace: she liked to put on the dog." Evidently "Mac" was an indication of ancient Scottish ancestry, proud clans, castle battlements—whereas "Mc" evoked a murky past among Irish peat bogs. However, Gordon Rogers, unofficial Rogers family historian, tells me it was Grace's son Arthur W. Rogers who assumed the "Mac."[3]

The Nova Scotia McLeods distinguished themselves in literature and in the law. Arthur McLeod was the author of *The Notary of Grand Pré* (1900). His daughter, my great-aunt Grace, was a productive author (*Nova Scotia Folklore; Tales from the Land of Evangeline*) and a formidable defender of the Scottish connection. She and her sister Agnes were two of five sisters; their father, a Harvard law graduate, served as commissioner for Nova Scotia in Boston. He spent half of the working year there and the other half in Liverpool, where his wife Eunice and daughters resided. An odd arrangement; spousal correspondence included in Gordon Rogers's researches suggests an undercurrent of family tension. He spent his retirement years at Clementsport in the Annapolis Valley. One of the daughters married and settled in Boston. Grace married Wyckoff Rogers, and their four sons all had distinguished careers in law, journalism, and politics.[4]

How did my grandparents meet? A puzzling question, since the Beckwiths lived in the Annapolis/Minas Basin region and the McLeods some distance away in the south coastal region.

My grandfather's business career in Victoria had its ups and downs. In the 1890s the family lived at five different addresses, and John Leander was often "on the road" on behalf of his latest enterprise. He travelled, according to Aunt Grace Beckwith, "taking his samples and getting his orders" as far east as Winnipeg and (in 1898) "even to the Klondike."[5] In the early 1900s he served two or three terms as a city alderman and gained a reputation for public-spiritedness. The Beckwiths moved into a prominent home on Fernwood Road, tokening a certain level of luxury and elegance; the family's Buick touring car was a widely remarked innovation. The family consisted of my grandparents and three children, Harold Arthur (my Dad), born in 1889; Alfred Edward (Uncle Fred), 1894; and Grace, 1901. A fourth child, Kate, born between Dad and Uncle Fred, died in infancy.

In 1912 my grandfather won election as mayor of Victoria. The previous incumbent, for four successive one-year terms, was Alfred J. Morley. In 1910 Morley's victory was extremely close, in a four-candidate race. In January of the following year, when there were three candidates, his more decisive win was questioned, but in a "special election" held in April, the result proved much more definitely in his favour. During the brief but heated election campaign, the *Daily Colonist* had commented obliquely in an editorial (11 January) of the city's misfortune "that certain persons in positions of prominence and certain aspirants to municipal honors display a total lack of every principle of honor," and after the result of the "special" repeat election was announced (8 April) hoped that "the

The Beckwith family, Victoria, circa 1895. Left to right: Agnes Smith McLeod, my grandmother; Alfred (Fred); Harold, my father; John Leander Beckwith, my grandfather.

business of the city will be conducted in a business-like way during the remainder of the year, and that there will be less reason in the future than there has been in the past to talk of one man rule." Voter turnout was slight. In a city of over 40,000 there was only one polling place, with limited hours of access.

John L. Beckwith, "commission merchant," was Morley's sole opponent in January 1912, and won by a slim majority of forty-nine votes. The next year, however, Morley was again a candidate, and the rivalry between the two factions intensified. The *Colonist*'s sympathies were clear: "Mr Beckwith is better fitted than his opponent for the Mayoralty" (editorial, 14 January 1913); at a rally at the Victoria Theatre, "hundreds were turned away," and Beckwith met with a "magnificent reception, his remarks repeatedly interrupted with hearty applause" (16 January). But the following day the election result was headed "Change in the Office of Mayor: A.J. Morley Squeaks In." The former mayor was reinstated for a fifth term on the basis of a five-vote margin over his opponent. The editorial page reduced this to four votes, deplored the small number exercising their franchise, and predicted a recount. Beckwith presumably refused to concede, and within a few weeks a court application by Morley's supporters in the Voters' League "to restrain banks from paying cheques

My grandfather, John Leander Beckwith, as I remember him.

signed by Mayor Beckwith" was reported to have failed (5 February). In lieu of a simple recount, a by-election was held "by order of the court of appeal" on 13 February, in which Morley triumphed by 112 votes. It was the last mayoralty contest for both men; starting in 1914 and throughout the war years, Alexander Stewart held the office repeatedly, several times by acclamation.

My grandfather returned to public service in a lower political key as a school trustee, winning his first two-year term in 1920 and, regularly re-elected, held this position until his death fourteen years later. Although he had little formal schooling, John Leander made education one of his main causes. His three children all attended McGill University. On the school board in the early 1920s he led the campaign to revive Victoria College as a junior-level affiliate of the University of British Columbia, culminating in its establishment at Craigdarroch Castle. The students dedicated their annual, *The Craigdarroch*, to him in 1933 in gratitude.

I find little evidence of music in the Beckwith/McLeod family lore, although education and literature loom large. A photo of the McGill Mandolin Club *circa* 1915 depicts a serious tuxedo-clad ensemble of nine mandolins, two cellos, a flute, and a snare drum. One of the mandolin players is my Uncle Fred. In 1916, midway in his medical studies, he went overseas with the second draft of the McGill siege artillery, transferred to the Royal Navy as a "surgeon probationer" after a few months, and died in a naval hospital in England during the flu epidemic of 1918.[6] Dad was the first family member to learn of his death and said one of the hardest tasks of his life was having to convey the news to his parents. Dad's own war service consisted of singing, playing the piano, and performing monologues in concert parties organized to entertain the troops training in BC. Though of appropriate age, he did not enter the fighting forces.

When my father drew himself up to his full height—for example when emphasizing a point in public speaking—he stood not quite five feet tall. From a childhood bout of poliomyelitis, he had a deformed middle back; the spine was stunted. Often when making such emphases, he would get up on his toes. He was in every sense strong and agile, and his walk was steady and erect; he had no limp. He was keen about sports, and in his youth an avid participant even in games such as basketball where his short stature might have seemed most handicapping. If he found he could not play, he volunteered as a referee. He was a good swimmer.

His deformity was never mentioned in the family. My mother claimed never to have discussed it with him and did not know its cause. It was only after Dad died that my sisters and I learned the background from our Aunt Grace. He contracted polio around the age of nine or ten, and his parents took him to San Francisco to consult a specialist (this was in the late 1890s). The recommended treatment was frequent warm baths and a series of exercises; he may have worn a brace. My grandfather had gymnastic equipment installed in the family garage, and my father followed a rigorous program to develop his chest and limbs.

I was able to amplify my sense of Dad's disability and how he and his family dealt with it in talking with Dr Michael Hutcheon.[7] I showed Dr Hutcheon photos of Dad at various ages from adolescence on, and from these and from my description he identified the spinal condition as kyphoscoliosis—a curvature caused by pre-puberty polio that may be either lateral (side-to-side) or front-to-back. The polio virus arrests nerve and therefore muscle and bone growth in a specific body area: one may find cases where one leg develops and the other does not, or, as with Dad, where the spine is prevented from normal development. Today such conditions are rare, since we have not only a polio vaccine but also sophisticated bone surgery techniques.

The hunchback, or humpback, in literature and drama, is generally depicted as either evil or crazy. One thinks of Richard III ("Crookback

Dick"), Quasimodo, Rumpelstiltskin, Quilp in *The Old Curiosity Shop*, the magician Cipolla in Mann's story *Mario and the Magician*, or, in opera, Rigoletto, Tonio, Alberich. Dad was the opposite—a social personality, a veritable pillar of the community, a leader, and moreover a person of sharp intellect and benign disposition. I have difficulty speaking of his "disability" or "handicap" because it was never acknowledged as such. Not only was his stunted back never referred to in the family circle, I cannot remember any community situation where it was recognized or remarked on in any way. Nor do I remember ever being taunted by schoolmates with "your Dad's a freak" or similar expressions, and it would have felt inappropriate rather than rude to hear him called "little Harold Beckwith." There was nothing either freakish or diminutive about his presence in the family, in his profession, or in the Victoria community as far as I was aware, and I don't think this was because I was especially "sheltered" in my view of him.

(The story has a sort of Canadian-historical parallel. The geologist George Mercer Dawson, 1849–1901, for whom Dawson City in the Yukon was named, played a vigorous leadership role in the development of western and northern Canada despite an early spinal tuberculosis which stunted his growth and deformed his back.)

My father's acceptance in a "normal" social role was skilfully prepared by two women in his life, his mother and my mother. I never knew his mother; she died one month before I was born. Obviously during his childhood and youth she nourished his sense of his own worth and helped him develop a positive mental outlook. Adolescence was more of an upheaval for him than for most boys, and somewhere there arose a rumour that he considered suicide at that time. No doubt both his parents showed concern, love, and support to carry him through, if indeed there was such a crisis. He attended Boys' Central School and later Victoria High School, and made good academic progress. In a photo of a Victoria High School production of *She Stoops to Conquer*,[8] he appears as Tony Lumpkin; this was a cherished outlet for his sense of comedy. The family attended Centennial Baptist Church, where at age thirteen or so Dad "took the pledge." He remained a lifelong teetotaller.

Dad was enrolled in Victoria College in 1907–8 and 1908–9; the institution had been established only in 1906. At that time the only post-secondary institution in British Columbia, it offered a two-year liberal-arts program affiliated with McGill University, Montreal. Classes were held in a wing of the Central School. After a brief hiatus during the war years, a new affiliation was set up, with the then-new University of British

Columbia in Vancouver; my grandfather's role in that phase of the College's history has already been noted. Not until the 1960s did the program expand into the present University of Victoria. Peter Smith's history of UVic reproduces an archival photo of Dad and his classmates.[9]

In 1910–11 Dad was an undergraduate at McGill. His nickname was "Becky"; he played lacrosse and basketball on college teams, and sang baritone in the college glee club. Stephen Leacock was one of his professors. At his graduation, he moved to Toronto, lived in a rooming house at 46 Dundonald Street, took the law course at Osgoode Hall,[10] articled with the Wellington Street East firm of Beatty, Blackstock, Fasken, Howard, and Chadwick, and was called to the Ontario Bar in 1914.[11] It seems not to have been his intention to practise in either Quebec or Ontario; he returned to Victoria and hung up a shingle in his law office, on 1 August 1914, a fateful few days before the onset of the Great War. His parents clearly helped him get started, but before long he was involved in productive partnerships and was becoming known for his work in numerous community activities. He was a natural joiner, and his participation often led to a stint as president of whatever group he happened to join. His legal partners included at various times John Clay, Marshall Gordon, Herbert Davey (later a justice of the BC Supreme Court), Alan Baker, and Ian Horne. Some of the organizations in which he was active: the Gyro Club[12] (founding president), the Native Sons of British Columbia Post No. 1[13] (secretary), the Arion Male Voice Choir, the Victoria Musical Festival Association (president), the Clan McLeod Society, and the Victoria Lawn Bowling Club (president). He developed skill as a debater and speaker, and at one period led classes in public speaking under YMCA auspices.

Politically in his youth he was a Conservative like his father before him. But in the mid-1930s, partly owing to the influence of Herbert Davey, he switched to the Liberal Party. He became an admirer of Mackenzie King and regularly campaigned on behalf of Liberal candidates, for example helping to manage the successful election bid of the local member of Parliament, Robert Mayhew.

His legal career reached its most active peak in the Depression years, and he never became wealthy from his work. At the time of his retirement, his young partner Ian Horne said he should have been charging for his services at a higher rate. In the 1930s, payment was often in goods rather than cash—a dozen eggs, a box of apples, a sack of potatoes, once (I remember) a used typewriter. At the start of the Second World War, he received a major contract with the federal government to negotiate expropriations of property in connection with the expansion of the airport at

Patricia Bay. The assignment demanded not only legal know-how but speed, and Dad was commended for his handling of it. I had my first experience of office routine, and my first indications of the esteem with which his clients regarded him, when at age thirteen I was brought in as summer office help. My responsibilities included filing and land-office searches.

The other special legal role Dad became known for was that of labour conciliator: he was a good listener and knew how to keep his cool. Other than that, through most of his working days he seems not to have specialized—handling wills, divorces, financial disputes, and whatever other tasks in a small city came his way as either a barrister arguing a court case or a solicitor writing cogent and persuasive letters. He had a deep love of language and a gift for verbal expression. Some members of the profession still recall his invention of "Beckwith's Annotations." These were the annual changes in the provincial statutes, printed on gummed paper, which he sold by subscription to his colleagues to help them keep their law books up to date. Though a tireless worker ("I have to pull my weight," he responded when my mother in later years tried to get him to ease up) and well regarded by his colleagues, he was always passed over when the annual King's Counsel appointments were handed out (a professional honour widely regarded as a political plum). He claimed this did not upset him; but I later came to think that it did.

I have vivid, if imperfect, memories of two cases he argued. In one, he successfully represented a school principal in a suit for wrongful dismissal. The man had been an election candidate for the Canadian Commonwealth Federation (the CCF, forerunner of the New Democratic Party), and the trustees who fired him, Dad proved, had been prejudiced by his leftist sympathies. The other situation was the defence of an Aboriginal youth accused of murder, where Dad was able to persuade a degree of leniency. I was a spectator of a court case of his only once: his competence and his polished and resonant speaking style were no surprise to me, though I reflected they might have been to others. At home he seldom shared his work experiences, and I suppose the periods of summer office employment and the occasional glimpse of his court activities were meant to acquaint me with a pattern of life that might be my own in the future. He discussed the appeal of the law with me now and then, and it was clear I could inherit his practice if I chose that direction as my career. It was not in his nature to insist, or to present barriers when later I told him such was not my inclination; he was disappointed, I feel sure, but characteristically he never said so.[14] He supported my music studies and took a genuine interest in piano pieces I was practising and in my fledgling efforts at composing. If he had further disappointments in my development, they concerned my clumsiness and lack of athletic ability. He spent a year or more building a beautiful sailboat in our basement, and, while I admired the careful work, I was not only lazy about helping (as he wanted me to) but awkward in taking my first turn at sailing it when it was finished (I capsized the thing). There were many occasions when "he never said so": it was Dad's habit to keep contrary opinions to himself. If he expressed anger, his brief outburst would be followed by an apology for having "spoken sharply" (as he put it). The most severe expletive I ever heard from him was "Rats!" He was no prude, certainly, but rather a person for whom discipline and control were of supreme importance.

He and Mother were clearly thrilled to be parents. Dad conveyed his fatherly precepts mostly through example rather than verbally. Central was to recognize the feelings of others. In action the watchwords were control and deliberateness, a reminder I constantly needed in my bouncy and show-off early years.

Dad's recitation repertoire included the "by gar" dialect verses of Drummond as well as "Cohen on the Telephone," both of which would be rejected today as ethnic putdowns. He would have been surprised if told they represented intolerance. He was not an intolerant person, but conformed to the restrictiveness and stratification of Victoria society, conscious of the Songhees reserve across the harbour, the Japanese tea gardens along the Gorge, and the vibrancy of Chinatown, in all of which he had client dealings.

Our family vacations in the 1930s ventured gradually farther and farther from Victoria. First of all, a cottage by the beach at Cordova Bay, now a Victoria suburb but at that time still a wilderness area. Later, another cottage at Vesuvius Bay on Salt Spring Island, with fascinating sandstone caves and an orchard of yellow-transparent apples from which we invariably developed stomach ache. Later still, a more primitive cottage at Kye Bay, north of Comox (though none of the other locations had either electricity or running water), where the sandbar extended half a mile and the water at high tide was therefore unusually warm for swimming. Gathered round the evening bonfire, we nearly always had a singsong, in which Dad would be the leader. The repertoire comes back to me: First World War songs, English and a few US pop songs, Harry Lauder songs (Lauder had included Victoria in his tours of Canada in the 1920s), no drinking songs except "A Tavern in the Town," no patriotic or religious songs except perhaps a spiritual or two ("Swing Low, Sweet Chariot").

a

b

c

Dad, (a) age ten, (b) the McGill graduate, 1911, and (c) in law practice in Victoria circa 1940.

Dredging these titles from the depths of memory, I find I can reproduce the tunes and most of the lyrics:

Keep the Home Fires Burning	Moonlight Bay
Tipperary	Shine On, Harvest Moon
Let Me Call You Sweetheart	In the Good Old Summertime
Daisy, Daisy	All the Nice Girls Love a Sailor
Clementine	Old Grey Bonnet
Roaming in the Gloaming	By the Light of the Silvery Moon

There was the usual quota of silly songs. In "I Wish I Was a Fish" (to the tune of "A-Hunting We Will Go"), the leader (Dad) sang each verse straight, and then invited the chorus to repeat it with a lisp. The second verse was "I Wish I Was a Ship." The third verse went as follows:

I wish I wasn't a simp
I wish I wasn't a simp
I'd sing a song that made some sense
I wish I wasn't a simp

It really was as dumb as it sounds, but at the end Dad would have us in fits.

Driving to Kye Bay in our 1928 Pontiac was an all-day adventure, though the trip can be made these days in three hours. The Malahat climb combined with the load of luggage would likely result in a rest stop while the radiator cooled down. Dad, at the wheel, would regale us with a stream of excerpts from his Gilbert and Sullivan repertoire: his memory ran to not only the famous numbers from *Pinafore*, *Mikado*, and *Pirates* but also rarer songs like that of Wells from *The Sorcerer*.

Hilarious, innocent fun in such holiday moments was a mark of home gatherings as well. Dad was always a central performer in our bouts of charades. In Victoria we pronounced it in the French manner, and instead of playing it in mime fashion we divided into teams and improvised little spoken scenes to illustrate each syllable of the mystery word, followed by the whole word. Teetotal Dad was especially effective in drunk impersonations. My parents could sometimes be persuaded to play a duet on the piano, their signature tune being "Bright as a Button Polka," which they treated as deadpan burlesque.

But they also had a keen appreciation of serious music, and treated me and my sisters to concerts by local artists and by the many outstanding visiting performers who played the Royal Theatre more often then than they do today. Among programs I have preserved from my childhood and adolescence are recitals by Marian Anderson, Richard Tauber, Amelita Galli-Curci, Richard Crooks, Mischa Elman, Yehudi Menuhin, Josef Hofmann, Arthur Rubinstein, the duo-pianists Vronsky and Babin, the Don Cossack Chorus, and the Salvatore Baccaloni company (in an abridged *Barber of Seville*). In some seasons, film personalities were among the artists who appeared (Nelson Eddy, Allan Jones). The events were a stimulus and more often than not a real thrill: our parents were intent on sharing with us their enjoyment of the finest in music.

Where did Dad's musicality come from? He studied piano to a fairly advanced point, and though I was never able to verify that he had formal voice training, in his youth he performed as a soloist, and always demonstrated an assured vocal production and a handy sight-reading ability. I have his copy of the Schirmer *Operatic Anthology*, volume 4.[15] Alongside Valentin's "Even Bravest Heart" from *Faust* there is a note in Mother's hand: "Sung by H.A.B. at opening of Capitol Theatre, Victoria. M.A.D. in audience heard a man behind say: 'He's good!' 1921." (My parents were married the following year.)[16] The Arion Club, one of the oldest choral organizations in Canada, remained an active performing group in 2011. A 1933 photo of the Club, reproduced in Dale McIntosh's *History of Music in British Columbia*, shows Dad in the second row from the back, his head just visible.[17] One of my family souvenirs is the thick wooden baton with which Dad conducted, for a short period in the 1920s, the Fairfield Methodist (later United) Church choir.

During my growing-up years Dad was a non-churchgoer. Having been raised in a strict Baptist household, he quoted the Bible frequently: "Much learning doth make thee mad" (Acts); "A soft answer turneth away wrath" (Proverbs). But he described himself as a fatalist. His religious thoughts and attitudes were practically never revealed in family conversations. Mother attended Anglican churches, but asked a Baptist minister to read Dad's funeral service.

Dad was neither an avid reader nor a linguist, but he had an extraordinarily precise feeling for language and speech. For him, it was unacceptable usage to say "it looks like it's going to rain." Dad would correct us: "looks *as if* ..." "Like" was an adjective or a preposition, but not a conjunction. In the late twentieth century this distinction broke down, and the given sentence would be considered okay by many, perhaps most, writers. Dad would insist on the difference between "due" and "owing," another largely ignored nicety of usage. In the biblical phrase mentioned above, he pronounced "wrath" to rhyme with "cloth," rather than with "bath." "Clerk," in a retention of English legal pronunciation, rhymed with "dark," rather than with "jerk"; "aunt" with "daunt," not "rant" (is that from *New* England, by way of Nova Scotia?); "attorney" with "corny," not "journey." Dad was in good health all through his thirties and forties—that is, the years when we were growing up. His hearing started to deteriorate when he was about fifty; this was judged at the time to be the result of problems with extraction of a wisdom tooth (I am told such a diagnosis is doubtful and there would have been other causes). Eventually he adopted a rather cumbersome hearing aid, similar to the one used with comic effect by Charles Coburn in the Carole Lombard–James Stewart movie *Made for Each Other* (1939). He continued to lead a busy professional and social life. A letter of 10 July 1950 expresses pleasure over his newly established partnership with Ian Horne and mentions that he has been in Vancouver as chair of a Board of Conciliation in connection with a railway dispute. (In my student years in Toronto and Paris he wrote me far less regularly than Mother did, but always deliberately and warmly.)

In his early fifties Dad began to show symptoms of Parkinson's disease. This is an exceptionally early age for such an occurrence. It would not have been connected causally to his early polio and the resulting

Dad in the mid-1950s.

kyphoscoliosis. Available Parkinson's treatments in the 1940s and '50s were limited to medications delaying the progress of the disease or offering short-term control of typical effects such as the tremor, whereas more effective procedures have been developed since.

In the mid-1950s he suffered a mental breakdown. The growing deafness and the knowledge that the direction of the Parkinson's affliction was not reversible made his burden a heavy one. He had years of a happy marriage and the enjoyment of his children, and had the satisfaction of knowing that his clients and associates appreciated his professional efforts. He took great pleasure in his regular lawn bowling matches and continued to sing and attend musical events. But as he faced his body's rebellion, he also faced professional retirement and the flight from the family nest of his youngest child. The mental crisis and the ensuing (again, unusually early) decline into senile dementia had psychological causes, including depression. *Sup*pression, of disappointment and even of anger, was a technique he learned for dealing with the extraordinary demands life imposed on him. He certainly dealt with them superbly: but here, it seems, was the toll. By mid-1953 Mother was unable to cope with caring for him, and he became for two or three years a patient in Essondale, the provincial mental hospital near New Westminster. His humour and rationality had disappeared, and he would pace up and down enacting imaginary courtroom scenes, bowing now and then to a judge no one else could see. In 1958, when I spent the summer in Victoria, he was in a nursing home there. I visited him regularly but was not always able to get him to recognize me, let alone converse. He died that fall. Rev. G.R. Easter, who conducted his funeral, said in a letter to me: "No one would wish him back to be as he was of recent years. He was surely a courageous soul."

2

Mother

In the same year, 1977, as my visit to the Beckwith ancestral haunts of Old Lyme, Connecticut, Grace Dunn, my mother's English cousin, paid me a visit in Toronto. The previous year had seen the first Parti Québécois victory in the Quebec provincial election, and Ms Dunn said: "John, what is all this about Quebec? They don't seem to like us." It was difficult to persuade her that both francophones and anglophones in Canada considered themselves Canadians and that there was no longer any strong feeling of "we/us" bonding the anglophones to their long-ago imperial motherland.

Ms Dunn lived her whole life (into her early nineties) in the small Hertfordshire village of High Wych, serving the local county family, the Buxtons, and doing volunteer work for the local Anglican church. The church is not old as English churches go; it was constructed in the early nineteenth century in the religious upsurge following Waterloo. High Wych is a short distance from Cambridge, and only about an hour's journey by car from London, but Ms Dunn travelled seldom. Her two or three trips to Canada were visits to her brothers and their families. The churchyard has markers on the graves of her parents and other close relatives.

Two of her uncles had emigrated to Canada in the 1880s—George Ironside Dunn (born 8 October 1863) and Thomas Ironside Dunn. A generation later, two of her brothers did the same. The recurrent middle name "Ironside" suggests a seventeenth-century connection to the followers of Cromwell. Sarah Dunn, my great-grandmother, was born Sarah Bunyan and evidently claimed descent from the author of *Pilgrim's Progress*, John Bunyan. The Dunn brothers found employment in Winnipeg, and George was married there, it seems only briefly; details of this episode, and the fate

The Dunn family, Victoria, circa 1909. Left to right: Bob; Bessie; George Ironside Dunn, my grandfather; Agnes; Mary Elizabeth Richardson, my grandmother; Margaret, my mother.

of Mary Jane Alexander, his wife, never formed part of the family story. In a sad recurrence of a familiar Victorian experience, she died of consumption on 31 March 1894, aged twenty-eight, having survived their infant son by only about six weeks.[1] George Dunn returned to England and married Mary Richardson at Tunbridge Wells on 17 June 1896, following which the two of them—my future grandparents—sailed back to Canada and travelled by rail across the country to Victoria. They welcomed their first child, Margaret Alice, on 2 November 1898, and in fairly orderly fashion three more: Robert George ("Bob"), 1900, Mary Elizabeth ("Bess" or "Bessie"), 1902, and Agnes Emily, 1906, who being the youngest was called "Babes."

Like Dad's parents, my mother's parents were mature people in their early thirties when they married. On the evidence, they were resourceful and hard-working. My grandmother's family, the Richardsons, like the Dunns, were small-town English: she was born (31 December 1863, eldest of thirteen children) in the village of Catsfield, Sussex, where her father was the local constable. One of her brothers, Charles (Uncle Charley) emigrated to Canada and farmed in the Fraser Valley. At the time of her marriage she was a lady's companion, and my mother was named "Margaret Alice" after her well-to-do employer, Margaret Alice Rogers—perhaps in expectation of an endowment; if so, it never came.

George I. Dunn seems to have been an entrepreneur of the same type as John L. Beckwith, though I imagine him as a less aggressive, less ambitious personality. At the time of Mother's birth, he was manager of a travellers' hotel, the Occidental, on lower Johnson Street. In later days that part of Victoria became a rough waterfront district and during the Second World War was the locale of several brothels: Mother was always circumspect therefore in describing her earliest family home. Subsequently the Dunns moved to a house on Pembroke Street and then to a larger house on Fernwood Road, just a few blocks north of the Beckwiths. Their father was now running a classy tobacconist shop at 1116 Government Street for the Vancouver owner, E.A. Morris. The elegant storefront still survives, and the name "Morris" has been retained.

I picture Mother in her growing years as brainy and athletic. Tall and long-legged, she excelled at both grass hockey and basketball. At George Jay School her principal was Henry B. MacLean, later a leading educator in British Columbia and initiator of the MacLean Method of handwriting, which was still taught in BC schools when I was a boy. In 1970 in response to congratulations on his eighty-seventh birthday, he wrote to "My dear lovely Margaret," recalling her as "a dear young girl ... seated at the Eastern part of Division 1 classroom, and ALWAYS an inspiration to me as teacher and friend." He enclosed a copy of a letter which her father wrote in 1912 thanking him "for the kind and personal interest you have taken in Margaret's welfare." George I. Dunn's note, demonstrating spectacular penmanship, adds: "Although a certain amount of credit is due her for the good showing she has made, far more is due to the teachers (and to yourself personally) ... I trust Sir that Margaret may look back in after years upon this period with pleasant remembrances and that she may prove herself worthy of having received such tuition." If the thought crossed his mind that she would make a good teacher, his insights were correct. She evidently responded to the appeal of romantic poetry, judging from the quotations (Wordsworth, Browning, Tennyson) she would effortlessly produce in later life, and to music: she learned to play the piano[2] and in adult years sang with a rich alto voice (in choirs, not as a soloist).

In the summer of 1913, my grandmother took all four children across Canada and across the ocean to visit the English relatives. The venture bespeaks a fair state of affluence for the family at that time. Mother kept

*My grandmother, Mary Elizabeth (Richardson) Dunn,
as I remember her.*

a travel diary. It was a memorable trip for her, not only for the contact with uncles, aunts, and cousins who had been known only by name, but also for the sense of historic upheavals in the country: during one of the suffragette demonstrations in London, my grandmother had her umbrella searched by the police. It was a change from quiet colonial Victoria.

Shortly afterwards, the Great War broke out, and many Victoria families sent male members overseas, including fellow students of Mother's from Victoria High School—among them Fred Beckwith, Spencer Dee, Ray Parfitt, and Kingsley Terry. Some returned; others, including Dad's younger brother, did not. On graduation, at seventeen, Mother took a normal-school course and was soon engaged (1916–17) as a substitute or "supply teacher." It was a low-paid apprenticeship; she was not yet old enough for a regular appointment. In one stint, for two weeks in the middle of an unusually cold January, she took charge of the one-room Glenore School, near Duncan, with twenty pupils in all grades; mornings, she trudged through snow to arrive before the children and start the stove.[3]

But a year later she was assigned to Willows School in Oak Bay, then a Victoria suburb. On her father's early death (in 1919, from cancer), she was in effect promoted to head of the family.

Her mother had two significant changes in her life around that time, perhaps as a result of her early widowhood. The Dunns were low-church Anglican, but after George Dunn died my grandmother ("Gran") became experimental in her faith, attending evangelical meetings and even reading Christian Science. The other change was physical: she developed cataracts, but the Christian Science studies persuaded her to refuse eye surgery and she became totally blind. Dad, who was courting her daughter, offered to pay the costs, but she would have none of it. In her later years, she ran her own household, cooking all her own meals and chopping her own kindling, and learned "modern" skills such as operating the radio and the dial telephone, but was dependent on others for help outside her home. She never learned Braille, but regular volunteers would come and read to her—my older sister recalls often reading to her from the works of Mary Baker Eddy. She struck me in childhood as a bright and cheerful person; she enjoyed all the songs and charade games as a sightless "onlooker" and created an atmosphere of affection for us children. She died in 1939.

Mother's first full-time teaching appointment, at Willows School, lasted five years, from 1917 to 1922. The original school of 1910 was a converted farmhouse, to which ancillary buildings were added, replaced by a larger and more permanent brick school in 1920. She had charge of a class of forty children in grades two and three. A photo shows the pupils rigidly at attention at their desks, hands behind their backs; another photo shows the teaching staff of six young women teachers with principal William Hoadley.[4] Among her fellow teachers, Marjorie McGillivray ("Gilly") became a close friend. Mother's salary was fifty dollars a month. By convention, female teachers resigned when they married.[5]

If it is a mystery, at this distance in time, how my Beckwith grandparents or my Dunn grandparents actually met, as to my parents the circumstances are clearer. The families not only lived mere blocks apart on Fernwood Road, but also summered in neighbouring cottages at Cordova Bay. A legendary scene takes place at the twilight campfire. Babes, Mother's youngest sibling, has suffered a splinter, and Harold Beckwith quietly calms her and removes it. Mother is impressed by his mixture of authority and sensitivity. For his part, it seems he was concerned with the emergency situation rather than with trying to impress her; but impress her he did. His baritone solo at the Capitol Theatre opening was further persuasion, as already mentioned.[6] There were dates—notably canoeing excursions along the Gorge. In one of these he proposed marriage, setting out as a reasonable debater his qualifications (health, solvency) and asking her to think it over.

The only unkind comment about my parents' relationship I am aware of I learned second-hand: one of her former classmates from Victoria High is said to have remarked that marrying Harold Beckwith was "the sort of thing Margaret Dunn would do"—meaning that it was offbeat or eccentric. But it evidently did not strike the families that way. Often recounted in later years was the reaction of Aunt Nan, Uncle Tom's (second) wife, an American from Parkersburg, West Virginia, known for a brashness that contrasted to the general Anglo-Canadian reserve. "Do you love him, Margaret?" "Yes." "Well then—go to it!"

The wedding took place on 3 August 1922 in St Barnabas's Church, then located on Quadra Street. Under the headline "Popular Victoria Couple Married," the *Daily Colonist* devoted nine paragraphs to the "unusually pretty wedding." "The church," we learn, "was filled to overflowing," and the reception at the Dunns' residence "was attended by about one hundred and fifty guests. A blinding rain of confetti showered upon the happy pair as they set out by motor for a honeymoon trip of the Island."[7] A wry running gag of Dad's, concerning the date, was, "no, the *other* war started on the 4th." Their relationship was not free of disagreements, but it was certainly no "war." In a favourite malapropism, he would refer to their "animosity" rather than "anniversary."

Domestic life in the 1920s and early '30s for my parents consisted of caring for a growing family, cherishing a wide circle of friends, and cultivating a small garden in their rented bungalow in Fairfield. My sister Jean was born in 1923; a couple of years after that, Mother had a miscarriage; I came along in 1927, my younger sister Sheila in 1930. Money was tight, but we had a regular maid to assist with household chores, meals, and the children. It was only later, at the height of the Great Depression, that I heard Mother pronounce the classic bourgeois comment to a neighbour, "You can't get good help these days." The maid, though paid a pittance, was certainly good; she also accompanied us on our summer vacations. But help, whether good or not, became less essential as we grew up and took more responsibility in the family unit. Dispensing with the maid, we had a succession of part-time cleaning women, but otherwise Mother attended to most of the household duties herself.

Like Dad, she participated in a chorus: in her case, the Victoria Ladies' Choir, whose director, Ira Dilworth, was an inspirational leader. Teacher

My parents' wedding photo, 3 August 1922.

of English and later principal of Victoria High School, he eventually left Victoria for an executive position with the CBC but retained some of his local ties, exemplified in his work as Emily Carr's literary executor. It was partly through Dilworth that Mother learned of Carr and her remarkably individualistic paintings, though she had sent me in early childhood to the kindergarten operated by a sister, Alice Carr. Mother used to recall that some time around 1930 she viewed an exhibition of Carr's work in a wing of the Crystal Gardens. Carr was there, but, perhaps symbolizing the artist's ostracism by the community, Mother was the only visitor. The paintings impressed her deeply, and she considered buying one, but wondered if she could live with its powerful images. The prices of the canvases seem now ridiculously low—she could have had the one she fancied for something like thirty dollars—but another reason for hesitating was that she could scarcely afford it.

Local history became an enthusiasm for her. She and Dad were friends and followers of W. Kaye Lamb, the historian and provincial archivist, later founder of the National Archives in Ottawa. She joined the Native Daughters of British Columbia Post No. 3 and in 1933 served a term as "Grand Factor" or president.[8] One of the society's projects was the preservation of historic buildings, and Mother's favourite was the Old Craigflower Schoolhouse. This one-room clapboard structure had been built by the Scottish pioneers of the Craigflower settlement in the 1850s, and it was now transformed into a museum illustrating the careers of the pioneer families. Mother volunteered many hours to its development and loved showing visitors around.

When we outgrew the Fairfield bungalow, we moved across town to a large rented house at the top of Smith's Hill. This rocky rise no longer bears the name, and the surrounding area has been subdivided and built up unrecognizably. There is a small park now where the house used to be. In the early 1930s it stood in mostly uncultivated grounds of close to an acre (oaks, underbrush, many wildflowers). Mother's energy ran to raising chickens and rabbits; Dad put his foot down when a goat was proposed. Part of her motive was procreational instruction for us little ones. Just down the hill was the temple of the local Sikh community, and, also as an instructional venture, Mother took us to one of their festival ceremonies: one fundamental we learned was to take off our shoes at the door.

On J.L. Beckwith's death, there was a small legacy, and my parents could contemplate building a home of their own. In the mid-30s you could build a four-bedroom architect-designed house for under $8,000 (with a mortgage at 0.5 percent!). The location in Oak Bay, Oliver Street, was a pleasant residential street, and though it had no view to boast of, the ocean was only half a dozen blocks away in two directions, south and east. Dad and Mother took pride in developing a lovely garden: fruit trees, berry vines, gladioli and roses, and a small "natural" plot where wild lilies would appear every spring.

Mother threw herself into activities, most of them enlargements of her role as parent. She organized a rhythm band, held on Saturdays in our living room. The neighbourhood children were given miniature percussion instruments—cymbals, triangles, drums, clappers, sticks—and would march or dance while Barbara Fraser, the Ladies' Choir accompanist, played the piano. Both my parents helped behind the scenes in the running of the annual music competition festival and, among other duties, hosted receptions in our home in honour of the festival adjudicators, distinguished musicians from the UK such as Harold Samuel, Steuart Wilson, Harry Plunkett Greene, Sir Hugh Roberton, Arthur Benjamin, and Harold Darke.

Our school experience was, Mother felt, unimaginative. Reading about the parent-teacher movement in the United States, she raised with other parents the possibility of forming such a group in Oak Bay and was surprised when the local principal poured cold water on the idea. She and her friends went ahead anyway. The Monterey Parent-Teachers' Association held its first meetings during 1939–40.

The principals of both local schools were British émigrés, F.G. Dexter at Monterey School (elementary) and D.H. Hartness at Oak Bay High. (A decade or so later, the boundary between Victoria city and the district of Oak Bay was aptly nicknamed "the Tweed Curtain.") The board of school trustees consisted also of male Brits who regarded managing public education as a sort of white man's burden and re-elected one another annually by acclamation. Not only a group of fellow parents but also several teachers in the system agreed with Mother that the school programs needed modernizing and that the "family compact" deserved to be challenged. Accordingly, in 1942 she became a candidate in the first school board election to have been called in many years. She addressed meetings, formed a committee to mount a phone campaign, distributed posters bearing her photo, and, on voting day, stimulated everyone to "get out the vote." She of course topped the poll, and the board admitted its first woman member and, perhaps, its first Canadian accent.

Her political life may have begun in a mood of tension, but it was not long before she earned acceptance and wide respect for her obvious dedication, awareness of educational trends, and willingness to work hard. She was re-elected to the Oak Bay board, and after that to the amalgamated Greater Victoria board for ten years (1943 to 1953). Her service as a trustee and as an executive in the parent-teacher association brought her into contact with officials and activists in other parts of the province. In 1948 she served a term as president of the BC School Trustees' Association and was later named a life member. There was constant travel and organizational work, on which she thrived. Dad was proud of her. But her official services never had a salary attached: compensation to elected officials was some years in the future. Mother did not find this especially unfair, but she once said, "If only they'd pay the *phone bills*."

In her middle years she was a force to be reckoned with—a bundle of energy, enthusiasm, and humour. Her laugh, at her own expense as often

*Mother's campaign photo in her first successful
run for school trustee, 1943.*

as not, sometimes became uncontrollable, ending in tears of hilarity. Her sneeze was heavily vocalized, a signature sound. When photographing a group of family, friends, or colleagues, with a large folding camera, she stood like an artist before an easel. A dip in the cool Pacific became a ritual of adjusting her body to the temperature in slow stages, first splashing her arms and neck; the final plunge, always backwards, would be accompanied by theatrical screams from her and loud applause from the family. A possible remnant of an English family trait was her habit of standing with her back to an open fire rubbing her bottom. "Fiddlesticks!" was a frequent expletive, of nineteenth-century English derivation, as was her habit of referring to us as "young Turks," a term no doubt used by her forebears since the 1890s, if not since the Crimean War years. Though liberal in principle, and a stickler for fair play, she was readier than Dad, I reflect, to acknowledge a stratification in local society: when the Chinese vegetable vendor came up the street with his cart of wares, she would address him in pidgin English, "Hello, Jim, you gottee nicee lettuce?" (All Chinese were "Jim.")[9] This racist streak came and went: she showed affection for our Japanese cleaning woman, used no special diction or tone of condescension, and called her by her name, Kinu.

After Dilworth's departure (*circa* 1934), his choir disbanded[10] and Mother joined the choir of Christ Church Cathedral under the dynamic Stanley Bulley. I became a chorister in the same choir, and on the formation of Bulley's Victoria Choral Union, Mother and I both sang with that group and experienced some of the highlights of the Western choral/orchestral repertoire (Bach, Handel, Mozart, and Brahms, as well as, of course, Parry and Vaughan Williams).

Her Anglicanism might be called selective. To Dean Spencer Elliott, she cited the words of the General Confession—"we have left undone those things which we ought to have done, and we have done those things which we ought not to have done, *and there is no health in us*"—and asked him, "Do I *have* to say that last part?" However challenged he may have felt by such questions, Elliott respected both my parents. He called on Dad for legal advice now and then and persuaded Mother to serve on a crucial citizens' committee in the early war years. The influx of service personnel, especially in the Esquimalt Naval Station, had created an alarming increase in venereal disease, and the committee, representing health workers, politicians, and social and church agencies, was asked to recommend ways to deal with the problem. Her curious children learned a new word, "brothel." Mother defined it for us as "a place where men go for excitement."

One of Mother's innovations was the Oak Bay summer playground program. It was then a fresh and untried idea to give children some organized activities—games, performances, craftwork—in the vacation months, equivalent to what later came to be called a day camp. She formed volunteer teams to supervise the hired instructors, commandeered local park space, and persuaded municipal authorities and local businesses to help out. We were admonished not to discard Popsicle sticks or toilet-paper rolls, but to collect them for the art classes. Mother found local police constables on their rounds were willing to deliver such bundles of equipment to the various park locations and she became notorious for calling on their help. She once alarmed the neighbours by arriving home after a delivery trip in the sidecar of a police motorbike. The playground planning was work she especially enjoyed, and her initiative earned her a lot of gratitude.

In late summer every year, whether at home or at a holiday cottage, Mother had her annual orgy of blackberry picking. There is no other way to describe this obsession. She could sniff out the location of woodland wild berry patches and had a knack for exploring them to their depths. We energetic youngsters would give up after an hour or two, but Mother would often stick at it all day and return with bushels of fruit, undeterred by torn clothes, insect bites, sunburn, or scratches. It was her favourite way of communing with the earth.

Close affection, between spouses and between parents and children, was central to Mother's view of life. "He married the Parfitt girl and they have three," would be her approving comment on being asked what had happened to a local acquaintance. Unmarried people or married couples without children were okay but somehow "odd." Sexuality was a means for expressing proper affection; sex without that was in her view "sordid."

There was a heartening reception to celebrate Mother's and Dad's twenty-fifth wedding "animosity" in August 1947. But the succeeding years brought tension and hardship for Mother. Her menopause was a crisis neither she nor Dad knew how to handle. Finances continued to be a concern; since the middle war years they had had a "paying guest" in the house, and this continued. Mary Baldwin, later Mary Young, was a bright young nutritionist with the Department of Health who became a lifelong family friend; Mrs Moffatt, an elderly widow, was an English war refugee, Charles Palmer an organist at the local Anglican church, St Mary's. By 1953 Dad's emotional state had become unpredictable. He experienced hallucinations, and his occasional wild outbursts were a terrifying contrast to his usual disciplined manner. His committal to Essondale was a solution, but awful for Mother to have to bear. At the end of 1954 she spent Christmas there and had several visits with him. Her long letter reporting on her trip begins in typical upbeat fashion: "I'm so happy to tell you that Dad is a lot better." On an outing with her to my sister Sheila's home in Vancouver, he read and responded to Christmas messages from friends, and for Mother this represented "a great step forward." "[He] looked at me," she wrote, "& smiled & took my hand & said 'just like old times.' He was so completely happy for those few hours ..." After her "wonderful holiday," her New Year's resolution would be "*not* to commit the unforgivable sin of being sorry for myself."

The years of Dad's illness were unsettled ones for Mother. She let rooms to single gentlemen, partly so as to have company in the house and partly for financial reasons. She signed up for a night course on the Beethoven symphonies, and then for another night course in wood-lathe work. Each summer she helped manage the playgrounds she had inaugurated. After his death, she felt a vague yearning for travel. One night, as she later told it, she dreamed Dad advised her to go to England. On this vivid directive (a wish fulfillment, perhaps), she sold the house, planning to leave Victoria for an indefinite time, and spent the following year in England. It turned out to be a year of tumultuous ups and downs.

She could afford her passage, but counted on finding some sort of employment once she arrived. From September 1961 to early January 1962 she was housekeeper to an elderly couple, the Backs, in rural Hertfordshire. Housekeeping was hardly her strong suit, but as a visitor to Britain she had few alternatives. Mr and Mrs Back had responded to her advertisement and had interviewed her for the position. The interview was pleasant, but after only a few weeks Mother found herself plunged into unexpected confrontation with the English class system. She had not held a job where she was answerable to others since her teaching days forty years earlier. In the interim, in most of her varied activities, she had operated as either an equal partner or a boss. Adding to the shock of sudden change, the Backs, her employers, turned out to be mean and miserly to an almost Dickensian degree.

She recorded her distress in a seventy-two-page letter addressed to her family at home, written in diary-like instalments over the last month of her ordeal (11 December 1961 through 12 January 1962). Here are excerpts from this remarkable document:

> • Today at lunch Mrs B said, "The potatoes are tepid. Don't you know we like things hot. Don't you have food hot in Canada. Why can't you remember?" All this at the table. And I had tried so hard to have things nice.
> • When Mrs Back's daughter & son-in-law were here recently they all went out & he—the s-i-l [—] stayed to look after their dog. I told him I was worried that I could not please them. He said he doubted if anyone could. He said he & Gwen (the dtr.) stayed with them for a few days & it was the worst few days he's ever spent ... I was prepared to put up with a difficult person ... but I am not prepared to put up with conditions which tire me physically & spiritually. No conversation, no music to lighten the atmosphere. My days off are nice—but not as frequent as promised.

When her replies to criticisms proved unacceptable, she began to fabricate ones that might be more pleasing—but hated feeling the need to do this, hence her "spiritual fatigue."

> • Mrs B called me into the lounge & proceeded to lecture me about "behind the pictures" &c &c. "When you came I told my friend you were a lady

and she said—'Then Mrs Beckwith will fulfill all her obligations.'" ... I had asked her about the pictures & she had said "never mind them." So I had left them—knowing there was dust behind & fly spots on front. Now I get scolded for it. "Mrs Beckwith—what has happened to the clock? It has stopped." That's where I made a mistake—I replied—"I looked at it." But she has no sense of humour & "This is no time to be funny."

• I asked [Mrs Back] if she'd mind if I had some of my lettuce for lunch. I had bought some shrimps in London to go with it. Made salad for myself. There was hot steak & kidney pie (canned) for Mr & Mrs B & fried potatoes & cabbage from the garden. Mr B set his voice as low as poss.—he must think God is down below—& said grace. He looked at my plate & said—"Will you want special diet at Xmas?" I thought he was joking & started to laugh, but the steely look in his blue eyes made me stop. "Isn't the food we serve good enough for you?" Mrs Back did not come to my rescue. She seemed to enjoy my discomfort. I just sat, I was so mad & so hurt I couldn't eat. Mrs Back said to me "Eat your dinner." I replied "I can't." Tears dropped. I kept my eyes closed. I couldn't speak, I couldn't get up. They went on eating & talking. How could they. Have they no feelings?

• [D]uring the morning Mrs B said—in an artifical honeyed tone—"Mrs Beckwith, we don't want any unpleasantness about this—but Mr Back made me turn off the heater in your room last night. You know, it's dangerous." Now—she must have gone into my room to see if the heater was on. *I* turn on her electric blanket at 7 p.m. and Mr B's electric stove at 8.30 p.m. And they are not in the room till 2 hrs after that by which time it is almost warm! And I (for the first time) left my heater on—and they turn mine off! You know what my room is like when I get home! "Blow, blow, thou wintry winds [*sic*],—Thou art not so unkind as man's ingratitude."

• I had worked hard ... doing extra cleaning ready for the family coming. Mrs B was in a bad mood when she came ... I wanted her to sit down & get her breath, but she said "No, I must make up the beds." "May I help you?" "No, you don't see what needs doing. Look at these doors! and ledges." "I have just done the stairs with the little hoover & the dusting—but I did not do the doors. Would you like me to do them now?" "Yes please. And I'll need the cover for the little boy's bed which I loaned you." I used it as a window cover to keep out the cold air. This she did not like ... There were some pins in it which I did not put there ...

• One day [Mrs Back] asked me to take her shoes to be resoled. When I went to get them I could not find the ticket & asked her to describe them to me. "Of course you wouldn't know what they were like. You never cleaned them!" She had never asked me to. She had asked me to clean Mr B's shoes. And I said I had not expected to do that. I wanted to say— "In Canada everyone cleans his own. Mr B is crippled in his legs but he's got two good arms and hands!"

• Stephen [grandson]: "What's that noise in the kitchen?" "It's Mrs Beckwith sneezing." S: "Is that a Canadian sneeze?"

• This a.m. the taps in the scullery froze. A small elec. heater was placed there to thaw them out & I was warm for once (only) but Mr B said it wasn't doing any good & asked me to put it back in the hall. Tonight after tea he was about to give me my weekly pay when he launched into a recital of all my sins—and they consider them *sins*—of omission & commission. What a memory the man has. "You sometimes bolt the front door—though it is not your job ... At Xmas the turkey was not properly cleaned inside ..." (Such a bird ... I *did* wash & wipe inside ..., so they blame *me* for a bird not in condition to cook!) ... I waited a long while after he finished—he expected me to say I was sorry—but I said—"I have upstairs a letter, asking to be relieved of my position with you. I have been considering it for some time & perhaps this is the time to present it."

Mother had in fact consulted with a lawyer recommended by her cousin Grace, in the preparation of a resignation letter.

• I'm all packed, just have to take the boxes & cases down in the a.m. to the garage & then clean the room ... I took the books I've been reading back to Mr B at tea time. He was gruff & said "Are they all here? Well, put them on the chair, there." ... I'm not going to tell them I'm taxiing all the way to H[igh] W[ych]. It would shock them. And Mr B would bawl me out ... My self confidence is returning. Visited 3 friends here yesterday, Mrs Read, who loaned me the red umbrella, Mrs Fewster & Mrs Hill who went to N.S. [normal school?] Drank tea at all 3. Just got home in time—for you know what! [A reference to a recurrent bladder problem.]

• Mr Back: "Mrs Beckwith, I don't know if you have noticed it—but all the time you have been here Mrs B has given up her seat so that you could sit by the fire." ... I guess he expected me to say I was grateful. Mrs B hung her head. I said nothing. "So you haven't noticed it!" he said. Still I said nothing—He thought I was ashamed, I suppose. I was—ashamed of his smallness! ... At dinner had asked if I were going all the way by car. I felt like telling him it was none of his—biz. but I quietly told him I'd had some £ s d as a Xmas present from Can. & I was using it this way to go by car. On his way back from the garage he said—"I wouldn't have embarrassed you by asking if you were going all the way by car if I'd seen your boxes with no string. It is evident you are not parting with them." Still I said nothing. I'd had a towel ready to give Mrs B as a parting gift. She doesn't get it. I go. I'm glad. Sorry for these poor people.

"These poor people": it seems in addition to provoking *her* to battle in ways they regarded as "beyond her station," they also constantly battled *each other*. Mother understood such domestic tension but had had no personal experience of it. For the next few months she looked for another position. In March she wrote about the results of a promising interview:

> I thought it was all settled but in a few days a letter came to say the little old lady with whom I was to live had decided after all that she wanted to be alone!! The family tried to persuade her that the time had come for a companion and that I was "suitable in every way" but she was adamant! I was SO disappointed. I was floored. When I had got my breath I went up to my room and knelt down—flopped would be a better word. And I stayed there, I laid the problem before The Lord. I talked to Dad, to my parents and to Bess.[11] I asked their help and asked what I could do to keep myself.

She placed advertisements in a couple of neighbourhood newspapers, and after further interviews was engaged by a family named Gibb. They turned out to be warm-hearted and congenial, as different as possible from the Backs.

Back in Victoria in late 1962, she began to get used to living in an apartment—a sunny one with a window facing east (on good days you could see the tip of Mount Baker across the water in Washington State—a mark of identity for Victorians). She missed her garden in Oak Bay, and it distressed her that the new owners were making changes in it; the family had to persuade her not to drive past. After a month or two she approached the superintendent of the apartment block and asked his permission to make a rock garden on the property. He was only too delighted, and in a short while she had transformed the plot into a handsome and colourful display of shrubs and blooms.

She contacted various friends in the teaching world, offering her services as a coach or tutor, and soon found she had more work than she could handle, guiding children with learning difficulties through their grammar and arithmetic problems. In order to be *au courant*, she signed on for a course in the "new math" (the US neologism took some getting used to). Like most Canadian cities in the 1960s, Victoria welcomed increasing numbers of immigrants from many countries, and there was a demand for teachers of English as a second language (ESL). Mother came under contract with the Victoria School Board to teach evening classes. In this she was notably successful. She loved language, loved teaching, and above all loved meeting people. Through the class contacts she could feel her professional self-confidence, damaged by the English experience, gradually returning. Added to this was the closeness of my sisters and their growing families, a constant source of pleasure to her.

In 1972 there was a province-wide competition: the education ministry offered to support travel and tuition for two teachers to attend a summer course in ESL methods in Toronto. Mother, aged seventy-three, applied and was awarded one of the two places. The course was given in a school near College and Grace, in the "Little Italy" neighbourhood, and she roomed close by with an Italian family. Life in a big-city downtown area was new to her, but she thrived on the bustle, the closeness of the community, people enjoying the summer evenings on their porches. At the end of the program she accompanied us in a short family vacation near French River, and I have a photo of her, in her element, picking ripe blueberries on the rocky river bank. During her stay in Toronto, she learned that Allen Lambert, one of her grade two pupils years ago at Willows School, was now president of the Toronto-Dominion Bank; dropping in unannounced at his fifty-fourth-floor office, she was delighted at his warm greeting of "Miss Dunn." In the fall she resumed her night-school duties in Victoria but in 1975 received word that she would be asked to retire. She had expected the notice, she said; at seventy-six, she could look back on a long, active, and varied teaching career. Not that it was entirely over: she continued with tutoring at home for several more years.

Dad's cousin, Arthur Rogers, formed the habit of spending a few months in Victoria each winter, after his wife Irene died (the climate was recommended for his asthma); during his visits he called on Mother regularly. They enjoyed animated Scrabble games and kept a "perpetual score." They were fond of each other and had a good deal in common. Relatives speculated they might eventually marry, but both said they were content to be just good friends.

With greater freedom in her schedule of activities and a slightly easier financial situation, Mother was able to travel for pleasure, and during the 1970s visited the UK and Ireland, Italy and France, South Africa and New Zealand. When various ailments caused her to quit cycling and other

Mother did her teaching rounds in Victoria by bicycle. A news photographer took this picture in June 1971. Mother was seventy-two.

physical routines, she moved into a retirement home, calling this "a new chapter in my life." Her ninetieth birthday in 1988 was a joyous celebration for many of her friends. At eight o'clock one morning in March 1990, my phone rang, and it was Mother wishing me a happy birthday. She had just learned direct dialling and had set her alarm for five a.m., Victoria time, in order to talk to me before I left for work. She reminded me, as she had often in the past, that I was born at nine in the morning, "just in time for school."

Later that year, hospitalized for surgery after a serious fall, she asked the attendants why they were doing so much for her at her advanced age.

Weren't there other more pressing cases? Her death that October was peaceful. At her memorial service I met teachers from my elementary and high schools and several University of Victoria professors. At her stated request the organ postlude was an arrangement of the "Hallelujah Chorus" from *Messiah*.

In the summer of 1958, shortly before Dad died, when Sheila and I were both visiting Victoria with our young families, Mother gathered us all at his nursing home for a photo—the children and their spouses and all eleven grandchildren. The expressions in this photo range over a wide gamut, from pride and happiness to distractedness and even perhaps fear. Dad looks sadly bewildered. I find it hard to view this document now, and can't help wishing she hadn't organized it, though it was totally in character for her to do so. There were eventually three more grandchildren, making fourteen altogether. In the years to come, two of the children experienced divorces; of the fourteen grandchildren two never married, and, of the twelve who did, all but two underwent divorces and further marriages. Those statistics are symbolic of how society has evolved in our lifetimes; they are not an indictment of my parents' ideals.

Mother's will provided a bequest of fifty dollars to each individually named grandchild and twenty-five to each great-grandchild, of which by 1990 there were already several.

Victoria: Childhood and Adolescence

Existence waked me here. (James Reaney)[1]

Where is here? (Northrop Frye)[2]

[W]ho, if I may be so inconsiderate as to ask, isn't egocentric? (e.e. cummings)[3]

I entered the world in a maternity home ("lying-in hospital" would be the English term) off Cook Street in the pleasant city of Victoria, British Columbia. The names resonate oddly. James Cook, on his last round-the-world voyage in 1777, sailed by the strait flanking the future site of the town in a fog and declared in his journal that the earlier claim by Juan de Fuca was an error: there was obviously no such body of water. His navigational genius is commemorated in many parts of the globe, as I was often reminded in later travels. Perhaps he can be forgiven this one blooper. Overlooking the inner harbour is a statue of the Great White Mother after whom Victoria, like countless places far and wide, was named. I saw an almost-identical statue of her in Albert Park in Auckland, New Zealand, in 1978. The one in the British Columbia capital is surrounded by redwoods and the one in Auckland by palms. Both settings have clashing cultural associations, imperial power versus "foreign" wilderness.[4] The local daily in Victoria is still called the *Times Colonist*. As for the province, it may be a matter of time before some nationalist calls for renaming it: "British" and "Columbia" both echo European intrusions in the so-called (by the intruders) New World. A colourful premier in the mid-1900s, W.A.C. ("Wacky") Bennett, replaced "B.C."

with "Beautiful British Columbia" on vehicle licence plates so as to remind everyone of their heritage and simultaneously of the scenic splendours of rocky inlets, rainforests, and high mountains. It was a good place to be born and a good place to grow up.

How much of what I retain of my childhood is memory and how much family legend?

Probably a genuine memory: aged about three, I run into the street and Dad grabs me out of the way of an oncoming car. A photo records this one: I am tied to a stake in the backyard and wailing loudly (my histrionic streak emerging) at this "unfair" punishment. The legend is that slightly later Mother discovered me, trailing rope and stake, begging cookies at a neighbour's back door. Another photo (I hope no longer extant) shows me aged three or four as ring bearer in a friend's wedding, wearing a suit of pink satin. Another legend: I'm supposed to have said I liked Mother's women friends because they wore soft fur coats. At age five or so, I heard a gossipy woman ask Mother if I was listening or would understand their talk ("pas devant ..."). Sometimes I would show off without concern for whether or not I understood. In a volume of howlers from

The Beckwith family, Victoria, 1931. Left to right: Jean; Margaret Alice Dunn, my mother, holding Sheila; John; Harold Arthur Beckwith, my father.

school essays, I read a funny quotation, "Great are the pleasures of childhood, but greater still are the pleasures of adultery," and repeated it for some of my parents' friends. They roared, but I doubt if they regarded me as precocious. I had no idea what "adultery" meant, though clearly it *didn't* mean "adulthood."

My only personal recollection of Grandad (Beckwith): when I was four or five he would take me on his knee after Sunday lunch and we would "read" the funny papers together (Dinglehoofer, Maggie and Jiggs, the Katzenjammer Kids, Tillie the Toiler, the Toonerville Trolley). I have a fuller store of retained images of Gran (Dunn): the tree in her backyard in the spring, bursting with Royal Anne cherries ready to be picked; her admonishments to passersby not to throw their litter on her verandah (as she detected their approach by ear—she was blind); her "old country" expressions such as "duck your tup'ny" (mind your head). When I was five and my sister two, we were baptized together in Gran's living room, by a popular evangelist, Dr Clem Davies.[5] It seems there was an Anglican baptism in Christ Church Cathedral too, but this more intimate occasion is the one that stuck in my memory. I recollected it many years later, and when I mentioned it to Mother she added that we all sang Gran's favourite hymn, "Shall We Gather at the River?"[6]

Aged six, I started piano lessons with Ogreta Ormiston McNeill,[7] who lived near Windsor Park in Oak Bay. I was proud to take the long streetcar ride, alone, to her home from our house in the north end of the city.

We were in the Great Depression. G.H.E. Green,[8] principal of my first school, Quadra Street Elementary, stood in front of the school assembly with a basin of water and a roll of paper towels, demonstrating that *one* towel was all you needed to dry your hands. Mother collected butter wrappers to grease baking tins with, and saved vegetable stock for soup, though most of her soups were *not* homemade. I was walking along Government Street one day with Dad and he brushed off a panhandler. I was in tears that evening, thinking of Dad's brusque treatment of the poor man. (What "poor men" did I know, except in imagination?) Dad delivered comfort in a brief lecture, an antidote to my sentimentality; I was persuaded that individual charity is no solution to large social problems.

Our home life was an active one. We were encouraged to express our independent personalities, but we joined in recreations such as (in winter) table games—double solitaire (Mother called it "Canfield"), mah-jong, or, when friends and relatives were present, charades.[9] Dressing up and acting were favourite pastimes. We had an antique Edison windup phonograph and a small collection of half-inch-thick shellac discs. We danced, processed, and cavorted to "The Whistler and His Dog" or the "Coronation March" from *Le Prophète*. When I was about nine, a classmate and I put on a program of skits in the family garage. My sisters and I were sometimes called on to play children's parts in adult plays. Once I was the Caterpillar in a dramatization of *Alice in Wonderland* at the Empire Theatre, and on another occasion Sheila and I played two Aboriginal children in a one-act play based on a tribal tale and written by a local playwright, Reby Edmonds. This piece won placement in the local drama festival, and we had the excitement of travelling to Vancouver to play in the finals. (The smell of the greasepaint ...)

Family summers were full of adventure. In my preschool years we would spend a month or more in a rented cottage on the waterfront at Cordova Bay, at that time a rural area in relation to the city. We knew all the neighbour families along the shore. We would buy fresh corn at fifty cents a dozen from the Japanese truck farm across the road, and Mother would boil it in sea water over a bonfire on the beach. We would sing rounds— "Row, row, row your boat," "My dame had a lame, tame crane." In later summers (when I was, I guess, seven, eight, nine) our temporary summer home was at Vesuvius Bay on Salt Spring Island. I can picture the ferry ride and the sandstone caves we loved to play in. The cottagers formed a little community. In one beach-party skit, Dad's role required him to be chased off the dock into the water; this was sensational. Another Salt Spring memory: my first (maybe only) glimpse of Mother in the nude.

When I was about six Mother spent a few weeks in hospital and I was boarded at Miss Alice Carr's nursery school in the Beacon Hill Park area. Miss Carr's sister Emily, the painter, lived close by and would drop in for tea. My letters to my mother from that time are already in cursive script rather than printing; evidently I had no trouble learning to read and write. Some of my "stories," three or four short sentences in length, appeared with my byline[10] in the "children's corner" of the *Colonist*, submitted either by me or (more probably) by my parents.

My *doting* parents. I was a holy terror, hyperactive, and it was a strain to discipline me, but they doted all the same. Mother used to say "don't get a swelled head" and (over and over) "you're not the only pebble on the beach." But clearly in her eyes I *was* the only pebble on the beach. At school, I was always the smallest boy in the class, though generally among the two or three brightest pupils. I often needed to be told to simmer down; excited feelings tended to get out of hand, and teachers found this an irritation. Once an exasperated teacher taped my mouth to make me shut up. A report card comment (February 1938): "John persists in being the class clown." At twelve or thirteen, I made a conscious decision to exercise control, in the interests of social acceptance.

That decision coincided with, or perhaps inaugurated, a religious phase. Between thirteen and about seventeen, moved by confirmation and regular participation in the church choir, I reflected much on the Christian story—to the point where our Dean, Spencer Elliott, wondered if I might be heading for ordination and a church career. One Holy Week the weather was awful and there was a violent storm on Friday afternoon, after which Easter Sunday was brilliantly sunny. I followed all this with the appropriate readings of the gospel, and felt deeply affected. The feeling was mysteriously joyful and akin to my awed reaction to listening to Flagstad and Melchior sing *Tristan* on the radio, and also to my wonderment at what was then happening to my body (the "accumulating sexual yeast," as Reaney puts it).[11] Elliott, another émigré from Great Britain, had a flair for drama, gave readings from Shakespeare's plays and Dickens's novels, and once delivered a series of sermons giving a Christian view of *Macbeth*, *Othello*, and other works. A parishioner remarked of him that "the church's gain was the stage's loss." He was an influential personality in Victoria during the 1930s and early '40s but I think was not happy there and fared better during a late-career renewal in Winnipeg.

I remember the names of all my grade school teachers: Miss Vye and Miss Bradshaw at Quadra, and, at Monterey, Miss Murray, another Miss Bradshaw (sister of the first one), Mr Warnock, Mr Gillie, Miss Creeden, and Mr Brynjolfson. The last name is the only non-British one; though Icelandic, he pronounced it as if it were British ("Brindleson"). The principal's name was Dexter, and he was addressed as "*Captain* Dexter" presumably from a military or naval title acquired in the First World War. He was a laconic senior figure, distinctly English in accent and manner. At the daily school assembly, in between announcements and prayers, he would accompany us all at the piano as we sang "O God, Our Help in Ages Past," "The Maple Leaf Forever," or "Land of Hope and Glory." He knew the songs by heart and expected us to, but his piano playing was haphazard; the tempos dragged painfully. (As a seasoned grade 3 pianist, I already showed signs of a critical streak.) In "Land of Hope and Glory," no one ever taught us the correct lyrics or what they meant: "How shall we extol thee, who are born of thee?" is terrible musical prosody; in addition, no kid could make it out, and "extol" was beyond our vocabulary.

My sisters were whizzes at sports and always took the top prizes on track and field day. In the boys' games I had little ability, and my track and field participation was a bit of a joke. I enjoyed the softball and in the soccer tried at least to follow the principle of "play up, play up, and play the game," despite my meagre aptitude. The teachers called the girls by their first names but the boys by their surnames. Two brothers from the same family would be differentiated in the British manner as "Smith Major" and "Smith Minor." We sometimes played against teams from the private schools (Glenlyon, St Michael's), which were even more British. The names of my schools, Quadra and Monterey, like many other names along the BC coast, reflect the Spanish explorations of the late eighteenth century, but I don't think anyone ever pointed this out as being relevant to our cultural history. We were educated as British subjects. (Even the one Canadian song in our morning repertoire celebrated "Wolfe the dauntless [British] hero," and its maple is entwined with the thistle, the rose, and the shamrock.) For a time, I kept a scrapbook of clippings about the royal family. The death of George V and the abdication crisis were vivid happenings, even though far away. It was an apt preparation for the royal visit of 1939, when we all lined the Victoria streets and waved flags, and then sang "Will Ye No Come Back Again?" as the visitors' boat pulled away from the harbour.[12]

Victoria had, and still tries to have, a reputation as the most British of Canadian cities. In my childhood, unlike now, there were no red double-decker buses to make the tourists imagine they were in Britain; we didn't need them: much of the population was still first-generation British or second-generation and trying to retain the south-of-England accent. It was as if the distinction in tone between public and private schools were defined by the accent of the teachers, imitated by their pupils.

However we felt no contradiction in being at the same time fascinated by US radio, and we listened to a wide range of programs none of which were remotely British. On Sundays, the New York Philharmonic at midday, and Charlie McCarthy and Jack Benny in the evening; on Mondays the *Lux Radio Theatre* with Cecil B. DeMille; on Tuesdays Fibber McGee and Bob Hope; on Wednesdays Fred Allen and the troupe from Allen's Alley; Thursdays were, I think, Bing Crosby and the slightly highbrow *Information Please*; and Fridays perhaps *Grand Ol' Opry*; on Saturday the truly grand and truly old operas from the Metropolitan at midday, and the NBC Symphony with Toscanini in the early evening, followed later by *Your Hit Parade* with Kay Kyser and the unlikely sensation of Frank Sinatra. Daytime and late-night serials (*One Man's Family, Ma Perkins, The Green Hornet*) were also an occasional attraction, as were live sports events (baseball mainly; we didn't follow hockey). Gradually (late '30s, early '40s), a Canadian element seeped into the repertoire as the CBC brought us the weekday Happy Gang show from Toronto and various musical features—the Toronto and Montreal orchestras, live solo and chamber music recitals, the Grenadier Guards' Band from Montreal, Mart Kenney, and others. We listened as a family to this miscellany of offerings, much in the same way that in later decades people watched television. Britain, the US, Canada—where *is* here?

The symphony concerts and operas on the radio were one of three main causes of my early enthrallment with music. The other two were piano lessons with Gwendoline Harper and singing in the Christ Church Cathedral choir. Victoria had bands but no regular orchestra; if you wanted to hear orchestral repertoire "live" you had to go across the water to Vancouver. Similarly, there was no regular opera, although the touring San Carlo Opera Company would visit the Royal or the Empire occasionally with standard works (*La traviata*, *Faust*), and once, I remember, a group of local singers did the Nile scene from *Aida* quite effectively. But radio was a rich source—for access to performances of the classics and also for talks (Walter Damrosch, Deems Taylor, and in Canada Harry Adaskin) that made you appreciate their wonders. If I later had to agree when critics exposed the hokey salesmanship of the music-appreciation movement, at the time and at my impressionable age it genuinely grabbed me.

The absorption of music via radio would not have had such a strong effect, though, without my direct involvements in learning the piano and in singing.

My lessons with Gwendoline Harper spanned nearly a decade in what are for musicians the most crucial formative years (ages eight to eighteen). It dawned on me only gradually what an excellent teacher she was: from her, I acquired a grounding not just in playing but in theory and analysis as well, such as I later found my peers from other centres had not. Gwen Harper, herself a fine performer, was positive, generous, but at the same time exacting. She had a broad-repertoire approach to music. There was a huge fount of wonderful repertoire to enjoy and to challenge a young person, and rather than endless repetitions to perfect one little party piece she encouraged curiosity and adventure. She had a studio attached to her parents' home on Bank Street, but later bought a corner bungalow on Oliver Street just across from our house and made her studio-home there.[13] Her teacher, Gertrude Huntley Green, lived in Victoria at that time in semi-retirement after a notable career, and when I started doing bigger concert pieces I would sometimes audition for her.

I think the first piece I played in public, at a recital of Gwendoline Harper's pupils, was Mozart's Allegro in B♭ (K3). The date was 22 March

1935. I recollect as signposts of my growing acquaintance with the repertoire several Bach Inventions; four or five preludes and fugues from his *Well-Tempered Clavier*; Mozart's Fantasia in D minor (K397); Beethoven's Sonatas op. 49, no. 2, op. 10, no. 1, op. 90, and op. 2, no. 2; pieces from Schumann's *Jügend-Album* and *Fantasiestücke*; waltzes, the Prelude in D♭, and the Polonaise in C minor by Chopin; Mendelssohn's Rondo Capriccioso in E minor and several of his *Lieder ohne Worte*;[14] Liszt's *Un sospiro*; Brahms's Waltz in A♭ and Rhapsody in G minor; music by Sibelius and MacDowell. My awareness of newer music—my curiosity as to what happened after Wagner—advanced by way of impressionism: I played moody numbers by a composer then much in fashion but now forgotten, Selim Palmgren, and Debussy's *La fille aux cheveux de lin* was a favourite. Poulenc's *Mouvements perpétuels* seemed the perfect, cheeky answer to Wagner and became one of my show-off pieces, representing my idea of "modern"—at least until, one day in 1944, I heard on the radio the premiere of Schoenberg's Piano Concerto, op. 42, by the NBC Symphony under Stokowski with Eduard Steuermann as soloist. I found it incomprehensible but mesmerizing.

The curricula for music studies in Victoria mirrored the English/Canadian or private school/public school dichotomies I have observed. There were two systems: that of the Royal Schools, London, and—the more prevalent one—that of the Toronto Conservatory of Music. Examiners from both London and Toronto travelled across Canada yearly to listen to young performers (predominantly pianists) and distribute grades and eventually diplomas (LRSM or ATCM). Gwen Harper guided me through the stages of the Toronto syllabus, and over time I presented myself for seven performing examinations and an equal or larger number of written papers in harmony, counterpoint, history of music, pedagogy, and "musical form" (i.e., analysis). You didn't have to do the written stuff, and some teachers cut it short, but she took a more thorough view, and I've always been glad she did. The examiners were formidable authorities, not just in the eyes of a callow candidate like me: their annual visits were regarded as cultural renewals by the local musical community, moments of contact with the bigger world of—*Toronto*. Those for whom I played over the years were Norman Wilks, Boris Berlin (twice), Alberto Guerrero (twice), Ettore Mazzoleni, and Sir Ernest MacMillan. A local agent rented a suite in the Empress Hotel for the lineup of exam sessions and also invigilated the three-hour written papers. It was a discipline everyone took seriously. Candidates' standings, but not the actual grades, were published in the *Colonist*. I will give an account of my diploma exam (ATCM) later.

The annual competition music festivals were another yardstick of progress. I took part both as a young pianist and (to the extent that my soprano voice held out) as a singer, and often won a top place. In my teens I also travelled to compete in the Vancouver festivals. The adjudicators at these events were usually experts from Britain, but when the war curtailed their travels, personalities from Canada or the US would come instead. There was an opportunity to hear and compare musical performances by one's peers, but there was also the inartistic attitude of tension, the off-putting competitive element, which in later years of the festival movement (after my time of involvement) became criticized and to some extent modified.

I was lucky as a kid to have Gwen Harper's encouragement. It was also my good fortune to sing in choirs conducted by Stanley Bulley, a musician of splendid ideals and a dynamic leader. It had a big impact emotionally and intellectually on a child of eight or nine not only to learn the church repertoire from Lassus and Gibbons through Bach to Holst (one of Bulley's teachers) but also, with his Victoria Choral Union, to be part of choral-orchestral productions of great pieces like the Mozart and Brahms

With Gwendoline Harper in Victoria, circa 1945.

Requiems and the *St John Passion* of Bach. Dale McIntosh recounts the controversy over Bulley's performances of Handel's *Messiah* in the middle 1930s, in which I was an involved young chorister: the rapid tempi reflected his awareness of Handelian style but were an affront to the Victoria establishment's ideas of sacred music.[15] Bulley and Harper worked together a few times when she played continuo for performances he conducted. Bulley, a product of London's Royal College of Music, communicated an elevated sense of musical values through his conducting, organ performances, and choral know-how (apart from the Union and Cathedral choirs, he served as supervisor of music in the Victoria public schools). I admired him and was influenced by him but—for reasons I find hard to fathom—never looked on him as a model for whatever musical future I might have.[16]

My luck with my growing musical obsession extended further. Through a fellow singer in Bulley's choir, the soprano Peggy Walton, I became perhaps the youngest member of an extracurricular circle which gathered at her studio (she was developing a career as not only a professional singer but also a painter and sculptor). To the musical love and appreciation of my parents, my piano teacher, my choirmaster, she added a new dimension, an attitude where music and the other arts were not just edifying and a part of the good life but a *passion*. Sunday afternoon at her place meant tea, tennis on a grass court, avid debates, updates on Victoria's visual art, theatrical, and musical life, and—what I most recall—sight-reading accompaniments to vocal music by Bach, Handel, Schubert, Schumann, Brahms, Debussy; sight-reading four-hand arrangements of symphonies by Haydn, Mozart, Beethoven; and comparing radio listening experiences (Flagstad, Pinza, Toscanini's Beethoven cycle). Peggy's friendship and example left their mark.[17]

I didn't choose my vocation; as I've often said, it chose me. I see my former self developing an obsessive enthusiasm for music and luckily finding friends and mentors who could show me, early on, both how exciting it is and what tough discipline is entailed in getting to know it from the inside.[18]

When I was fourteen, an accident threatened whatever vague musical ambitions I was harbouring, at least in performance. Invited to Gwen Harper's home for a social evening, I offered to chop kindling for her fireplace and managed to chop my left index finger, almost severing it at the nail joint. My parents were out of town for the weekend, so Gwen rushed me to emergency at the Royal Jubilee Hospital, and a doctor put the bones and tendons together temporarily. The next day I travelled to a hospital in Vancouver, where the delicate job was completed and I was fitted with a cast. The joint no longer functioned, but the finger was otherwise okay. It was some months before I had normal use of it, however, and I practised meanwhile from a book of pieces for one hand. The loss of action in the end joint was no handicap to piano performance; indeed, Alberto Guerrero later told me he wished all his fingers were like that: one of the aims of practice is strengthening the end joint so as to prevent its collapse.

I remember the names of all my teachers at Oak Bay High School too: Miss Beveridge, Miss Burridge, Mr Gibbard, Miss Gordon, Mr Lister, Mr Mattock, Miss Mole, Mr Sanders, Miss Smith, Mr Tanner, Mr Wallace, Mr Whittemore. Again, all had British surnames, but most were Canadian, the exceptions being Miss Smith (Scottish), and Mr Tanner, Mr Whittemore, and the principal, Mr Hartness (all three English). According to a rumour, Whittemore had been passed over for the principalship, which may explain his evident lack of interest in teaching (science); he took up much class time recounting his First World War service in the Falkland Islands (existing on a diet of "salt pork and 'ard tack"). Miss Beveridge and Mr Sanders took us through basic Latin. Fraser Lister, our maths teacher,[19] was well known as an actor with the Victoria Little Theatre, and he and Margot Gordon coached (extracurricularly) our drama productions. Patricia Hamilton Smith (history) had a thick Scots accent and a volatile temperament, making her the butt of student jokes. Mr Mattock was the aptly named shop teacher; he had lost several fingers in pursuing his specialty. Edward W. Tanner taught the "commercial" subjects; in typing class he barked his orders in sharp military fashion and once gave me a dressing-down for continuing to bash out stencils by pick-and-peck while in the process of learning touch typing. The principal, D.H. Hartness,[20] taught us chemistry. He was unsuited to administration, had a short temper, and was awkward with young people, though cultivated and well read. We called him The Cue behind his back, because of his baldness, and it humanized him that he found out about this and referred to it humorously in assembly. The best classes, in my recollection, were those of Gibbard (English) and Burridge (French). They were both dedicated to their subjects and enthusiastic about teaching. Gibbard's readings of poetry and enactments of Shakespeare scenes were memorable, partly perhaps because we were made to learn passages from memory; there are several that I can still recite ("O for a muse of fire that would ascend / The brightest heaven of invention ..."). Miss Burridge spoke French well and had a repertoire of little jokes to instill correct usage ("y" before "en"—

any donkey knows that). An excellent teacher, she had an exuberant personality, with boundless energy: she coached the girls in grass hockey and rode a Vespa (we called it a "putt-putt") to and from school.

Outside school, I was increasingly absorbed in music—lessons, choir practices, performances. But Oak Bay High had no music program and little in the way of extracurricular musical activity (no choir, orchestra, band, or music club). Now and then students who were developing musical abilities would contribute to an assembly or school show—Patricia Straughan[21] and I would team up in violin and piano numbers, for example—but that was about all. There was no drama course in the curriculum, either; however, there was a good deal of after-hours play production in which I found a lot of satisfaction and enjoyment. My friend Frank Lindsay and I wrote and produced a farce based on Holmes (Frank) and Watson (me). It was a huge success, but he complained afterwards that he had all the feeder lines and I had all the laugh lines. There was no school newspaper, so a few of us started one: Jean Hopkins and I were the co-editors. I also worked on *The Oak Leaf*, the school annual; alongside the

*Aged sixteen, co-editor of the student newspaper
at Oak Bay High School.*

smell of greasepaint I began to like the smell of printer's ink (we produced the annual with a downtown printing firm).

These were, for me, good years. On the occasion of the fiftieth class reunion (which I could not attend), Bob Peers asked us to recall our "most embarrassing moments" from high school, and I wrote that one of mine was "rehearsing an adagio-dance scene in [A.A. Milne's] *The Man in the Bowler Hat* with Georgina Moore (on whom I had a crush), and in my nervousness dropping her on the stage floor." I learned that when this was read out at the reunion Georgina, in the audience, was amused but couldn't recall the incident and didn't know of my infatuation. My note to Peers contained the following further "embarrassment":

> I didn't see the movie *Class of 44*, but compared to others in the same vein of would-be nostalgia I'd say the real experience was much more innocent. Our mating rituals were dancing two or three times a year to Len Acres's band; kisses; limited fondling. Our health classes included no reproduction unit. In the growing community concern over venereal disease we were once assembled (segregated, of course) for a special lecture on the subject by someone from the Provincial Health Department. This is my *most* embarrassing teen-age recollection: I fainted. Locker-room jokes were one thing, but the graphics of male–female sex—nowadays common knowledge to anyone over twelve—came as a complete shock.

Our graduation banquet had taken place at Terry's on the day after the D-Day landings in Normandy. I told Peers he deserved credit for organizing the reunion, exactly fifty years later (7 June 1994):

> Are you typecast after being named all-round best student in our class?— an award everyone applauded, I think. After Audrey Usher as best scholar and Jim Kinghorn as best athlete there was a "special" citation of yours truly for journalism, drama, and music: another embarrassment, because not only did I not feel I deserved it but I was sure there were those who connected it with the presence on the [graduation ceremony] platform of my mother representing the school board—though she knew nothing about it. (Maybe one way and another the teen years were just *always* embarrassing.)[22]

Oak Bay High had an enrolment in my time of less than five hundred students—small by today's secondary-school standards. In the Depression and war years its material resources were limited (there was, for example, no school library), but the human resources were, I believe, rich—a staff of strong personalities with genuine communicative skills. The well-known author Pierre Berton was a student at both Monterey Public and Oak Bay High about five years before my time, and, contrary to my experience, he refers to this in his autobiography as a disagreeable episode; he mentions few details apart from an altercation with Principal Hartness (whose name he misspells).[23]

Yes, these were the war years. At high school the boys had cadet training (mostly marching drill) instead of gym classes. At home we accustomed ourselves to food rationing and blackout curtains. Victoria, like other west coast communities, felt vulnerable to enemy attack from across the Pacific. The expulsion of Japanese-Canadian families to inland camps was a shameful response to these fears, but I don't recall that it was even debated. There were war-bond sales campaigns. We listened to Churchill's speeches on the radio as the Nazis closed in on Great Britain and strongholds in the Far East fell one after another. Names of students from higher years started appearing in the casualty lists. Refugees (stranded Brits, escapees) from Hong Kong and Singapore came as temporary residents. Reading about Dame Myra Hess's inspiring daytime concerts in London's National Gallery, I hit on the idea of raising some money for the fund she had started in their support. As a young pianist, I was active with the junior branch of the Victoria Musical Arts Society, and with fellow members I organized a few concerts; from the proceeds, we were able to send approximately $1,000 to the Myra Hess Fund. I treasured Dame Myra's kind letter of thanks; she enclosed the program of the 1,000th National Gallery concert, which had just taken place (23 July 1943). She was, she said, "deeply touched by your warm & generous tribute to my work during the war" and she expressed thanks to the participants in our "lovely concert."

> I think we are all proving that music is one of the great forces in the world ... My work is very strenuous & leaves me very little spare time, but I felt I must write to you myself. The war news is so encouraging now & perhaps it will not be too long before I can cross the water again & come even as far as Victoria![24]

When my voice cracked, I continued to attend church as a server—the low-Anglican term for acolyte. Servers wore surplices, lit and extinguished candles, carried crosses or banners in processions, and transported the unsanctified bread and wine (and the collection plate) to the altar for blessing. At first devout and absorbed in these "sacred" duties, I began to feel confused and put off by the apparently routine attitudes of the clergy, especially our bishop. Harold Sexton was a pompous Australian with a booming bass voice. When he started a supplication with "O God! ...," you couldn't be sure if he was praying or blaspheming. In the vestry between services his chatter was (unexpectedly to my adolescent sensibilities) worldly and even crass, though not exactly vulgar. In contrast to Dean Elliott's intellectual and theatrical sharpness, his demeanour, as I observed it, was scarcely that of a churchman. This was, I guess, the beginning of a turnoff for me in religious thinking. In my college year, I stopped regular church attendance.

For three summers in my high-school years I had an unusual job. I was joe-boy at the summer school of the Department of Education, held in Victoria High School. My duties were a combination of publicity, stage management, and janitoring. I had a basement office where I created posters for school events, and at those events (including daily noon-hour recitals) I toted music stands and chairs; at the Friday night dances I took tickets at the door. I exercised what I fancied was artistic imagination in the posters, and made efforts to improve when I heard that an art teacher had pointed them out as examples of poor design. The recitals had a strong professional lineup. Performers included the pianists Arthur Benjamin and Gertrude Huntley Green and the violinist Jan Cherniavsky. Nicholas Goldschmidt came from San Francisco with a program of self-accompanied lieder. An appearance by Bonnie Bird, from Seattle's Cornish School, was a captivating introduction to modern dance by an artist who had been associated with both Martha Graham and John Cage in their Seattle years. (In the later 1940s, I was to take part in some of the summer school concerts as pianist.)

From taking a role in a school play in my final year, 1943–4, I won a scholarship to the summer theatre course at the Banff School of Fine Arts. The month of study was the longest time and Banff the furthest distance I had been away from home. I shared billeting with about a dozen other guys in an old house off Banff Avenue. The School didn't yet have its own quarters and was housed for the summer in the Banff High School. Our instructors were Sydney Risk from Edmonton for acting and mime, Burton James from Seattle for stagecraft, and Joseph Smith from Salt Lake City for speech. Smith, as the name and hometown might suggest, was a Mormon. He spoke with a finely cultivated Oxbridge accent, which he presented as the ideal for stage delivery: some of the students became flummoxed in their attempts to produce the distinction he demanded between the two a's in the phrase "brass tacks." In the major production, a melodrama called *Death Takes a Holiday*, one actor had the line "I'm half mad," and Smith insisted it should be pronounced "hoff med." We had some terrific parties, including one where we ended at dawn at the summit of Tunnel Mountain. I met some bright and attractive girls. There was no drinking that I can recall. Burton James told me he thought I had the makings of a professional actor. He said the same of another student, Henri Bergeron, from St Boniface, who in fact did go on to a career in theatre and became a well-known personality in radio and television in Montreal. Bea Goldberg (Bea Leonard) and Marcia Diamond were also later prominent names in the acting world. It was for me an enjoyable and stimulating interlude.

In the fall of 1944, I enrolled in first-year arts and science at Victoria College. I was seventeen. Life was my oyster: I was said to have talent in piano playing and acting, I was socially involved and full of beans—and— I had a steady girlfriend. Pamela Terry was a year ahead of me in school. We acted together in plays and both studied piano with Gwendoline Harper. She was beautiful, and her standoffishness in our first few dates only increased my feelings of wanting to explore with her all the things we both liked. We became close friends and regular companions to movies, concerts, plays, and even sometimes church services. We performed piano duets, rode bikes, swam (either in the ocean or in the saltwater pool of the Crystal Gardens), played tennis, listened to her classical record collection, and endlessly talked. In a later age we would naturally have become lovers, but, while we petted a lot and love was the name I gave to the fever I was experiencing, we observed the physical limits that were customary in our society at the time. We developed a strong sense of devotion to each other, and people said we were a nice-looking young couple. The Terrys were a prominent Victoria family. The pharmacy started by Pamela's grandfather, Wallace Terry, grew to include an ice-cream parlour and eventually a restaurant, and became a popular meeting place at the centre of town, the corner of Douglas and Fort Streets. Her father, a doctor, was stationed in Victoria as an officer with the Canadian Army medical corps. During my year at Victoria College, she went to the Provincial Normal School.

Around this time I had a first brief assignment as a teacher of piano. A group of parents in Happy Valley, a rural district west of Victoria, wanted someone to teach their children, and Gwendoline Harper, thinking it would be good experience, recommended me. Every Saturday morning I would go out by bus and spend the day giving lessons to the youngsters in the living room of one of the mothers, who also provided

Peggy Walton did this pastel portrait of me,
aged seventeen, in Victoria, in 1944.

me with lunch. The experience *was* useful, and it earned me a little money, but I became frustrated with my own ineptitude. There were published methods to guide me, but I never knew which to introduce first, the physical tasks of suiting little fingers to the keys or the visual/mental tasks of reading musical notation. There are supposedly those who teach but can't do; in this case, I found I could do but couldn't teach. As a result, I have always had great respect for successful piano instructors.

In emotion and in imagination I believe my world expanded greatly in 1944–5. The college courses opened my eyes to wonderful and boundless intellectual horizons that I had only dimly suspected at high school. The freer discipline, the greater dependency on personal application in studies, the sense of worth that it gave to be addressed by instructors as "*Mister* Beckwith"—all this was new and tremendously nourishing. The instructors were scholarly specialists of a quality higher than one might have expected in such a small and modestly endowed institution. The maths professor, Bob Wallace, conveyed a spark of real enthusiasm: "Isn't this great stuff?" he would exclaim, demonstrating a complicated theorem. Harry Hickman was the brilliant and resourceful professor of French. He had made many extended visits to France, and his francophilia was contagious. His *dictées* were gems of performance art; he introduced us to poetry and drama from Ronsard through Molière to Verlaine and had us memorize key portions. In particular, I was entranced that as pronunciation models he used Maggie Teyte's recordings of the songs of Debussy and Duparc (he was an avid music lover). Ruth Humphrey, our professor for English "lang & lit," similarly revealed wonders of English literature. I had always liked reading, but her classes turned casual interest into a kind of urgency: there seemed to be so much that you *had to* read if you wanted to be an educated person. As in our English classes at high school, and as in Hickman's French classes, we had memorization assignments, and passages have stuck in my head ever since.

Our textbook for the "lang" of "lang & lit," *The Reading and Writing of English*, was written by an Australian, E.G. Biaggini.[25] His earlier study, *English in Australia*, had a lengthy subtitle: "taste and training in a modern community: a preliminary enquiry into the power of the adult to recognize good and logical English, with some reference to the common way of thinking."[26] Both volumes have prefaces by F.R. Leavis, the transatlantic critical guru of the period. The author's procedure was to compare examples of writing to illustrate both "good and logical" qualities and the opposite: Thomas Hardy, D.H. Lawrence, good; H.V. Morton, Warren Deeping, and some unidentified hack journalist, bad. Professor Humphrey devised exercises for us along the same lines. The aim was not just proper usage but the development of taste and critical discrimination. A sort of finishing school to turn us into literary snobs? No; as interpreted by our instructor, it was a path to clarity in communication and in "the common way of thinking." A unit of the course focused on examples of good and bad advertising copy.

Ruth Humphrey's judgments were solid, but her criticisms could be sharp: "For goodness sake, call a spade a spade," she wrote in the margin alongside some arty paragraph I turned in. I needed a few such jabs of plain speaking at that stage of my life, as she no doubt recognized. I was grateful for her prodding and advice, and we later became good friends.[27]

Music and theatre occupied no regular place in the college life, but there was a literary club, and I found that, as at high school, I was called on to help edit the college yearbook. I contributed short examples of prose and maybe some poems. I formed new friendships, one of which, with Ronald Shepherd, has lasted a lifetime.[28]

The college occupied the old Dunsmuir mansion, Craigdarroch. The wartime military drills were more intense than in high school: male students, approaching conscription age, were enrolled in the Canadian Officer Training Corps, wore uniforms, and had rifle practice and mock-battle manoeuvres that required crawling over rocks and mud at the suburban Rithet's Farm. An army sergeant was assigned to put us through our exercises. In one, we were required to leap over the twenty-foot stone wall on the Craigdarroch grounds and then haul ourselves back up stone by stone with our bare hands; there was an impossibly short time limit; it was excruciating. I hated the rifle practice and was a hopeless shot. For the rest, as in school sports, I tried to keep cheerful and do my best. A notice was posted one day calling us to report "in mufti." I had no idea what this meant (it means "ordinary dress") and created hilarity by turning up in full uniform. Towards the end of the 1945 spring term came the sudden news of Roosevelt's death. In May we were sent to a two-week training camp at Chilliwack in the Fraser Valley. I had asked to be excused because my Associateship piano exam was coming up in June and I didn't like the thought of an interruption in practice time. My request was turned down, but I was allowed time off at the camp so that I could practise on an ancient upright in the chapel. We slept in barracks, took turns on kitchen duty, and spent our days in various military workouts. I recall an overnight assignment to "guard a bridge," which I found hard to take seriously, though it must have had relevance to the realities of war. Many of my companions either took sick or pretended to, but I managed to get through all of it. During the last few days of the camp, VE Day was announced; the European War was over.

I had a few weeks to prepare for my TCM exam. My examiner, I learned, would be Alberto Guerrero. I was trying for the combined performer's and teacher's diploma; you could do one or the other, but I was ambitious and entered for both. I put in more than my habitual hours of practice and rehearsed my program for family and friends as a recital. It included works by Bach, Beethoven, Chopin, Debussy, and Poulenc. Gwen coached me from her knowledge of the usual questions asked in the viva voce on pedagogy. On the day, I felt quite nervous. Guerrero had a natural and friendly manner, but I played less well than I thought I could have and became tongue-tied in the pedagogy part. From his examiner's written remarks, which arrived in the mail a few weeks later, I had to face that I wasn't as well prepared in piano playing as I had imagined. He pointed out basic discrepancies in my technique as the cause of my occasional stumbles and lapses. In particular, he was not convinced that I had prepared well enough for the teacher's requirements. (My unhappy Happy Valley experience should have persuaded me to give them deeper study.) He commended my musicality and made encouraging general comments but gave me a grade just under "first class" for performing, and under "pass" for pedagogy. Pamela Terry, in the same exam session, entered for the teacher's diploma only, and passed it. Dad and Mother were bewildered: if this was to be my chosen path in life, why hadn't I done better? In my scholastic subjects at high school and college I had never had a *failing* grade.

There was a silver lining: a letter came from the Conservatory offering me a piano scholarship. Guerrero, though rightly denying me a first-class mark for my playing, had detected promise—an aptitude, a talent—that led him to recommend me for further study. It was an attractive prospect. The only comparable music program close to Victoria was that of the University of Washington at Seattle, where I couldn't be sure of admission; the University of British Columbia had no music department or degree offering until several years later. Despite their misgivings, my parents agreed to support me in my next move. Instead of continuing for the second year in my Victoria College program, I would go to Toronto and study music full-time. The scholarship was for piano studies at the Toronto Conservatory of Music (an affiliate of the University of Toronto), and I would enrol at the same time in the University's Faculty of Music; my ATCM diploma in performance would admit me to the second year of its bachelor of music (MusB) course and my credit-conscious parents thought a degree sounded better than a diploma. It was in some ways a shaky start, and the indefinite separation from Pamela was hard to contemplate, but I was excited. This was what I wanted to do, what I felt *compelled* to do, at this stage of my life.

STUDIES

Toronto: Youth

I had travelled little. I knew a good deal of my native Vancouver Island, but even there the furthest west I had been from Victoria was Sooke, and the furthest north Campbell River. Excursions off the island had taken me as far south as Portland in northern Oregon and as far east as Banff in Alberta. Now, as a young music student during the years 1945 through 1949, I crossed the continent in Canada or the US as far as Toronto, by train or bus, twice a year, spending the school season there and the summer in Victoria. My first trip, by Canadian Pacific, included stops in Kamloops to visit my mother's sister Agnes Carmichael and her family and in Regina to visit my father's cousin David Rogers and *his* family including at that time his mother, my formidable great-aunt Grace Dean McLeod Rogers, who took it as her duty to warn of the dangers lurking as I set out on my life's path and to instruct me in behaviour and status: McLeod men, by her rules, didn't help with the dishwashing but were expected to make their own beds.

The only city larger than Victoria I had known was Vancouver; Toronto was bigger and different. Miss your bus in leisurely Victoria and you waited twenty minutes for the next one; in Toronto the tandem streetcars rumbled up Yonge Street at the rate of one every *three* minutes. The drivers called the stops in an Ontario twang, "Callege and Carten" for "College and Carlton," or "Blooah!" for "Bloor" (like a drill sergeant's shout, "March!"). The *Star* and the *Tely* (i.e., *Evening Telegram*) sold on the streets ("Star/Tely paper here!") for three cents, *The Globe and Mail* for five. Size and pace took getting used to. People's attitudes were different, too. I had, I suppose, unconsciously absorbed the nuanced coexistence of Canadians, ex-Brits, and Asians in Victoria and Vancouver society but had observed no intolerance or prejudice against Jews. Victoria's Jewish population was minimal; there was one synagogue, and the few Jewish families I knew had changed their names (Meyerstein to Marston, for example) and observed no distinctive lifestyle. In Toronto it surprised and puzzled me to hear openly anti-Semitic comments from adults I regarded as intelligent and humane. Such talk bore no relevance to the friendships I formed with Jewish fellow students in music.

Alexandra McGavin, formerly a piano student of Gwen Harper's in Victoria, was now studying with Alberto Guerrero and living with a fellow student in a row house on Aylmer Avenue.[1] They kindly gave me a room while I looked for somewhere inexpensive to stay. There was a women's residence attached to the Conservatory building at College and University, but nothing comparable for men. After a few days' search, I took a room at the College Street YMCA for five dollars a week; that was to be my home for three school years.[2] From it, I could walk in ten minutes to the Conservatory and in five to Alberto Guerrero's studio on Grosvenor. Directly across the street was the art deco grandeur of Eaton's College Street, the department store's classy uptown branch, with the Eaton Auditorium on the top floor. I took low-cost meals in either the "Y" cafeteria or Eaton's basement café; alternatives were the cafeteria in the basement of the Conservatory, the Honey Dew restaurant nearby, or, a little further away, Mary John's in the Gerrard Street artists' quarter. The butter tarts at Mary John's were a nickel each; coffee was usually ten cents, but you could get something approximating coffee at Kresge's for five. Coached by my parents to be thrifty, I budgeted carefully and tried to spend no more than a dollar a day on food.

At the Conservatory I was offered a choice of which teacher I wanted to study with. Otherwise, Principal Ettore Mazzoleni would assign me to someone. I said I wanted Guerrero. He had been my examiner, and I appreciated his assessment of my talent, respected him, felt grateful to him for having recommended me. Alex McGavin enthused about her lessons with him. Whether I had heard any of his solo performances on the radio I can't recall, but I certainly knew of his high reputation. He accepted me in his class and became in the next few years a powerful influence in my development, a force in my life comparable, I believe, to that of my parents.

Mazzoleni said the scholarship[3] would cover further lessons, so (never having had the chance to study another instrument) I signed up with Perry Bauman on the oboe. This was a disaster. Perry was a marvellous player and a patient teacher, but I had no aptitude and became discouraged at the terrible quacks I was making, so after a few months gave it up. I enrolled for the second year[4] in the three-year MusB course, which meant assignments in harmony and counterpoint, and classes (they were called "tutorials") twice a week, with the two professors in the University's Faculty of Music, Healey Willan and Leo Smith. There were optional lectures, attended by advanced Conservatory students as well as those in the Faculty program, and the history of music series by Arnold Walter deservedly attracted big attendance: he was widely knowledgeable, played fluent piano examples, and persuasively introduced us to a variety of music; his presentations of medieval works and of Wagner and Mahler were highlights. The teaching of Willan and Smith had a notably English outlook: the former called you "old man," the latter "dear boy."[5] Contacts with the Faculty dean, Sir Ernest MacMillan, though irregular, were more stimulating; his criticisms had a more practical base.[6]

The core experience lay in my weekly private sessions with Guerrero. He analyzed my playing and showed me more efficient, more relaxed, more dependable ways of applying my arms and fingers to the keyboard. I felt awkward and became easily discouraged, but after some months gained confidence. Did I see myself a few years hence as a solo performer on the tour circuits? Thinking back, I believe I regarded the piano as a means of Learning Music, rather than a specific career goal—but I was keen to become as good a pianist as possible. The learning laid out by Guerrero used no boring exercises but was all done through wonderful piano repertoire (Bach, Scarlatti, Mozart, Beethoven, Chopin, Schumann, Brahms, Debussy). As a scholarship holder, I was expected to perform in Conservatory concerts. On one occasion (10 April 1946) I shared the program with the organist Roma Page, the soprano Lois Marshall, and a fellow pianist from Guerrero's class, thirteen-year-old Glenn Gould. It was encouraging to place in or near the top in the annual competition festival, winning a first for my performance of Mozart's Fantasia in C minor, (K457) and a third for Bach's Prelude and Fugue in G♯ minor (WTC 1). The first for the Bach class went to Glenn.[7] Dad and Mother were especially impressed with these "winnings," from their experience of such festival competitions in Victoria. I may have been starting to redeem myself in their view after the mixed results of my ATCM exam.

If, as noted, the Conservatory had no residence accommodation for male music students, in fact there were few male students to be accommodated. Arriving in September 1945, I found I was one of a small minority of men then enrolled. The war had just ended. Applying for practice-studio time, I learned that the morning and afternoon hours were

Toronto Conservatory of Music Alumni Association
Toronto Chapter

EVENING MUSICALE

Concert Hall, Toronto Conservatory of Music
Wednesday Evening, April 10th, 1946, at 8.30 o'clock

Programme

GOD SAVE THE KING

I.

Scherzetto .... Vierne
Sonata IV - Andante .... Bach
L'Organo Primitivo .... Yon
Musette and Minuet .... Handel

ROMA PAGE
(Marion Ferguson Scholarship 1945-46)

II.

Five Préludes .... Debussy
    Bruyères
    La Puerto del Vino
    La Sérénade Interrompue
    Canope
    Minstrels

JOHN BECKWITH
(Hazel Ireland Eaton Scholarship 1945-46)

INTERMISSION

III.

Recit.: Marble My Heart Is .... Handel
Aria: Flawless as Noonday .... Handel
Alleluja .... Mozart
Sweet Chance That Led My Steps Abroad .... Head
Silent Noon .... Vaughan-Williams
Aria: Un Bel Di Vedremo, from Madame Butterfly....... Puccini

LOIS MARSHALL
(Conservatory Singing Scholarship 1945-46)

IV.

Prelude and Fugue in B flat minor .... Bach
Rondeau and Caprice, Second Partita in C minor........ Bach
Impromptu in F sharp .... Chopin
Waltz in E minor .... Chopin

GLENN GOULD
(Heintzman Scholarship, Piano, 1945-46)

Coffee will be served in the Rotunda

Program, Toronto Conservatory of Music, 1946, by scholarship winners.

all booked by the women residents, so I had to be content with practising in the early mornings and early evenings when the women were at either breakfast or supper. During the war years, people recalled, there had been few male students in the advanced levels—Godfrey Ridout and Robert Fleming were the main composers whose names I heard. Fleming had moved to Ottawa to work with the NFB,[8] but I formed a friendship with Ridout. Another active figure was George Hurst, a composer from

Scotland who was studying conducting with Mazzoleni. I got to know the composition students, especially Harry Somers and Harry Freedman, who were in the class of John Weinzweig. Weinzweig and Barbara Pentland, the main composition teachers, were radicals in the eyes of our faculty professors. Among congenial fellow students in the MusB program were Howard Brown, a year or so ahead of me (a fine pianist studying with Lubka Kolessa, he was later head of music at Bishop's University), and, in my year, Don Ryerson, a teacher whose wife Edna was the only Communist member of the Toronto Board of Education (he was I believe a descendant of Egerton Ryerson, the Ontario education reformer), Kelsey Jones, a gifted pianist and committed composer and later a professor in the Faculty of Music at McGill, and Brock McElheran, who went on to an outstanding career in the US as a teacher and choral conductor. Brock was a war veteran, and years later wrote a vivid memoir of his service in Britain.[9] As art, music, and drama editor of the undergraduate newspaper *The Varsity*, he gave me a few reviewing assignments. In Guerrero's class I found stimulus in the company of Oskar Morawetz, a Czech refugee then becoming well known as a composer; he had a nice sense of humour and I was floored by his musical memory. Serious piano students then enrolled, besides the young Gould, included Malcolm Troup, Victor Dell, Florence Dahl, Neil Van Allen, Colleen Sadler, and Margaret Sheppard; we traded lesson experiences, attended master classes and each other's recitals, and talked together about repertoire. I came to regard Margaret as a "feminine presence" in my life. Originally from Windsor, she was my senior by a few years, and we seemed to hold similar views on music and on the world. Wrapped up in the exploration of music and struggling with the piano, I appreciated her performances of advanced pieces like *Carnaval* and the Polonaise-Fantasie, and her accounts of their technical challenges. We went together to concerts and plays and shared the occasional dinner or Sunday brunch. It was friendship rather than dalliance (though Margaret was an attractive young woman), and I expect I bored her with talk of my girlfriend Pamela at home, with whom I exchanged frequent letters.[10] An old friend from Victoria, Marjorie Lea, was another regular contact; she studied with Ernest Seitz, had her own recital series on local radio, and was George Lambert's studio accompanist. My father's cousins, the Arthur Rogers family, and their friends the Grays (the family of one of Dad's Osgoode classmates), extended dinner invitations now and then, socially involving and budget-saving.

I got to know Conservatory performers—singers (Marguerite Gignac, Mary Morrison, Pierre Boutet) and instrumentalists (the violinists George

Pyper and Andrew Benac, the cellist Rowland Pack)—and often also their teachers, by making myself available as an accompanist. In these early student years I did a great deal of accompanying and coaching of singers, and also collaborated now and then with violinists. I acquired quick sight-reading ability and good knowledge of the standard song repertoires. For a season or two I was the studio accompanist of one of the most active voice teachers, Eileen Law (alto soloist in some of MacMillan's *Messiah* and *St Matthew Passion* performances); I frequently accompanied recitals, and was on call for the annual Kiwanis competition festival.

I joined the usher corps at Eaton Auditorium. You had to supply a dress shirt, black bow tie, and tuxedo pants, but they gave you an usher's uniform consisting of a jacket and cap. There was a small honorarium and you received a share of the evening's tips. In addition to showing patrons to their seats, you served them non-alcoholic punch at intermission and helped out in the checkroom. With these slight duties, you got to hear some first-rate concerts without having to buy a ticket. Several fellow music students ushered along with me.

My routine consisted of piano practice, study hours (often in the tall-ceilinged reading room of the Toronto Public Reference Library, a couple of blocks west of the Conservatory on College Street),[11] lessons and classes, and evening concerts, whether as an usher at the Auditorium or as a student audience member at Massey Hall. Having heard few live orchestral performances, I was eager to make up for this gap in my musical experience, so bought a student subscription to the Toronto Symphony Orchestra concerts, added regularly to my personal score library, and went to as many of the rehearsals as I could manage. The conductor, MacMillan, was also dean of the Faculty of Music, and students were usually permitted to sit in on his rehearsals.

From my college classes with Ruth Humphrey I acquired a love of books, and also of bookstores, particularly second-hand ones. My literary choices usually ran to novels and plays rather than didactic fare. My music instructors—Guerrero, Smith, Walter—impressed on their students, by example and advice, the importance of building your own music library. Books and scores were cheap (sixty cents for a Penguin reprint of George Eliot, eighty cents for a miniature of a Haydn symphony). Toronto had sheet-music shops and publisher outlets, and I became familiar with them. Among my purchases were Donald Francis Tovey's *Essays in Musical Analysis*, all six extant volumes. There was a postwar effort to produce previously unpublished writings of his (for example, someone had edited a seventh volume of the *Essays*) and I was eager to have these. Freda

Ferguson, who handled music in the Toronto office of Oxford University Press (called Amen House after the one in England), seemed surprised by my interest. There had not been any great Canadian call for Tovey (she pronounced the name to rhyme with "lovey-dovey"). From the local branch of Boosey and Hawkes I bought newly released scores by Bartók and Stravinsky. I got the name of a bookbinder from Guerrero and had him put hard covers on my Bach and Beethoven piano scores; I wanted them to last.

A keen concertgoer from my childhood, I lapped up the opportunities to hear leading performers in Toronto. These included, in my first year or two, the violinists Nathan Milstein and Josef Szigeti, the Budapest String Quartet, and the pianists Rudolf Firkusny, Alexander Brailowsky, Claudio Arrau, Rudolf Serkin, and Mieczyslaw Horszowski. Arrau was a fellow Chilean and personal friend of Guerrero's, and practised on his piano when visiting Toronto. Horszowski gave a massive rendition of the *Hammerklavier* Sonata—astonishing in view of his diminutive size and evidently small hands. Among the singers were Jennie Tourel, Paul Robeson, Ezio Pinza, Marian Anderson, Jussi Bjoerling, and two remarkable artists then past their prime, Lotte Lehmann and Maggie Teyte, both of whom made deep impressions. Monteux and Mitropoulos were among the TSO's guest conductors. There was little new or avant-garde music, and almost none by Canadian composers. The touring San Carlo Opera Company, known from their Victoria visits, offered an annual week of warhorse repertoire in full-scale if conventional productions.

I took in plays fairly regularly at the Royal Alexandra Theatre, which was gaining back its reputation as a tour stop of US and British companies (no Canadians). Second-balcony seats were cheap. A small live orchestra (five or six players) performed during intermissions—gems from *Oklahoma!* and the like. During my student period, *The Importance of Being Earnest* with John Gielgud as Worthing and Margaret Rutherford as Lady Bracknell was unforgettable, while, also from England, Donald Wolfit brought a Shakespeare repertoire, which was my cue to study the plays I didn't know, such as *As You Like It* and especially *King Lear*, engrossing even when routinely done. In another season, *Macbeth* featured Flora Robson and Michael Redgrave, and from New York there was an *Anthony and Cleopatra* with Katherine Cornell, as well as *A Streetcar Named Desire* with Uta Hagen and Anthony Quinn, and several musicals.

Hart House Theatre announced its postwar reopening and the appointment of a new director, Robert Gill. I learned that their inaugural show would be Shaw's *Saint Joan*, a play I had studied in Ruth Humphrey's

English class; so I read for Gill and he assigned me a small role. Charmion King was Joan; she and other cast members later became prominent professionals in Canada (David Gardner, Araby Lockhart, Donald Davis). John Walker, who took the demanding Inquisitor's role, was later a distinguished member of the university's French department and used his theatrical voice as a summer-relief announcer for the CBC. This was for me the first of several acting involvements—an outlet for my energies that contrasted to my main concentration, music.

A few months in Toronto opened a wider and deeper world of music. I felt more than ever convinced that music was my future, and early in the new year, 1946, I got up courage to say this in a letter to my parents. Dad's letter to me, in reply, bespeaks his character and our relationship. Here is most of it:

Dear John:

[M]any thanks for the Gagnon book[12] ... His paintings interest me very much. Some of those in the book I remember, but others were quite new to me. Several, which show Quebec country scenes in Winter, remind me of the trip I made once from Montreal to Lachute, Quebec, in mid-Winter, to see Mrs. Massick[13] ... She was a brilliant woman and a real character at the same time. Talked a streak, but never tired the listener. It was a mixture of wit, profound thought, reminiscence and plain interesting conversation. One minute she'd be discussing her reasons for disapproving of St. Paul and his writings, and the next she'd be telling of the fun she had when her husband was a member of the press gallery at Ottawa and he and she helped with members' speeches ... How she ever got landed in a little house in the village of Lachute (and seemed to like it) I never did know. Probably she enjoyed her books and writings and her thoughts so much that her surroundings made little difference.

The letter starts with this recollection as a warm-up. He then mentions that Pamela Terry and Ron Shepherd were their recent guests for dinner. He continues:

All went over to the Harpers' (Gwen's house) to play your record.[14] Very good. I'd like to hear it a few more times...

Pamela played your three compositions.[15] Here's my comment, for what it may be worth (as that of the "man in the street" musically).

The Frolic for Ronaldo is really clever, if light-ish, and I like it very much.

The other short piece I like even better. There is much more to it of originality and of real musical value ... I feel it will grow on me as I get to hear all there is in it ...

The longer piece is very interesting but just hearing it a couple of times left me feeling as if I'd been hearing a speech in a language that I only knew imperfectly ... I'd like to hear it a number of times more ... It is quite definitely interesting.

I hope you are keeping your compositions in some sort of binder— and dated. If not, you should start at once.

He then turns to the topic of my letter. The support he and Mother had promised was for an initial scholarship year. When I said I was serious about a musical future, it was tantamount to asking their further support for completion of the bachelor's course and perhaps more.

The announcement of your decision to make music your life work did not surprise me. I agree with it most heartily; in fact, I'd come to the opinion myself that that would be your wisest decision. It would be grand to have you with me in the office. I know we'd get on well together and you could be successful. But at the same time I'm convinced that you'd never be entirely happy practising law—and I wouldn't want anyone to go into it unless he really enjoyed it.

Your other year in Toronto should be quite possible to manage, especially with your summer earnings and any possible scholarship help. You may have to break off for a year or two [i.e., take a steady job] before going on with the rest of your educational program, but you should stick to it ... if you feel it is needed. For a final goal radio and university music faculty appeal to me (in that order) with composing and critical writing on the side.

Better start soon looking into placement for summer work this year. If you want me to make any enquiries ... let me know.

Love
Dad.

The mixture of reassurance, affection, and practical advice is Dad to the life. My father seems here to be describing my career in advance as he envisions a "final goal" (!) of involvements in radio and post-secondary teaching, "with composing and critical writing *on the side*." This is almost exactly the way it turned out; how did he know? Clearly radio music was a flourishing activity. John Avison in Vancouver was like a role model with his constant radio appearances as piano accompanist or conductor. There was talk of expansion of existing music faculties and the creation of new ones. These may have been the practical opportunities I spoke of in writing my parents. They recognized my growing ambitions for composing and the critical bent of my forays into journalism, but regarded them as sidelines rather than serious ways to earn a living.

My summer job in 1946 (and again in 1947) was allied to the journalism streak. I was a summer replacement in a lowly department of the *Victoria Daily Colonist*—the "morgue," the office where photos were filed. The photos were in the form of metal or cardboard "cuts" (i.e., offset engravings) and were filed alongside clippings of items in the paper where they had been used. It was boring work and the pay was not much, but I liked being part of the busy atmosphere. A bonus was a series of lunch-hour talks the editor, Sandham ("Sandy") Graves, gave to interested junior members of his staff, on do's and don't's of newspaper writing. I had already known how to touch type; I now knew as well how to put a news report together succinctly, and who was who in a professional newsroom. In the second summer, Graves gave me a few reviewing assignments (of some of the summer-school recitals).

A series of solo piano performances on the local Victoria radio station CJVI gave me a first taste of radio broadcasting. In 1947 I must have auditioned for the CBC network affiliate in Vancouver, CBR, because I was given four half-hour recitals. I included a few of my own piano compositions in these programs. Pamela and I played a recital of two-piano music for the summer school that year.

The Toronto academic season of 1946–47 had been in several ways quite different from that of 1945–46. The Royal Conservatory Opera School began operations, with Nicholas Goldschmidt as its first musical director, and an enrolment of bright and eager young singers. The Faculty of Music more than doubled its student ranks in adding a new vocational program, music education. In both the opera program and the music education course, as throughout the university, students were older than the peacetime norm, many completing their formation on veterans' grants. It was a stimulating atmosphere: everyone was strongly motivated both for their personal futures and for the future of Canada.

Practice time on the Conservatory pianos became increasingly hard to book, and Irene and Arthur Rogers offered to let me practise in their home; my daily routine now included a streetcar journey to and from the Lawrence Park area in North Toronto. I worked hard in my piano studies with Guerrero (winning two firsts in the Kiwanis festival) and towards the completion of my degree. Somehow I found time to play Collins in a Hart House Theatre adaptation of *Pride and Prejudice*. Kay Hawtrey was Elizabeth, and our proposal scene was deemed a highlight. David Gardner was Bingley, Araby Lockhart Aunt Gardiner, and Bea Leonard Mrs Bennett. At a cast party, I was introduced to James Reaney, a campus *enfant terrible* whose writings and personality were already legendary.

We found we had much in common, with his background in music and my enthusiasm for literature and theatre. Through him I met other budding writers: Colleen Thibaudeau (later his wife), Phyllis Webb, Phyllis Gotlieb, Robert Weaver and Robert Patchell (both of whom joined the CBC), Diana Goldsborough, William Toye, and Margaret Gayfer (all of whom became active in the publishing world). At the *Varsity* office, where I continued to write reviews of music, and also sometimes of drama, I encountered Norman DePoe and Mark Harrison, both later well-known figures in the journalism world. A prominent new talent in the Guerrero "stable" was Ray Dudley, and we became close friends. Guerrero was

James Reaney, at his farm near Stratford, 1949 (photo by me).

interested in the classical duet literature and put the two of us to learning this interesting repertoire, including the big four-hand sonatas of Mozart and Stravinsky's *Pièces faciles* (we took turns playing the "facile" part). Dudley, then seventeen, had a sunny disposition and driving ambition for music—an exceptional combination. Reaney, Thibaudeau, Gayfer, Dudley, and Helmut Kallmann (whom I met the following season) all remained among my most valued friends.

Social gatherings often included alcoholic drinks, requiring an adjustment from my upbringing in a booze-free household. I handled my first preprandial sherry cautiously, but could not suppress making a face at my first beer, causing hilarity (it was a family dinner at Araby Lockhart's). At a gathering of students at Trinity College which I attended with Keith MacMillan, I managed a rye and ginger with greater aplomb. It was a matter of not only acquiring the taste but learning my limit. At a cocktail party at the home of Godfrey Ridout and his wife, Freda Antrobus, I was

Ray Dudley, in front of the Ontario legislative buildings, Toronto, 1948 (photo by me).

invited, as the youngest man present, to help serve the martinis. Helping myself in the process, I soon became plastered, "high," and terribly talkative, but fortunately not sick. In a performance with Ray Dudley later that evening my playing was quite reckless. Enjoy, but don't overdo, was the message—and don't try to play the piano.

In May I had to prepare for my examinations. There were papers in history of music, "form," advanced harmony, and fugue, and you presented yourself for a "viva voce" session where you were expected to play something from *The Well-Tempered Clavier*, read a score at sight, and answer questions on assigned scores (one of which that year was the Brahms Fourth Symphony). In the fugue exam, you were given a subject and asked to compose a fugue on it in three hours; few candidates ever finished that one. When someone in our class asked Healey Willan how to prepare for the fugue test, his advice was "Write fugues, old man, write fugues." You established a formula and then practised getting it down on paper fast. Willan was, in my experience, not a helpful teacher. He had many favourite sayings, one of which was "Don't take yourself too seriously." His affable manner disguised the fact that he took himself and his career *quite* seriously: some years later Ron Napier, of BMI Canada, told me of Willan's constant phone calls about the promotion of his opera *Deirdre*. Leo Smith, Willan's colleague, was a genuine scholar and a kind man, though not, again in my experience, a notably communicative teacher. He was famous for dropping hints in the last few weeks before the exam period from which you could gather what questions would be on the paper. I topped the class when the results were announced, even though I barely earned a "pass" for fugue. The Faculty had a high failure rate, and often even experienced and hard-working candidates were obliged to repeat subjects they had missed. One of my fellow students in Willan's harmony class, a nun named Mother Lucy, from Windsor (she also studied piano with Guerrero), said before the exams that she was going to pray for me; she might better have sought divine help for her own success, because she was one of the casualties. The other graduation requirement was an "exercise," your choice of either a twenty-minute composition (a string quartet or a piece for chorus) or what would later be called a "major paper," an extended essay. Composing was more and more my chief goal, but I felt inadequately prepared for the first option, so chose the second. I had just added the Sonata in A, op. 101, to my piano repertoire, so my essay topic was "Beethoven's fugues," and, leaning heavily on Tovey, I analyzed this and other relevant works, large and small, mostly from his "third period," trying to arrive at original observations if not actual research findings. My approach was musical analysis, not historical sleuthing. The exercise was accepted, and I had some good compliments on it from Leo Smith.

I had my degree but wanted to be free to study further. The U of T had as yet no graduate offerings in music, but another degree was not essential, to my thinking. I had made good strides in piano and was ready to give a full solo recital; there were encouraging comments on my first serious attempts at composing,[16] and I wanted especially to pursue this avenue. I auditioned for, and received, another RCM scholarship award, the Heintzman Scholarship. My parents agreed to support me in open-ended music studies for the season 1947–48, and I was able to supplement this funding with various part-time earnings: I gave up ushering but continued my activities as an accompanist and coach, including now rehearsals with the Opera School; and I succeeded Brock McElheran as art, music, and drama editor of *The Varsity*, a commitment for writing and scheduling for which there was a small weekly fee (smaller than those of my fellow editors, on the grounds that I had my choice of free tickets to all those wonderful plays and concerts).[17] With the authority of my baccalaureate, I put prospective student reviewers through a test of musical knowledge. One of the applicants was Helmut Kallmann, from second-year music education. Raised in pre-war Berlin in a cultivated family, he was well versed in the classical repertoire and dissected my questions minutely. We formed a solid friendship and in later years worked together on many projects. When looking back on his career as the pre-eminent historian of Canadian music, he told me that I was responsible for his first writing assignment.

My piano studies had progressed to the point that I could play a fairly demanding recital. This took place on 3 December 1947. Colin Sabiston, music critic of *The Globe and Mail*, gave it a full review, commending not only my playing but also the extensive program notes I had written.[18] The notes, which he described as "scholarly," were a turgid and opinionated reflection of the sort of notes Tovey wrote for his performances in Edinburgh. My program was severely classical: Mozart's Sonata in D (K311); the preludes and fugues in C♯, E, A, and F♯ minor from Book 2 of Bach's *Well-Tempered Clavier*; and two "third-period" works by Beethoven, the Six Bagatelles, op. 126, and the Sonata in A, op. 101. In his end-of-the-year roundup in the *Globe*, Sabiston singled out two young artists as especially worthy of future attention—Lois Marshall was one and I was the other. This was extraordinarily lucky; I wasn't sure I deserved such praise, but Lois certainly did. I had covered for *The Varsity* her appearance with a Conservatory chamber orchestra in an Alessandro

Scarlatti cantata a few weeks previously and was bowled over like everyone else by her beautiful voice and compelling stage presence.

I joined Nicholas Goldschmidt's class in conducting. With a fellow pianist in the class, George Crum (later music director of the National Ballet of Canada), I performed classical symphonies and overtures arranged for piano duet, while the others took turns conducting. When it was my turn or Crum's, Goldschmidt would take over as second pianist. His criticisms were sharp (to me: "You're too inhibited!"), and he didn't always provide a clear demonstration of what was required; but it was valuable experience. My perception that conducting was something a budding composer ought to be able to do, at least decently, has proved to be accurate.

One of the events I reviewed for *The Varsity* was the TSO's all-Canadian concert on 27 January 1948. This was a brave, if conservative, bow to the growing repertoire by the country's composers. Other contemporary pieces appeared rarely, among them the symphonies of Roy Harris and William Walton. As a striking exception to the prevailing program blandness, Harry Somers played two full solo recitals, one of his own piano music and the other of Barbara Pentland's. Such live examples of current music appeared only seldom, of modernism even less frequently, and students relied on score study and listening to what recordings were available in the small Conservatory library collection (I recall as revelations the quartets of Bartók, the ballets of Stravinsky, and several then-brand-new scores by Copland).

The New Play Society, then in only its second season, introduced (2 to 5 April 1947) a recent London success, Ronald Duncan's verse play *This Way to the Tomb*, and Howard Brown and I performed the incidental music by Benjamin Britten, scored for piano four hands. We read it from a rented manuscript copy; evidently it has never been published. I remember it as a series of witty musical pastiches. This was my first of several contacts with the NPS company as both pianist and actor.

My family in Victoria had supported me during three years of music study, but now, starting in the fall of 1948, I undertook to support myself. The Royal Conservatory principal, Ettore Mazzoleni, offered me a position as staff publicity officer. The salary was modest but steady, and he agreed to let me have an upright piano in my office on which I could practise after hours. I continued my piano lessons with Guerrero, while filling my days writing press releases, setting up interviews, and designing brochures. There were opportunities to expand my knowledge of printing and graphic design, through almost daily liaisons with a downtown print shop, the Haddon Press, and with the printing department of the U of T Press. The Conservatory had published its own journal in the past, and I proposed to revive something of the sort. The resulting four-page newsletter (all the budget could stand) was called the *Monthly Bulletin*, and circulated not only internally but to the widespread network of examination centres across the country. I tried to incorporate both news items and short discussion papers, and was successful in persuading some of the leading teachers to contribute. In a *Varsity* column I had referred sarcastically to the "bureaucratic jargon" of the Year Book, and Mazzoleni took delight in telling me it was now my job to edit it: I believe the new one was an improvement. My small office was located in the western annex of the RCM alongside that of Anna McDonagh, the concert manager. Anna (later Anna McCoy) and I became firm friends.

My studies with Alberto Guerrero had a continuing, strong influence during this period.[19] He was an active solo and chamber-music performer, and I was always profoundly impressed with his public and private readings. The private ones arose spontaneously in the course of lessons, and in the public ones I was occasionally conscripted to turn pages for him. In the circle of fellow students, Glenn was astonishing everyone and becoming insatiably curious about music and a lively companion. A new arrival from Saskatchewan was the gifted and effervescent Stuart Hamilton. His already-strong passion for opera prefigured his later career successes, especially as the founder of Opera in Concert. His disparagements of his own piano playing were always a comic camouflage: he is an exceptionally fine pianist.

I had returned to Toronto in early September 1948 in a sweltering heat wave. I decided to quit the "Y": the weekly rate for a single room was increased to seven dollars, and I thought for that price I could find something better. Sweatily tramping the streets, I found an attractive small room on Aylmer Avenue. My new landlady, Pola Forster, was a nurse at the Toronto General Hospital and shared the house with a cousin, Mary Corbett. Friends called her "Pola" because of a supposed likeness to the silent-film star Pola Negri; her actual name was Ruby Hainstock before she married the painter Michael Forster. He was English; she was from the Wingham area in Huron County. The house was full of Forster's intriguing canvases, and she spoke often of their life together before the war. Without asking, I took it that she was a widow. Many years later I learned, not from Pola, that he had left her and was living with someone else in Mexico.[20] In later years she was a devoted friend to me and to my family. Her quiet, comfortable home was one of a dozen or more row houses built in the late nineteenth century as an off–Yonge Street continuation of Belmont Avenue on the fringe of Rosedale; they were originally residences for the servants of wealthy families across the ravine in Rosedale proper. The one-block-long street contained only these houses, nothing else, and there was no street sign at the Yonge intersection, so you had to give careful directions, and people often got lost trying to find it. The row had a reputation as a kind of artists' colony. Robertson Davies spent part of his youth there; several Conservatory staff members were our neighbours, as were other musicians, including the organist Richard Tattersall and his wife Kitty, a piano teacher; next door was James McNaught, a magazine journalist who, as "James Bannerman," was a well-known CBC personality. I lived there happily for a year and a half, until we all had to move because the block was to be demolished to make way for the new Yonge Street subway. At this point some crackerjack at City Hall ordered a street sign; it's still there as a pointer to the non-existent Aylmer Avenue.

That fall I resumed my avocational activities in theatre by playing Dr Einstein in *Arsenic and Old Lace* at Hart House Theatre, with an accent modelled on Peter Lorre and Oskar Morawetz (Oskar was much amused). In February I played Mr Dangle in Sheridan's *The Critic* for the New Play Society. For that role, my accent was upper-class English, and the experienced Josephine Barrington, cast as Mrs Dangle, complimented me on it. The Society had programmed *Oedipus Rex* together with *The Critic* after the success of the English National Theatre, with Laurence Olivier, in the same double bill. In *Oedipus* I remember writhing on the floor as a member of the speaking chorus. The director of both plays was Dora Mavor Moore, but I found most of the guidance we received came from her son Mavor Moore. She was in my observation an effective booster but short on technique (the actors had to figure out their own blocking). Charles Tisdale and I were the duo-pianists for the NPS's *Spring Thaw* the previous season (1–3 April 1948, the first run of this popular annual revue). I had by that time joined the Toronto Musicians' Association (Local 149 of the American Federation of Musicians), but we didn't have a contract. The Society was intent on establishing itself as a professional organization, but funding was a struggle. Mavor Moore wrote that they weren't able to pay me, but he pledged to send me a cheque as soon as finances improved—for fifteen dollars. I wish I had kept the letter; the cheque never arrived, and I refrained from ever mentioning it to Mavor in later contacts with him.

I auditioned for Norbert Bowman, the CBC radio producer, and performed the first of several half-hour piano broadcasts in his series *Sunday*

Morning Recital. With Guerrero I prepared another solo recital and a duet program with Dudley, both of which included my own compositions. The two major items on the solo recital were the cycle of Inventions and Sinfonias by Bach and the *Valses nobles et sentimentales* by Ravel. Guerrero had featured the Bach pieces some years before in his own performances, and he and his wife Myrtle invited a number of musical friends to hear me play them. It was still a common attitude among musicians that they were "exercises" rather than real music, illustrated in the mechanical way many pianists, for example, rattled off the B♭ Invention, instead of giving it a singing presentation such as might suit an aria in one of the cantatas. "Singing" is a specific indication in the composer's introduction to the cycle. In the event, various factors prevented me from giving my best performance. In Victoria a few weeks before, Pamela's mother died after a long illness, and I was distressed at hearing of the upset in her family life; the evening of the recital (in early January) was bitterly cold, and I was unaccustomed to caring for my hands under such conditions. I gave good accounts of the Ravel and of my own pieces, but the Inventions and Sinfonias had uneven moments, not up to the standard I had achieved in tryouts. I received nice comments from the party guests afterwards (including the MacMillans and the Leo Smiths) but felt as if I had fluffed the assignment. In a review in *Saturday Night*, John Cozens voiced exactly the view about the Bach pieces I had hoped to combat: I had not demonstrated, he said, that they were anything more significant than "teaching pieces." Most of all I had, I thought, let Guerrero down; but assessing the evening in my next lesson he put a positive spin on it and made the suggestion that my next repertoire challenge should be the *Goldberg Variations*—from which I judged that he had by no means lost faith in my abilities.

My duties at the Conservatory kept me in Toronto for most of the summer of 1949. In early July Victor Feldbrill conducted the Conservatory Orchestra in a reading of Barbara Pentland's Symphony No. 1, and Harry Somers and I were conscripted for the percussion parts. I remember the work but have forgotten what particular instruments I was called on to play. For several years the RCM had rented a booth to hand out pamphlets at the annual Canadian National Exhibition. I suggested a better use of the funds would be a series of short recitals by some of the school's best students, and when the proposal was accepted I set about organizing the programs. The young performers included names like Marshall and Gould. I spent the August holiday period on the west coast, partly in Victoria and partly in Vancouver, where Pamela was taking a summer

With Alberto Guerrero, Vancouver, August 1949 (photo by Pamela Terry).

theatre course at UBC. I stayed in one of the campus Quonset huts and spent my days copying the score and parts of my orchestration of a new work, *Music for Dancing.* The Guerreros had rented a summer home in West Vancouver, and Pamela and I visited them there. She had decided to come east with me in the fall for further drama study in Toronto. I looked forward to introducing her to the city and to my circle of friends. We arrived back in time to say farewell to Reaney, who was leaving for Winnipeg to take up his new position in the English department of the University of Manitoba. Pamela found a comfortable furnished room in the St Clair–Bathurst district. She registered for the inaugural year of the theatrical school of Ernest Sterndale Bennett and his wife Hilda. Bennett (grandson of the nineteenth-century English composer William Sterndale Bennett) had operated a course in stagecraft and acting through the Royal Conservatory and had trained a number of prominent performers, among them Jack Medhurst, George Luscombe, Kate Reid, and Hugh Webster. He had lately decided to set up an independent school in a loft near Church and Queen. Pamela and I had busy schedules, and she had occasional part-time work in a movie theatre and later a book store; we met for outings and meals and enjoyed parties, both musical and theatrical. It was a welcome change from having to communicate by letter. That Christmas we were invited to dinner with the Guerreros, and in the holidays the two of us put on a party for friends in Pola's living room.

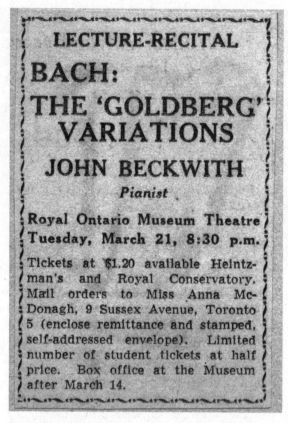

Newspaper advertisement for my piano "debut," March 1950.

The early months of 1950 were eventful for my musical development. The *Music for Dancing* suite was performed several times both in its original piano-duet form and in the orchestral version; I was one of the winners in a CBC songwriting contest; the CBC presented my music in a half-hour network feature in the *Wednesday Night* series; and I gave, in March, in both Hamilton and Toronto, a well-received lecture-recital on Bach's *Goldberg Variations*. Reginald Godden, whom I had known as a piano teacher in Toronto, was now principal of the Hamilton Conservatory and generously invited me for a trial run of the *Goldbergs*. In Toronto, the venue was the basement theatre of the Royal Ontario Museum. I rented a less-than-full-size Heintzman grand for the occasion, having found it suited the piece better than the boomier concert grands on offer. Anna McDonagh, my Conservatory colleague, helped by circulating a flyer and looking after ticket sales. Given on

21 March (Bach's birthday, and in his bicentennial year), it was an independent production, and we were gratified at the response, even though the hall was less than full: we had what can fairly be described as a distinguished audience. The event elicited a rave from Pearl McCarthy in *The Globe and Mail*.[21] She and her husband, Colin Sabiston (he was the regular music critic; she wrote mainly on art but also occasionally reviewed music), had had me to tea and to dinner and introduced me to some of their circle. Sabiston knew of my work on *The Varsity* and gave me a few reviewing assignments for the *Globe*. He also sometimes covered theatre events and had reviewed a couple of plays in which I had acted. The connections of friendship and the extravagant terms of McCarthy's *Goldberg* review ("one of the finest recitals in decades") may have made some readers suspect undue favouritism; however, the lecture-recital format was novel and my playing was the best I had done up to then. McCarthy's praise was exaggerated, yes, but in later years my efforts—whether as composer or performer—sometimes met with critical abuse that was just as exaggerated. I wasn't sure it was ethical or proper for me to thank her, but Guerrero said it was, so I called her. This time at the Guerreros' after-concert party, I felt elation rather than chagrin.

All these activities cut into my devotion to my day job, and I began to get complaints from Mazzoleni. No doubt he was starting to realize that his vision of my making a career as (as he put it) "the Mark Schubart of the Conservatory"—a reference to William Schuman's right-hand man at Juilliard—was unlikely of realization. I took his criticisms to heart and tried to do better. Around this time, Géza de Kresz approached me and asked if I would help him with a manual on violin playing he was writing. A former member of the Hart House Quartet, he was one of the principal violin teachers at the Conservatory and a frequent recitalist with his wife, the pianist Norah Drewett de Kresz. He had spent a large part of his career in Canada, and his wife was English, but his native language was Hungarian. He knew, I suppose, of my writing and the editing I did for the *Bulletin*. It was an interesting task: I was able to suggest improvements in the writing but had almost no understanding of violin-playing technique. The manual was unfinished when de Kresz died, but (according to a biography of the de Kreszes) completed portions were privately published in 1969.[22]

Looking back, I am surprised that I did not curb my theatrical spurts in this busy period, but I had a role in an independent production of James Thurber's *The Male Animal* and later played Chasuble in Wilde's *The Importance of Being Earnest* for the University Alumnae at Hart House

Theatre. For this the director was William Needles, and William Hutt played Algernon; both became among the foremost performers at the Stratford Festival. Needles loved the play and insisted that we say our lines exactly as written. It is indeed a brilliant script, and the habit of quoting from it has never left me.

Around the time of my *Goldberg* performance, we all faced removal as the homes on Aylmer Avenue disappeared in the path of the city's new subway. The Tattersalls moved to a house on Balmoral Avenue near St Clair and Yonge. Shortly after they took possession, Richard Tattersall suddenly died: he was ill, and it seems the move upset him. Kitty offered me a front bedroom with an adjoining sunroom, and I lived there until my departure for France in the fall. Irish-born, she was a vivacious personality and a great fan of MacMillan's. In her new home she continued her work as piano teacher to (as she liked to say) the "carriage trade"—children of the Rosedale families across the ravine from Aylmer. She would bring me tea in the mornings and pass along all the latest musical gossip.

A further piano-playing venture had a certain link with Conservatory interests: I performed a solo recital at the annual Summer School, including what was perhaps the first performance in Canada of the Sonata by Aaron Copland. I found this work both original and eloquent, and also introduced it in a CBC *Sunday Morning Recital*.

But by now composing was taking a larger and larger amount of my time and energy.

5

Composing

A publication of 1974, *Colombo's Canadian Quotations*, included a saying of mine from an interview of 1967: "From about age eight I had the idea I wanted to be a composer—mainly, at that time, in order to become very, very famous." This awful, but true, statement was repeated in *Colombo's* under an attribution to another Canadian composer, Harry Somers.[1] In my usual bossy way, I wrote a correction to the editor, John Robert Colombo; he agreed that there had been some mixup and that I was the one who deserved credit (blame?) for the remark.

Longing for fame, or at least for recognition, is an unworthy but often-felt motive in my work life, and probably does date back to childhood. It even affected the prayers I used to whisper as a child. As a young adult I wasted a good deal of creative energy on visions of self-promotion. The other part of the childhood declaration, the aim to compose, is a distinct memory from my early years, but I was slow to act on it. During a visit to cousins in Portland, Oregon, when I was ten or eleven, I performed for them a short piano piece which I had not only improvised but even managed to write down. It was a one-page reiteration of the triad and harmonic-minor scale on C, to be played with determination and a certain amount of rhythmic fury, and I think the title was "Gnome's Dance."

The only other attempt at "composition" alongside my piano practice and studies in elementary harmony and counterpoint dates from my thirteenth or fourteenth year. This is a quite unoriginal set of piano variations—not that the "Gnome's Dance" was original in any way—on the Lutheran chorale, "Seelen-Bräutigam" ("The Soul's Bridegroom") by Adam Drese (1620–1701). In church we sang it under the title "Arnstadt" to the text of an evening hymn. Was it prophetic, in view of my much later interest in and use of hymn tunes, that this little effort was based on a chorale? I showed the variations to a fellow student and asked if she might include them in her recital program (she politely declined); I couldn't have imagined performing them publicly myself and didn't even play them for family or my teacher privately. If a copy exists (I sincerely hope not), it will portray a student who earnestly wanted to compose but had not the slightest idea how to go about it.

During my first year of full-time music study, in Toronto (1945–46), I produced some short examples—six little one- or two-page piano pieces, a few songs. They reflect what little I knew of musical modernism—slightly witty bagatelles or short-winded atmospheric effects.[2] During 1946–47 these were followed by a few more examples of similar miniature scope and also a couple of attempts at choral music. My versions of two lyrics from *Twelfth Night* exhausted any interest I might have had in setting Shakespeare to music and are the only compositions I ever showed to Healey Willan. He was encouraging but rightly criticized one cadence as being too much of a cliché. The other older musician to whom I turned for advice, Arnold Walter, was also fairly encouraging ("You seem to have something to say"). I had further approving comments from my piano teacher, Alberto Guerrero, for whom I played some of the pieces. I entered a group of the piano compositions and the choruses in the annual CAPAC (Composers, Authors and Publishers Association of Canada) contest for young composers and was awarded second prize, a small amount of cash. Clermont Pépin, a student of Walter's, was the first-prize winner. In my solo broadcasts on local radio in Victoria and Vancouver during summer holidays I played some of my own piano pieces.

In 1947–48 I began to feel more like a composer and had my first experiences of performances of my music by others. In December of 1947 I became interested in classical Chinese poetry—the motivation for this interest escapes me, but I read various English translations and was drawn to the idea of setting some examples as songs. Those by Arthur Waley were the most admired, but I found greater rhythmic stimulus in the versions of the US poet Witter Bynner. The text I chose for the first setting in my little cycle is, though I did not realize it, one of the most famous lyrics of Li Po, a delicate *aubade*, for which Bynner's title is "The Staircase of Jade." By New Year's Eve I had completed a set of five songs and gave them the title *Five Lyrics of the T'ang Dynasty*. The Victoria College Music Club announced an evening of music by campus composers, and I submitted my cycle. Freda Antrobus agreed to perform it with me but took ill a few days before, so the first performance—the first concert exposure of *anything* I had composed, in fact—was by the tenor Arthur Bartlett. Both Freda and Arthur were students of George Lambert, and George had included me in a group of colleagues and students he and his wife Gretchen invited to their Saturday dinner parties now and then. His enthusiasm for my *Lyrics* and his coaching of the first performance were a valuable boost. The performance went surprisingly well considering the shortness of learning time Bartlett had had, and in a review in the University of Toronto student newspaper, *The Varsity*, Doug Valleau singled out my work for special praise. That must have been my first public criticism; unlike many of the subsequent ones, it was positive.

In March 1948 a group from the Conservatory attended a student composers' symposium at the Eastman School of Music in Rochester. I was lucky that my songs were included in the program, performed this time by Freda Antrobus. Other Conservatory composers attending were Somers, Freedman, and Pépin. The symposium was a three- or four-day immersion in new music. A number of the students from US schools later became quite prominent: Lee Hoiby, Ned Rorem, Howard Boatwright, Arthur Frackenpohl, Yehudi Wyner.

The Royal Conservatory (Toronto) delegation at the first Student Composers' Symposium, Eastman School of Music, University of Rochester, March 1948. Left to right, standing: James Innes, Morry Kernerman, James Hunter, John Mair, Rowland Pack, Andrew Benac, Joseph Pach, James Pataki, Clermont Pépin, Harry Somers, Victor Feldbrill, John Coveart, Gordon Jocelyn; at the piano: John Beckwith, Freda Antrobus.

What stayed with me from the music I heard? The melodies and harmonies seemed to consist of perfect fourths more than any other interval. Later that spring I wrote a piano piece in which I put quotation marks around a perfect-fourth motive which stuck in my head as a kind of symposium prototype. Hindemith was teaching at Yale then, and some of the symposium participants were his students. The prevailing interval quality was attributed to his influence. Forty years later, in 1988, as a visiting composer at Memorial University in St John's, I coached a group of students for a concert including some of my earliest works—works I hadn't heard in a long time—and it hit me how often my instinctual melodic ideas in that period emphasized perfect fourths and fifths: many of the melodic lines in the *Lyrics*, especially the first and last songs, illustrate this, as does also, for example, the horn fanfare at the start of the Five Pieces for Brass Trio, composed four years later. When we repeated the *Lyrics* in a Toronto presentation of the Conservatory's symposium concert, Pearl McCarthy's *Globe and Mail* review included the comment that they were "worth a publisher's notice." Jean Howson, music editor for the just-started publication program of BMI Canada, read this and said she "could take a hint." She asked me to submit the songs, which meant sending them to BMI in New York for approval. Howson contacted the representatives of Witter Bynner, the translator, and received permission (I hadn't thought to ask previously), and the songs appeared in an attractive format with the Chinese characters spelling "T'ang Dynasty" in red on the cover. It was some years before the firm issued the whole set under one cover; the initial publication was of five separate songs, which seemed to me nervy, considering that the longest of the five lasted scarcely two minutes.

This project was my initiation into the performing-rights scene of the late 1940s. BMI Canada was a new organization, a Canadian branch of Broadcast Music Inc., ASCAP's rival, formed in the early 1940s by US radio interests.[3] In Canada it soon developed a competitive position with the established agency, CAPAC. Since I had been a contest winner with CAPAC, that association's general manager, St Clair Low, summoned me for an interview and gave me a lecture about the evil practices of BMI and its Canadian upstart partner. However, since I knew that both established and younger composers in Canada (Champagne, Willan, Somers, Morel) had signed agreements with BMI Canada, I felt safe in doing so. No other music publishers in the country appeared to take an interest in the younger generation of composers, or for that matter in "serious" repertoire. Unlike CAPAC, BMI Canada set out to be both a performing-rights body and a publisher.

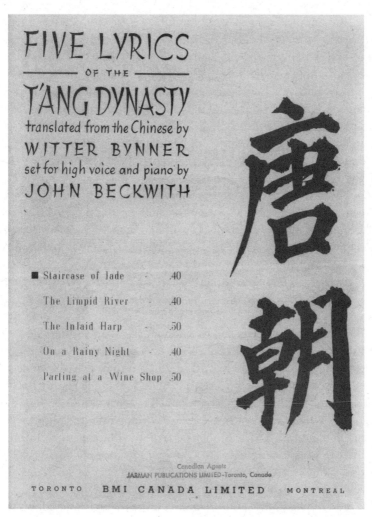

Cover of my first publication, Five Lyrics of the T'ang Dynasty *(BMI Canada, 1949).*

The *Lyrics* are indeed slight. Despite obvious technical shortcomings, I believe they achieve a convincing musical crystallization of the poems' vivid moments of feeling, and this without perhaps overdoing the "oriental" coloration. The published songs soon appeared on examination and festival repertoire lists and over the years have been sung by many students. Almost always the performances are by sopranos, although the first performance was by a tenor, and I always considered the songs more suited to the tenor voice. When acknowledged as the composer, I often want to ask whether the young performers know any of my other—meaning *later*—

music, but am pleased if they still find these little works interesting and performable. Among the four recordings of the set,[4] the most surprising to me, and in many ways the most gratifying, was that of a Hong Kong artist, Barbara Fei. When I met her years later in Hong Kong, I was able to thank her and say how happy I was that a distinguished performer of Chinese background would find the songs appropriate—meaning culturally unintrusive. The recording by Jon Vickers occurred almost by accident. Though a great admirer of his voice, I felt the *Lyrics* did not suit him, and the performances, evidently hurriedly prepared, are not in my view definitive or a good model.

On another visiting-composer stint, this time at the University of Alberta in October 1997, I heard a touching performance of the *Lyrics*, and became momentarily choked up when asked to say a few words. It had suddenly hit me that *fifty years* had passed since I wrote them.

My next two composing enterprises arose respectively from my frequent activities as an accompanist to singers and my studies in piano-duet repertoire with Ray Dudley—namely, the set of Four Songs to Poems by Edith Sitwell and the suite *Music for Dancing*.

The Edith Sitwell songs had touches of drama and mystery lacking in the *Lyrics*. I may have been led to her writings by my friendship with James Reaney, for whose early work she was to some extent a model. The songs, for soprano and piano, were taken up by Marguerite Gignac, Lois Marshall, and (I think) Mary Morrison, all fellow students of mine at the time. There were originally five songs,[5] but Weldon Kilburn, Lois Marshall's teacher, thought the fifth was not as effective as the others, so I dropped it. It had, I recall, a more rigid structure (was it a ground bass?) which he felt was out of keeping with the other more spontaneous-sounding songs. There was no immediate surge of interest for publication of this set, but I realized I should obtain authorization for my use of Dame Edith's texts. Her representative in London asked me to submit a score, and I did, and some months later received word that the poet declined her permission, offering as her reason that she had just signed an exclusive contract with William Walton. The denial of permission included a prohibition on further public performances of the songs. When I asked for the return of the manuscript, the agent apologetically told me Dame Edith had lost it. The exclusive contract with Walton was apparently short-lived, if it ever existed, since within a few years there was a setting by Humphrey Searle of her *Gold Coast Customs*.

Music for Dancing came about not only by my immersion in the duet medium but also by the offer of a commission. Herman Voaden, Toronto teacher and playwright, was active in the Forest Hill Community Centre concert series, which had inaugurated a policy of giving annual commissions and first performances to local composers. Weinzweig, Somers, Adaskin, and Pentland had received such awards, and I was surprised to be considered alongside these established names. Voaden invited me to write music for a ballet to be danced by the Volkoff Ballet troupe and choreographed by their director, Boris Volkoff. The committee accepted my suggestion of the medium of piano four-hands. The commission fee, fifty dollars, sounds extremely small, but it was a gesture—an honorarium—and composers appreciated it in a period when there was as yet in Canada no recognized principle of payment for new works, and indeed little interest in programming them. The prospect of a public performance meant more than the money. I composed most of the cycle of seven dances in Victoria during my summer break in 1948. For some reason there was no advance consultation with Volkoff. Herman Voaden probably should have arranged this; at least I should have asked about it, but was too shy and inexperienced. The music shows my inexperience but isn't especially shy in spirit. My models—Ravel, Debussy, Poulenc, the Walton of *Façade*—are easily recognized. The "Valse" (my youthful francophilia dictated the French form rather than "Waltz") suggests another model, namely Erik Satie; however, I had heard none of his music, so this was a secondary reflection, maybe from members of the Satie circle—Poulenc or Milhaud. The continuity of the cycle depends far too much on repetition and sequence, but there are some not-bad melodies and the harmonies show some effective moments of brashness. Alberto Guerrero said after Dudley and I rehearsed the final "Round Dance" with him that he couldn't get the repetitive main tune out of his head for days. He also made the astute comment that the suite seemed to be music "of the dance" rather than "for dancing."

Ray Dudley was my partner at the concert premiere, in January 1949, during our duet recital at the Conservatory, and later he and I travelled to Boston as part of the Toronto delegation to another student symposium, where *Music for Dancing* had a good deal of success as a "fun piece." We performed it several more times during the next two seasons at the invitation of various Toronto music organizations. But the ballet Voaden had envisioned never materialized. When I went with another pianist, Marjorie Lea, to play it for Boris Volkoff (that must have been some time in the fall of 1948), the choreographer's reaction was outspokenly negative. He said he couldn't imagine where a ballet to such music might be set, unless in a madhouse. The Volkoff company may have been under pressure to produce a new Canadian ballet ("a Can*add*ian ball*ett*," in Volkoff's Russian-accented way of saying it), because within a year they commissioned and premiered John Weinzweig's *The Red Ear of Corn*.

During the summer of 1949 I made an orchestration—my first such attempt apart from class assignments—of *Music for Dancing* and copied the parts. The following season there was a reading by the Conservatory Orchestra conducted by a fellow student, Victor Feldbrill, and a full performance on radio by a professional group under Samuel Hersenhoren. The suite (in full or in part) was played at the 1950 Canadian music symposium in Vancouver, and there was a broadcast performance by an orchestra in Oklahoma. I submitted the score to Sir Ernest, and a few seasons later he placed some excerpts on a Toronto Symphony Orchestra program. Through these performances, I came to realize that the spirit of the music was contradicted by my heavy hand as an inexperienced orchestrator; therefore I withdrew the orchestral version. (An opportunity to make a more suitable transcription, this time for smaller forces, came along in 1959.)

In that same summer of 1949, I composed most of the chamber-music setting of Reaney's *The Great Lakes Suite* from his first volume of poems, then in preparation, *The Red Heart and Other Poems*.[6] This score—calling for soprano, baritone, clarinet, cello, and piano—apparently inaugurated my move in two new directions: echoing popular music and reflecting particular Canadian ways. My composing was almost entirely instinctual, and my experience included a great deal of popular music, but I had up to then resisted any feeling that I might draw on such a store. It is also a mystery why in my earlier searches for song texts I did not investigate CanLit. Having a gifted poet as a friend and listening to his ideas about popular culture (*The Red Heart* includes, pre-McLuhan, a cycle based on comic strips) were valuable stimuli as I extended my approach. *The Great Lakes Suite* was certainly an advance over my previous pieces: the poems gave me structure and the chamber-music ensemble gave me opportunities for colour. I chose the group after encountering Ravel's *Chansons madécasses*, for voice, piano, flute, and cello, in a live performance. I knew little about either the clarinet or the cello but my ear was evidently a reliable guide, and the two players in the first concert performance, Leslie Mann and Rowland Pack, were helpful. That performance formed part of the Conservatory's program at the annual (March 1950) student composers' symposium, held this time in Toronto. The singers were Lois Marshall and Glenn Gardiner, and I was the pianist. Pearl McCarthy's review in *The Globe and Mail* was again highly complimentary.

But the actual premiere of the *Suite* occurred earlier, in February of that same year. *CBC Wednesday Night*, the radio network's cultural series, featured periodic half-hour recitals as one-person showcases of Canadian composers, and it was my good luck to be offered one of these. The program included the *Suite* (we were preparing it for the symposium concert,

Page 8 from the manuscript score of the "Lake Michigan" movement of The Great Lakes Suite, *to Reaney's words (1949).*

CBC WEDNESDAY NIGHT
FEBRUARY 15

MUSIC BY JOHN BECKWITH

Program

1. Excerpts from 'Music for Dancing', for piano four-hands.

2. Four Songs to poems by Edith Sitwell (first broadcast performance).

3. 'The Great Lakes Suite', for soprano, baritone, clarinet, 'cello, and piano, to poems by James Reaney (first performance).

Performers

Lois Marshall, soprano; Bernard Johnson, baritone; Leslie Mann, clarinetist; Cornelius Ysselstyn, 'cellist; Ray Dudley, Weldon Kilburn, and John Beckwith, pianists.

7:30 to 8, EST. 11 to 11:30, CST. 9:30 to 10, MST. 9:30 to 10, PST.
Check time in your daily newspaper.

Postcard-flyer for the February 1950 half-hour on CBC Wednesday Night.

but Pack and Gardiner were unavailable, so the cellist was Cornelius Ysselstyn and the baritone Bernard Johnson), two of the Sitwell songs performed by Lois Marshall and Weldon Kilburn, and two excerpts from *Music for Dancing* played by Ray Dudley and me. The broadcast gave rise to a short review by Chester Duncan in the literary magazine *Northern Review*—a cautiously worded gesture of encouragement.[7] Looking back, what was really encouraging, given my limited skill and small output at age twenty-three, was the sheer fact that my music would receive this coast-to-coast exposure.

The reception of my work gave me increased confidence, but I realized how much I still had to learn about composing. When I heard that the scholarship that had taken Somers to Paris for composition studies was being offered again, I determined to apply. The award was sponsored by the Canadian Amateur Hockey Association; a month or two later I learned my application had been successful. In a note of congratulation, Harry wrote that he looked forward to showing me around Paris but jokingly warned that I might find the weekly hockey practice strenuous.[8] In fact during my west coast upbringing I never learned to play the Canadian national game.[9]

The CBC ran a songwriting contest that year. I submitted *The Great Lakes Suite* and also a new baritone song, "Serenade," set to a poem by another literary friend, Colleen Thibaudeau. The *Suite* was rejected, but the song received a prize and a broadcast premiere by Charles Jordan (who later recorded it). Among other prizewinners were Pierre Mercure, Jean Coulthard, and Lionel Daunais.

At the end of the school year in June, the Conservatory announced that Lois Marshall would receive the senior school's Eaton Graduating Award. The prize, $1,000, was intended to help finance the recipient's professional debut concert in Eaton Auditorium. Lois and Weldon offered me a commission to compose some new songs for this occasion, scheduled for October. I chose four poems by e.e. cummings, a poet I was just discovering. Lois performed the set beautifully. From my experience working with her in preparing *The Great Lakes Suite*, I realized that she didn't really like to rehearse: she invited me to a run-through of the Four Songs to Poems by e.e. cummings only a couple of days before the concert. But she had obviously assimilated them quickly and fully. She later included them quite often in her programs, and in the mid-1970s after her rebirth as a mezzo I had the pleasure of performing the accompaniments, transposed, for her, in a concert at the St Lawrence Centre arranged by Franz Kraemer. Among other singers who also gave early performances of this set are Mary Simmons and Mary Morrison. When published by Waterloo Music (the score has a few misprints), they were, like the *T'ang Lyrics*, taken up by students and teachers and performed fairly widely.

The cummings songs represent a more modern approach than either the *T'ang Lyrics* or the Sitwell set. They also express more clearly and more convincingly the poetry's young-love elements, with which I was ready to empathize. The final song conveys lovers' springtime joy, and the long, serious song that precedes it is a kind of youthful credo of the post–First World War years, to which I could attach post–Second World War feelings as I dropped out of my Conservatory position and ("with straight glad feet") headed to Europe for more full-time study, vaguely confident that it was all leading somewhere. Lois's Eaton Auditorium concert took place on Thursday 12 October 1950. The next day Pamela Terry and I were married at the Toronto City Hall (Floyd and Jean Chalmers, at the after-concert party at their home, had been aghast: "Do you realize tomorrow is Friday the thirteenth?"), and the day after that we sailed from New York on the *Île de France*.

6

Paris

Compared with other European cities, Paris in 1950 showed few outward signs of having survived a war. But if you looked, the walls around the main open spaces displayed plaques marking where nineteen- and twenty-year-olds had died in the street fighting just before the Liberation in August 1944, and if you listened, residents would recount stories of life under "les Boches." In Eugène Ionesco's play *La Leçon*, a murderer dons a mourning armband for his victim; in the 1950 premiere production it carried a swastika. Inflation caused hardship for those on fixed incomes such as pensions. There was a brisk black-market traffic in Lucky Strike cigarettes and nylons.

The previous Canadian Amateur Hockey Association award winner, Harry Somers, and his wife Kay, were living in Montparnasse. They met our boat train and took us to a hotel on the boulevard Raspail where they had booked us a room. Then we all went for a late-afternoon walk through central Paris—down to the Seine, across the Île de la Cité, along the Quai du Louvre, through the Tuileries to the Place de la Concorde with its magnificent view up the Champs-Élysées, the monuments and public buildings by this time (early evening) floodlit. Back on the Left Bank we took supper at La Coupole, overwhelmed by this stunning intro-duction to the city.[1] Harry and Kay were in fact preparing to return to Canada, so we saw them only a few times more in the following couple of weeks. They introduced us to their circle, one of whom, the US pianist Eugene Gash, became a close friend during our stay.

In correspondence with the Canada Foundation I learned that Nadia Boulanger had accepted me as a composition student. Within a few days of arrival, I presented myself at the fabled studio-apartment, 36 rue Ballu,

97

where she received her students. From the corridor waiting area I could hear her commanding baritone voice as she concluded a lesson. She emerged, greeted me warmly, and immediately donned a coat and strode out the door, explaining that she had an errand to run and we could talk along the way. I kept pace with her as the two of us traversed many blocks to what my memory tells me was the rue du Faubourg Saint-Honoré (it was certainly a good hike, to a street of fashionable shops, but maybe not quite that far). She shot questions over her shoulder: Had I found a place to stay? I was married? Was my wife musical also? She stopped at a jewellery store and asked to see some silver christening mugs, picked one, paid for it, wrote out a card, addressed it, and handed the package to me. Would I be so kind as to deliver it, since it was not far from my hotel? We agreed on a time for my first lesson, and she was gone.

The address indicated on the gift package was just off the rue du Bac. I went there, found the number, and pushed the button for the appropriate floor. The elevator was one of those where you land right in the apartment, to be met by a servant. It turned out to be the residence of the Prince of Monaco, just then a new father. Mademoiselle, among other affiliations, was honorary music director to the royal family in Monte Carlo (some years later she played the organ at the wedding of Prince Rainier and Princess Grace).

She had heard of a couple of possible living quarters and suggested I inquire about (as I gathered from her rapid talking) "48 rue Jacob and 66 Monsieur le Prince" (or whatever the numbers were). At a later meeting, with a group of other students, I reported to her that the space at 48 rue Jacob was taken and that when I asked at 66 rue Jacob for Monsieur le Prince there was no one there by that name. Everyone enjoyed this hilarious faux pas: my knowledge of the Saint-Germain-des-Prés quarter didn't as yet include the rue Monsieur-le-Prince.

My first lesson was both an assessment and a procedural discussion. I showed her *The Great Lakes Suite* as my most ambitious attempt so far at an ensemble work. I must have shown her also the new cummings songs, because I recall she pointed out the (unconscious) quotation of Beethoven's Seventh Symphony in the fourth one. She asked me to prepare an analysis of the first Prelude in Bach's *Well-Tempered Clavier*. From my scores and my answers to various questions, she judged that for a while I should compose for single-line instruments only, avoiding the piano since I was a pianist and the medium was "too easy" for me. This was good advice. Among other composition students at the time, I later learned, some were expected to take semi-weekly classes with her assistant, Annette

Dieudonné, in conventional harmony and counterpoint; she evidently felt I was adequately prepared in those areas. When I brought my paper on the Bach Prelude, she approved it, and we discussed alternative ways of viewing the exceptional and controversial bar 23. I asked a question that has always intrigued me about this piece but that goes unanswered in published analyses I have seen, namely, why is each chord sounded *twice*? She said she thought it was a matter of acoustics: it allowed each step in the harmonic plan a chance to resonate. A good spur-of-the-moment answer, certainly; I still wonder.

These businesslike exchanges set the path I was to follow in the succeeding months. I brought her week by week pieces for two wind instruments, then for three, and eventually produced a quartet. It was good for me to concentrate on making musical sense in parts playable only a note at a time, thinking also of players and (to a more limited extent) of idioms. Her criticisms were based on sight-reading of my work at the piano and would consist of questions about form and note choice—why this harping on $E\flat$ here? or, could there not be some extension of the phrase there? or, did I *really want* this pause?—or else illustrations from models (Bach, Chopin, Schubert, Stravinsky, Ravel, played almost always spontaneously and from memory). Her musicianship was extraordinary.

She wanted me to hear what I was writing, so arranged for readings and even performances. She sent me to the bassoon class at the Conservatoire, where the professor (Gustave Dherin, who twenty years previously, I was impressed to learn, had played one of the bassoon parts in the first recording of the Stravinsky Octet) led his fourteen pupils, seven to a part, in my Four Pieces for Bassoon Duet. As I arrived, they were rehearsing in unison a famous fast passage from the finale of Ravel's Piano Concerto in G—a mighty sound. I was introduced as a pupil of Mademoiselle Boulanger ("elle est quelqu'un, vous savez," the professor told the class), and quizzed in front of the group as to my status as a foreign *boursier* (my modest scholarship was judged enormous by French standards). The pieces pleased him, but he found one of them "too long": on hearing it, I agreed and made some cuts. It seems from documentation I later ran across that there was a public (or maybe semi-public) performance by members of his class; my memory of this is dim. With the later Five Pieces for Flute Duet, however, I recall an effective performance in a program arranged by Mademoiselle at the Union interalliée. The program was of music by her "British" students, among whom I was grouped—I suppose because I wasn't from the US. It was sponsored by the British Council. One of the flutists was a then-star at the Conservatoire, of whom I saw a good deal in Paris, Alex

UNION INTERALLIÉE

CONCERT
donné
A L'OCCASION DU FESTIVAL OF BRITAIN

"JEUNES COMPOSITEURS ET VIEUX MÂITRES ANGLAIS"

LE MERCREDI 16 MAI 1951   33, Faubourg Saint-Honoré

Three of my Five Pieces for Flute Duet were performed in Mlle Boulanger's concert at the Union interalliée, Paris, on 16 May 1951. Also featured were two fellow student-composers, John Lambert and Thea Musgrave.

I — Capriccio   Lennox Berkeley
                                      (1903)
   Nocturne   "
   Polka   "
           Mme Luise Vosgerchian
           M. Noël Lee

II — Deare if you change   John Dowland
                                   (1563-1626)
   Come again   "
           M. Doda Conrad

   Flow my tears   "
           Mme Massignon et M. Doda Conrad

III — Fanfare and March   John Lambert
                                     (1926)
       MM. Maurice Rigole, Carrol Stitt

   A cycle of songs on the Nativity of Jesus
                (1re audition)   "
   Prologue : from the "Prioresses tale"
        (Geoffrey Chaucer 1340-1400)
   1 - O sweetest night (Myles Pinkney 1599-1674)
   2 - Shepherd, shepherd hark that Calling
           (Et. Teresa 1515-1582)
   3 - Upon my lap (Rickard Verstegan 1565-1620)
   4 - A maid pearless (Anon Pointed in 1530)
   Epilogue : Ave Maria
       Mmes Flore Wend et Marie-Claire Jamet

IV — Three Pieces for Flute duet   John Beckwith
                                        (1927)
   Allegro moderato
   Andante
   Vivace
           Mme Odette Ernest et M. Murray

V — Sweet was the song   Anonyme
                                      (C. 1594)
           Mme Flore Wend

   O Nata Lux   Th. Tallis
                                    (1520-1585)
           L'ensemble vocal
       sous la direction de M. Karel Husa

VI — Be in me (Ezra Pound)   Thea Musgrave
                                        (1928)
   Dance figure (Ezra Pound)
   Aubade (Louis Macniece)
   The return (Ezra Pound)
   An immortality (Ezra Pound)
           M. Doda Conrad et l'auteur

VII — King Arthur, fragments   H. Purcell
                                    (1658-1695)
       Mmes Flore Wend et Massignon
           M. Doda Conrad
   Mme Luise Vosgerchian et M. Noël Lee
           et l'ensemble vocal
       sous la direction de M. Karel Husa

           Pianos Pleyel

Murray, a young English performer who went on to a distinguished career. These duets covered a variety of approaches and helped me develop fluency in linear composing. Often the two instruments would exchange ideas and cross registers somewhat in the manner of the two violins in a baroque sonata or the upper two voices in a Renaissance madrigal. One of the flute pieces was a ground bass in which the "bass" line migrated from one part to the other as well as to various pitch levels. I seemed to have a fondness for dance rhythms, not always standard or identifiable ones.

The Five Pieces for Brass Trio had affinities to specific models, among them a smart little work for trumpet, horn, and trombone by Poulenc, and a Hindemith sonata (I forget which) with unbarred cadenzas. The first piece opens with a horn figure covering the same wide range as the well-known *Till Eulenspiegel* motive, but built in Hindemithian perfect fourths.[2] One of the pieces took the form of a block-chordal chorale, and in another each instrument in turn played what I fancied to be a characteristic solo cadenza. Mademoiselle was especially pleased with that one. It wasn't until my return to Canada, however, that I had a chance to hear this work played.

To the sets of duets and the trio I had by the spring of 1951 added a solo piano work (Mademoiselle's proscription on piano composition must have been relaxed by then). The initial title was *Rhapsody* but I later renamed it *Novelette*, because it turned out not rhapsodic but more like a musical narrative. Gene Gash performed it in his solo concert at the American Students' and Artists' Center in December 1951, and I sent a copy to Ray Dudley, who also performed it that season. It may represent an advance on the wind music I had been writing, in that it derives from the octatonic scale. I hear in it some Bartók influence but can't recall whether I was practising Bartók at the time.

Lessons were scheduled at a variety of times, sometimes 8.30 a.m. and sometimes as late as 9.30 p.m. A fellow student, Hector Campos-Parsi, said that he once arrived at the rue Ballu when Mademoiselle was feeling under the weather but insisted on looking at his work in bed. In Pamela's journal for 19 February 1951 she writes: "John phoned Mlle's secretary to cancel his lesson because he thought he hadn't enough prepared ... but as soon as Mlle came home from the Conservatoire at noon, and heard about it, she immediately phoned John to tell him he must come—so, he did."[3] If you missed a lesson one week because she was otherwise booked, she would meet with you twice the following week.

Besides lessons, we students were invited to sign up for the weekly *mercredis musicaux* in the studio. These innovative open classes, noted by

THE AMERICAN STUDENTS' AND ARTISTS' CENTER

261, Boulevard Raspail — PARIS - 14ᵉ

Métro : Raspail

presents

GENE GASH

PIANIST

Thursday evening, December 13, 1951, at 9 o'clock

PROGRAMME

J. S. Bach	Chaconne, D Minor
	(Transcription by Busoni)
L. van Beethoven	Sonata, Opus 101
	Allegretto, ma non troppo
	Vivace alla Marcia
	Adagio, ma non troppo, con affetto
	Allegro

INTERMISSION

Harry Somers	Sonata, No. 4 (First performance)
	Andante
	Allegretto
	Adagio
	Andante
John Beckwith	Rhapsody for piano (First performance)
Claude Debussy	La Cathédrale Engloutie
	Feux d'Artifice
Maurice Ravel	Jeux d'Eau
	Toccata (from Le Tombeau de Couperin)

Gene Gash included works by two Canadian composers, Harry Somers and me, in his piano recital in Paris, December 1951.

everyone who has written about Nadia Boulanger, were a joy. Mademoiselle would preside at one of the two pianos in a concentrated musical experience that might include reading, spoken analysis, and participatory singing and playing of scores by Sermisy, Purcell, Rameau, J.S. Bach, Berlioz, Debussy, or Stravinsky (I mention those I can remember; there were others). Purcell's *King Arthur* was a revelation, followed by another, his *Hail, Bright Cecilia*. Bach's cantatas nos. 4, 105, and 161 also remain in my mind indelibly; again, there were others. Of Stravinsky, there were the choruses from *Perséphone*. I find I can recall phrases and whole sections from these works over half a century later. Attending the sessions were not only her composition students but a sprinkling of interested professionals including some of the singers heard on her recordings. Usual turnout was thirty to forty.

From time to time the members of the Wednesday class would prepare a public presentation. During my winter of study, I participated in three or four. The first was a memorial concert for the pianist and composer Dinu Lipatti. A favourite student of Mademoiselle's, he died in early December 1950, of leukemia, aged only thirty-three. She was visibly upset by the loss. The concert at the Union interalliée included Bach's Cantata 161 (*Komm, du süsse Todestunde*), a eulogy by Roland-Manuel, and a recording by Lipatti of one of his own works. A happier occasion was an evening at the home of the Princesse de Polignac, a fabled patron of music and one of Mademoiselle's great supporters, honouring the musicologist Henri Expert. The event was attended by the president of the Republic and Madame Auriol, which meant that everyone was in formal dress and the grand circular staircase leading to the salon was lined with members of the Garde Républicaine in dress uniforms. Appropriately, the program consisted of works from the French Renaissance repertoire—I recall "O joly bois" by Sermisy, the amusing "Chant des oiseaux" of Janequin, and Claude le Jeune's "Revécy, venir du printems."[4] At another Union interalliée concert, Mademoiselle led us in a mixed program (excerpts from *Perséphone*, I think; a chorus from *Les Troyens*; some Rameau) with her idiosyncratic juxtaposition of idioms and styles. Debussy's *Syrinx* for solo flute formed a prelude to one of the classical pieces, on the grounds that the harmony and the flute colour, to her ear, demanded it.

Nadia Boulanger's guidance came at a good time for my development as (or *into*) a composer. I was often astonished at the rapidity of her musical responses. She spoke French and English fluently (and sometimes alternately, for example in the *mercredis* where there was a bilingual attendance); Italian with the young couple who looked after her apartment and her meals; some Spanish; and maybe a bit of German. But she claimed that her *native* language was music, and one could believe it when her fingers produced an instantly recalled phrase of Fauré or Ravel to illustrate a point or when she nodded impatiently to her page turner about ten bars from the end of a page in something she was sight-reading. She encouraged me, took my work seriously, and made me feel I was making progress. "I see you are a real composer," she said one day. This was however a comment not on a score but on the meticulous razor-blade erasures in a fair copy I was making in India ink on transparent paper; she was curious about the process, in which most students were then developing similar skills. "You will someday write a very good symphony" was a startling prediction, perhaps a standard one made to others; in later years I felt that there were enough symphonies in the world without my producing one.

Towards the end of her long life Mademoiselle came to be regarded as a seer, and people listened almost reverently for her pronouncements about music and about life. I think especially of the film documentary by Bruno Monsaingeon.[5] By the time of her death, to the general hagiographic strain a few dissenting views circulated: Virgil Thomson considered her rigid and out of touch, and for Elie Siegmeister she had a "mean" personality (both were US students of hers in the between-wars period).[6] In my experience, in the early 1950s she was full of conviction and energy, and delivered her opinions forthrightly, but didn't speak in apothegms as if for posterity, as she was evidently encouraged to later on. Some of my fellow students worshipped her; I deeply admired her.

At the same time I resisted some of her general opinions and attitudes. Her world view differed from the one I was putting together. She was a devout Roman Catholic and in her social and political ideas a conservative. Students received a black-edged invitation to the annual memorial service at La Trinité for her sister, the composer Lili Boulanger, who had died in her twenties, and to whose memory Nadia's whole career was dedicated.[7] The studio during that period was filled with floral tributes and sympathy cards. During an election I asked her if she would be voting. She said she never voted and believed things were run better in the eighteenth century when you just found the best person for the job, appointed him, and left him to it. From the war in Indo-China came news of the death of the son of a renowned French military leader, the Maréchal de Lattre de Tassigny. Mademoiselle was in tears for his parents.[8] A number of her most successful students were homosexuals, and some commentators on her influence have depicted the "Boulangerie" as a hive of gay culture and even speculated that she herself had lesbian tendencies.[9] In my year the percentage of gays was, I think, no greater than in any other student group. It was if anything an asexual atmosphere. A member of the class, unnamed, revealed to her that he and his friends enjoyed now and then dressing up as women; Mademoiselle expressed severe distaste in telling me of this.

Working on a piece by Debussy, I said I found it "very French," but she corrected me: it was well done but too undisciplined; more typically "French" was the music of Ravel. She had been a classmate of Ravel's and had also known Debussy, so her judgment was no doubt partly personal. In a concert, I heard an orchestral work by Messiaen. It was new to me, and I gave her my impressions, hoping to hear hers; but she dismissed his music as an unimportant aberration. Messiaen was her most prominent rival and held a professorship in composition at the Conservatoire (despite her international prestige, she was appointed there only at a lower rank and only to teach solfège, the reason being her sex). He was the organist at her parish church, the Église de la Trinité, just down the street from her home, which indicates that they must have met now and then. Aaron Copland sent her an article from the *New York Times* about celebrations of his fiftieth birthday. The outline of his career mentioned that he had studied with her in Paris in the 1920s and had been exposed to, and influenced by, new developments in French music at the time, including works by Erik Satie and his cohorts. "Nonsense," was Mademoiselle's reaction. Satie was no influence—a clown.

Copland visited Paris in 1949 and again in the spring of '51, his first visits since the war. He appeared at one of the student concerts (26 May) and spoke a few words. In his memoirs he says he found the musical atmosphere greatly changed since his student years.[10] The new paths of the 1950s described by historians were just in formative stages. In the Boulanger circle we were hardly aware of the activities of Messiaen and his pupils (including, at this time, Stockhausen and Boulez) or of the *musique concrète* experiments which were hatching. Likewise we knew little of Leibowitz and the interest in serialism he had begun to stimulate. Intrigued by what I read about Messiaen, I bought his *Technique de mon langage musical* and the score of the huge piano work *Vingt regards sur l'Enfant-Jésus*, then newly published, and studied them, but knew better than to mention them to my teacher. My contacts with the music of Boulez and with the electro-acoustic pieces of Pierre Schaeffer and others came only after I left Paris. It may have been the news of Schoenberg's death in the summer of 1951 that led me to take up certain of his works—*Pierrot lunaire*, the Suite op. 25, and the Orchestral Variations. I had heard *Pierrot* but never looked at the score, and the later, serial, scores were quite new to me. Again I hesitated to discuss them with Mademoiselle. That year she attended a festival in Germany and came back denouncing Ernst Krenek's serial opera *Karl V*, a featured work.

To Copland, Paris may have been less exciting then than in his youth, but for Canadian students it was a beautiful and tremendously inviting environment. Pamela and I treated seriously the opportunity to explore the rich variety of cultural offerings. While I worked at my musical projects, she attended French-language classes at the Alliance française. We had realized staying permanently in the international quarter of Montparnasse would soon deplete our means, so took a ground-floor flat in the block-long rue Jacques-Offenbach in Passy. After a month or so, it proved unsatisfactory and we started to look for other accommodation. Fiona Millar, whom I had known slightly as a member of the Reaney-Thibaudeau circle at the University of Toronto, was giving up her flat to marry the painter Paul Buttigieg, so we took it over. Situated on another composer street, the lovely avenue Mozart in Auteuil,[11] it was hardly anyone's idea of a "flat" or apartment, but rather consisted of two sixth-floor *chambres de bonne*; one had a sink and a small wood stove, and the other didn't; access was by a rear *ascenseur*; the WC was down the hall. We turned the larger room into a combined kitchen, bedroom, and living room, and the other into a working space or studio (the Bechstein upright I rented had to be dismantled and carried up the back stairs), calling it the "music room."[12] The windows, facing southeast, gave glimpses of the Seine and the Eiffel Tower. We enjoyed the challenge of making this into our home. We got to know the shops in the neighbourhood, including the one with the sign *Vins, charbons, bois* where we placed orders periodically for a

Pamela Terry in Paris, 1950.

supply of wood for our stove (carried up on the delivery man's back). We developed ingenuity in cooking our meals on the stove and a little hot plate, and also in bathing in the sink—it was either that or a visit to the public baths. These surroundings, though meagre, began to feel like home, and soon we were confident enough to invite dinner guests and even overnight visitors. Of the other occupants of the building, we had cordial relations with Monsieur and Madame Petit (our landlord and his wife), and especially with the Voisin family—Madame, a published poet, exchanged language lessons with Pamela, and I attempted to give piano lessons to the youngest of their six children, the unruly ten-year-old Pierrot ("*insupportable*" was his mother's word).

We frequented expatriate locales like the American Library and the American Students' and Artists' Center, and sometimes the Maison canadienne at the Cité universitaire. Through Clermont Pépin, whom I had known in Toronto, we were invited to perform *Music for Dancing* at the Cité in a concert of works by Canadian student composers. It was attended by Madame Vanier, wife of the then ambassador, later Governor General. Pépin played his *Danse frénétique*. We formed friendships with US music and theatre people at the Center, and Pamela was cast for a role in a production by their theatre wing of Gertrude Stein's *Yes Is for a Very Young Man*. This late work received its world premiere in March 1951, and in the audience on opening night was the late author's companion, the wiry, birdlike Alice B. Toklas. She commended the company afterwards, bubbling with enthusiasm.

Looking back, I am surprised to recall what an active social life we had in Paris. We made friends with some of Mademoiselle's students, and with other music students—John Lambert, Thea Musgrave, and Alex Murray from the UK, and Hector Campos-Parsi, Miguel Gomez, and Al Tepper from the US. I had encountered the latter group at the student-composers' symposia at home. I shared a score now and then at the Wednesday classes with a student named Gabriel, and we enjoyed exchanging comments about our work and about the repertoire we were studying. A few years later I was surprised to run into him in Montreal. I hadn't known his surname, Charpentier, or that he was from Canada. We have remained not only professional colleagues but good friends. Eugene Gash was a frequent companion to concerts and other events. A former pupil of E. Robert Schmitz, he was pursuing his piano career on a scholarship and had a keen interest in new music.[13] On special occasions we would take dinner with him at the Sainte-Beuve, a favourite restaurant in Montparnasse which the Somerses had introduced us to. Bob Russell, who had been a

CONCERT DE MUSIQUE CANADIENNE

à la Maison Canadienne, le 28 Mai 1951

1. Musique pour la Danse — John Beckwith
      Prélude
      1ère Pantomine
      Valse
      2ème Pantomine
      Polka
      Pas de deux
      Ronde

         John et Pamela Beckwith

2. En pensant à elle (Samain) — Jean-Paul Jeannotte

   En Mer (de Grandmont) — Jean-Paul Jeannotte

   Intimité (Jammes) — Jean-Paul Jeannotte
         a) le Bêchage
         b) le Mysogêne
            Jean-Paul Jeannotte
         au piano : Colombe Pelletier

3. Gnomes — Jean-Yves Landry
            Josephte Dufresne

   "Reel à quatre" — Sylvio Lacharité

   Danse rustique — Victor Bouchard
            Victor et Renée Bouchard

   Etude en sol dièse mineur — Victor Bouchard

   Danse Canadienne — Victor Bouchard
            Victor Bouchard

4. Les Oiseaux de Mer (Charpentier) — Jocelyne Binet
   L'Adieu (Apollinaire) — Jocelyne Binet
   Mon père me veut marier — Jocelyne Binet
            Réjane Cardinal
         au piano : Madeleine Gareau

5. Nocturne — Clermont Pepin
   Danse Frénétique — Clermont Pepin
            Clermont Pepin

6. Nocturne — Jocelyne Binet
   Ave Maria — Clermont Pepin
   Cantique des Cantiques — Clermont Pepin
            Choeur des M.C.P.
         Direction : C. Pepin
         au piano : Raymonde Gagnon

Concert de musique canadienne program.

fellow drama student of Pamela's in Toronto, was taking classes in mime in Paris and often dropped in, sometimes with the piano student Sue Davidson (later Sue Polanyi). We met Ian and Cecilia Mackinnon-Pearson, an older Canadian couple to whom Alberto Guerrero had given us an introduction, occasionally joined them at a meal or a musical event, and were later invited to their country home near Dourdon. We regularly exchanged visits with the Buttigiegs and followed Paul's progress in the art world and the birth of their first child in late 1951. From Paul's exhibit in a gallery in the rue de Seine we bought one of his canvases, a portrait of Fiona, in soft colours but with heavy black outlines somewhat after Rouault (Monsieur Petit's reaction was, "alors, si les femmes étaient comme ça ..."). On New Year's Eve we held a party for friends in our little flat, apologizing afterwards to some of our sixth-floor neighbours who had been upset by the noise.

Visitors included a close friend from college days, Ron Shepherd; Anna and Bill McCoy, on their honeymoon; Betty Jean Hagen and her teacher Géza de Kresz, in town to participate in a *concours*; Pamela's brother Robin Terry; and Colleen Thibadeau, who was spending the year teaching at a girls' school in Angers and would now and then stay with us for a weekend. In the summer Pamela signed up with an agency to take care of children of tourist families. It was not through the agency but through Colleen that she received her biggest assignment, to look after Nancy and Edward Jackman, children of the Toronto magnate Henry Jackman. As a university student, Colleen had been a live-in nanny at their Rosedale home. The kids, aged approximately ten and twelve, were thrilled to sleep on the floor of our back-stairs "music room" and to do the sights with us by *métro*, bus, or on foot.[14]

Paris was continually fascinating. With memberships in Les Jeunesses musicales, we were entitled to free tickets to educational musical and theatrical events, and to discounts at the concert halls and the opera. We bought the weekly guide *Une semaine de Paris* and soaked it all up. In particular, the opera offerings were a constant attraction, and a novelty for us. At the Opéra I can recall *La damnation de Faust, Boris Godounov, Thaïs,* Milhaud's *Bolivar* (in its world premiere), and a *Faust* with live horses and the Garde Républicaine band in the Soldiers' Chorus scene; at the more intimate Opéra Comique, *Louise* (with sets by Utrillo), *Figaro* (with a spoken-dialogue insertion of the trial scene from the play), *Madame Butterfly, Manon, Pelléas,* and a double bill of *L'Heure espagnole* and *L'Enfant et les sortilèges.* When I reported to Monsieur Voisin that we had seen *La Flûte enchantée* at the Opéra, he said no, it must have been at the Opéra Comique, since it's a comedy with spoken dialogue. A music-loving professional engineer and *père de famille*, he had a sure sense of genre, but the conventional repertoire distinctions were starting to break down, and in fact it *was* at the great Palais Garnier that we saw this work. It was spectacularly mounted. The productions varied; in a larger active repertoire than most opera companies would these days maintain, some were beautifully realized while others tended to be routine or even slightly tatty. In our cheap seats, sometimes with only a partial view of the stage, we loved being there, whether to marvel or to criticize. In addition there were occasional visiting opera companies from Germany at the Théâtre des Champs-Élysées, and in that famous hall we also heard concert versions of Falla's *El Retablo* and Stravinsky's *Les Noces*. My first acquaintance with the latter made a profound impression, a sound-world distinct from the concert *Sacre* and the *Petrushka* of the Opéra ballet.

We went to a lot of movies and plays. English-language movies, shown in English, were available periodically at some theatres (not as many as in present-day Paris), and there was a cinema in the Champs-Élysées which showed French-language movies with English subtitles. Dubbing was an alternative, but by no means standard, practice; I preferred subtitles, which allowed for the sound of the original voice and language, and I still do. Actors we knew in Paris used to pick up assignments to dub English soundtracks for French films—a more lucrative source of income than their stage roles. With French theatre offerings, our command of the language usually wasn't up to the test, so we would prepare by reading the script ahead of time. We were thrilled to see Louis Jouvet in *L'École des femmes* and *Tartuffe* (he died in the last months of our stay). Anouilh's *La Répétition* with Barrault at the Marigny and Racine's *Britannicus* with Jean Marais at the Comédie-Française stick in my mind, as (also at the Comédie) *Le Médecin malgré lui* and the inevitable *Cyrano*, and, in a suburban theatre (I forget which) a simplified and highly effective *Le Cid* by Jean Vilar's TNP (Théâtre national populaire) with Gérard Philippe in the title role: in this, the acting was vivid but the sets minimal, consisting of two chairs, a plain one for peasant scenes and a high-backed one for the palace; no chair, you were outdoors. After a movie, play, or concert we sometimes met friends for guitar or folk music at a Left Bank bar; favourites were L'Abbaye and the Bar Vert.

The "Bach year," 1950, was observed in a cycle of chamber music concerts with spoken commentary by Norbert Dufourcq. We heard several of these. The flute works featured Jean-Pierre Rampal and the cellist was Paul Tortelier—both artists then still young and at the start of their careers. Enesco and his former pupil Menuhin played the Double Concerto. The Végh Quartet gave a cycle of the six Bartók quartets, which I had studied but heard only on records. German performers who had been under a cloud during the war were welcomed—Fürtwängler in Bruckner and Beethoven (a heavily mannered *Pastorale*), Gieseking in the last three Beethoven sonatas. A favourite venue was the elegant, medium-sized Salle Gaveau in the rue la Boëtie: we heard superb concerts there by Isaac Stern (another "rising star" at the time), Clara Haskil, Jennie Tourel, and the baritone Charles Panzéra, a fine artist though past his prime. Symphony programs in the Salle Pleyel or the Théâtre des Champs-Élysées conducted by Markévich, Désormières, and others, included sometimes dynamic performances (*Le Sacre du printemps*, for example) but could also be perfunctory. The several local orchestras were often under-rehearsed, and it took a firm-handed visiting conductor (like Munch) to bring them to life. We listened and criticized, glad for the chance to hear both familiar and unfamiliar repertoire. There was, as the above summary indicates, little avant-garde music available: the "Domaine musical" concerts were still a few years in the future. The city had many noted residents, and the homes of Colette, Cocteau, Sartre, and others would be pointed out to us. We once recognized Françoise Rosay in the audience at a play, and another time, in a concert featuring a new quartet by Honegger, we picked out the composer—though it appeared that, like us, he was less than thrilled by the performance; he ducked out a side door when asked to acknowledge the ovation. (Most of this I recall spontaneously from memory, prompted only by a few surviving letters of the many I sent home. I didn't keep a journal or a scrapbook.)[15]

We lived sparsely but wanted to pursue every avenue in what I guess was our youthful culture quest. As a break from Paris life, we took three short vacation trips, one in March to London for a week of (mostly) theatre, and the other two in July—to Perpignan for the Casals festival and to London again for the Festival of Britain. Gene Gash accompanied us in the March junket, and in the second London trip we joined a party with Fiona Millar and Colleen Thibaudeau and met Reaney, who had come over for a British holiday excursion with Colleen. Our Perpignan stay was extended by a few days on the Côte Vermeille (Collioure, Banyuls; we had wanted to add Barcelona, but Spanish visas were difficult to obtain). In the late summer we contemplated trying to attend the premiere in Venice of *The Rake's Progress* but found the trip was beyond our means.

Mademoiselle was there; her verdict: the new Stravinsky work "could almost be popular." I resumed my lessons with her on 16 October, but after one or two sessions decided not to continue. One reason was shortage of funds. Another was that in showing her the still-incomplete Woodwind Quartet I found I could almost predict what she would say. She had evidently given me increased confidence: Was it ungrateful of me to leave at this point? Those last months of 1951 were uncertain. I pressed on and finished my Quartet. Reluctantly, we booked our passage to return to Canada in January.

But in December Pamela was invited to join a theatre troupe for a tour of US army bases in Austria and Germany, and it seemed I could also have a part in the company for a walk-on or as backstage crew. We cancelled our boat tickets. The Gomezes, Mike and his wife Ginny, signed up to take over our flat. Then, a week or so later, we learned the tour plans were off. An alternative idea to returning home had been to go to London and try to find work there in order to survive a few more months: so in mid-January we left Paris, went to London, found digs in the Finchley area, and started haunting the labour exchanges—not an encouraging enterprise for non-Brits, in midwinter, under the newly changed government. We must have had *some* resources because I remember splurging on opera performances (*Figaro* and *Wozzeck,* both at Covent Garden, the latter under its first conductor, Kleiber)—if our usual cheap seats can be called a splurge.

Ups and downs. Word now came through that the tour was revived, and we were needed in Germany in mid-February. I felt shaky about accepting, but Pamela insisted, and since it was her opportunity it seemed fair that the decision should be hers. George VI had just died. Shortly before our departure we were part of the audience for a modern-music concert in the Hampstead Town Hall. Organized by the Society for Contemporary Music, a group headed by Humphrey Searle, this inaugural concert was (despite the royal mourning) attended by the Lord Mayor of Hampstead, in full evening dress with his elegant chain of office. Called on for a few words at the start, he said what a fine thing it was to support contemporary music—works such as, for example, the noble "Solemn Music" of Walford Davies, played at the king's funeral service. When he sat down, the program began with a performance of *Octandre* by Edgar Varèse—about as far a cry from Davies as you could conceive—and His Worship's face and neck, viewed from the back, became quite flushed. The main feature of the program was *Pierrot lunaire,* with Hedli Anderson in the speaking part.

A day or two later, we took our travel orders to the Northolt airfield only to find our plane had been commandeered to fly General and Mrs Eisenhower back to SHAPE headquarters in France after their appearance at the funeral. We were accommodated overnight in a local inn and told to report again the next day. This time the flight did take place—in midday to Orly, and then in the late afternoon to Wiesbaden. In the dark at Wiesbaden instead of the anticipated passport inspection we deplaned with a few other personnel onto the tarmac and found our way to a truck which was to transport us to a hotel for the night. Our advance images of what a visit to Germany (the wartime enemy) might be like weren't at all like this. Our papers called for spending the following day in a long train journey through southern Germany to the Austrian border and from there to the village of Wels in Upper Austria, where the Army had taken over the main hotel, the Hotel Greif.

Wels became our headquarters for the next four and a half months. We rehearsed in the hotel ballroom. When not rehearsing, I had permission to use the only piano, in an adjacent salon. At Foyle's in London I had bought Alfred Einstein's edition of the ten mature quartets of Mozart, works I scarcely knew; this volume became an object of study and enrichment during my spare hours. The troupe was directed by Amram Novak, with whom Pamela had worked in Paris. The other performers were a varied bunch, and in daily rehearsals and bus travel on the tour we came to know them all. Some, including a former child actor, had had Hollywood experience; others were just entering the profession. We and the one Australian were the only non-US members. The initial presentation was a topical Broadway farce, *John Loves Mary*, written by Norman Krasna for Nina Foch, about a young war veteran returning to the States to be reunited with his fiancée. We both had small parts and helped with backstage tasks. We enjoyed leisure hours in the interesting Roman-walled town of Wels, and found the tour also full of interesting new discoveries. We performed in Salzburg, Munich, Regensburg, Augsburg, Stuttgart, Frankfurt, Mainz, Ulm, Nuremberg, Saarbrucken, Bad Kreutznach, Worms, and Wiesbaden, either in camp halls or in local theatres.

Audiences ranged from a few hundred to (in Wiesbaden, for example) over 1,300. In Salzburg we did our little play on the stage of the Festspielhaus (!) and were accommodated not in the town but in the mountains across the border in Berchtesgaden, the location of Hitler's hideaway villa. At the end of the tour we were flown in an army transport plane over the Alps to Trieste for a performance there, and then back through the narrow air corridors of this occupied territory to Vienna for a couple of performances there. The German towns showed still many signs of wartime destruction. When I told a waitress in Nuremberg how much the town impressed me, she sighed, "Ja, Nürnberg *war* schön." I was thinking of the marvellous Dürers on display in his birthplace; she was thinking of the rubble. The train station in Munich was only partly in operation; the roof had not been replaced since its demolition by Allied bombs. One of our fellow actors, Jake, was Jewish. He had served in Germany during the war and had a good command of the language. He obviously had a severe emotional reaction to this return visit to cities he had known, some of them

With Pamela, theatrical tour, spring 1952, at a railway station in the Tyrol.

scenes of atrocities, and he would sometimes seize up in silent anger. In Vienna, our bus was subjected to a demonstration against the alleged use of poison gas by the US in the Korean War (then in progress). In the rotating four-power administration of Vienna, the Soviets were in charge during the period of our visit, and the army had had to ask permission to use the theatre in the centre of the city. It was hard to put across light comedy in an atmosphere of suspicion and hostility.

In all the cities we played, we took what chance we could to see the sights—galleries, churches, restaurants, even the occasional opera (*Zauberflöte* and *Boris* in Munich, *Onegin* in Augsburg, a striking *Freischütz* in Wiesbaden). Our US companions were not all as gung-ho for such experiences, and we were surprised that the troops stationed at the various bases seemed to keep to themselves rather than mingle with the populace. In Munich we found some of the best beer, and beer halls alive with atmosphere and history, but the guys seemed to prefer going to the dimly lit army bars and ordering their favourite Milwaukee brands. Of course, our second-hand Broadway shows could be regarded as another example of providing a stateside, never-left-home atmosphere. For many of the soldiers, movies were a common experience but live theatre was a novelty. Female members of the cast were greeted with loud whistles, and swearing (never heard in the movies) usually brought outbursts of raucous laughter. In our second show, one character was identified with the recurrent exit line "God-damn it," and this always brought down the house. Once, however, a base commander insisted we substitute "Gol-dang it," which, despite exaggerated efforts by the actor, never had nearly the same impact.

For a second tour, starting in April, the vehicle was *Room Service*, a farce well known from the film version by the Marx Brothers. It was a faster show than *John Loves Mary*, without the sentimentality. There were some changes in the company, but we were kept on, and even had better parts (Pamela played the ingénue, and I did a funny cameo). After rehearsing in Wels we visited most of the same towns as before, but this time travelled to Vienna by train rather than plane. Given the way the borders of the occupied areas were drawn, US personnel could travel direct via Linz in about six hours; but we Canadians, the lone Australian, and Beryl, the pregnant English girlfriend of one of the actors, were classed as "British subjects" and therefore had to travel through the French, British, and Soviet zones—that is, through Innsbruck, Semmering, and Graz, changing trains twice, taking more like eighteen hours, with a lot of tight security, waiting on station platforms, and passport stamping—a wearying roundabout trip, much of it through marvellous mountain scenery. In Vienna we were fortunate to hear a *Fidelio* in the Theater an der Wien, the site of its premiere; the Stadtoper had not yet reopened.

Towards the end of June we returned to Wels, packed our luggage, and said goodbye. The ISCM Festival was in progress in Salzburg, and we spent a week there attending several interesting concerts. I wrote a report of this for *The Globe and Mail*. I remember a performance of Schoenberg's *Erwartung* with Ilona Steingruber (who later sang the title role in the first recording of *Lulu*), and another of Boulez's *Le Soleil des eaux*, the first work of his I had ever heard. One concert came to an abrupt and upsetting conclusion when the conductor, Herbert Häfner, had a heart attack while conducting, fell backwards off the podium, and died. At some of the festival events, I was able to meet with fellow composers—the Austrian Sonia Eckhardt-Gramatté (later a prominent personality in Canada), Don Banks from Australia, Milton Babbitt from the US (the program included his song cycle *Du*), and others.[16]

We had changed our boat reservations and were now to sail home on the *Queen Elizabeth* at the end of July. We made our way by train to Zurich (an exhibition of paintings by Edvard Munch, an artist I had never heard of, made a lasting impression)[17] and then to Paris, where we put up in a pleasant small hotel on the Left Bank close to the Seine and the Île. On Bastille Day we had a farewell meal in Montparnasse with Beryl and Lyle and other friends from the tour, and the next day went to England to spend a few days with Pamela's father at his home in Surrey before our departure.

When I had informed a German fellow traveller, on the train through Switzerland, that we would soon be sailing to Canada and would then spend four days on the train to the west coast he had refused to believe me. "*Four days?*" There was much about our European adventure that I would have refused to believe if told of it in advance.

CAREER

7

Writing

As I returned from Europe in the fall of 1952, what were my prospects? Colin Sabiston had written that Leo Smith was seriously ill (Smith died that spring) and suggested I should apply for the position of music critic on *The Globe and Mail*.[1] I contacted the editors but received no reply; later, I learned that they looked unfavourably on my letter, which was not so much an application as a statement of terms. I had a good deal to learn about how to present myself. Another possible avenue was teaching. An appointment in music was advertised at the University of Saskatchewan, and I applied, hoping my studies with Nadia Boulanger would be taken as equivalent to a graduate degree.[2] In Toronto, Richard Johnston said he found it shocking that some job didn't immediately open up for me. I was neither shocked nor surprised. I hadn't imagined a place in the music community would simply be handed to me on a platter.

From September 1952 until March 1953, I was a freelancer in Toronto. I taught a weekly one-hour class in "musical form" for the Faculty of Music. On a Conservatory contract, I gave private lessons in music theory to a few teenagers. I accompanied opera rehearsals. I wrote concert reviews for *The Globe and Mail* at $7.50 per assignment. (Under Leo Smith's regime the paper had published several reports I sent from France, but when I proposed an advance article for the Schoenberg concert by Glenn Gould the editors were not interested.) I even undertook concert management, for a couple of Conservatory staff members who recalled my work for the publicity bureau. A friend from student days, Robert Weaver, was a talks producer for CBC Radio, and through his contacts Pamela and I presented a series of short radio talks about our European adventures—three titled "Apartment in Paris" and another three titled "Roadshow in

Germany."[3] I played a Sunday afternoon recital at the Art Gallery and repeated the repertoire, in part, on my former CBC radio spot, *Sunday Morning Recital*. Practicalities intruded: the *Globe* work sometimes entailed travel to and from a suburban venue, and eventually the cost in time and transit fares made the fee not worth the trouble; the solo recital work demanded hours of practice, for which again the skimpy remuneration scarcely repaid the effort. In February 1953 my monthly earnings reached a low point. Another friend at the CBC, Fraser Macdonald, mentioned that there was an opening in his department, not imagining that I would be interested. I decided to apply, got the job, and held it until the fall of 1955.

The department was called Radio Continuity. Macdonald and four others were assigned to write scripts for live and recorded music programs on the two CBC stations, sometimes for local series or special occasions and sometimes for the networks. We shared a large office in the Jarvis Street headquarters building. Ostensibly we put in nine-to-five working days and were expected, like all staff members, to sign in and out. But the work was not heavy. Producers would send us program sheets for coming broadcasts, with indications of timing so that we could calculate how long to make the announcer's script. There was a small reference library elsewhere in the building, and on the office shelves were the major music dictionaries, a selection of the standard program-note compilations, a few critical collections, and (curiously) back issues of periodicals such as *Modern Music, Music and Letters*, and the *Musical Quarterly*. When literary research sources were scarce, we could look up scores in the music library or crib from record jackets in the record library. Scripts for daytime recorded-music programs were rather routine ("here is ..., that was ..."), but live solo and chamber-music recitals and the weekly broadcasts of the CBC Symphony Orchestra presented a greater challenge. The pay was low, but it was regular.

A few weeks after I started with the department, Ira Dilworth, one of the top network executives,[4] called the producer of the Symphony concerts, Terence Gibbs. He said he had understood the Corporation didn't contract with freelance writers for program notes, so what was this credit to Beckwith he heard on a recent broadcast? Gibbs had to explain that I was now on the staff. Dilworth's office was in the posh annex, often called the Kremlin, a parking lot and several corridors away from our department's basement quarters in the main building. I recalled this years later when I had administrative responsibilities and tried to make it a principle to know the personnel and where they were located in the plant.

In front of the CBC Jarvis Street headquarters, 1954.

Because the demands weren't onerous, I did a good deal of browsing in the publications at hand in the office. I enjoyed the *Modern Music* articles and reviews, and through them and the published volumes of Virgil Thomson's *Herald Tribune* reviews I added considerably to my knowledge of the US new-music scene. The *Quarterly* articles broadened my horizons, and Paul Henry Lang's all-knowing editorials increased my awareness of musicological trends. I also listened to a good deal of recorded music that was new and unfamiliar to me. If it was hack work, it was at the same time a learning opportunity. ("Hack" was the term Glenn Gould used one day in 1955 when, fresh from his debut triumph in New York, he dropped in to the department to say he needed sleeve notes for his coming Columbia recording of Bach's *Goldberg Variations* and couldn't find the time to write them, so "would one of you hacks like to do it?" He received a cool response, so ended up finding the time after all.)

Though now a regular at the CBC, I didn't give up all my freelance work. After sign-in, I would often take the Carlton streetcar a few stops along to the Conservatory building for a class or a rehearsal, and then scurry back to the CBC to meet a script deadline. With department colleagues there was an understanding for mutual cooperation; sometimes we even faked each other's sign-ins. In 1954 my Faculty class load became suddenly much heavier,[5] requiring sometimes several streetcar junkets in one day.

Another involvement had already arisen in 1953, largely from my own ambition: a half-hour slot in the radio schedule became vacant, and I made a bid for it, proposing a series devoted exclusively to modern and avant-garde music. The idea was accepted, and, full of enthusiasm, I chose an inaugural program consisting of *Octandre* by Varèse and the String Trio by Schoenberg. The program time, Saturday at the early supper hour, was not at all appropriate for concentrated absorption of new music, with the result that many listeners phoned or wrote to protest. But the management, instead of cancelling the series forthwith, found another, more suitable, spot for it in the schedule. The series, *Music in Our Time*, continued for several years and remained my responsibility (on contract) after I left the Corporation in 1955.

Later I became responsible for two other radio music series. The summer replacement program *Music of the Church*, on Sundays around the lunch hour, aimed to illustrate a broader repertoire than was available on other programs, at a time when the immense historical scope of music of Christian (and other) liturgical traditions was becoming more and more accessible on discs. Sometimes in fact I borrowed recordings from the Faculty Library's collection which were not (or not yet) part of the CBC Record Library. A given Sunday program might feature chants, Renaissance motets or masses, baroque cantatas, or modern liturgical works. The breadth of repertoire was probably dictated by my teaching preoccupations at the time. The same might be said of the series *The World of Music*, which succeeded *Music in Our Time* and lasted in a regular late-evening time period well into the middle 1960s. Program length was one hour, rather than the thirty minutes allotted in the earlier series. Here my programming ideas emphasized contemporary works but delved into corners of the classical (and sometimes non-Western) repertoire that had had little broadcast exposure but were starting to achieve a presence in the recording catalogues. Listening to unfamiliar but significant musical works became part of my commitment, both in my teaching and for these radio series, and occupied a greater amount of my time than before or since. It was another challenge, and an enjoyable way to expand my knowledge.

There were signs that I was regarded as a maverick broadcaster. Helmut Blume in Montreal, whose *International Concert* had a popular following, would occasionally send me broadcast tapes he received from Europe that he found too far-out for his audience. For *Music in Our Time*,

I borrowed a tape recording someone had obtained from Paris, featuring Pierre Henry's *musique concrète* composition *Orphée*. It was, I believe, the first electro-acoustic work ever broadcast on the Canadian airwaves. The deep growls were strange, but I supposed them to be evocative of the supernatural elements of the Greek myth; and why were the tempos so draggy? I was unfamiliar with European tape calibres, and they were new to the CBC technicians; we aired the tape at the *wrong speed*. There was unfavourable listener response and a gentle rap on the knuckles from management on that one. A different case was the reception of John Cage's *Indeterminacy*, which I presented almost in its entirety on *The World of Music*; it aroused more letters and phone calls than any other broadcast, most of it positive. When the first recording of Schoenberg's *Moses und Aron* was released, I wanted to broadcast excerpts, but the composer's widow refused to give her permission without a hefty royalty, and we had no budget. She said she was content to wait, and the subsequent success of the piece has proved her right; in the 1950s it was hardly known. One of my concerns was to include music by Canadian composers whenever possible. The transcriptions released now and then by the CBC's International Service were virtually my only source. They included valuable works that other programmers found too difficult or too long but which I judged suitable for "my" audience: regular, if small, feedback convinced me that such a following existed.

Known for writing radio scripts and newspaper reviews, I was approached to prepare background notes for concert programs. After my full-time appointment to the Faculty of Music in 1955, the Faculty's chamber-music series became a frequent assignment, and I especially liked putting together comments for the Mozart cycle in his anniversary year, 1956, covering live presentations of the big quartets, the string quintets, and other major works. Articles and scholarly papers were not yet my style, but new invitations brought opportunities for these: the editor of the *University of Toronto Quarterly*, Douglas Grant, read my Mozart notes and asked if I would like to contribute something. Imitating the survey articles I had been reading in the US journals, I submitted "Composers in Toronto and Montreal," a commentary on the work of eight contemporaries, four in each city—including (an innovation for the *Quarterly*) music-notation examples.[6] At this period also I wrote the chapter on "Recordings" for MacMillan's book *Music in Canada*[7] (as editor, he wrote the epigraph and opening paragraph, setting the scene in a literary way, which I would not have been able to do) and, perhaps as a result, was asked to write a survey of the current musical scene for a book on Canadian culture edited by a US historian, Julian Park.[8] One thing again leading to another, a year or two later Park suggested my name to the organizers of the annual conference of the Society for French Historical Studies, in Cleveland, who wanted something about nineteenth-century French music for a panel discussion. I made up a talk about three composers—Berlioz, Bizet, and Debussy—illustrated with a few piano excerpts.[9] Devoid of scholarly originality, it resembled my presentations to history-of-music classes in its attempted humour and my radio scripts in its superficial observations; but it was warmly received. In 1957 I had attended my first Learned Societies conference, in Ottawa, to give a paper on current Canadian composition for the Humanities Association, which Morry Kernerman and I illustrated with a short program of violin-and-piano works. The chairman, Malcolm Ross, was preparing yet another collection of essays on the state of the arts[10] (in those years following the Massey Report and just before the birth of the Canada Council, the pundits were constantly examining Canadian culture): Would I write the essay on music? In retrospect I am prouder of the radio series than of these early attempts at scholarship, but it was all good formative experience.

Geoffrey Payzant had by this time persuaded the Canadian Music Council to sponsor his concept of a national serious-music magazine, and the result was the *Canadian Music Journal*, published first in Sackville, New Brunswick (Payzant was then with the department of philosophy at Mount Allison University), and then in Toronto, after his move there in 1959. Payzant and I and our families formed a lifelong close bond of friendship. He asked me to edit the *Journal*'s record reviews and I did this from 1958 to the publication's regretted demise in 1962. I also contributed a couple of articles, one a profile of Jean Papineau-Couture and the other "A Stravinsky Triptych," based on the composer's recent compositions and writings and his spring 1962 visit to Toronto.[11] These were, I believe, an advance in seriousness and originality over what I had done previously—an improvement no doubt attributable to Payzant's critical influence. His lectures on musical aesthetics attracted a large student following. In a talk I heard him give once, he depicted the field of criticism as a series of circles, all interrelated—the research-and-analysis papers influencing the professional newsletters and the newsletters influencing the daily press reviews and chat columns, which in turn provided fodder for the chroniclers and analysts. He viewed it as a concentric or spiral pattern, rather than a hierarchical one. Our debates are a pleasant memory. The *Journal* under his leadership, though it survived only six years, is now regarded as having set a new benchmark for national music publications in Canada.

Though few if any of my "serious" writing and speaking assignments had fees or honoraria attached, the radio scripts brought in a fairly regular supplement to my teaching salary. Intermittently, I was asked to join the panel of critics on a popular local program called *CJBC Views the Shows*. It was an engaging format: each reviewer, in addition to his or her own assignment of the week, was expected to sample one or two other topics (read a book or attend a film or an art gallery opening), so as to be able to join the discussion following each short formal review. Jack Batten, Kildare Dobbs, Joan Fox, Robert Fulford, William Kilbourn, Elizabeth Kilbourn, and Ross McLean were among the frequent panelists, while I alternated on music with Geoffrey Payzant and Richard Johnston. The producer, Wendy Michener, was one of the most perceptive script editors I have ever known. She remarked once that she thought my trademark as a critic was my "naturally bitchy personality." The series was discontinued when the station, CJBC, was transformed into the CBC's French-language outlet for Toronto. Wendy, fluently bilingual, thought they should keep it on under the homonymous title *CJBC vue les choses*. Her early death was one of those sad, inexplicable losses.

In 1959 Nathan Cohen, newly appointed as entertainment editor of the *Toronto Daily Star*, invited me to review concerts and opera, and write a weekly column on music. I had many other commitments apart from full-time duties in the Faculty of Music, but he was willing to let me have my choice of events to cover, as many or as few per week as I thought I could manage. (My acceptance was based partly on a special financial need. Reaney and I, fresh from the broadcast premiere of *Night Blooming Cereus*, were trying, with the help of friends, to raise funds for a staging of the opera,[12] and I decided to put my *Star* earnings in a separate bank account for that purpose.) I averaged two or three review assignments a week during the season, and undertook reviewing of Stratford Festival and other summer events as well. In my Saturday columns, I had freedom to write about any topics that seemed to me of interest. They were dashed off hurriedly, but represented comments on music and especially on local musical life that were not the domain of the paper's *other* musical columnist, Leslie Bell. (On a couple of occasions, Bell voiced sharp opposition to my championing of radical new works.)

Cohen, a notoriously outspoken drama critic, was in my experience a generous person and an encouraging editor. Once when another stringer was unable to attend a Rodgers and Hammerstein gala at the O'Keefe Centre, he asked me, on just a few hours' notice, if I would take it on. Reading my review the next day, he took the trouble to phone and congratulate

JOHN BECKWITH on Music

LAST SATURDAY'S COLUMN attempted not so much to write an "Inside 12-Note Music" as to counter some charges commonly levelled at the products of this technique—their alleged excessive dissonance, lack of melody, and hyper-intellectualism.

The subject of today's sermon, as announced, is a capsule survey of the classics of 12-note writing.

Another common anti-12-note thrust—"It's all very well for expressions of tortured emotion, but could never be a vehicle of humor"—went unnoticed last week; so it might be a good idea to begin our list with some examples of happy 12-note music.

If there's humor (of a Chaplinesque kind) in Picasso's harlequins, then Schoenberg's suites for piano, Opus 25, and for chamber ensemble, Opus 29, also show it. These are 12-note line-drawings, as it were, deliberately modelled after 18th-century dance-forms. Berg's "Lulu" (which is genuine 12-note music, though his earlier "Wozzeck" is not) has, in the music of its central character at least, a powerful quality of ironic humor which, though wildly eccentric, often touches on high comedy.

For rib-tickling wit, a rare quality in abstract instrumental music of any period, there are Anton Webern's Concerto for Nine Instruments and Quartet with Saxo-... The latter, I wish to testify, produced audible ... Toronto concert audi-

My column in the Toronto Daily Star, *headings from 1962 and 1964.*

JOHN BECKWITH ON MUSIC

CBC symphony due back; few expect it

IN APRIL THE CBC Symphony Orchestra, Geoffrey Waddington's splendid creation, sole surviving network-broadcasting symphonic orchestra in North America, will cease to exist.

I know, the press release yesterday said the orchestra's activities were being suspended for the season 1964-5 only; but the chances of its renewal after a year are remote. Even the most sympathetic and optimistic observer can hardly expect the CBC's financial state to improve that markedly in so short a time. And the CBC brass in general is known to have had its hooks in the orchestra (long considered a "luxury" of Canadian radio) for some years. It is a tribute to Mr. Waddington, CBC director of music, that he has managed to keep it going this long.

Even though the CBC promises to broadcast symphonic music with the Toronto Symphony Orchestra, ...owers of past CBC

Symphony Orchestra is also the death of new and challenging live-orchestral repertoire in Canada.

• • •

CONGRATULATIONS ARE IN order for Walter Susskind, whose contract as TSO musical director has been renewed. The suggested absorption of CBC players into the TSO and the use of the TSO for broadcasting next season place him in a position of more pivotal importance in Toronto's musical life than ever before.

(The announcements did not explain whether this contract's one-year term was at Susskind's request or at the TSO directors. His last contract was for three years.)

It may be a timely moment to review some of the disapproving comments Mr. Susskind's leadership of the orchestra has roused lately. How valid are they? If valid, what can he be expected to do to correct matters in his new ... ion of power?

forget that in his first year here he produced the most harrowing presentation of Berlioz' "Damnation of Faust" most of us have ever heard? Do we forget the thoughful, musically illuminating, performances he drew from the TSO in other seasons in such standard symphonies as the Beethoven Fifth and Ninth, the Brahms First, the Haydn "Military," or, a work I personally never expected to enjoy again, the Dvorak "New World?"

This is not meant entirely by way of defense. I sometimes feel at Susskind concerts that his basic musical instincts are rather insensitive and crude, and that the occasional inspired performance happens just by accident.

I get the sense of a completely professional orchestral technician who sometimes exerts himself and sometimes just doesn't care to.

But the most fundamental complaint is the third one: Mr. Susskind has not made the average TSO subscription concert a different ... of ... from what it ...

me; it surprised him that my scope extended to the Broadway repertoire. From time to time during my five years with the paper,[13] he would take me to lunch at Winston's and ply me with arguments for quitting the Faculty and joining the *Star* full-time. I was always resistant, and when I discontinued the connection I felt my main reason was a growing dislike of the role of critic. "Bitchy personality" or not, I found greater fulfillment in my teaching than in the journalistic work.

Once after a performance of Brahms's First Symphony at Massey Hall an audience member near me remarked, "Wasn't that lovely?" It was an excellent performance, but "lovely" is not the word I would have used for that ponderous and multi-faceted work. Another time, from someone else, came the question, "Well, is it yes or no?"—indicating the common perception of the reviewer as a thumbs-up-or-thumbs-down evaluator or judge. In my approach, a review was a description, not a judgment or a consumers' report. I became adept at the task, hurrying to the *Star* office on King Street after the concert, writing out my six or seven paragraphs of comment, typing it, and handing it in before the deadline of 11.30, which meant arriving home around midnight. Later I learned to go directly home, type my review, and send it to the office by cab, so as not to be quite as late.

It was a lively period in the *Star*'s history. Staff writers included Cohen for theatre, Robert Fulford for books, Elizabeth Kilbourn for art, and the "star" columnists Pierre Berton and Ron Haggart. There was a certain satisfaction in seeing my byline in such company. I became noted for correcting the style guide's musical spellings: "Tschaikowsky" was an outmoded and illogical transliteration, and "obligato" an error for "obbligato" (my objections were ignored). There was satisfaction, too, and the occasional thrill, in many of my self-chosen assignments: Glenn Gould with the Toronto Symphony in Schoenberg and Mozart (K491); the Oistrakhs, *père et fils*; Anna Moffo in *La traviata*; distinguished recital work by leading local figures such as Rowland Pack and the conductor Heinz Unger; the 1962 concert of Schoenberg and Stravinsky conducted by the latter and Robert Craft. I enjoyed strong editorial support and good feedback from readers—with the occasional exception: when I criticized the young Joan Sutherland for programming nineteenth-century "claptrap," an anonymous fan phoned to give me a foul-mouthed piece of his mind; and the TSO conductor, Walter Susskind, hit the headlines with a podium speech denouncing the three local music reviewers (John Kraglund of *The Globe and Mail*, George Kidd of the *Telegram*, and me) as "yapping puppies" chasing the heels of the musicians. I seldom took notes during a concert, but nearly always found something to say. Covering a solo concert by an earnest but untalented local performer, I went back to the office feeling an honest description would mean tearing it to pieces, and what would be the point of that?—the player evidently had some standing as a pedagogue, and who was I to attack him? (Sutherland was famous; she could take it.) I asked the city editor if I could write about something else instead, and he agreed. Included in my *Star* assignments were two or three trips to New York to cover the Metropolitan Opera (Vickers in *Die Walküre*; the premiere of Menotti's *The Last Savage*, which I hated), the Philharmonic, and offbeat musical presentations such as *The Play of Daniel*. The *Star* liked the occasional out-of-town "special report" by its writers.

Cohen took it as part of his standing as a drama critic that he wouldn't attend the parties or otherwise mingle in the profession. I wasn't able to assume a similar high moral tone but tried to avoid possible real or perceived conflicts of interest. As my editor, he gave me a free hand to write about, for example, the opening of the Edward Johnson Building and the inauguration of the Ten Centuries Concerts series, in both of which I was closely involved. Of course he relished controversy. In talking with players I knew in the TSO, I sensed an unhappy working atmosphere and wrote a Saturday column about it. Contract negotiations between the orchestra and the Toronto Musicians' Association were in progress, and I was summoned before the TMA board and threatened with expulsion unless I revealed the sources of my article. I didn't depend on my union membership for my livelihood, so the threat was not as severe as it was meant to be, and I knew that journalists' sources are generally (and legally) regarded as confidential, so I refused. The controversy was an early indication of the decisive change of management which occurred in the next year's TMA election. When I wrote a "mixed" review of a new orchestral work by Oskar Morawetz, the composer, a long-time colleague, took it personally and complained to the League of Composers; it was some years before our former, friendly relations were restored. Another colleague said I should have passed that assignment to someone else.

I sometimes devoted my Saturday space to mini-lectures about musical questions that interested me. When I wrote a pair of columns on the musical theories of Heinrich Schenker and Donald Tovey, trying to rationalize for *Star* readers why their findings were influential, Cohen said I was becoming "too academic." He seldom suggested topics but once said why not a column on the fiftieth birthday of Benjamin Britten, and I was glad to oblige, even though it wasn't an event I had planned to write about. The journalist in my background, going back to school days, responded on cue.

In addition to my *Star* commitment, my radio scripts, and the various miscellaneous writing chores mentioned, I started in the early 1960s to contribute programs on special topics to various other CBC series. There were then several serious talk shows about music: *Music Diary* from Vancouver, *New Records* from Toronto, and the national arts program *Critically Speaking*. During this time I prepared a documentary about Harry Partch,[14] another about Wanda Landowska, programs on the music of Webern and on electronic music, and various reviews of recordings. In a talk about the mazurkas of Chopin, I played my own piano illustrations. By the mid-60s, I was assigned to prepare and write documentaries on Boulez (on his visit to Toronto), Bartók (on the twentieth anniversary of his death), and Hindemith (on his death), involving research and interviewing. My interview with Pierre Boulez was only partially successful: he responded volubly to the series of "deep" musical questions I had thought up; however, his English proved rapid but not yet fluent, and with my lack of interviewing experience I found myself interrupting him too much of the time. For the Bartók program I went to New York to interview Victor Bator, Bartók's executor, the composer's son Peter, and the musicologist Paul Henry Lang, who was among Bartók's colleagues at Columbia University. I was astonished to learn of the composer's complex legacy— at the time, the estate was earning hundreds of thousands in royalties, all of it consumed in lawyers' fees for various unresolved international litigations—a cruel irony when one thinks of the strained finances of his last years.

Occasionally I would submit one of my radio reviews, or an expansion of one in the *Star*, to Milton Wilson, editor of the *Canadian Forum*, and he would give it print exposure. He also invited me to review a few books on music for the *Forum*.

A specially pleasurable involvement for me around 1966 was a year-long radio series called *The Music of Chopin*, produced by Diana Brown. Allan Sangster's *The Music of Mozart* had occupied a popular late-evening radio slot for a number of seasons, and on its completion he went on to *The Music of Beethoven*. The aim was to air as far as possible with available recordings every work the composer wrote, in however many broadcasts it might take. For Mozart and Beethoven several years of weekly one-hour doses were needed, but one could cover Chopin's comparatively slender output in about twelve months of half-hour shows. Diana selected the recordings and I wrote and spoke the short introductions. Besides presenting the repertoire in recordings by leading players, we devoted one program to Chopin arrangements (ranging from various composers' contributions to *Les Sylphides* to Barbra Streisand's vocal rendition of the *Minute Waltz*) and another to popular songs adapted from works by Chopin, of which there were a surprising number. I was no Chopin expert, but the programs immersed me in music I felt I knew well and greatly liked, and there was positive feedback from listeners. One listener, Mateusz Gliński, *was* a Chopin expert and invited me to lunch to discuss the controversy over the notorious "Delphine letters." He took the (I believe untenable) scholarly position that the letters were genuine.[15]

A seemingly incurable urge has led me to contribute to the "letters to the editor" columns of many publications. At one point William Littler quipped that I seemed to be making editorial-letter writing a second career. Poor judgment, bad taste, inaccuracy, faulty usage, historical error, injustice all sparked my comments. I once slammed the *National Geographic* for a badly researched feature about the blues. I took *The Globe and Mail* to task for repeated use of the term "English Canada," a futile protest in view of its almost universal adoption (it continues to irritate me). In the University's staff bulletin I berated the audience at Northrop Frye's memorial service for chattering all through a magnificent organ performance by John Tuttle. I wrote to the same paper deploring the introduction of advertising posters in campus washrooms and the ugly "Toronto" sign on the otherwise striking graduate residence on Spadina Avenue. Another letter writer to the *Globe* said he would attend a Canadian opera if the COC ever produced one that was half as good as Verdi, and I responded that I knew several Canadian operas that good; the paper didn't print that one. Letter space used to be generous; more recently, editors have come to expect a type of letter that is condensed and cryptic, designed to be instantly grasped on the Internet rather than savoured in print. I'm only occasionally successful in imitating the new style.

From 1966 to 1970 I took on another regular writing assignment, as program annotator for the subscription concerts of the Toronto Symphony Orchestra. Walter Homburger, the orchestra's manager, approached me when Marcus Adeney decided to relinquish the position which he had held for several years. I created a routine format for the notes—a brief identification of the piece and its composer, in small print, followed by relevant quotations from the literature and whatever comments seemed appropriate—and I relied a good deal on my experience in radio continuity. It helped that I had ready access to the Faculty of Music library, then in a period of rapid expansion. Homburger said he didn't see the need

The bug and John Beckwith

Again this season the Toronto Symphony
Program includes the very informative "program
notes" by John Beckwith. Our thanks to
Volkswagen Canada Ltd. for so generously
sponsoring these notes.

— your editors

II

*The Toronto Symphony Orchestra house programs for the
season 1968–69 carried this advertising notice.*

for program notes, but subscribers seemed to expect them. He found a sponsor for the house program in the Canadian branch of Volkswagen, and programs started to feature a regular full-page ad with the catchy line "The bug and John Beckwith." Much of the program content was familiar symphonic repertoire, but now and then a premiere entailed special score study: during this period, the regime of Seiji Ozawa, the orchestra introduced new pieces by Takemitsu, Nono, and others. On the first Canadian performance of Messiaen's *Turangalîla,* in the presence of the composer, my notes included a tasteless quotation from Stravinsky about the Ondes Martenot, and Homburger passed on to me that Messiaen was offended. It was indeed bad judgment on my part.

Helmut Kallmann's *A History of Music in Canada, 1535–1914* was published in 1960 and drew a lot of favourable reviews (I wrote one for the *University of Toronto Quarterly*). Nothing half as thorough or as finely documented had ever been produced, either in English or in French, on this topic. Kallmann took a broad historical view of "music" as meaning not merely the country's written and performed repertoire but the role of musical activity in the life of its people. He had spent a decade gathering evidence in all parts of the country. We were close friends since student days and had collaborated on several projects, and I had followed the evolution of his *History*. Now the question was, as I put it to him, what to do for an encore: Where would his research now lead? I sensed that, unlike me, he always had a vision, a plan. He said he thought his findings suggested two directions—towards some sort of alphabetically organized dictionary of information about music and musical life in Canada, and towards a Canadian musical *Denkmäler* or Monumenta collection, a scholarly edition, probably in several volumes, that would preserve the most significant published music of the country's past. This rational prediction amounted to an outline of his work for the succeeding quarter-century or more, first in the *Encyclopedia of Music in Canada* and then in the twenty-five-volume *Canadian Musical Heritage* series. I feel grateful to have been able to play a part in both, under his leadership.

From observations of the poor showing of Canadian composers in international reference works on music, I wrote a critical article, "About Canadian Music: the P.R. Failure." It concluded that "if you want the job done well" (i.e., the job of documentation) you should "go to one of the country's own musical experts."[16] The article caught the eye of Floyd Chalmers, the publisher and cultural philanthropist. Keith MacMillan and I met with Chalmers to hear him outline his views on a possible Canadian-music reference publication. My remark, in "The P.R. Failure," concerned information sources on *composers* (composers like me, though I modestly refrained from saying this), but what we identified in our discussion was a broader need—for a general encyclopedia that would cover all phases of the country's music, past and present. The obvious person to develop such an enterprise was Helmut Kallmann. He had just moved to Ottawa as head of the newly founded music division at the National Library of Canada, but was eager to take on the encyclopedia task, and the National Library agreed to free up part of his time. Over the next several months, Gilles Potvin and Kenneth Winters were conscripted as co-editors, and Michael Koerner assumed the position of board chairman. Chalmers, MacMillan, and I, along with half a dozen others from various parts of the country, became board members, and Mabel Laine and Claire Versailles joined the team as managing editors respectively for the English and French editions of the book. (We argued strongly that as a Canadian encyclopedia it should appear simultaneously in both national languages, in versions as closely identical as possible.) Chalmers pledged a large sum of his own money, and in meetings with granting agencies in Toronto, Montreal, and Ottawa he proved a persuasive pleader for the substantial funding that was required. Lists of topics and sub-topics were circulated for opinions and suggestions. Offices in Toronto and Montreal recruited researchers and translators, and the editors started holding "triangle" meetings every month or two to review progress.

Progress? It turned out to be slower than we had foreseen. In various writings and talks I produced in that period I kept saying (starting in 1975) that it would be out "next year" or "in a year or two." The English edition, *Encyclopedia of Music in Canada*, appeared late in 1981, the French edition, *Encyclopédie de la musique au Canada*, over a year later, in early 1983.[17] Many of the articles, as Winters was fond of pointing out, were on topics that had never before been researched. Contributors had variable expertise, and some who had earned reputations as journalist-critics (and therefore were presumably able writers) were stymied by their assignments—a further indication, if we required one, that the publication was sorely needed. I contributed several entries, and helped with copy-editing and with the tricky task of checking the translations. In 1979, when finally everything seemed ready, Ken Winters announced that he wanted to read the whole manuscript through (all 1,300 pages) one more time before sending it to be printed, which would have delayed us further; he was voted down.

The longer-than-anticipated preparation time meant constant upward revisions of the budget. When a bank overdraft in six figures threatened to put a halt to everything, Floyd Chalmers told us to relax; he would make a phone call to "Bill" or "Frank" or whatever the bank president's first name was. He himself ended contributing nearly half a million dollars, an exceptional donation at the time for such a project. He attended almost every board meeting, constantly urging us on to completion, but he refrained from making editorial suggestions. The book is dedicated to him, and I recall Mabel Laine's description of his delighted reaction when she handed him his copy.

The need for more and better writings about CanMus struck me over and over in my teaching, from the late 1960s on. The *Encyclopedia* project was one fulfillment that I was glad to help bring about. Another, only partly achieved, was the series *Canadian Composers*, initiated around the same time by the Canadian Music Centre.

The profiles of contemporary US composers in the *Musical Quarterly* and *Modern Music* had provided a model for similar articles in the *Canadian Music Journal* (as already mentioned, I contributed one on Jean Papineau-Couture). In the '50s and '60s an increasing number of monographs appeared in the US dealing in greater depth with the careers of individual composers—for example, Arthur Berger's book on Aaron Copland. I felt various Canadians merited similar treatment. The reactions to the "P.R. Failure" article in 1969 and my new connection as a board member of the Canadian Music Centre led me in 1971 to propose a series of such volumes. Keith MacMillan as CMC director was dissatisfied with the effectiveness of his newsletter *Musicanada* and suggested the money be diverted to cover other types of publication. The board then formed a "publications committee" and asked me to chair it. The committee's mandate was to develop a plan for commissioning both a series of individual-composer monographs and a biographical dictionary of contemporary Canadian composers. The dictionary, treating of the music of 144 composers, was prepared by a team of a half-dozen writers and edited by MacMillan and me. It was published by Oxford University Press of Canada in 1975.[18] The series had a longer and more difficult gestation.

The committee was an excellent one, consisting of the composers André Prévost and Robert Aitken and the writer/commentators Gilles Potvin and Lyse Richer-Lortie; MacMillan was a lurking ex-officio presence. Our first commissions, in December 1971, were for monographs on Serge Garant, John Weinzweig, Harry Somers, and Pierre Mercure. Each of the writers would receive an honorarium and a small advance for research expenses. In 1972 we approved further commissions for studies[19] on Jean Papineau-Couture and Barbara Pentland. In a memorandum to the authors in October 1972, I wrote: "It is planned to have [the studies] appear at the rate of two or three a year, starting in 1973." As in so many phases of my working life, I had a lot to learn—this time about authorship and the publishing process. Even more than with the *Encyclopedia*, progress was slow, with many delays and postponements. As time went by and no books appeared, members of the Centre board who had been unconvinced of the need for our series at the outset became understandably impatient. In early 1975 the board voted to discontinue its support. The committee was in the position of having to realize the already-committed projects and retained enough confidence to continue with a few further commissions, undaunted though financially unsure.

That same year, 1975, in fact saw the appearance of the dictionary and the completion of two of our monographs. That on Somers, by Brian

Cherney, was the first to be published.[20] That on Garant, by Udo Kasemets, was turned down by the publishers' readers, who considered it "too technical." Keith and I proposed it for revision and translation into French for consideration by a Montreal publisher, but our francophone colleagues were unenthusiastic about this. We had worked together harmoniously through a series of meetings, but when the idealistic notion that the entire study series could appear in both languages proved impractical Lyse remarked dramatically, "Nous sommes trompés encore!"—an echo of the *Révolution tranquille*. This work on Garant survives only in manuscript;[21] a different sort of book about this composer and his music appeared in the 1980s.[22]

In 1976 commissions went out for studies on Rodolphe Mathieu and R. Murray Schafer, and we began exploratory talks with writers on Violet Archer and Gilles Tremblay. In 1977, *Contemporary Canadian Composers* appeared in a French translation.[23]

What did I and my colleagues learn from this enterprise? One, that writers on Canadian music are rare; and, two, that most of them are academics with limited time for research and authorship and *un*limited habits of procrastination. The Mercure study was never completed.[24] The Schafer and Pentland studies appeared in 1983 and the Papineau-Couture study in 1986, more than a decade after the original commissions.[25] George Proctor's work on Archer was well advanced when the author suddenly died; his research was published posthumously as an article.[26] The Mathieu and Tremblay studies were never started. The Weinzweig study became a saga: first contemplated in 1971, it passed from a first author to a second author and, after another delay, to a *third* author, Elaine Keillor, and after further vicissitudes appeared from a US publisher in *1994!*[27] By that time the original series had ceased any signs of expanding; I had relinquished my position as "general editor" in the late '80s. Though arduous to produce, the few volumes which emerged may have inaugurated a literary sub-type, represented since in a succession of studies on other Canadian composers, produced in different formats and under different auspices.

Shortly after Glenn Gould's untimely death in 1982, John McGreevy invited me to write something for a memorial volume he was editing (Geoffrey Payzant had suggested my name to him).[28] Payzant's 1978 study of Gould's musical thought[29] had contributed greatly to making Glenn's work known and seriously regarded. It may indeed have initiated a whole literary genre, Gould Studies, in view of the unabated flood of publications about Glenn in later years. As the pioneer authority on Glenn's career, who had been in close touch with him, Payzant was frequently called upon for interviews in the early 1980s, but by the mid-80s he had taken to refusing both Gould interviews and appearances on Gould panels. (Glenn's long-time manager, Walter Homburger, made a similar resolve.) Around that time, Payzant asked me to join him in talking with the editor of an Italian music journal, then visiting Toronto, who was preparing something about Glenn. I answered a few questions from my early acquaintance with Glenn, and Payzant gave an eloquent synopsis of his research concerning Glenn's ideas on music and musical performance. The editor appeared to be listening and took a few notes. At the end, he said he had a further question for us: "I would really like to know, please, what were Glenn Gould's last words?" It was an early warning of the sentimentality and voyeurism that have so often passed for commentary in the vast output of Gouldiana that followed.

The realization of Helmut Kallmann's vision of a Canadian musical "Monumenta" series came about in an unexpected way. Clifford Ford, who had been my composition student in his teen years and later as a University of Toronto undergraduate, had a teaching position at Dalhousie University in Halifax and, in introducing a course in Canadian music history there, had written a textbook on the topic, bringing Kallmann's work up to the present and emphasizing the composed repertoire.[30] To complement such a course he thought there should be a series of reprints from Canadian music published in past generations, and around 1980 he approached Kallmann and several others with similar interests to test possible support for this idea. In 1981, in Toronto, five of us had a lunch meeting: Ford, Kallmann, Elaine Keillor from Carleton, Fred Hall from McMaster, and me. We outlined plans for what was to become the Canadian Musical Heritage Society (Société du patrimoine musical canadien), with the aim of producing the sort of anthology Ford saw as a need and Kallmann years ago had imagined. Kallmann had already drafted a list of the volumes required if we wanted to do the job thoroughly: separate collections of piano, organ, chamber, orchestral, and band music, solo songs, theatre music, and choral music in large and small forms. We soon invited Lucien Poirier of Laval as a sixth member of the team. We formed a board of advisers with a national purview and started exploring sources of funding; luckily, the time seemed opportune for a sympathetic response from the arts councils and the Social Sciences and Humanities Research Council in Ottawa, and several private foundations also came through with grants. Ford left Halifax and set up an office in Ottawa to pursue the project as our full-time executive secretary.

Editorial board, Canadian Musical Heritage Society, Ottawa, circa 1990. Left to right, standing: Lucien Poirier, Elaine Keillor, John Beckwith, Fred Hall, Clifford Ford; at the piano: Helmut Kallmann.

Over the next couple of decades we worked volume by volume on our series, entitled *The Canadian Musical Heritage / Le patrimoine musical canadien.* We each took assignments to edit a volume or two, and invited other experts as "guest editors." The potential contents of every volume (there were eventually twenty-five) were circulated to all six members of the group for comments aiming to guide the volume editor in the final choice. Periodically a bundle of photocopied scores would arrive in the mail and I would spend a couple of days at my piano playing them over and pencilling my reactions and yea-or-nay votes. The committee's bilingual notes form a unique, candid assessment of the CanMus repertoire and could furnish a future research topic.[31] The system had its hazards: once a sheaf of my notes was lost in the return mail and I had to spend another couple of days redoing them. We met in Ottawa three or four times a year to discuss progress. It was an unusually harmonious team; the flow of energy was remarkable, and I found I learned an enormous amount about Canada's musical past and developed great respect for my colleagues' knowledge and judgment. My assignments were volumes 5 ("Hymn Tunes / Cantiques") and 18 ("Oratorio and Cantata Excerpts / Extraits d'oratorios et de cantates").[32]

The Society was its own publisher and distributor. We took 1950 as a cut-off date for music to be included, which meant that still-living composers would be represented in some volumes—and this in turn obliged us to confront problems of permissions. The *earliest* examples went back three hundred years—earlier than might have been expected. These were pieces not *published* in what is now Canada but somehow relevant through adoption and use. We aimed at scholarly editions that would also have practical usefulness to performers.[33] Introductions and notes appeared in both English and French: Kallmann and I were "style editors" for the English, and Poirier (and later Marie-Thérèse Lefebvre)[34] for the French. The repertoire made no distinction between "classical" and "popular": both the turn-of-the-century symphonic poems of Clarence Lucas and the 1930s recorded hits of La Bolduc were grist for our mill. Reviews of the volumes in Canada and abroad were encouraging: we were thrilled when Thurston Dox, in *American Music*, started one notice with "The Canadians have done it again."[35] I was told by a US colleague that our series served as one of the models in the planning of the series *MUSA* (*Music in the United States of America*), inaugurated in 1993.[36]

However, getting out our message to potential users—students, researchers, and teachers—was slow and often frustrating. Ten years into the project, a performer would ask, "Do you know of any early Canadian music for organ?" and would register surprise on learning that one or two volumes of organ repertoire were already in print as part of *The Canadian Musical Heritage* and available for purchase or on library loan. Even after publication of the concluding volume 25, in 1999, the series could be described as having earned only moderate recognition and respect by Canadian performers and music educators. Cultivation of the national musical heritage remains a minority interest in Canada, compared with other countries.

Again, what to do for an encore? One useful by-product of our efforts was a coil-bound anthology of extracts, a cross-section of highlights from our two dozen volumes, with the title *Historical Anthology of Canadian Music*.[37] After the final volume of the series, the Society had envisioned shifting its efforts to compact disc recording. A number of CDs had appeared on various labels offering performances of this or that historical work, but there was no systematic survey series from which the whole repertoire could be illustrated in sound. We managed to commission and release two discs in what we decided to call the "Lavallée Series." The committee chose the repertoire, and Ford and I were on-site representatives at the recording sessions. The first was *Le souvenir*, a CD of songs from the nineteenth and early-twentieth centuries, and the second *Noël*, a collection of Canadian music associated with Christmas.[38] We drew up plans for several further recordings, but in the late 1990s and early 2000s arguing the case for substantial long-term funding was much harder than it had been in the early 1980s. The rules governing recording-subsidy programs of the granting agencies were set up to assist living performers and composers, and our historical approach to the repertoire fell in the cracks. After a discouraging reception in meetings with those responsible, we had to give up. Twenty-five volumes, a two-volume anthology, and two CDs later, I am proud of our achievement—and getting there was a lot of fun.

In these projects—*CMJ* reviews, the dictionary and composer studies, the English-language introductions to the *Heritage* volumes, the Institute's *CanMus Documents* series (see p. 160)—I regularly found myself in the position of editor. Before publication I would scan the manuscripts and send the authors my comments—lists of little mistakes and suggested improvements, such as texts always need before being published. My own manuscripts always required such scanning by at least one other pair of eyes. I inherited Dad's sense of proper usage and clarity of expression in language, and my work had come under scrutiny by fine professional editors such as Francess Halpenny and Margaret Parker at the U of T Press. The process demanded diplomacy: some authors found me merciless and considered my notes an attack on their precious work; others were grateful for my help. My field was music, in the view of the complainers, so what business did I have making these specialized comments on their writing? In my arrogance I evidently thought my experience with writing and with publisher contacts was of value. To students who resented my pointing out incorrect usage or fuzzy expression in their history-of-music essays, on similar grounds (it was a course in music, not in writing), I used to reply that whatever the subject you had to strive for clear verbal communication. Publishers often sent me manuscripts they were considering, for my opinion.

My critical writings and talks accumulated to the point where I considered gathering some of them for a possible book. I made a selection and showed it to Margaret Gayfer and William Toye, asking advice from their experience in the publishing world. They both encouraged me. I tried one or two of the avenues they suggested, without success. Eventually Michael Gnarowski, editor of a small independent press in Ottawa, The Golden Dog, expressed interest, and the collection (entitled *Music Papers*, after the *Papiers de musique* of the early-twentieth-century Montreal critic Léo-Pol Morin) appeared in 1997. A year later Gnarowski sent me what he called "a small royalty cheque" and said he was delighted at the annual sales: ninety-nine copies.

Encyclopedias date rapidly. Preoccupations in the 1980s and '90s were a second edition of EMC, and then discussions for a third. The initial EMC had been the largest single publication undertaken up to that time by the University of Toronto Press. $EMC2$ was inevitably larger, and the French edition emerged in a boxed set of three volumes instead of a single nine-pounder.[39] Ken Winters had relinquished his former post, and Robin Elliott came aboard as an associate to Kallmann and Potvin. There was considerable dependence on newer technology in the editing process. The first edition was remarkable (and ahead of its time) among musical reference works in its generous treatment of popular and commercial musics, and Mark Miller's role as "jazz and pop" editor was even more heavily emphasized in the second. I was responsible for several writing, revising, and editing chores. A rare aspect of EMC was its national focus— unlike other musical dictionaries, it concentrated on the music and musical life of one country. Maintaining that focus was not always easy. New board members in the 1980s thought the idea of editions in two languages, and the corresponding travails of translation, could be dispensed with. As an alternative, one member, an up-to-date businessman, thought the translation could be handled by a computer program, and he had to be persuaded that in view of the special vocabulary of music this would be a disaster. Notably, in our drive for funding we had a more generous response from the Quebec government (then under the Parti Québécois) than from that of Ontario.

It seemed for the prospect of a third edition we would, like so many similar enterprises, abandon print production in favour of an ongoing online reference work. The National Library, which since Kallmann's day had been a close partner in EMC research, became a centre for updating of entries, and in the early 2000s the board turned the work over to the electronic reference organization Historica. Helmut Kallmann had retired from the Library in 1987 but headed the preparation of $EMC2$. He and I, along with Michael Koerner, Joan Chalmers (Floyd's daughter), and Rod Anderson, veterans of the early days of the project, gathered in 2002 to see it handed on to the future in a new form as $EMC3$.

Miscellaneous writing invitations continued to come my way. Kevin Bazzana, editor of the Glenn Gould Foundation's journal *GlennGould*, asked me for a contribution, and I sent him some Gould memories and a summary of corrective notes I had made in recently published Gouldiana.[40] Out of curiosity, I started researching the 1940 name change, from "Gold" to "Gould," and eventually produced another, shorter article.[41] Hoping to verify some points in this second piece, I rang Bert Gould, Glenn's father. We had not been in touch for fifty years, but he remembered me and agreed to meet for a short interview. However, when the time came, his wife called to postpone; Bert was unwell. Another message came a week or two later; he was in hospital. He died there shortly afterwards, aged ninety-four. His funeral, in early January 1996, was a small service in a United Church in Don Mills. The two speakers, Robert Fulford and John Roberts, both dwelt more on Bert's role as a father than on any other facet of his life—his business success or his work with the Kiwanis Club for example. A "choir" of five sopranos and one bass (no altos and no tenors) attempted "Jesu, Joy of Man's Desiring" by Bach, to an excruciatingly inept electronic-organ accompaniment. I imagined Glenn squirming. It was of course all well meant: as Virgil Thomson once quipped, God doesn't necessarily insist on professional standards.

During the years 2004–8, I was an intermittent contributor of compact disc reviews to the Toronto monthly concert guide *WholeNote*. The review editor, David Olds, established a policy of including only "positive" reviews—meaning that your review was expected to indicate why your disc was worth recommending. He circulated lists each month to his stable of reviewers asking for their preferences. I liked the challenge of trying to say something fresh about a new recording in a limited space (Olds kept rigidly to a maximum of 250 words), and my choices ranged over a broad repertoire from Rameau to Brant.

My more substantial writings of later years were either the results of research projects or accumulated critical views that for one reason or another stimulated me to some kind of organized expression. Returning to my earlier work on hymnody, I thought of trying to explore further the very earliest Canadian publications, from the first decades of the nineteenth century, each of which had distinct characteristics. The known editions of Humbert's *Union Harmony* had never been compared; the substantial *Nouveau recueil de cantiques* of Daulé had never been analyzed; little background had been produced on Jenkins's *Psalms of David* and its compiler; and, unknown to me or anyone else, there was a real discovery to be made in connection with Burnham's *Colonial Harmonist*. When Kathleen[42] and I sat in the farmhouse of one of Burnham's descendants and were handed a large, bound manuscript containing what was apparently a draft of a never-realized second edition, I understood the satisfaction scholars and researchers feel from such unexpected breakthroughs.[43]

Occasional talks have sometimes flowered into publishable papers. I felt this sort of potential in the talks I gave in 1993 and '94 about the history of the University of Toronto Music Faculty, mixtures of research and personal recollection. The Faculty was marking its seventy-fifth anniversary, and I had been closely attached to the institution for more than half of those years as student and later staff member. The talks went over well, but when I approached the University of Toronto Alumni Association for a small grant to help publish them, I was cold-shouldered, so assumed the cost myself.[44]

In 1996, the Société québécoise de recherche en musique asked me to speak at a conference at the University of Sherbrooke centred on the tenth anniversary of Serge Garant's death (Sherbrooke was Garant's hometown). There had been a good deal of media attention to a new Montreal composers' group, Les Mélodistes indépendants, whose anti-modern manifesto rang the bell for stylistic "accessibility" and spoke of a *rupture* between avant-gardists and the musical public. I decided to imagine what Garant's response would be to this mini-controversy, and the result later reached print in both languages.[45]

Some years earlier, Gordon Smith had given me a photocopy of an extensive and intriguing music manuscript, *Annales musicales du Petit-Cap*, from the late nineteenth century, whose editor was Mgr. Thomas-Étienne Hamel. I had made arrangements of some of its tunes (the book contained over a hundred) but had not taken the time to explore them systematically or delve into the work's provenance. I found it odd that no one else had done so, although the volume, housed in the Archives du Séminaire in Quebec City, was cited in several reference works. I made a poor start by locating Petit-Cap on the north coast of the Gaspé peninsula and picturing Hamel as an obscure music-loving priest in that unlikely and remote place. This romantic image was shattered when I learned that Hamel was one of the great figures in nineteenth-century church history and specifically in the history of Laval University, and that the Petit-Cap in question was a retreat near Quebec City owned by the Séminaire and frequented by its students and staff. Hamel was indeed a music lover and evidently compiled his collection for group singing at the retreat. My findings, described in a talk I gave for the Society in both Montreal and Quebec City, were eventually published in both French and English.[46]

For some time I was intrigued that two composers from the Canadian past whose work I had come to know well, Joseph Quesnel and Calixa Lavallée, were the subjects of musical theatre works written and produced in Montreal in the 1940s by the organist, composer, and writer Eugène

Lapierre. The pieces had not been revived, and no one apparently had investigated them. In a couple of visits to the Bibliothèque nationale in Montreal, I found in the Fonds Lapierre what remained of the scores and librettos, as well as background documents, and produced an essay which was published in a collection dedicated to my former student Beverley Diamond on her sixtieth birthday.[47] The resourceful Marie-Thérèse Lefebvre helped with information and advice. Lapierre turned out to be a less-than-attractive figure—a mediocre composer, a fanciful writer rather than a genuine historian, and a product of the paranoiac nationalism of the Duplessis era. However, I thought his two productions marked a significant phase in Canadian musical life, and in Canadian life generally, despite their distorted portraits of Quesnel and Lavallée.

In talks to student groups and others, I had vented my reflections on areas of music that were of concern to me, notably in a few convocation addresses, a paper at the CUMS conference in 1997 at Memorial University in St John's called "Accessibility, Elitism, or Oblivion: Options for the Composer," and a talk in 2004 for the Women's Musical Club of Toronto called "The State of Composition." The most far-reaching attempt along these lines was my presentation at the CUMS/CAML meeting in Montreal in 2007, where a fuss was made over my having reached the age of eighty. Echoing Charles Burney, I titled my remarks "The Present State of Unpopular Music," recalling that term from its ironic use by Harry Somers on a number of occasions. My address was a critical defence of modernism, live performance, and perseverance in a period of seeming decline for serious music. "Small is beautiful" was one of my optimistic comments. The paper attracted the attention of the Canadian Music Centre and for some months was posted on its website; it subsequently appeared in two different journals.[48]

A major preoccupation was my first real book, a short biographical study of my teacher Alberto Guerrero. I should have written it thirty years earlier—or someone should have—when key figures in his life story (Myrtle Rose, Glenn Gould) were still alive. In 2002 his daughter, Mélisande Irvine, donated a collection of his papers to the Faculty of Music library, and I spent a weekend perusing them. They included concert programs and newspaper clippings from his early career in Santiago. It appeared that a great deal of his background was unknown either in Chile or in Canada, and that there were mistakes and contradictions in the available accounts. Encouraged by conversations with two former Guerrero students, Ray Dudley and William Aide, I started to organize a "search" for primary documents that might clarify the record. In January 2003 Kathleen and I spent ten days in Chile. We found Guerrero's birth and marriage certificates and made contact with archivists and music researchers at the Biblioteca nacional, the music department of the Universidad de Chile, and the diocesan archives in his birthplace, La Serena. In October of that year, I presented a talk called "In Search of Alberto Guerrero" (the eventual title of my book) at the Faculty of Music in Toronto. The topic caught the attention of Nieves Carrasco, a Chilean artist living in Toronto, and after my talk she offered to help with Chilean and Spanish-language aspects of the project. Her grandfather, an architect, was a member of the artistic group Los Diez in Santiago in the 1910s, along with Guerrero. During our half-year leave in Santa Fe, New Mexico, in 2004, I added to my research (it helped that the University of New Mexico library in Albuquerque had almost-complete historical files of the Santiago newspaper *El Mercurio*) and wrote the first draft of the book, finishing it in Toronto later that year. It differs from most biographies in its combination of narrative and personal memories—and I forewarned readers of this in my introduction. The book was turned down by several publishers but eventually accepted— and produced in exemplary style—by Wilfrid Laurier University Press in Waterloo.

In May 2006 the Press and the Faculty of Music in Toronto co-sponsored a launch party, and both Mélisande and her son Tony Irvine were able to attend. I had not met Tony previously; he was on a visit from his home in Mexico. Mélisande, then in her late eighties and suffering from a heart condition, died in September of that year. That was another shadow of several that hang over the project when I call it to mind: two close friends from student days in Toronto passed away during the years I worked on it, who followed its progress and greatly helped with remembered information and criticisms—Margaret Sheppard Privitello in 2003 and Ray Dudley in 2005. *In Search of Alberto Guerrero* has been well received but has drawn less attention beyond Canada than I think the subject deserves. In my planning, I realized the book would attract a larger readership with a title like *The Man Who Taught Glenn Gould*. But I chose to picture Guerrero as an outstanding musical personality—for his own achievement and wide influence as performer, teacher, and (in earlier years) composer—rather than as a vague figure in the shade of his most renowned pupil.

In March 2006 I attended a party celebrating John Weinzweig's ninety-third birthday. I came away thinking it was time I tried to set down my thoughts about his music and memories of our association.[49] Brian Cherney had visited Weinzweig around the same time and told me he was

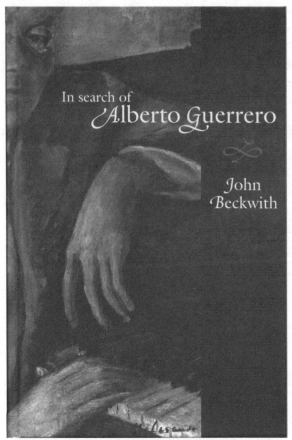

In search of
Alberto Guerrero

John
Beckwith

P.J. Woodland's cover design for In Search of Alberto Guerrero
(Wilfrid Laurier University Press, 2006) incorporates
Mélisande Irvine's oil portrait of her father.

considering something along the same lines. We both felt that Weinzweig's own public pronouncements and the various accounts of his personality and career by others had left an incomplete and unbalanced picture, and that he deserved more. He had remained active as a composer and musical advocate (some would say agitator) for over sixty years, and his legacy seemed in danger of fading away. We drew up a plan for a collection of biographical and analytical essays, and in August I was able to tell John and his wife Helen what we hoped to do. He had been in gradually failing health, and died only a couple of weeks later. Our book[50] brought together research and comment by fourteen writers, and as both co-editor and one of the contributing writers I found it absorbed much of my time and energy over the succeeding three years. Research, especially in his papers at Library and Archives Canada in Ottawa, solidified his stature as a single-minded and virtually "self-made" composer, and considering closely a number of his works I had not previously known well increased my respect for his remarkable, indeed unmatched, achievement. Cherney,[51] who had been in my class half a century before, proved an ideal collaborator—a meticulous researcher with excellent musical knowledge and writing skill. We found we shared a similar point of view as composers and also a keen admiration for Weinzweig.

Academia

As teachers, Alberto Guerrero and John Weinzweig both strongly influenced my musical formation. Guerrero's only piano teacher, as far as anyone knows, was his mother. Weinzweig's only composition instructor, for a limited time, was Bernard Rogers in Rochester; his other teachers, in Toronto, left him feeling bitter and frustrated. How did they become such outstandingly successful teachers? Similar questions arose constantly in the 1950s as I found myself taking up responsibilities as a teacher: for example, What is teaching? and How do you become a good teacher?

Northrop Frye's definition of education was "repeating something over and over until you know it by heart."[1] I used to wonder how I could tell whether my teaching had any effect. The one sure evidence I could produce was that I taught my son Symon how to drive a car and he passed his driver's test on the first try. Music has both scientific, right-or-wrong qualities and elusive, unmeasurable ones: the difference between an eighth note and a quarter note, or between C and C$\sharp$, may be exactly quantified, but the differences between *allegro* and *allegretto*, staccato and semi-staccato, or *forte* and *fortissimo* are matters of judgment, taste, and feeling. Teaching music isn't a simple matter of dispensing information and testing whether it gets across.

For Guerrero, teaching was a mysterious process. You knew, he said, when you got across to your student, but you didn't really know *how* or *why*. Moreover, what worked for one student didn't always work for another. Compatability between teacher and student seems to be essential for effective communication and influence. Student reactions about a teacher can vary widely. As noted earlier,[2] Nadia Boulanger achieved great renown as a teacher, but not all her pupils emerged from her classes with the same views of her or the same musical attitudes and habits; the same might be said of both Guerrero and Weinzweig.

My first teaching assignments were university classes and private lessons in musical theory and the history of music. Apart from knowledge of my subject, there were no qualifications; I had taken no courses in educational methodology, had undergone no criticism from experienced teachers, endured no sessions of "practice teaching." I read Gilbert Highet's *The Art of Teaching*[3] but little of the more fundamental educational literature. I skimmed the music education journals occasionally, but found their contents were mainly how-to articles aimed at school-music teachers. I plunged in, trying to be guided by what I had observed of my own teachers and feeling lucky to have had so many fine ones. I used the piano and, less often, the phonograph to illustrate, and I distributed paper copies of music-notation examples or else drew them on the blackboard, because I knew that developing an inside knowledge of music required you to be constantly in touch with the sound and the look of it, not just with descriptive words about it. From observing the best musicians I had encountered, I told my students that knowing music from the inside meant being able to hear what you read, and sing (or play) and write down in notes what you hear. In common with most novice teachers, I had to work hard to keep ahead of the students. This was especially true when, in the middle of my second season of teaching, I assumed an almost-full courseload on the sudden departure of a colleague, George Loughlin, who took up an appointment in Australia. Inheriting his class in medieval and Renaissance music, I sat up late every night reading Gustave Reese and searching out music examples in the Apel-Davison anthology.[4] My own spotty undergraduate preparations had not included these wonderful areas.

My part-time engagement to the Faculty of Music in the fall of 1952 coincided with full-time appointments to Kenins, Morawetz, and Weinzweig. The Faculty director, Arnold Walter, could be seen as bolstering the institution's strength in composition studies, although we were hired to teach theory subjects to all music undergraduates, not just budding composers. Bolstering of music history studies came a few seasons later, with further appointments—Harvey Olnick, Myron Schaeffer—Canada's first professional musicologists. My teaching responsibilities grew, and in 1955 I was accorded permanent (full-time) status. As a junior member of the staff, I was expected to be versatile. The load included craft courses and study courses—that is, courses like traditional harmony and even fugue,[5] but also courses in history and analysis. Most of my students were music majors but some were enrolled in either honours or general programs in the Faculty of Arts and Science. My first assignment had been a course in contemporary-music analysis. Then I was handed an undergraduate course in counterpoint and fugue and another in basic musicianship (meaning traditional harmony and analysis with concurrent sight singing and dictation).[6] The latter program, for first- and second-year performance majors, is one which I enjoyed and continued to teach for more than thirty years. I also taught (when asked) a variety of undergraduate history-of-music courses as well as graduate courses in special topics. After the first few years of keeping a week or so ahead of history classes and responding to the varying demands of this period or that period designed now for music majors and now for general arts enrollees, I used to boast that I could serve up a survey of Western music history in a half-course or a full course, in one, two, or three hours a week. In the full course, Beethoven got three lectures, in the one-hour-a-week arts option, twenty minutes. I was a sort of musicological custom tailor. I called myself a composer and was fairly steadily productive, but it wasn't until my sixteenth year of teaching that I faced my first composition class. In terms of my value to the university, then, I was a generalist, not a specialist.[7]

I was scarcely older than my students and had to work to earn their respect. University procedures were more formal in the 1950s than in later decades. In our Faculty we didn't insist on wearing gowns, as was the custom in some colleges, but I had to ask members of my class to please refrain from calling me "sir." There were other ways to acknowledge authority. Once I referred to some feature in a score by Bach and a student interrupted; he knew the score well, he said, and he questioned my point about it. Feeling on the spot, I returned the challenge: Would he please stay for a few minutes after class so we could look at the score together? It turned out I was right, but I had not wanted to waste class time having to prove this. I soon learned that awareness of time was a vital part of classroom technique. I prepared notes but in the lecture style of the day found my natural gift of the gab sometimes resulted in a scramble to complete the class before the actual or imaginary bell.

My assignments intrigued me, and the constant association with bright and committed colleagues and students was stimulating. Without spelling it out, I was aware of a developing loyalty to the institution. For Frye (an outstanding teacher), the university undergraduate program was "the engine room of society."[8] In my experience the music faculty was no ivory tower, sheltered from "the real world." I attended council and committee meetings and appreciated playing a part in decisions. I spent spare hours with the head librarian, Jean Lavender, perusing the monthly Schwann catalogues and developing lists of long-playing records to be ordered (Olnick had instituted a push for vast improvements to the library's collection). Conscious of my limited paper credentials, when the Faculty announced a new Master of Music degree program in 1955, I signed up. Weinzweig was my main adviser, and I took courses as well from both Olnick and Schaeffer. Language study was obligatory, so I enrolled in introductory Italian. Spreading the degree work over two years, I still found it impossible to finish the composition thesis while juggling full-time teaching and family responsibilities; my graduation didn't take place until 1961. At the final oral exam, Dr Walter as chair posed a single question: What were my views on modern-music aesthetics? Though tense, I must have held my own in the ensuing lengthy debate. There was little reference to my thesis, a three-movement work for piano and orchestra.

Surveying the Faculty's founding and early history in two talks in the 1990s,[9] I made a study of examination questions as a way of observing the changes in course demands over the years. The essentials of an advanced music education program in the 1970s and '80s, I found, were not the same as those of the 1920s. The exam papers confronting candidates in the spring of 1953 reflected the new composer appointments in the first references to works by Schoenberg, Hindemith, and Stravinsky. Where in later periods students would study assigned music by listening to cassettes or CDs, in the 1950s they equipped themselves with scores: in the first course I taught, Schoenberg's *Pierrot lunaire* and Suite, op. 25, were required. I formed the habit of copying score excerpts on stencils and running off copies of them (on a purple-ink spirit duplicator) for class discussion. Cheap photocopying (not to mention websites) were as-yet-unknown teaching tools. I savoured the sound of music in class and found satisfaction when the freshman harmony studies were sufficiently advanced that we could spend a whole hour analyzing a Beethoven sonata movement, Bach prelude, or Schubert song. Using Schubert's "The Erl King" in one such session, I was delighted when, with six minutes to go before dismissal, a singer in the class volunteered to sing it to my (largely faked) accompaniment. It brought the dissection to life. Now and then I was bold enough to invite an older member of the performing staff to a class to join me in a live illustration of some work we were studying. Kathleen Parlow played a Mozart sonata and talked about it, and Ernesto Vinci sang the entire *Winterreise* after I had devoted a couple of lectures to it. Analyzing Ives's *From the Steeples*, I contrived a classroom reading, with glockenspiels in each of the four corners and brass soloists in the middle.

The administrative separation of the Royal Conservatory and the Faculty was many years in the future, and they continued as "sister institutions" within the university. Principal Mazzoleni set up a series of musicianship classes for Conservatory scholarship students (gifted teenagers who looked likely to pursue a musical future), and he asked Tali Kenins and me to teach them. The late-afternoon sessions for groups of half a dozen students turned out to be animated encounters with keenly motivated youngsters, most of whom entered the Faculty and went on to prominent careers—I recall Brian Cherney, Patricia Perrin (later Krueger), Terence Helmer, Anahid Alexanian, and others.

My first sabbatical, in 1965–66, was only the second granted in the Faculty of Music. Dr Walter took pains to impress on me how lucky I was; in his career he had never had a *whole year* to spend on his own musical pursuits. We later learned to call it "study leave," since "sabbatical" sounded too much like holiday goofing off. My partial salary for the period, supplemented by a Canada Council study grant, proved not quite adequate support for the twelve months, so in the spring of '66 I took on a number of CBC assignments—both talks and piano performances. Robert Aitken, at that time first flute of the TSO, recommended me to Maestro Ozawa, and I was one of the keyboard players in his performance of Charles Ives's Fourth Symphony (23–24 March 1966). In its New York premiere the previous year this sprawling score had required three conductors, Stokowski and two assistants. But Ozawa chose daringly to do the one-conductor version, as devised by Gunther Schuller. The score calls for solo piano, piano four-hands, and organ; Pat Krueger played the solo piano and the organ, while Carol Pack and I were the duettists. In the second and fourth movements, the parts were atonal, dense, and tough to play. The textures were unusually involved, so that in rehearsal the players found it at times impossible to hear themselves. In some passages, a dozen different rhythmic or harmonic motives occur simultaneously (psychologists dealing with musical perception put the limit for human ears at three, or four maximum). I asked Seiji Ozawa how he managed to keep it all together, and he said he found the trick was to concentrate on one part of the orchestra at a time, more or less tuning the others out. In analyzing this extraordinary piece with students later, I referred to this pragmatic approach as a possible way of *listening* to such passages: it's possible to visit aurally the various strands in the wonderful thicket of notes one or two at a time, acknowledging them in turn as if walking around a monumental and complex piece of sculpture. Participating in that performance was a thrilling experience.

The Faculty had occupied its new building, named after Edward Johnson, in 1962. The following few years brought curricular changes, new content to be absorbed, and a new, more informal way of communicating with students. Stockhausen, Berio, Cage were new personalities to be reckoned with; the Faculty appointed its first ethnomusicologist, Mieczyslaw Kolinski; the three-year undergraduate degree expanded to four years; and, belatedly, a new sub-discipline, performance (sometimes referred to by the US term "applied music"), became recognized with its own degree stream. The old fugue course disappeared as a requirement—one professor, Godfrey Ridout, voiced a fervent but unsuccessful plea to retain it on the grounds that it made the students "better citizens." Classes became rap sessions rather than lectures. Male staffers started appearing without their jackets and ties (one professor, the Austrian-born Gerhard Wuensch, even sported Lederhosen). The basic survey in the history and literature of Western music metamorphosed into a consideration of music's nature and social purpose, a context incorporating current popular musics and non-Western musics. It was a novelty for the Faculty Council to discuss a proposed course offering which defined its topic geographically rather than by genre or era—not a course in lieder, or baroque music, but a course tentatively called "Music of North America." Dr Walter asked whether such a course would deal with—he could hardly bring himself to say the word—*jazz*. In the Council debate, I argued in favour of the proposal, without anticipating that I would be asked to teach the course. Starting in the 1966–67 academic year, it became my specialty for the next twenty years or more.[10]

In designing the course, I found it was possible to develop useful comparisons between the settler cultures in New Spain, New England, and New France in musical terms and project them into succeeding eras. The consideration of Aboriginal musical cultures I mainly left to a later point in the chronology, roughly when investigators began studying and documenting them and (especially) when field workers began recording them; within a decade or two, discussion and illustration from a broader historical perspective would become feasible. I benefited from then-new writings on music in Latin America by Robert Stevenson, and on US musical history by H. Wiley Hitchcock, Richard Crawford, Eileen Southern, and others; for Canada there was Kallmann. In the accounts of early psalmody, I found stimulus for investigations of my own, which eventually led to publications. At the start, though, I didn't try to hide the fact that I had more

In this photo of 1980, I am apparently meeting with my "Music of North America" class (photo courtesy of Rick MacMillan).

enthusiasm than expertise. With the students, I covered much of the continent's repertoire (both the "cultivated" and the "vernacular," to use the terms Hitchcock had introduced); digging out scores and recordings required sometimes a good deal of ingenuity and instinct, especially for early musical Canadiana. The listening I had done for my radio series had made me familiar with at least some of the relevant pieces, and happily a few good anthologies, both published and recorded, were just emerging. Reading about Scott Joplin's opera *Treemonisha*, I learned that the Toronto jazz musician Ron Collier actually possessed a copy of the out-of-print vocal score. He loaned it to me so that I could discuss it with the class; there was at the time no recording. My self-accompanied renditions of Henry Russell's song "The Old Arm Chair" and numbers from the late-nineteenth-century Canadian operetta *Leo, the Royal Cadet* proved more memorable to the students than some of the more profound topics. (*Leo*, immensely popular in its own era, has lately been successfully revived.) In class discussions, we developed comparisons between prominent musical figures in the US and Canada—for example, Stephen Foster and Calixa Lavallée.

In 1970 Toronto played host to annual meetings of two professional societies—the American Musicological Society and the Music Library Association—providing a valuable glimpse of enthusiasms and standards from elsewhere, particularly the US universities. During the AMS gathering, there was a special meeting about the future of Canadian-music studies, chaired by David Sale, who had done an excellent master's thesis on concert life in early Toronto; the keynote speaker was Helmut Kallmann. With this inspiration, I assigned my "Music of North America" students research in facets of local musical history—church choirs, military bands, dance halls, publishing and instrument-making ventures—and interviews with senior musicians. The course attracted an enrolment varying each season from eight to twenty or more. In the first year it was offered, the class included Eric Chafe, John Kruspe, Doug Riley, and Timothy Maloney. Beverley Diamond remembers that almost all students in the course the year she took it emphasized the music of Canada in their later careers as researchers, theorists, or composers.[11] Members of that group included, besides Diamond, Jay Rahn, Clifford Ford, Dorith Cooper, Ruth Pincoe, and John Fodi. Indeed, among the participants over the years, a surprisingly large number have gone on to do original research in Canadian music, which is perhaps the most gratifying result of my efforts as a teacher. Historically I believe "Music in North America" marks the beginning of incorporation of local repertoires and local historical accounts in university music studies in Canada, alongside courses first offered in the mid-1960s at the University of Alberta and the Université de Montréal. It was part of a trend: there were soon to be similar courses at almost every university music department in the country.

Working with student composers was a new responsibility starting around 1967. The increased popularity of the composition major (we were in the creative sixties), together with the enlarged graduate program, necessarily involved more staff composers in the undergraduate offerings. Weinzweig, Kenins, Morawetz, and later Lothar Klein, Derek Holman, John Hawkins, and Walter Buczynski all participated. We each had our own methods and approaches, but met every few weeks for tryout sessions with student performers (the communication with performers was less than perfect, with the result that, as often as not, the student composers were their own performers). After my first year in this new role, I inaugurated a series of open noon-hour workshop readings devoted not primarily to student works but rather to works from the broad modern repertoire, with which students appeared to lack close acquaintance. The series became popular and continued for several seasons. Alex Pauk, conductor of the Esprit Orchestra, once told me those readings were a main stimulus for his passion for new music.

The composition classes were different from other teaching situations, their emphasis being on creativity and individual experience. There is a widely held opinion among composers that composition can't be taught. Certainly creativity is an urge or an instinct, but it can be stimulated, nurtured, by a teacher's practical tips and criticisms. I asked Reaney about his experience teaching creative writing. "I start by asking them their world view," he said. When interviewing music students for the composition concentration, we would get them to submit whatever pieces they had already composed. If an applicant demonstrated ambition but hadn't yet attempted to produce any music, it seemed a bad augury. No matter how elementary or faulty, the early tries were evidence of a musical "world view" ready to be developed. The classes were often more like therapy than formal instruction. Students felt free to criticize each other, with the teacher as referee. Some students composed reams; others would sweat several weeks to produce a couple of phrases. I liked to refer to models—Copland, Webern, Ravel, Berio—often assigning for class discussion particular scores relating to whatever creative projects were in progress. While it was obviously important to encourage a knowledge of recent music, I found it distanced the discussion of a technical problem if I illustrated it from a Handel sonata or a Mozart string quartet, where articulation of phrasing or curve of melody could be divorced from "style." (Here perhaps is evidence of Boulanger's influence.) "Style" was like "world view," the hoped-for personal stamp of the creative artist. Occasionally I used an example from my own music, something I was working on or had recently finished. Dealing with a student work-in-progress, I liked to sight-read it at the piano, or get the student to. A favourite assignment was an ensemble piece for the students' own instruments, which they could then read together. I tried always to include assignments for solo voice or choir; they not only raised special problems (text choice, prosody) but also provided music which the group could try singing at sight.

If it was a period of increasing demand for the composition program, it was also a time when new trends appeared to challenge the radical modernism of the mid-century. The teacher's role, it seemed to me, was to encourage *originality* in whatever musical avenue the student chose to explore. In the early 1970s a vogue for classical tonal reference arose, mainly after the success of George Rochberg's Third Quartet, a work deliberately modelled after the late quartets of Beethoven. When someone asked Elliott Carter, around this time, for his opinion of younger composers, he observed that they all wanted to sound like Brahms but didn't know how. My students attempted to make their pieces "tonal" by introducing root-position major and minor chords, bypassing the larger implications of tonal relationships as illustrated in Beethoven or Brahms. To demonstrate this point, I once took the time to play for the class the slow movement of Beethoven's Sonata, op. 106, perhaps his longest; in it, multiple ideas are masterfully exposed, varied, and repeated, along a broad arc of related tonalities. Stravinsky compared this kind of composing to the construction of a suspension bridge. I wanted to show that it wasn't easy. Quoting T.S. Eliot, that new poems are made from old ones, I admitted there was nothing really new in music, but at the same time always hoped for original solutions to creative tasks, fresh ideas, avoidance of well-worn lines or idioms.

As with the "Music of North America" classes, over the years the undergraduate (and later graduate) composition seminars attracted some talented young composers, many of whom went on to active and productive careers. Clifford Ford as a dedicated teenager had studied privately with me before entering the Faculty. He was one of an outstanding group in my very first composition classes, along with John Fodi, Gary Hayes, Bob Bauer, and David Nichols. (In previous years several students from my other classes went on to careers as composers, notably Robert Aitken, Bruce Mather, and William Douglas.) In the early 1970s, a group of graduates and senior undergraduates—Ford, Hayes, Marjan Mozetich, and others—formed a new-music performance organization to which they gave the name Array. Most had been my students, and I helped sponsor some of their first events. The programs featured mainly their own works; audiences were small at first, and the level of success varied, but eventually the annual series became an established and recognized feature of the Toronto musical landscape, later under the name Arraymusic. With similar motives of making a showcase for their own music, in the 1980s a younger group initiated a series with the name Continuum, again mainly from my classes and to a certain extent with my help (as an advisory board member in this case). The group included Omar Daniel, Clark Ross, James Rolfe, Timothy Knight, Alastair Boyd, and the flutist Jennifer Waring. Both Arraymusic and Continuum were still mounting new-music events in 2011. Ross, Rolfe, and Daniel all became productive figures in later decades, as did other former students such as Kristi Allik, David Passmore, Elma Miller, Tom Dusatko, Henry Kucharcyk, Peter Hatch, Chan Wing-Wah, John Burge, Ronald Bruce Smith, and Alice Ping-Yee Ho.

Just as the old formality of dress and of class-time communication gave way, university programs in the late 1960s started to offer students more choice, more electives. While there was, some thought, a danger of weakening the basics, there was now more opportunity for staff to present courses in their areas of specialization and research. Many were given once only, but in a few cases popularity led to repeated offerings. I designed a graduate course in the history of hymnody, with an emphasis on its North American phase. Among my other undergraduate and graduate electives were courses on Bach's *Well-Tempered Clavier*, on opera in the twentieth century, on the music of Ives, the music of Debussy, and music between the two world wars. With one group in the 1980s I examined the twentieth-century status of "two musics," popular and classical—a tentative consideration of what later became a contentious issue. It was a common complaint that graduate students had aptitude and talent but often lacked "background"—that is, an awareness of the scope of classical repertoire. The curriculum contained a course in "music literature," seemingly in answer to this perceived need. It became my course, and soon one of my favourites. I would cover each year a different set of five or six general topics (dance genres, the violin sonata, microtonalism) and illustrate each with appropriate historical and contemporary examples. We might spend several seminars examining a question like "What is tonality?" in the light of selected passages from early and modern scores. A colleague, Carl Morey, had observed the students' lack of experience in handling orchestral full scores, so one of my topic units always touched on the symphonic repertoire—two or three weeks with the big Schubert Symphony in C, Brahms's Fourth, Mahler's Fifth, or Beethoven's Sixth, bar by bar.

The traditional lecture format and the trendier rap session are two different ways of imparting or developing knowledge, both (ideally) using the Socratic method: that is, interrogation. My gift of the gab led me at times to forget to draw my hearers out with questions. Once a student detained me after a history class and, referring to her notebook, asked, "What was your third point about Corelli?" I gulped; I hadn't recalled saying Corelli was important for two points let alone a third. Evidently I had droned on without checking class attention in question-and-answer fashion and (an important consideration) without even maintaining eye contact with the students. Such educationally poor examples were, I hope, rare, but I remember one graduate seminar when I gave out a long, flowing discourse (on what topic I forget) and suddenly stopped with a realization I had been asleep on my feet—for how long I couldn't say. What the

With John and Helen Weinzweig at a reception, 1974.

students wrote in their notebooks on that occasion I can't imagine. Well, I was *tired*. I loved the work but, often on the same school day, found I had to leap from a Rameau keyboard suite to *Lulu*, or from the rules for the augmented-sixth chord to criticism of a student brass-ensemble piece. The exertion, the mental effort, was fatiguing.

The Canadian Association of University Schools of Music (CAUSM) began operation in 1965. Although I was not among the several faculty members from the U of T who helped set up the organization, I attended its annual meetings regularly for many years and sometimes presented papers on subjects that interested me. In 1974 I served on the program committee. The meeting that year was in Toronto, and we succeeded in making "Canadian music" the central topic for papers, discussions, and performances.[12] In 1981 the name was changed to Canadian University Music Society (CUMS). Its journal, the *Canadian University Music Review* (after 2005, *Intersections*), is an exceptionally durable survivor among serious music periodicals in Canada. Academics were increasingly encouraged to engage in research and to produce articles and conference papers: the organization provided an outlet. For a composer, composition projects are the equivalent of original research, but I, like many other composer-teachers, felt drawn also to writings in scholarly areas such as history, criticism, or analysis. The annual contact with colleagues from other campuses was a valuable bonus. In 1987 I joined the Sonneck Society (later the Society for American Music, SAM) and attended *its* annual conference in Pittsburgh—the first of a dozen or more. I was successful in proposing Toronto as the site for the 1990 meeting and in turning it into a joint gathering with yet another newly founded scholarly body, the Association pour l'avancement de la recherche en musique du Québec (ARMuQ; later the Société québécoise de recherche en musique). The journals (*American Music, Les Cahiers de la SQRM*) and the annual conferences were always stimulating, and again I valued the contacts—and sometimes real friendships—that developed.

At the start of my career, academics were known as teachers or perhaps professors. The designations "educator" and "scholar" were just coming into common use. In Victoria, Ruth Humphrey, I remember, considered the term "scholar" hifalutin, an affectation of her male colleagues; she put a lot of energy into her teaching but published little. Though vastly knowledgeable in her field, she was no pedant such as those Yeats ridiculed in his poem "The Scholars," which she had us study ("They'll cough in the ink to the world's end" is a line I recall). I delved into special topics and issues for articles and talks, but was not moved to call the process "scholarship." Partly this was because I had no secure sense of method aside from what I had gathered from Olnick's teaching and from collaborating with Kallmann.

Canadian music became by the early 1980s a significant field of study, as articles and dissertations began to appear with greater frequency and more and more departments instituted courses. Two Faculty colleagues, Carl Morey and Timothy McGee, approached the philanthropist Floyd Chalmers, remembering the major financial backing he had provided for the *Encyclopedia* in the 1970s. They asked if he would consider endowing a centre for CanMus studies at the U of T. The suggested price tag was a million dollars. Chalmers agreed, and the university accepted an endowment for a new study and research program to be called the Institute for Canadian Music, and for a Chair, whose holder would be the Jean A. Chalmers Professor of Canadian Music (after his late wife). Dean Morey asked me if I would accept the position of director of the Institute and the inaugural Chalmers Professorship. He was surprised when I asked for time to think it over. In fact, *I* was surprised by the invitation. I had known of the proposal, but assumed the appointment would go to someone from musicology, rather than a composer—someone like McGee or Morey himself, both of whom had published major works in the field. Unknown to me, they had assumed I was the person for the task, and had even mentioned my name to Chalmers. There would be a slight reduction in my teaching obligations, and I would have a free hand to spend the Chalmers money on whatever projects I fancied. I decided to accept, figuring it was a challenge, and possibly an appropriate final contribution I could make to the Faculty before retiring. (I was then fifty-eight. A journalist reporting the appointment wrote sixty-eight, leading my friend Margaret Gayfer to remark that she could understand why I needed a Chair.)

The Institute was a part-time venture with no office and no secretary. Within a short period, however, it managed to create an identity, through invited guest lecturers, annual conferences on special topics, and a publication series. I worked with a few colleagues and three or four graduate research assistants. When not managing conferences or editing publications, we developed team research projects, notably one on Canadian college songbooks. I was a complete novice in computer technology, but several of the students brought skills in the then state of the art, limited though it was in comparison to what emerged a few years later. Our guests included Richard Crawford, Nicholas Temperley, Robert Stevenson, and Vivian Perlis, all of whose works I had read, read about, and admired, and all of whom I had encountered at the Sonneck gatherings. Our conference subjects were hymn tunes in Canada, the dissemination of Canadian composers' works abroad, Canadian ethnomusicological studies (a joint enterprise with the music department of York University—a case of "hands across the 401," as a York colleague, Bob Witmer, called it),[13] and the relationship of classical and popular idioms in new music (with the music faculty of Wilfrid Laurier University). We gave the publication series the name "CanMus Documents," at the suggestion of a colleague, the ethnomusicologist Timothy Rice. CanMus was a term I liked to use, analogous to the well-established CanLit, and Rice thought "documents" would allow for the possible inclusion of other forms such as films. Volumes were devoted to proceedings of the conferences and to a selection of reports on researches the Institute had sponsored—including Rebecca Green's on the songbook repertoire, and others by Gaynor Jones and Colin Eatock.[14] A proposed volume on Canadian orchestral composition in the 1980s was to have consisted of invited talks by five composers. The talks were delivered, but the publication encountered various snags and delays and has never appeared.

Funding for the Institute's programs came from Chalmers's pledged annual grant of $50,000. In 1989 he decided to hand over the entire endowment, as one of ten gifts of a million dollars each to ten Canadian arts organizations. The gift consisted of stock rather than cash, and the returns, less than anticipated, were not available immediately, so as I prepared for my early retirement I found the Institute's future uncertain. It soon recovered its stability and has survived under the resourceful and enlightened management of, first, Carl Morey, and then Robin Elliott.

Starting in 1975, when Françoys Bernier asked me to teach part of a summer course devoted to Canadian music at the University of Ottawa, I have had a number of guest-professor or composer-in-residence invitations from other universities—notably Memorial in 1988, Mount Allison in 1992, the University of Alberta in 1997, and Brock in 2000. The opportunities to hear students perform my music, listen to theirs, and generally discuss my work, have always proved rewarding.

My researches and writings on the history of tunebooks and hymnals began around 1973 and have occupied much of my energy and interest at various times since, including my post-retirement years. Istvan Anhalt once asked me, "Why hymns?" It seemed to him, and has often seemed to me, a curious choice of specialization. The hymns themselves—that is, the texts—were not my concern, and religious factors were no part of my motivation. Working with Reaney, I sensed how in former generations people retained familiar hymn-tune melodies, alongside pop songs, hardly distinguishing between the two. In many of our collaborative projects, hymn singing has been an important element, again not primarily for religious reasons. Through teaching and reading, I felt the strong significance of psalmody and later hymn singing in the lives of early North Americans. The *Bay Psalm Book* in the seventeenth century, *Urania* in the eighteenth, *Southern Harmony* in the nineteenth, and other historic publications, had many offshoots, including in what is now Canada, from which my ancestors, among others, learned the fundamentals of music and a repertoire of tunes. I liked to point out that the tunebooks were produced not only for use in public worship, but also—perhaps *mainly*— for social and family use. I once posed the rhetorical question, "If hymn tunes and chorales are not 'people's music,' what is?"[15] Analyzing with students the earliest imported and indigenous tunes, I found both melodic and rhythmic traits that endured. The rhythms in particular behaved quite differently from the classical vocabulary of Europe: where the verses had a symmetrical formation in twos and fours, the tunes often proceeded in fives, sixes, or sevens. In a southern US field recording of the tune "New Britain" (to John Newton's words, "Amazing Grace"), the singing moves in seven-bar units. All this was intriguing. No one, as far as I could find out, had made a thorough investigation of the repertoire and the history of publications from a Canadian standpoint. My first attempts were haphazard, and possibly patronizing. The task of editing an anthology for *The Canadian Musical Heritage* demanded a more rigorous and more detached method. I made lists, scoured library collections, played and sang many tunes, compared early and late versions. An exercise I gave to my graduate seminar in the topic (a survey from St Ambrose to *The Hymn Book*—Anglican/United Church, 1971) was: compose a hymn tune in one of the standard metres. It wasn't easy. Several Canadian churches were in the process of revising their hymnals in the late 1980s and early '90s, and I hoped my anthology might inspire revivals of some of the early tunes I admired. My mother, when I told her I was editing this volume, thought it was wonderful: every church in the country would buy it and I would become rich. However, while musicological circles seemed to take my efforts seriously, the churches remained uninterested, and the repertoires I had researched went unvisited by the denominational hymnal committees.

(Anhalt's question "Why hymns?" related not just to my researches but to the hymn-like formations that kept cropping up in my compositions. I became an observer of the many instances of chorale textures that arose, sometimes when least expected, in works by others. The variations on a Bach chorale in the finale of Berg's Violin Concerto offer a striking example, and I noted comparable passages, either derivative or freely invented, in Mozart, Brahms, Stravinsky, Bartók, Copland, Lutoslawski, even a Chopin nocturne. The music of Ives was full of examples. What did they signify? solemnity? reflection? communion with the infinite? or perhaps simple nostalgia? Looking at my own list of pieces, it surprised me to find prominent chorale evocations in at least a dozen scores, including two of the operas and several large works for chorus. In an opera they could be associated with the spiritual mindset of a character; elsewhere I could only interpret their "meaning" in general and vague terms, although I recognized they often resulted from musical features that had fascinated me in my historical digging.)[16]

I had several reasons for taking early retirement from the Faculty of Music. Completing the opera *Crazy to Kill* had required a half-year's leave without pay, and I realized further major composing projects (and I had a few in mind) might again conflict with Faculty obligations. University appointments were becoming scarcer, and many bright young musicians were appearing on the horizon: maybe it was time for me to step aside and make room for one of them. Colleagues gave me a fine send-off—not a gold watch but a reception centring on a first-class program of my music, tendered by performers I had known and worked with. Organized mainly by Tim McGee and Bill Aide,[17] it was a truly heart-warming occasion. I had requested "no speeches," but in the end there were two—a short one by Joan Chalmers and an even shorter one by me, thanking her and everyone else.

For three or four years after my official retirement, I continued to take on teaching tasks, when asked—replacing an associate on leave, or developing a score-study program for student conductors. For the season 1990–91, I remained as director of the Institute until Morey returned from sabbatical ready to assume the post. As well, I served on the occasional graduate degree committee. By the later 1990s there were virtually no formal demands, but I felt comfortable with my round of frequent if irregular visits (working or browsing or attending concerts and talks) to the Faculty building, full as it is of memories and echoes. As dean of the Faculty in the 1970s, when welcoming new undergrads, I told them they would find the practice rooms in the lower basement and the library on the top floor (it has since relocated in a separate wing). They should expect, I said, to spend time in both areas every day, and in between they would likely pass in the hallways a performer just back from a tour of Russia, a music educator preparing to give a workshop in Mexico, a musicologist whose book had just appeared from a distinguished scholarly publisher, or a composer whose concerto had just received a notable premiere. I wanted them to appreciate all this musical quality and vigour— as I always did.

Discussion of the deanship episode belongs in another chapter.

9

Politics

The pie graph of normal adult life patterns includes large slices for sleeping, eating, working, and running errands. In my case there is another large slice for *attending meetings*. I became accustomed to the (often lengthy and verbose) decision-making processes of academia. The Faculty Council and its various committees necessarily imposed a burden of time. To these were added new obligations starting in the 1960s—tenure and promotion committees, grievance committees, appointment panels—whose meetings sometimes turned into oratorical marathons. I once heard the comment that where the carpenters' union covered a short agenda in a lunch hour (because everyone had to get back to work), an academic committee could drone on endlessly—semantic quibbles, legalese, classical quotations—and then adjourn having decided nothing except the date of the next meeting. During my term as dean of the Faculty, I had moreover to attend regular interdepartmental gatherings and found myself roped in for committee duties in the central administration and in other faculties and colleges. I believed strongly in participatory democracy and as head of an academic body became known for striking committees as a solution to problems (the "royal commission" ploy). Once I was even accused of being "too democratic." The price was a huge amount of time sitting and listening in meetings.

Thinking of the constant round of activities of both my parents, I think I must have inherited a "joiner gene." For several years starting in 1952–53, I took on executive responsibilities with the newly founded Canadian League of Composers, and in the 1960s I served on the rather ad hoc management board of Ten Centuries Concerts.[1] Shortly after becoming dean in 1970, I was approached to join several volunteer boards and committees, among them the boards of directors of the Canadian Music Centre, the Canadian Opera Company, and BMI Canada. Was I invited for my musical experience or as a representative of the university? I kept the question to myself and felt obliged to participate. The meetings were often tedious but the discussions were important. Now and then I would be asked to join one of the arts council juries, and I looked on this too as vital service, although it was often intense and wearing, especially as allocations of money became skimpier. It was also in the early 1970s that work commenced on the *Encyclopedia of Music in Canada*, and my involvement in that project, as a member of the editorial board, meant yet *more* meetings.

I was familiar with basic parliamentary procedure and *Robert's Rules of Order* but gradually acquired a keener sense of their fine points, sometimes through having to serve as chair (for example on the Faculty Council). James Reaney told me with glee of his experience in a term as chair of the scholarly body ACUTE (Association of Canadian University Teachers of English). "When someone moves an amendment to the amendment,"

The 1955 annual meeting of the Canadian League of Composers took place at my home in Toronto. Standing, left to right: Louis Applebaum, Samuel Dolin, Harry Somers, Leslie Mann, Barbara Pentland, Andrew Twa, Harry Freedman, Udo Kasemets; front, left to right: Jean Papineau-Couture, John Weinzweig, John Beckwith (photo by Helmut Kallmann, CLC archivist).

he said, "all hell breaks loose." I learned to vacate the chair if I wanted the floor (i.e., wanted to enter the debate), after seeing a university colleague heavily criticized for not doing this. On one occasion, with my heart in my mouth, I ruled a loquacious orator "out of order" and was relieved that no one "challenged the chair," as (again) I had seen happen in another context. A scenario demanding utmost patience was when you had to discuss amending the constitution and bylaws. I once sat next to Ben McPeek[2] at what I think was his first meeting as a member of the CMC board when we had to concentrate on a long list of such amendments, and at one point he whispered to me, "Is it always this much fun?" You thought: democracy in action, you have to have rules, someone has to do it; but you couldn't help wishing you were doing something else—like practising Bach.

The Canadian League of Composers was in its formative stages when I was corresponding secretary. The Ten Centuries series was a distinctive short-lived concert venture. In both organizations I worked with fellow composers of roughly my own generation. The League indeed had come into existence in 1951 in order to articulate the aspirations of the composing profession. We defined "professional" in drawing up rules for admission to membership: you had to have undergone a more or less formal course of study, written pieces of major length in a variety of media, and achieved recognition in performance. I could name two or three composers, later active and fairly well known, whose applications the membership panel turned down. As the organization grew, these conditions became less rigid and the concept of a professional standard more flexible. Apart from self-consciously defining who we thought we were, we also concerned ourselves with defining what we wanted the organization to do. Our main purpose was to promote our works; hence our sponsorship of public performances—orchestral and chamber-music programs, even an operatic evening—and our involvement in publication of an anthology of new piano music. Recording outlets were a dream of the future.

At the end of the 1950s, using various foreign models, we sketched a plan for a national library and information centre for our repertoire, for presentation to the newly created Canada Council; from this initiative the Canadian Music Centre emerged. It was a period of many new stimuli and ventures in the country's cultural life. Reaching out internationally was however not yet a high priority. The League dropped its membership in the International Society for Contemporary Music after only a couple of years, regarding it as a budgetary extravagance. I was one of only two members (Alexander Brott was the other) who voted against the motion to secede from the ISCM. It was many years before the connection

The program designs for Ten Centuries Concerts, by Peter Dorn, featured
a stylized Roman "ten" with ancient and modern details.

was resumed. On the other hand, the League earned special international recognition in the summer of 1960 with its week-long International Conference of Composers at Stratford, an initiative of Louis Applebaum. Udo Kasemets and I were conference secretaries and edited the proceedings afterwards.[3] The panel discussions and concerts were tremendously stimulating and timely, and we Canadians revelled in the opportunity to meet and talk with Krenek, Berio, Rochberg, Schuller, Blomdahl, Dutilleux, and so many other front-ranking composers from abroad. I was thrilled to be asked to interview Edgard Varèse for the CBC. The CLC now describes itself as "the oldest" professional composers' organization in the country, implying there are others. Indeed, the later decades of the twentieth century witnessed a diversification of protected interests in new (not necessarily rival) societies of women composers, film composers, electro-acoustic composers, Saskatoon composers, Nova Scotia composers, and more. The CLC membership stood at 350 in 2009.

Ten Centuries Concerts lasted only five full seasons but made a permanent impact on concert programming in Toronto. The series was Murray Schafer's brainchild. The organizers were almost all composers, and, as with the League, promotion of our own works was an important purpose, though not the most important. Rather than "all-Canadian" concerts, the series placed our music in a historical context, consisting of the entire repertoire since the Middle Ages, including pieces from Canada's own musical past. From a survey of the programs and the (almost exclusively local) performing groups who took part, I look on Ten Centuries as a forerunner of the specialist societies both for new music and for early music which arose in the 1970s. Among the suggestions I put forward and helped to produce were program segments of Satie, of Webern, of Morley, and of Italian Renaissance vocal music; concert versions of Purcell's *King Arthur* and Bizet's *Djamileh*; and several Canadiana presentations, among them Godfrey Ridout's restoration of Quesnel's *Colas et Colinette*. Helmut Kallmann was a frequent consultant to the series, and when he suggested mounting Franz Kotzwara's *The Siege of Quebec*, a curiosity of late-eighteenth-century London with a Canadian slant, he and I and Murray Schafer shared preparation of the score.

On the occasion of the Canadian Music Centre's fiftieth anniversary, I recorded briefly some recollections of its founding and early years.[4] As I noted, "Symbolizing the then-close relations between composers and CBC, the first four Executive Secretaries were all former CBC music producers" (Jean-Marie Beaudet, John Adaskin, Keith MacMillan, and John Roberts). My decade or so as a member of the board was during

MacMillan's tenure. In another chapter I have described my work with him on the dictionary *Contemporary Canadian Composers* and my efforts with the board's publications committee.[5] After a decade and a half of activity in Toronto, the Centre started to discuss the possibility of establishing regional offices elsewhere in the country. I recalled:

> In the board's deliberations, Dick Johnston argued for one in Calgary, and gained strong support from Paul Baby, whose main aim was to see one in Montreal. I took the minority view that the expansion would put a dangerous strain on available funding: federal politicians of the day talked simultaneously of national unity and decentralization, but I was a skeptic. The regional offices have succeeded brilliantly, but the national overview in music remains elusive.[6]

Like the CLC, the CMC has gradually revised the interpretation of its mandate, and particularly the requirements for associate-composer status. Submission of scores and recordings is no longer mandatory. Having completed my service as a board member, I nevertheless entered the debate in 1987 when it was proposed that associate composers should pay annual dues. In a letter to the then board chair, Allan Bell, I argued (contrary to the prevailing opinion in the arts councils) that the composers were not "members" of the Centre, but rather the creators on whose behalf the Centre was formed.[7] The Centre was, I said, "an organization *for* composers, not an organization *of* composers." Many of us were happy to contribute voluntarily to the Centre, but it seemed to me wrong to assume that all associates could afford to do this, besides which no system of sanctions was suggested for those who might fail to cough up dues—young freelance composers for example. Was the Centre going to punish them for nonpayment by removing their works from its library? I asked. After protest from the League, the board reconsidered the proposal and abandoned it—but succeeded in passing it six years later.[8] At this writing, the CMC lists approximately seven hundred associate composers.

The CMC board was a mix of musicians and individuals from other fields, mainly education and business. By contrast, I was, I think, the only musician on the Canadian Opera Company board, which consisted of men from the professions and the corridors of finance plus a few society matrons. It numbered thirty or forty members—a considerably smaller size than it later became. I understood Herman Geiger-Torel's frustrations as artistic director having to respect the views of the enthusiastic (and often well-informed) laypersons. Though often at sea during meetings about finance, I listened closely when new repertoire was under discussion. One ardent buff, a follower of international fashion, asked, was it not high time the company did an opera by Henze? But for the scheduled revival of a contemporary Canadian opera, Somers's *Louis Riel*, there was only token support: it was anticipated to lose money, although in fact I believe it didn't. I voiced my opposition when there was a motion for a minimum annual donation by board members. We all felt committed to support the company, but to state an obligatory figure as a condition of membership seemed to me discriminatory: it was tantamount to handing over the reins of operatic power to the rich. To my chagrin, my objection was misunderstood. The board chair thought I was embarrassed because as an academic on a modest salary I couldn't afford the minimum tariff mentioned (a fairly high figure); magnanimously he said he thought the chair could be granted the right to approve exceptions. Shortly afterwards, my term on the board was over, although I played a further role on the search committee for Geiger-Torel's successor. To my surprise, Torel himself was a member of that body. It was an effective committee, and I supported the selection of Lotfi Mansouri. We met in a variety of offices and board rooms, and I took a turn hosting the group at the university's Faculty Club. At the conclusion of our work, the board thanked the various law and business firms who had allowed their executives time off to serve on the committee, but there was no message of gratitude to the university—as an academic I was considered public property, with all the spare time in the world.

Geiger-Torel's leadership of the company in its first years has never been adequately assessed, in my view. He had a broad approach to repertoire and a good eye for performing talent. He became committed to the Canadian scene, partly through the early tours in which he accompanied troupes to many parts of the country, living up to the national name. He commissioned and produced more major operas by Canadian composers than any of his successors. In the early 1970s he realized a long-standing wish by mounting three of the four works in the Wagner *Ring* cycle, and took it as a devastating defeat when, on fiscal grounds, the board executive vetoed the production of *Das Rheingold* which would have completed the venture. The defeat could be interpreted as a fatal one: it was no doubt a contributing factor when Torel collapsed and died at the start of the fall 1976 season, which was anyway to have been his last.

If I felt like a representative of a respected but token minority as a director on these two boards, the CMC and the COC, on the BMI Canada board I found myself in the midst of the "music industry" with fellow members representing publishing and recording enterprises and the world of pop music performance; the chair was a brilliant lawyer, Gordon Henderson. It was a crucial period of change for this organization. During my decade or more of service, it first severed its connection with the US parent body, Broadcast Music Inc., to become an autonomous corporation under a new name, PROCAN (Performing Rights Organization of Canada) and then entered into talks for a merger with its long-time rival, CAPAC (Composers, Authors and Publishers Association of Canada); the merger was accomplished by the late 1980s, under yet another new name, SOCAN (Society of Composers, Authors and Music Publishers of Canada). I was an interested witness and participant in all these changes, and both Henderson and the general manager, Jan Matejcek, showed respect for my minority views, but I can't claim to have had much influence.

After an all-day board meeting, it was traditional for the PROCAN directors to gather with executives of the CBA (Canadian Broadcasters' Association) for a banquet. The broadcasters—representatives of the private networks and stations—were all men, as at first were all the PROCAN directors. The banquet was always lavish and always ended with a closed session of bawdy jokes. I found the musicians among my associates (Gene McClelland, Paul Horn, Hagood Hardy, and a few others) felt as aloof from this frat-party nonsense as I did. A few women appointed to the board in the 1980s evidently showed no similar distaste, but whether because their presence made the organizers feel awkward or because it was becoming outmoded social behaviour, the practice ceased.

After a couple of years with the new SOCAN Foundation in its fledgling years, I learned my term was up. I was among the "classical" composers present at the 1992 meeting in Toronto when a makeover of the organization's voting process gave virtually exclusive decision-making powers to the pop music interests. Referring to that meeting in a talk in 2007, I noted that "serious composers had been key players in founding and operating both parent societies [CAPAC and PROCAN]. The new structure guaranteed they would never have a majority voice in SOCAN."[9] After outlining the "loaded" voting system, I described the consequences:

> Within a year the new SOCAN board abolished the established policies for distribution of the performance royalties it collects. Former practice favored "serious" creativity, recognizing that writing a successful popular song demanded less expenditure of energy and skill but had a vastly greater chance of commercial compensation than composing a successful string quartet ... Recognition took the form of a sliding scale for the various

categories. But now ... there was to be no more sliding scale: popular songs and symphonic compositions were to be evaluated equally, the sole criterion being length (that is, timing).[10]

Shortly after the PROCAN/CAPAC merger, Eddie Schwartz, a songwriter on the board, had published comments urging that the "serious" or "classical" composers should be "weaned off the breast"—a reference to the massive subsidy support such members supposedly enjoyed from the arts councils and to what he considered the "unfair" sliding-scale policy. When I protested this flagrant insult, Schwartz said he had been misquoted.[11] When my remark about the different creative demands of popular and classical composition appeared, the Vancouver songwriter Jim Valance sent me an email message. As I later described it, he

> voiced strong objection to [my] claim ... He proposed a contest: if I would write a pop song, he would compose a string quartet. I would win if my song sold a million copies, but he would win if his quartet was completely ignored. I loved the idea, but told him I was too busy.[12]

Whether a nasty jab or a friendly tease, these were advance warnings of the decline of "classical" new music that became widely noted in the early years of the new century, especially in North America, when the term "music" came to mean almost exclusively commercial fodder.

In a review of this account, my "political" life sounds more like an exercise of my habitual critical bitchiness (see chapter 7, p. 125 above) than an example of effective leadership. I was often in opposition, often in a minority, and the issues which animated me were often, *too* often, concerned with money—how to avoid spending too much of it, how to be fair in distributing it, how not to let it override artistic values. In my seven years as an academic administrator, by definition I landed with inescapable leadership responsibilities (whether I carried them out effectively is for others to judge), and money was a constant worry. The annual budget went almost entirely on People; a small amount was left over for Goods and Services, but virtually nothing for Ideas. When the higher-ups foresaw tough times ahead the cuts they demanded came almost entirely from Goods and Services, not People. They wanted you to have Ideas, but you had to find a way to pay for them. They looked on the Faculty of Music's public halls as potential earners: Why couldn't we rent our space to more and more performing groups? There was however, as I saw it, a limit: the halls were part of an educational plant, not a pleasure arcade. To pay for a concert organ for one of the halls, I courted wealthy patrons. It was the beginning of the dependency of artists and academics on the so-called "private sector" that has preoccupied later administrators.

In developing loyalty to the Faculty, I had never seen myself as the head of it. In January 1969 I was appointed to the search committee for Boyd Neel's successor, chaired by one of the university's vice-provosts, John Hamilton. A former dean of medicine, he specialized in pathology but had a background of music study and was a concertgoer and a knowledgeable opera buff. Several meetings ensued, with long discussions of terms of reference, qualifications for the post, wording of a call for applications and nominations—the familiar academic snail's pace. At Hamilton's request, I gathered material to inform committee members on the background of music at the Faculty and the Conservatory. At length, in early May, we began to consider names of potential candidates, and Hamilton told me two nominators had suggested *me*.[13] If I allowed my name to stand, I would have to resign from the committee. I took a weekend to confer with family and friends. I had argued that the institution should have a leader familiar with the local scene, rather than a Big Name imported from the US or Europe. Two other committee members resigned at this time to throw *their* hats in the ring—Keith Bissell and Ezra Schabas—both older and more experienced. My recent work, especially on a committee charged with major revision of the Faculty's curriculum, had given me a useful perspective on the institution's future, and I had a long acquaintance with the program and the dramatis personae, though I lacked experience in management. It was a long shot, but I agreed, and sent Hamilton my CV as he had requested. In the fall, four external candidates visited Toronto for interviews, presumably the committee's short list. One was from another Canadian university, the other three from the US. If this was indeed the short list, clearly I wasn't on it. I was not invited to meet with Hamilton and company. There followed several weeks of silence; why this delay in the expected public announcement? Members of the search committee avoided one's glance. Then, just before the end of term in December, the provost, John Sword, called me to his office and asked if I would accept the appointment. I pondered for ten seconds and then said yes. The next day, he and President Claude Bissell came to the Faculty and made a public announcement. There was a hearty positive response from the gathering of students and staff. In a congratulatory note, Bissell found this "spontaneous enthusiasm" was "a good augury, as was your little speech for the new regime."[14] I had been in fact too tongue-tied to say much more than "thanks" and "I'll do my best."

As dean of the University of Toronto Faculty of Music,
circa 1972 (photo by Gustav Ciamaga).

Many people appeared to welcome the prospect that I might create a "new regime." I was touched by a number of messages of approval and good wishes. Schabas, writing from London where he was on leave, was "delighted in every way"; Rosevear expressed his "confidence" in my (as yet unproven) leadership. Robert Fulford, with whom I had collaborated at the *Star* and in CBC broadcasts, asked: "Can creeping respectability have overcome you at last?" Richard Johnston, newly appointed dean at Calgary, pictured for me a world of academic administration where "you will soon come to question your sanity [but ...] can occasionally see an idea come to flower." Colleagues from other parts of the country said they were pleased: Helmut Blume and Jean Papineau-Couture from Montreal, Leonard Isaacs from Winnipeg, Graham George from Queen's, George Proctor from Mount Allison. Murray Schafer, in Vancouver, advised me to give highest priority to appointing an assistant: "There must be some unvenomed and uncontaminated people around who love to go to meetings, write reports ... Get one!" The appointment received wider public coverage than a similar one would today. The *Star* mentioned my salary. For the *Telegram* (Ken Winters) I was "an arrogant little fighter." The *Globe* (Blaik Kirby) described me as the new head of a "strife-ridden organization." (Kirby had previously written a journalistic exposé of personality conflicts in the Faculty, some real and some imaginary.)

But what was the organization I was to be head of? Boyd Neel was retiring as dean of the Royal Conservatory of Music, which since 1952 had two administrative divisions, the Faculty of Music (under a director, Arnold Walter) and the School of Music (under a principal, Ettore Mazzoleni). Since Walter's retirement in 1968, Neel had assumed his duties as acting director of the Faculty. On Mazzoleni's sudden death the same year, David Ouchterlony had become acting principal of the School (popularly and confusingly referred to as the Conservatory, or "the Con"). The news release from Simcoe Hall called me "Dean of the Royal Conservatory of Music and the Faculty of Music, University of Toronto"—a redundancy equivalent to saying I was dean of the whole and also of one part of the whole. On the other hand, a note from the secretary of the board of governors, David Claringbold, read:

> Dear Professor Beckwith:
> It is a pleasure to inform you that the Board of Governors at its meeting held recently appointed you to the position of Dean of the Faculty of Music, effective July 1, 1970.

Two actions in the independently run but affiliated wing, the School, were the cause of this confusion. One, its board of directors had confirmed Ouchterlony as principal, even though there had been an undertaking not to do so until the new overseer, the dean, was selected; and two, the same board had decided to discontinue its 50 percent support of the dean's salary. Further, the university had eliminated the post of director of the Faculty. When, in an interview at Simcoe Hall early in the New Year, I asked Bissell what my position was, he said, "It's a good question." I thought I knew the answer: I was expected to direct the work of the Faculty and at the same time to express the university's link with the School by attending the odd meeting there. I did attend a couple of meetings with the Conservatory directors and felt decidedly unwelcome. As Winters's "arrogant little fighter," I was known to have critical views about the Conservatory's programs and style of management. Ouchterlony was effusively cordial but wanted to be free to run his own show. Besides, just supervising the Faculty was a demanding task. In the fall, I consulted with various responsible parties and talked with a couple of fellow deans, and at length proposed a new administrative plan, in effect separating the two wings but including checks and balances to ensure that they would both continue as valued units of the university, each with its own program and purpose. We could once again call the Conservatory by that name, and it would be a preparatory school, a community school, and an examining body, and the Faculty a degree-granting professional school. I was summoned to the University Senate to explain the background to its members (I said it was like explaining the plot of Wagner's *Ring*), and they approved the new set-up.

Historically what seemed to me and others a simple clarification of responsibilities may have set the Conservatory on its path to end its university affiliation, but that action came about only twenty years later, and only after three or four long and tense think-tank investigations. I thought, and continue to think, that the break was a mistake. In my time as dean, there were at least a few officials at Simcoe Hall, like Jack Sword and John Hamilton, who understood and valued the Conservatory's educational role; but in later decades they were replaced with business-minded leaders for whom it was more a commercial showplace than a school.[15] I attended Conservatory events, maintained good exchanges with Conservatory teachers (several of whom were cross-appointed to the Faculty), and once a year wrote my signature alongside that of the principal on a couple of hundred Conservatory diplomas.

Instead of Neel's office on an upper floor of the Edward Johnson Building overlooking Philosopher's Walk, I chose to resume use of Walter's old office, a large space on the main floor overlooking the front entrance. With a small budget for new furnishings, I ordered a round conference table and tried to vary the position of my chair (*the* chair)—hoping to express a *primus inter pares* approach. I compiled a list of Faculty operations that could function more smoothly: the opera division, the library, the music education program, the publicity office. These were management issues, and management was foreign to me, but I felt I had to tackle them. Opera was run by a stage director, a music director, an administrator, and a secretary—an expensive and top-heavy administration which needed streamlining. The library was supervised brilliantly by Harvey Olnick, as chair of the library committee, an advisory body which seldom met. His unofficial status placed the librarian, Jean Lavender, in a straitjacketed relationship to the rest of the university's library system; the situation called for clearer lines of authority. In music education, we were just beginning to react to a new set of guidelines from the Ontario Education Ministry affecting the structure of the Faculty's curriculum for aspiring teachers: How to play this one? Colleagues' differing views would need to be sorted out. The publicity officer, Edith Binnie, had excellent contacts and solid experience in concert management, but I reasoned that the office needed a broader outlook in order to speak on behalf of *all* departments of the Faculty, even though performance was the one the public would always be most aware of. It took a few years, but gradually I was able to see significant inroads on all these fronts.

At my appointment, one greeting gave me special pleasure: it came from Arnold Walter. He said he knew I would do things my own way but I should call on him whenever there was something he could help with. It was a warm gesture of support from my old teacher and former boss. It wasn't long, however, before he rang to suggest lunch, and plied me with advice. I should run the office myself, he said, and get rid of the advisory group Boyd Neel had assembled; in particular, I should keep the budget figures a secret and show them to no one except the Faculty secretary. But I didn't want to be, and couldn't be, a one-man show. It was against my temperament, as well as against the temperament of the times. Dynastic one-man positions were giving way to term appointments (mine was for seven years), and, like most universities, Toronto had introduced student participation (by vote) in many areas of its governance (there would shortly be elective seats on our own Faculty Council for students). I kept the committee (or "cabinet") of department heads because I regarded it as a source of consultation, support, and shared authority; and, while I didn't broadcast the budget information, nor did I feel the need to keep it a deep secret, especially later when cuts had to be made, and seen to be made, with fairness. Another voice of experience was that of Ernest Sirluck, the dean of graduate studies, who had served on the search committee which recommended me. He told me I should start my "new regime" by doing something unpopular—in order to show who was boss. I rejected this advice too: it would have struck me as play-acting.

Members of the executive committee, or cabinet, as originally convened by Neel, were the heads of the Faculty's departments: Harvey Olnick, history and literature; Ezra Schabas, performance (including opera); Gustav Ciamaga, theory and composition; and Robert Rosevear, music education. In time there were a few changes: Godfrey Ridout subbed for Olnick during a leave year, and Rika Maniates joined when she became the new chair of the department; Rosevear resigned as music education chair, to be replaced by a new appointee, Charles Heffernan; Olnick had doubled as chair of graduate studies, and when his term was up his successor, Lothar Klein, joined us as a fifth member. We met every other week around the table in my office. It was a gathering of strong natures, all passionately committed to their specialties. My part was to find a unifying voice that I could present to the world—and especially to the university administration—as that of Music. There were inevitable clashes:

members would accuse one another of betrayal, or storm out slamming the door (this happened only once). Listening to our discussions, I tried to make fair and equitable decisions but was often suspected of favouring one department over its rival. The parallel to a family dinner table was obvious. Northrop Frye had served a term as principal of Victoria College and described to me the role of an academic head vis-à-vis his associates: "They just want you to keep telling them how good they are." In confirming the committee as an advisory group I also confirmed the departmental structure, and by university policy the head of a department was entitled to a full year's sabbatical (or study leave) on completion of his or her term—at full salary—a generous provision whose strain on the Faculty's budget I hadn't anticipated. The policy was designed for large faculties whose departments often numbered over a hundred, whereas some of ours had only around a dozen. In the later 1970s the Faculty's departments became "divisions," whose "coordinators" had shorter terms.

A watchword of the times was "openness." Educational leaders were urged to consult widely and to signal their intentions, rather than acting arbitrarily. Reading the popular philosopher Alan Watts, I gathered it was unwise to listen to the loudest voice, or squeakiest wheel. I preferred to act on behalf of a consensus and not have to "pull rank." Once, though, I was successful in overturning the action of a colleague who had gone over my head to the president's office in order to "stack" the makeup of an appointments committee. On a couple of occasions, I accepted recommendations based on majority votes even though I had reasons for disagreeing with them; in retrospect I judge that to have been surface fair play but politically poor tactics. When rivalry bubbled up between the musicologists and the performers, the former bearded me en masse in my office with loud complaints that I was favouring the latter, a three-times-larger group. I had to listen patiently to the charges and demands, even though conscious of the role I had played, and continued to play, in the Faculty's musicology program—admittedly in what one scholar referred to as a "peripheral" capacity. Called on to chair a tenure hearing in the Department of Fine Art, I learned of similar festering factionalism just across the campus, between art historians and studio artists.

One series of meetings was unexpected and arduous. I was conscripted to serve, along with heads of other university divisions, on a disciplinary tribunal. Two students were charged with disrupting a scheduled guest lecture by a noted sociologist from the US. In an age of student riots (Berkeley, Kent State, Concordia), the administration took such attacks on academic life and on freedom of speech very seriously. At other campuses, the targeted scholar had been accused of expressing racist views, and the eruption at the U of T was inspired in part by the radical Students for a Democratic Society movement south of the border. The mechanism for hearing the case was an outmoded one, the so-called university "caput," a sort of band of chiefs; outmoded or not, it was the only forum the rules allowed. We sat for a total of nineteen days, listening to witnesses and arguments from lawyers for the university and for the accused pair. Our chair, a veteran professor of law, Albert Abel, was matched for toughness by the young defendants. For me, the situation had an added strain: one of the defendants, William Schabas, was the son of two close and much-valued friends, Ezra and Ann Schabas, both widely respected in the university community. The verdict and the imposed penalty were harsh, and it was years before the break in our relationship was healed. Bill Schabas went on to an exceptional career in international human rights law and, in 2006, an appointment to the Order of Canada.

The 1970s saw growth among existing music departments in Canada and the creation of several new ones. I was engaged to write assessments or reviews of music programs at a number of institutions—and similar requests continued up to and even after my retirement. For the CUMS gatherings I had visited many campuses; in this new capacity I was to visit many more, among them the University of Calgary, the University of Western Ontario (twice), the University of Ottawa, Dalhousie (twice), McGill, and Wilfrid Laurier. I did a good deal of homework on curricula. The Faculty's own curricular structure, I thought, needed updating and reform. The system of course credits had become over the years unbalanced; cases had arisen where participation in a relatively ad hoc performance activity earned equal degree credit with a course requiring hard study and preparation. I formed a curriculum task force and took an active role as its chair. After several months of discussion and consultation we presented our report to the Faculty Council, which voted its approval of only about half of the proposals—a disappointing result. It was difficult to battle the status quo. I began to see what Dick Johnston meant about leadership and ideas.

In a surviving file labelled "Deansville" I found a scrap of pencilled jottings, evidently the list I had made on assuming decanal duties, of areas needing attention. The main priorities I have already referred to—opera, library, music education, publicity. I also listed choral music, voice teaching, percussion, the electronic-music studio, Canadian music studies, jazz, an internal newsletter, and instrument purchases, and there were lines for

"Conservatory relations" and "Alumni." Heffernan, Rosevear's successor as chair of music education, was a choral specialist, fulfilling my sense that this side of our work deserved a professorial position rather than a reliance on part-time instructors. He was with us for only a few years before moving to another university, but his tenure brought marked improvement in the Faculty choirs. In the vocal music studios there were two issues to be faced: one, the principal voice teachers were nearing retirement, and, two, they strongly opposed choral participation by their students, arguing it ruined their voices. The percussion teachers needed a bigger studio, as both enrolments and instrument holdings increased. We were able to negotiate a large basement room of the Royal Conservatory building for this purpose. UTEMS (the electronic-music studio) had earned great prestige in the 1960s as the first installation of its kind in Canada and one of the first on the continent. It continued to do effective, creative work and to play host to visiting composers and technicians. I wanted it to be more prominent but lacked the technical background to be able to say how this might be accomplished. When I asked at budget time for departmental wish lists, Gus Ciamaga was the one head who regularly told me things were fine, that the studio needed no special financial boost. I had begun a course with, for the first time, a major focus on the music of Canada,[16] but I thought it called for expansion and found that a new appointee, Carl Morey, was already an active researcher, especially in the local music history of Toronto. He has since developed undergraduate and graduate courses and produced many publications in the field. I was happy when course credit could be offered for the Faculty's jazz ensemble, a long-time extracurricular offering under Phil Nimmons, now with the collaboration of a younger instructor, David Elliott. From my years-before stint as a fledgling publicist, I knew how important it was that members of a big organization be aware of each other's work, responsibilities, and accomplishments. Edith Binnie's office, with help from the Undergraduate Association, managed to issue for some seasons a weekly sheet of news, announcements of events, items about staff performances and publications, and the like, and, as sources of money and energy became scarcer, to keep it alive on a regular but less frequent basis. In addition to mounting a special appeal to buy a concert organ, I acquired further instruments for the Faculty's collection, year by year (sometimes by selling the old ones): a concert harp, a concert Steinway from Hamburg, and a number of early instruments. A happy gift, from the university's rare-books librarian Marian Brown, was a historic square piano that had belonged to her family. It was one of the earliest instruments of the nineteenth-century Boston maker Jonas Chickering. For a time, I housed it in my office.

Given my concern to preserve good neighbourly relations with Principal Ouchterlony and the "Con," I welcomed RCM teachers, singly and in groups, many of whom I knew well, for discussions and sharing of advice, and I served on the first review committee, chaired by John Hamilton. The report of that committee incorporated a number of my suggested "checks and balances" for the continuance of the university's voice in academic matters at the RCM. As time went on, Ouchterlony and others found them restrictive, necessitating further long deliberations in further review committees (meetings, meetings!).

The Faculty of Music Alumni Association, founded in the 1950s, had lapsed into inactivity, and, looking at the strong role played by alumni in other university divisions, I felt it needed to be revived. Alumni representatives on the Faculty Council, and alumni volunteers on think tanks or other short-term advisory groups—these were ways to reignite their interest in the school. Eventually we succeeded in resuscitating the association, with a program of musical and social events, although it was hard work. First, few professional performers or professional teachers in music are as affluent as professionals in dentistry or engineering, and, second, few can spare *time* (let alone money) to support their alma mater. Later deans did a fine job in building up this important facet of the Faculty's life; maybe in my time we at least gave it a kick-start. (Ron Chandler's "historical introduction" to the Faculty's 1990 directory of alumni contains a section on what he calls "the Beckwith years," summarizing the administrative and curricular changes of my decanal "regime.")[17]

Sir Ernest MacMillan, the Faculty's second dean, died in May 1973 after a lengthy illness. At a memorial ceremony in Convocation Hall, Lois Marshall sang Bach with a group of Toronto Symphony players. I gave one of the spoken tributes. In October of the same year, Arnold Walter suffered a severe heart attack and died after a few days. In a short eulogy during the memorial musical program in the Faculty's Concert Hall, I remembered his fondness for Latin quotations and thought "Si monumentum requiris, circumspice" was appropriate, only changing the last word to "circum*audite*." The inspiration for the Faculty's home was indeed his more than anyone's. A year later, we received university approval to rename the hall Walter Hall.

Walter's period as director saw slight staff turnover and almost no retirements. I now found that the university's rule for mandatory retirement

Addressing a meeting of secondary school teachers, circa *1975.*

of professors at the age of sixty-five would soon apply to some of his appointees, and it was up to me to bring this to their notice. The interviews took careful handling and touched on issues of health and income, not to mention personal vanity. These were long-time friends, senior colleagues I had learned to respect; it was awkward to address them as their new, young boss. Individual responses varied: while some had considered plans to retire, for others the notion was unthinkable or unthought of. Sometimes emotions flared. In several cases it was possible to offer continuing activity on a contract basis. Mieczyslaw Kolinski had been appointed on contract while already past the age limit and was carrying the equivalent of a full professorial load. When I broached with him the topic of retirement he smiled and asked, "Yes, what is the deadline?" Having lived in the 1930s and '40s under the Nazi death threats, he was serene about getting older and slowing down. It was not until 2007 that the University of Toronto abolished the fixed-retirement rule, one of the last universities in Canada to do so.

In his seventeen years as director, Walter had had freedom to hire, promote, and grant tenure, without reference to the committee processes that came into being around 1970. I learned of my own promotions and my tenure in notifications from his office; they entailed no specific action on my part. The new procedures regarding appointments were democratic but time-consuming; moreover, annual budgetary restrictions throughout the '70s made it hard to expand, and you were obliged to justify any hiring of new instructors. Wilfrid Bain, the powerful dean of music at Indiana University, was asked at his retirement how many of the appointments he made did he think had worked out successfully. "About half," was his reply. Bain was, like Walter, a one-man hiring team. Of twenty or so full-time appointments I approved, on committee recommendations, I would make the same evaluation. They proved variable, from brilliant to moderately disappointing. I would not claim that with a freer hand I could have done better; the brilliant ones were exceptionally strong additions. My views on appointments were not universally accepted. I had no great confidence in the star system whereby you tried to attract (and pay big salaries to) internationally famous performers or scholars, thinking of the glitter their names would add to your brochure; and I tried to hold a check on contracts to professionals who, while outstanding, might be able to offer only a few hours each week to the Faculty—weakening the institution's cohesiveness and continuity. I wanted colleagues, whether in professorial appointments or contract positions, who would regard the school as a major commitment and would even take part in running it (including a turn as dean). I was genuinely proud of the Faculty and took every opportunity to say so; but, unlike some deans and department heads, I wasn't an empire builder.

Also unlike many deans, I continued to carry a partial teaching load throughout my term in office, figuring it was important to keep closely in touch with students' attitudes and needs. During my term I was less active as a composer, but not completely *in*active. I appreciated that my co-workers understood my desire now and then to get away from the office and write music. There were new pieces in all but one of my seven years in "Deansville."

With an excessive love of neatness that others have sometimes pointed out,[18] I used to take periodic inspection tours with the building manager, noting changes in allocations of space and spots that presented a less-than-perfect scene for visitors. I looked for chances to display the Faculty's art collection and for ways to augment it. Though the University was fast relinquishing its long-time *in loco parentis* stance with students, I urged the kids to lead a regular routine and, opposing the automatic food machines, told them a honey bun and a Coke was no kind of lunch. Though not a hockey fan, I made an appearance at the odd game of the Faculty team, the Gustav Maulers (when their opponents scored, the band struck up the slow movement of the First Symphony). I emphasized social togetherness in events like the orientation meeting in September and the end-of-term party in December, and called for live music as an essential component (it was after all the Faculty of *Music*). At my first party as dean, I contributed a pair of solo rags by Joplin, which raised cheers and also brought a memo from the leading professor of piano, Pierre Souvairan: "Thank you for the polkas." I enjoyed being a greeter of guests such as Yehudi and Hephzibah Menuhin, Rudolf Serkin, Karel Ančerl, Lord and Lady Harewood, Rudolf Bing, Janet Baker, and the composers Luciano Berio, Steve Reich, Cornelius Cardew, Arthur Berger, Lukas Foss, Aaron Copland, and others. Serkin played a benefit concert for the Faculty's scholarship fund, a beautiful Beethoven program, and donated a collection of papers of his associate and in-law Adolf Busch to the Faculty library. Harewood was on a tour to report on the state of opera in Canada. I recall the moment when he stooped to kiss the hand of our leading professor of voice, Irene Jessner, exclaiming, "My first Sieglinde!" A group of us took Aaron Copland to a leisurely lunch at the Faculty Club and sat talking past two o'clock, at which point he (a graduate of no university) asked, "Don't any of you have to get back to work?" After the music librarians and the musicologists in my first year in office, we were hosts to further specialized symposia, festivals, or annual meetings—the guitarists, the carillonneurs, the opera producers, the Orff specialists, the saxophonists, the band directors, the double-reedists, the ethnomusicologists—and I began to appreciate as never before the multiple mystiques that make up the world of music.

Heading the Faculty would not have been possible without good support from my associates. Any remaining vestige of the prejudice against English accents I acquired in my growing-up years in Victoria disappeared when I found that the secretary of the Faculty, the dean's secretary, and the assistant dean (administration) (as the Faculty secretary was later called) were all English, and that all three—Carol Burke, Penelope Nettlefold, and David Keeling—were sympathetic and on my wavelength. Keeling especially, a music graduate of Cambridge, had the aptitude for paperwork and figures that I so badly lacked. We worked together happily, and I was always grateful for his steady and positive guidance when I found myself in political deep waters. When Penny Nettlefold retired,

Lynn McIntyre (a *Canadian* and a one-time student of mine) was her excellent replacement.

In 1977, when my period of service was up, in answer to a group of Faculty colleagues who wanted me to stay for a second term, I considered this possibility but at length told them I would prefer not to. Then a series of disturbing interruptions in the work of the search committee for my successor prompted the university president, John Evans, to ask if I would stay at least for another year or two. I gave the matter further thought, but again declined. It would be, I said, hard to act in a "temporary" capacity, and I foresaw a worsening of Faculty morale. I had future plans that I didn't want to postpone or abandon. Evans understood my position and refrained from twisting my arm.

As was happening in other parts of the university, my being a dean served as a precedent: rather than a lifetime commitment, the post became something academics could step forward and take a turn at. In our Faculty I was succeeded by Ciamaga, and he was succeeded by Morey: both had been students of mine, as was Morey's successor, Paul Pedersen. The selection process also changed, as search committees engaged professional headhunters, took longer and longer to deliberate, and leaned more and more to candidates with reputations as fundraisers. Back then, I considered it a tough job; nowadays I think I would find it an impossible one.

The successive Faculty of Music deans, 1970–97. Left to right: David Beach, Carl Morey, Paul Pedersen, me, Gustav Ciamaga, Robert Falck (acting dean).

In 1987 I received from Governor General Jeanne Sauvé an appointment as a member of the Order of Canada. Deserved or not, it was a nice stroke. I hadn't expected any resulting new activities, but in the next decade the government decided to call for volunteers from members of the Order to replace the overworked judges in citizenship ceremonies, and I had the distinct pleasure of presiding over about a dozen such gatherings. There were usually sixty or more new Canadians taking the oath, from several dozen different countries, and their attentiveness and smiles were inspiring. The format called for the singing of "O Canada" at the conclusion, so in my welcoming remarks I always threw in a few comments about Lavallée.

As will be clear from earlier parts of this chapter, the end of being dean by no means meant the end of going to meetings. My life was still full of them. I remained committed to SOCAN, the CMHS, the *Encyclopedia*; I took on committee work with the Sonneck Society, mostly by correspondence, as we all started using email; Keith MacMillan invited me to join the trustees of the Sir Ernest MacMillan Foundation; and I added to my calendar brief stints with other groups. My hearing loss, first detected before I was forty, became gradually more severe and made for strain in some gatherings, even after I was fitted with hearing aids. With weakening sight, glasses can restore 20-20 vision, but with hearing there are too many variables, and the aids—even those with sophisticated digital technology—can only offer *aid*, not restore hearing to perfection. At meetings I learned to sit in a front row and with a clear view of the chairperson's face. By the late 1990s I found I was feeling the strain more and more. Some projects were completed, so the meetings slowed down or ceased altogether (the *Encyclopedia*, the CMHS); with the few remaining committees, I decided to resign. Then in 2004 I received a call from Germaine Warkentin of the university's English department, whom I had known through her work on Reaney's poetry. She invited me to serve on a newly formed body. RALUT (Retired Academics and Librarians, University of Toronto) had inaugurated a Senior Scholars Committee to promote the work of retirees who were active in performance and research. It was an interesting assignment, Germaine was a dynamic chair, and several members shared my problem with hearing. I was a member of the committee for four years, during which we instituted an annual one-day symposium, got the administration to provide space for a "seniors' college," and succeeded in drawing attention to senior academics' needs (and rights) in local divisions of the university. Our meetings were both lively and harmonious.

A few pages back, I noted my possibly genetic tendency as a "joiner." Both my parents had strong feelings of social responsibility, even of activism, and there were marked instances of this trait among forebears. My composing and my writing, as well as my assumption of administrative tasks and my participation in the work of non-governmental organizations in my field, have been shaped by such attitudes—which I acquired without thinking much about them.

I reflect too that my world view has been deeply affected by my associations—including in a few cases life-long close friendships—with several survivors of the Nazi persecution. Walter, Geiger-Torel, Greta Kraus, and Oskar Morawetz were pre-war examples; a postwar case was Karel Ančerl, who spent his last few conducting years in Toronto and with whom I had several contacts. Mieczyslaw Kolinski's comprehensive grasp of music I found inspiring, in our many talks. His serene, scholarly demeanour gave few clues that he had spent the late 1930s in flight and the war years in hiding.

Helmut Kallmann came to Canada as a wartime "enemy alien" alongside Walter Homburger, Franz Kraemer, Helmut Blume, and others who, like him, were to play decisive roles in Canadian musical life. For several years after his retirement, Kallmann edited a newsletter for survivors of the New Brunswick prison camp where, ironically, such fugitives from Hitler's Germany—almost all of them Jewish—spent the early years of the Second World War. He rarely spoke of his personal wartime exodus saga but often reminisced about the Berlin of his youth, a city he loved, knew intimately, and eagerly revisited in the '90s. After leaving Berlin in early 1939, he had heard sporadically from his parents for a year or two. His father died in Theresienstadt, his mother in Birkenau; he never learned the fate of his only sister.[19] In a late essay, Kallmann examined his feelings of citizenship: was he German, Jewish, or Canadian?[20] He concluded he was all three. He said as a Jew he blamed the tragic upheavals of his youth on the Nazis, not on the German people. He remained passionately fond of the German language and the German literary and (especially) musical heritage. Taking the Canadian musical scene as his scholarly theme, he became just as passionate about Canada and played a leading part in many crucial events of its cultural life. Our comradeship was a natural one, based on mutual musical enthusiasms. He and his wife Ruth took a keen interest in my children, and we shared parties and outings. When they settled in Ottawa, he acquired a second piano, and on visits he and I would sight-read Mozart concertos, always a pleasureful experience.

Visiting Montreal in 1954 for a CLC meeting or concert, I was a guest at the home of Istvan and Beate Anhalt. He was a new member of the McGill music staff and a deeply committed composer. Our conversations were intense, and I was sharply impressed when he played his then-new solo-piano Fantasia for me. Over fifty years later, after his retirement as head of another music school, at Queen's University in Kingston, I had another memorable private reading by Istvan, of another just-composed solo-piano work, this time his *Four Portraits from Memory*. Those fifty years encompass many personal and family visits and several hundred letters. We developed a regular habit of discussing compositional interests and challenges, and of exchanging new scores. Istvan had spent the last war years in a work camp for Hungarian Jews, from which he escaped and lived several months in hiding, later emigrating to France (as a student of Boulanger's) and eventually to Canada. His wife, Bea, had arrived from Berlin as a teenager in the pre-war period. Their friendship and our shared experiences have brought me genuine spiritual nourishment over the years. In what probably sounds like some mutual-promotion campaign, Istvan has published sympathetic comments about my work, and I have on several occasions written critical appreciations of his, as well as an attempt at a character portrait.[21]

COMPOSITIONS

10

For Instruments
(I)

Arnold Walter once remarked that a composer may do many jobs in order to survive—writing, teaching, performing—but always regards himself or herself primarily as a *composer*. (A moment of self-revelation, perhaps? His own composing took a back seat to his administrative career.) Despite the considerable survival demands at the time of my entry into professional life in 1952–53, I continued to think of composing as my main ambition and aim. I might find little time for it, but it was a constant mental preoccupation. The main creative effort in the 1950s went for the opera *Night Blooming Cereus*.[1] From my decision to improve my academic credentials by applying for the MusM degree came two instrumental works, the Three Studies for string trio (1955–56) and the Concerto Fantasy for piano and orchestra (my thesis composition, 1958–60).

I was fortunate to receive in that decade four commissions for instrumental pieces. They kept the compositional wheels turning, and I could tell myself commissioning meant that someone *needed* my music. The first, in 1953, was a short contribution to John Adaskin's *Opportunity Knocks* radio series. For this musical talent program, Adaskin conducted a small orchestra and made a practice of ordering new works from local composers, four or five minutes in length. My piece was a freely conceived theme for solo clarinet with variations, and I called it *Montage*.

It was my first original work for orchestra. Glenn Gould phoned me after the broadcast, in some excitement; he thought it sounded like Webern, whose music was much on our minds at that time—a laughable exaggeration, but his and Adaskin's compliments were welcome encouragement.

*Example 1: This solo line for clarinet formed the basis
for my variational* Montage *(1953).*

The second commissioned piece probably no longer exists. Around 1953 or '54, Louis Applebaum had a surplus in his National Film Board music budget and offered small honoraria to various composers for "stock" music that he would record and use as required in future films. I remember nothing about my little work, but Applebaum did conduct a recording of it.

In 1956 the University of Toronto Music Alumni asked me to write something suitable for a school orchestra. This was the second in a proposed series of annual composer commissions; the first was Harry Somers's *Little Suite for Strings.* I produced *Fall Scene and Fair Dance*, for a string orchestra with solo parts for clarinet and violin. There followed both a premiere performance by Faculty of Music students under my direction and a publication (score and parts) by BMI Canada. I had little experience of school instrumental programs but had the impression from talking with teachers that student abilities varied; so I thought the mini-double-concerto format might be appropriate. The titles of the two movements suggest a vague pictorial background from rural Ontario. The *Fair Dance* was based on a motive I made up for my ear-training classes, one of many such, this one in a catchy 5/8 metre. The work has had a decent record of performances.

The remaining commission of the '50s was for a rescoring of my early piano-duet suite, *Music for Dancing*. George Crum, music director of the National Ballet of Canada, remembered the piece and persuaded the choreographer David Adams that it could be the basis of a ballet; however, my 1949 orchestral version called for more instruments than the National could afford. George made admiring comments on the instrumentation of *Night Blooming Cereus*, in which his wife, the soprano Patricia Snell, sang the part of Barbara; he thought a similar slender treatment would suit

Music for Dancing. It was, for me, a good opportunity to use the surer knowledge of the orchestra I had by now acquired (in the brief commission assignments, in my MusM studies with Weinzweig, and in the opera). This version has been widely performed, and the LP recording by the CBC Vancouver Orchestra under John Avison's direction had many broadcasts. Adams's ballet, called *The Littlest One* (a title I disliked), received a try-out in Hamilton, and there may have been one or two further performances in the National's tour of 1959–60, but the work never caught on and was soon dropped from the repertoire. I recall it only dimly as being a child's fantasy somewhat akin to *L'Enfant et les sortilèges*.

The Three Studies and the Concerto Fantasy, written in fulfillment of university degree requirements, might be expected to show more original invention and a more deliberate application of skill—and I believe they do. My adviser, John Weinzweig, thought the string trio medium was "putting one player out of a job," but, recalling my gradual progress with winds in studying with Boulanger, I found three lines enough to handle. Two scores I studied around this time were Mozart's Divertimento in E♭ (K563), and the String Trio of Schoenberg (that of Webern I didn't encounter until some years later). While the first study has a melodic kinship with the woodwind quartet I composed in Paris, the second is more freely chromatic. The third is my first attempt at serial writing. I had analyzed a number of the standard serial works and introduced them to my students. I was especially interested in the then-brand-new compositions by Stravinsky (the *Cantata*, the *Shakespeare Songs*, *In Memoriam Dylan Thomas*) with their non-dodecaphonic series. Weinzweig was known as a Canadian pioneer of serialism, but my move in this direction was not dictated by him, although I benefited from his advice and encouragement. When the Studies were played in a chamber concert by three Toronto Symphony members (Isidor Desser, Eugene Hudson, George Horvath), friends said they sounded unlike my previous music. I attributed this partly to the serial element and partly to the increased confidence in writing for strings which the classes with Weinzweig had given me.

I interrupted my pursuit of the MusM in order to finish *Night Blooming Cereus*. Walter told me he was preparing to promote me to the rank of assistant professor (after four years as a "lecturer") but couldn't until I completed my master's. In a later period the demand would have been completion of a doctorate and half a dozen refereed publications (if not performances by the Juilliard Quartet or the Boston Symphony). I embarked on what I figured would be a work in two movements for piano and orchestra. Again, scores I had studied and admired may have served as models or touchstones—the Concerto by Schumann gave me the idea of a "fantasy" approach to form, and that of Schoenberg illustrated how orchestration could delineate form.[2] Alberto Guerrero's remarks on various works in the classical concerto repertoire stuck in my memory.[3] My meandering first movement, with its octatonic patterns and its clangy chordal recollections of Copland's Piano Sonata, was followed by a variational second movement (the interplay between the soloist and an orchestral celeste, in one of the variations, was an original touch, and I managed an effective, long orchestral diminuendo). Further contrast was needed, as Weinzweig felt and I agreed. In adding a third movement, in a more animated tempo, I decided to use a twelve-note set—specifically one I had seen in an article by Henry Leland Clarke entitled "The Abuse of the Semitone in Twelve-Tone Music."[4] The all-interval set ($D\sharp - E - F\sharp - A - C\sharp - F\sharp - C - G - E\flat - C - B\flat - A$) contained only nine pitch classes and afforded an opposition of minor triads a tritone apart, changing colour to major when inverted. I worked hard to show what I could do with this, and even included a fugato middle section as a supposedly "learned" display. The fugue subject was related to the Coplandesque chords in the first movement in ways that Weinzweig found too abstruse. "Your listeners will never *hear* that connection," he rightly observed. The rapid continuity proved idiomatic for the solo piano but awkward for the woodwinds who introduced the fugue. Despite its shortcomings, I hear this finale as my most accomplished extended work up to this time. The Concerto Fantasy was first performed in Montreal in 1962 on a League of Composers program; the Orchestre symphonique de Montréal was conducted by Roland Leduc and the soloist was Mario Bernardi. I recall that Pierre Mercure attended and complimented me afterwards. He had just dropped his CLC membership in disagreement with League policies and perceived aesthetics, and he dismissed the rest of the program, but for some reason found my piece acceptable. Bernardi later repeated the Concerto Fantasy in a broadcast performance with the CBC Symphony under Jean-Marie Beaudet.[5]

I found my composing habits in these early ventures varied from one to the next, but there was a certain resoluteness about the way I produced the score when I was satisfied with it. In student days already I had observed that performers expected a readable fair copy of the manuscript, so I acquired a decent skill in copying my music in India ink on sheets of lined transparent paper. From fellow League members I picked up tips on the preferred type of pen nib and the handiest correction procedures (usually cutting or scraping with a razor blade). The resulting negative could be reproduced, similarly to an architectural blueprint, on large, smelly Ozolid machines such as the one favoured by Toronto composers at Phil Podoliak's Music Photocraft Company on Bathurst Street (their slogan caused unintended amusement: "Come to Us with Your Reproduction Problems"). The CMC adopted this process in its early years, and the librarian, Henry Mutsaers, a superb professional copyist, used to give instruction sessions for student composers. It wasn't until the early 1980s that I abandoned this laborious method in favour of dark-pencil copies on regular opaque paper. Xerox duplication up to that time didn't give a sufficiently clear or permanent result.

Two orchestral commissions occupied my composing energies in 1962 and 1963, one from the Victoria Symphony Orchestra and the other from the Vancouver Youth Symphony. Hans Gruber, then music director in Victoria, wrote a cordial invitation letter, expressing in a polite way that he wanted a piece that wouldn't be too shocking or far-out for his audience:

> How soon could you have something ready for us, and would you give me a rough verbal outline of what you may have in mind ...? Will it HAVE to be in the 12-tone system, and unrelievedly dissonant, or may we hope for something more classical, harmonically speaking, with the odd major chord here and there?! We want you to have a big success with our audiences, and, if your time allows, we should like to have you in the audience ..., advising us during actual rehearsals—or perhaps even have you conduct yourself your own work.[6]

I remembered that one Vancouver critic had considered *Music for Dancing* to be among the two or three most radical scores played at the Vancouver Symposium in 1950.[7] Gruber added detailed notes on the strengths and weaknesses of his (at that time) semi-professional orchestra, as a guide for me in making the instrumentation. He later repeated the invitation to conduct the work, but I said I thought that was his responsibility. Again (as in *Fall Scene and Fair Dance* and the original plan of the Concerto Fantasy) I came up with a work in two contrasting movements; the eventual title was *Flower Variations and Wheels*. The first movement, far from being "unrelievedly dissonant," had a sweet melodic character and unfolded in variations like flower petals, while the second had motoric rhythms suggesting the pleasures of cycling. Victoria is a city of gardens and I cycled a lot there as a kid.

I cycled again a good deal in the summer of 1962 when vacationing with my family on Lake Huron not far from Tobermory. Jamie and Colleen

Example 2: This melody (a) for solo flute, originally written for recorder, formed the theme for Flower Variations *(1962). It may have been suggested by a theme (b), also for flute, in Virgil Thomson's* The Mother of Us All.

Reaney and *their* family were staying in a neighbouring cottage, and we spent happy days together. Jamie was teaching his young sons the recorder, so I wrote them a little sixteen-bar melody, and then a second part to go with it, forming a recorder duet. The tune, in G major, is squarely shaped and has conventional (not to say trite) harmonic implications—a move towards the dominant in bar eight; another move in bar twelve, this time to the subdominant; and then a return to the original tonic. Some of the contours imitate a sixteen-bar melody from Virgil Thomson's opera *The Mother of Us All*. Probably the imitation was deliberate; if the Thomson tune (employed also in his score for the film *The Goddess*) was a parody of the Appalachian folk repertoire or perhaps of the shape-note tunebooks, was mine a parody of Thomson? Adapting this tune for my *Flower Variations*, I started, as Thomson did in his opera, with a solo flute in low register, a colour I was fond of. The tune gives off, I think, a quality of nostalgia. But the variations put it through various serial treatments in inversion, retrograde, and retrograde inversion (following Stravinsky, I found no contradiction in treating tonal motives serially), and there are highlighted duos that perhaps refer back to my wind-music exercises for Boulanger. *Flower Variations* may echo some of the more sentimental passages of *Night Blooming Cereus*. In *Wheels*, there are surprise percussion elements—a ratchet in one transition, and a gong underlining the climactic union of the two main themes. The other surprise is an epilogue passage for a high solo violin (in a tonality players have always found rather ungrateful). *Flower Variations and Wheels* has had regular revivals, fulfilling to some extent Hans Gruber's hopes for a "big success." Performances by various orchestras have been led by Victor Feldbrill, Alexander Brott, Karel Ančerl, and Andrew Davis, among others. I dedicated the score to my father's memory (he died in 1958), not as a *Trauer-Musik* but simply as a piece that he might have liked—not meaning to imply that I didn't like it myself.

For the Vancouver commission of 1963 my name had been suggested by the journalist Francine Campbell, whom I had known slightly in Toronto; she was a member of the Youth Symphony board. As with my earlier work for student players, *Fall Scene and Fair Dance*, my instinct suggested something for soloist and orchestra. The Concertino for horn and orchestra consists of a succession of six short sections. The first and last employ a rather pompous rhythm like the baroque *ouverture à la française*, while the others combine the solo instrument with string, brass, woodwind, and percussion sections in turn. The format, I now see, mirrors various scores by my teacher, John Weinzweig, but I believe this is a case of osmosis rather than specific copying. The twelve-tone set consists of six notes followed by the same six-note pattern inverted; in retrograde, four of the notes make up a well-known motive by Mozart, from the rondo-finale of his Horn Concerto in E♭ (K447), which I quote in the scherzo-like fourth movement. Eugene Rittich, first horn of the Toronto Symphony Orchestra and a former Victorian, was a helpful adviser on the solo part and performed it on two occasions, once with the CBC Symphony Orchestra conducted by Sir Ernest MacMillan (the orchestra's last public concert before its disbandment in 1964) and once with the TSO under Andrew Davis. The Concertino was never played

Example 3: (a) The basic set for the Concertino (1963) provides a four-note reference (bracketed) to (b) the finale of Mozart's Horn Concerto (K447).

by the commissioning ensemble. In a history of the orchestra, some years later, the author claimed that the score had posed "considerable difficulties"; this, I protested, was an unfair accusation.[8]

Between 1959 and 1962, besides the major projects mentioned, I produced a number of short piano pieces designed for young players in early stages of learning. A frequent complaint about composers in my generation, and still in later generations, is that their music is designed for professionals and therefore tough to perform; we're asked, why don't you just write some simple stuff that young pupils can understand and enjoy? Weinzweig once said he felt as if people were telling him that only the classics were allowed to be grand or profound. The need for easy learning pieces was of course real, but I didn't think it meant excluding the element of challenge or avoiding new modes of structure or expression. Moreover, to me, "instructive" and "enjoyable" were not necessarily mutually exclusive qualities. *Six Mobiles*, *Interval Studies*, and the *Suite on Old Tunes* were the first examples, all published by BMI Canada, along with a set of short songs for children, *Ten English Rhymes*. Over the years there have been more.

During the summer of 1965, I spent two or three months in the University of Toronto Electronic Music Studio (UTEMS), aiming to gain knowledge of the techniques of this new medium. I was guided by Gustav Ciamaga, who had been a student of mine in the 1950s. In a period of graduate study at Brandeis University, he developed expertise in electronic music, returning to Toronto and to UTEMS as Myron Schaeffer's associate and, soon, successor (Schaeffer died suddenly early in 1965). The resources were oscillators, filters, tape recorders, and various editing devices. Synthesizers and computer controls were still in the future. I was slow to develop skill but responded to the sense that fragments of music might be handled as a sculptor handles clay, time-lengths of musical sound being perceived as lengths of recorded tape. Some of the studies that I produced are in the studio's archives. The summer experience changed my outlook and my approach to form in works for live players, but I later incorporated electronic means in only a few compositions. The devices for treatment of pre-miked "live" sounds (in the classical radio sense of "sound effects" or in what the Paris group called "musique concrète") seemed to me more durable than the vocabulary of synthetic sounds; the latter struck me as limited, despite some undeniable masterworks, and (after only a decade or so) overused and full of clichés.

Putting together the incidental music for James Reaney's play *The Killdeer* early in 1960 had initiated my attraction to informal collage-like composition. I was further emboldened in this direction by the music I heard and some of the composers I talked with at the International Composers' Conference in Stratford that summer. A series of CBC Radio collaborations with Reaney—the first of which came along in the fall of that same year—provided the perfect opportunity to put such ideas into practice. I describe our words-and-music "collages" in detail in another chapter.[9] In a sudden commission in 1967 came a chance to apply what I had learned in these ventures to a purely instrumental medium. The call came again from Vancouver.

The English harpsichordist George Malcolm would be the guest soloist at the Vancouver International Festival, with a string ensemble led from the first desk by Norman Nelson. The concert was scheduled for mid-July. My invitation came in April: Would I compose something for harpsichord and strings to be premiered on this program? It was short notice,[10] but the end of the Faculty teaching term was near and I figured I could find the time. Moreover, I was intrigued to write something featuring the harpsichord. I had played the Faculty's harpsichords in demonstrations for my history-of-music students, cherished the repertoire, and included a harpsichord part in some of the radio collages. A further challenge in the request was that the ensemble was to perform without a conductor. I developed a plan whereby the soloist and the thirteen string players would all play from a full score, coordinating by means of visual and aural cues to be indicated by coloured markings. This allowed for the kind of informal mixes of tempos and metres I had discovered in the collages. I drew on traits I had observed in works by Charles Ives and in more recent "chance music" compositions. I had heard, and greatly admired, a performance in Cleveland of George Crumb's *Echoes of Time and the River* and remembered that Crumb had required each member of the orchestra to play from the score. I worked in the Faculty's harpsichord studio daily and within five weeks finished and copied the work and sent the score to Vancouver. I called it *Circle, with Tangents*—thinking of the harpsichord as the circle and the string parts as the tangents, but also of the rotating rondo-like musical structure from which stray fragments continually spin off.

Fresh ideas came quickly in this piece. A symmetrical twelve-note set supplied cohesion and a source of lines in the often complex textures. Each string part I considered a distinct strand, a solo; the first viola part was especially prominent, as a sort of foil to the harpsichord (Simon Streatfeild was the performer in Vancouver). The harpsichord makes its first statement in a glissando played with the forearm and later underlines a slow right-hand melody in six-note clusters (the thumb playing two notes together); still later, a rapid ostinato suggests stride keyboard. There had to be a compromise with the classic twelve-tone avoidance of the sonority of the octave, in view of the harpsichord's characteristic registral doublings at the octave. The instrument I wrote for had both 4' and 16' stops, and I wanted to specify these colours. The 16' stop is a modern invention, spurned by instrument makers of the later twentieth century, although called for in works of the mid-century by Frank Martin, Elliott Carter, and others. Rather than try to avoid octaves, I decided to *emphasize* them, and in the finale of the score there is a quasi-chorale intoned by the harpsichord entirely in octaves, answered by directional series of pizzicatos in the string ensemble (the passage is reproduced in part in the endpapers of this volume). I called for a seating plan with the harpsichord (the "circle") in the middle of a wide semicircle of string "tangents," making it possible to pass various sounds across and around the performing space—as in this quasi-chorale, for example. In a recurring refrain, three of the strings play the same line in octaves, uncoordinated as to tempo. The strings range over a fairly rich selection of timbres, in one section strumming like banjos. A passage in high, sustained violin harmonics reflects the hiss of the air conditioning in the studio that May.

On finishing the composition, I travelled to Montreal, where George Malcolm was performing at Expo 67. I had heard and liked several of his recordings of Handel, Scarlatti, and other classics. We met for the first time at Kenneth Gilbert's home. As I played through and talked over the score for him, I saw Malcolm becoming impatient. I had composed for an instrument with a non-standard disposition of registers, though I understood it to be like the one he would use in Vancouver. He was critical of

Example 4: In this passage from Circle, with Tangents *(1967) the same line is played in octaves by the viola in even notes, the cello starting fast and getting slower, and the violin starting slow and getting faster.*

some of my rhythmic notations. At length he said, with a tone of finality, "This isn't my kind of music." However, it seemed he was prepared to fulfill his contract: the performance would go ahead. He did not suggest adjustments, and in view of the tight scheduling I was not about to offer any. That evening I went to dinner at Istvan Anhalt's home, where John Cage (in town for Expo) was also a guest. I shared my crushed feelings with the gathering, and Cage's remark was, "Now you see why we found *our own* performers." He was referring to his similar experiences with international "big name" artists whose minds were closed to new kinds of music. (One of my motives in so eagerly accepting the assignment may have been the chance to have my work played by someone with George Malcolm's international reputation.)

A week or so later I heard from the Vancouver Festival management: Would *I* care to play the solo part at the concert? I answered that, first, it was Malcolm's concert, not mine, and, second, I was not a harpsichordist. I agreed to come a few days before the concert and coach the string players. This part of the preparation proved completely agreeable. The players were not only excellent but cooperative, and I had worked out a scheme of rehearsing part by part and section by section so as to accustom everyone to the sounds (often with several seemingly quite different musical processes going on at the same time). I felt it was working well. But on the soloist's arrival a day or two later the mood became more strained. He made no effort to disguise his dislike of the piece, though he had learned it thoroughly and in accordance with what I had asked. The other contemporary composition on his program was a fluffy pseudo-jazz work by Joseph Horovitz, from which I could surmise the sort of new music that was more to his taste.

After the dress rehearsal, I went for a long walk along the harbour to clear my head. One trivial point bothered me: the composer at a premiere usually receives a ticket for the concert, but by an oversight the festival had neglected to give me one. Should I make an issue of this? I sat eating a Chinese meal debating this question in my mind, and absently opened a fortune cookie: the fortune read, "Keep out of useless arguments." Sage advice; I decided to swallow my pride and buy a ticket. Lining up at the box office I heard a voice behind me. It was Barbara Pentland, with her husband. She barged forward and spoke to the attendant: I was the composer and it would be an outrage if I had to pay for my ticket. So I got one free after all.

The concert went extremely well. There was a full audience, including Barbara and Hally, Murray Schafer and Phyllis Mailing, and my old

English teacher Ruth Humphrey. Malcolm played the solo part in *Circle, with Tangents* flawlessly, and the string players were terrific. The piece had a rapt hearing and a warm reception. Elated by the applause, I went onto the stage and held out my hand to shake Malcolm's but found he had walked off. Backstage afterwards, I was unable to find him to thank him and had to conclude that he was avoiding me. His attitude was puzzling: If he hated the piece and hated having to play it, why not just sight-read it, treat it perfunctorily, go through the motions? On the other hand, having decided to play it well and professionally, why indicate in front of others (the players, the audience) that he hated it?

The colour coding of the *Circle* full score may represent my adoption of some of the revolutionary changes in musical notation that arose in the '60s in works by Stockhausen, Bussotti, and others in Europe, and the Cage-Feldman group in the US. To my surprise, Ron Napier of BMI Canada expressed interest in publishing it. Such an elaborate production was already unthinkable a decade or so later even in Europe or the US, let alone Canada. It was done by separate offset runs for each colour: I recall drawing the cues four times, in red, blue, green, and brown. The piece has had a number of revivals, and in the 1990s Colin Tilney made an excellent recording with members of the CBC Vancouver Orchestra.[11] I had considered it to be no longer performable with the virtually complete disappearance of modern harpsichords in favour of historical-replica instruments starting in the '70s; however, Tilney found ways to adapt my registral specifications to the then-more-prevalent type of instrument. In later harpsichord works I have made only general suggestions as to registrations and timbres, leaving specifics up to the performer.

In 1969 I was invited to be composer-in-residence at the late-summer Inter-Provincial Music Camp near Orillia. I had naive notions of what the title meant: You resided at the camp and you composed, no? As later experience showed, composers so designated rarely actually *reside* in the appointed place, and they usually produce already-written scores, only rarely composing new ones. I got little sleep, scrambling to produce a fresh set of short pieces in a few days, copying parts, and rehearsing them with members of the camp's junior band (including two of my children, Jonathan on clarinet and Symon on drums). The pieces were designed to give the young players a taste of collage structure—they consisted of independent components, with rhythms that were cued rather than conducted; one movement was a study in oddly grouped, fast eighth-notes. The title, *Elastic Band Studies*, derives from one of many remarks attributed to the conductor Sir Thomas Beecham. Exasperated at trying to lead the orchestral accompaniment for a soprano with a wayward sense of rhythm, he is supposed to have told her, "Madam, this is a symphony orchestra, not an elastic band." Funny, yes; but I sympathized with the poor woman (not that I suppose the story was true). Why not a flexible kind of ensemble music where the performers would play deliberately *not* together? After the dress rehearsal before the camp concert, I asked the band members if they had any questions. One young flutist put up her hand: "Is someone going to tell the audience ahead of time that it's kind of *weird?*" The *Studies* have had a number of subsequent performances, notably by ensembles led by my U of T colleague Stephen Chenette.

Being "in residence" at the camp entailed talking music theory and composition with individual students and small groups, and of course participating in social activities. My versatility was put to the test in improvising a piano accompaniment to a skit by the camp director, Harold Nashman, based on the Al Jolson hit "Sonny Boy," and in vamping a keyboard part in a combo accompanying a square dance, with the chording shouted in my ear by the bass player, Boris Kersting.

In my administrative position at the University of Toronto, one of the first appointments I approved was the tuba player Charles Daellenbach. When he and four colleagues formed the brass quintet called the Canadian Brass, they asked me to compose a work for them. The occasion for the premiere in the summer of 1972 was a late-evening outdoor concert on an island park in the Avon River at Stratford—the concluding event in a special "music day" at the Stratford Festival. I started to imagine five brass instruments interacting in collage-like groupings. That they were brass and would be playing outdoors reminded me of a film sequence I had liked many years before: the opening of Alexander Korda's version of Wilde's *An Ideal Husband*, with Paulette Goddard, sets the scene of late-Victorian London with a mounted brass band cantering splendidly through Green Park to period music by Arthur Benjamin. Maybe I could make a *processional* piece, have the players move around the stage, into the audience. Pressed for time, I accepted an invitation from John and Helen Weinzweig to use their lakeside cottage, just north of Huntsville, for a couple of weeks and while there developed a plan and sketched a good deal of *Taking a Stand*. The title is a pun: the five performers move during the music to and from fourteen music stands placed backstage, on the stage on various levels, and in the audience area. The music I conceived as creating action, prompting them to move. I had not tried to articulate exactly how it would connect with the meaning of "standing up for one's principles": however, there is a passage towards the end where the trombonist marches menacingly towards the other players as if in domination; he mounts a platform and the others pick up his march tune, but at length they start to fall away, indicating dissent, and the two trumpeters drag him off the stage (still playing);[12] in performance, this struck me as illustrating a warning against the dominating, loudest voice in a social situation—stand on your principles, okay, but not so rigidly as to force them on others; don't lose respect for others' views.[13]

The opening section, and several later passages, have a bluesy character. One day after a composition class I found on my piano rack a blues melody of some thirty notes. I couldn't recall whether I had made it up as a demonstration of the blues idiom, or indeed where it had come from; it wasn't copied from any examples I knew; when I asked the students later they could shed no light on the mystery. I liked the tune, started hearing it in a high trumpet register, and decided to explore its variational possibilities (including serialization) in *Taking a Stand*.

Preparing *Taking a Stand* for the concert was immense fun. The players responded enthusiastically and rose to the work's technical demands— including passages where, performing in motion, they had to memorize their parts. The performance, under a clear sky and a full moon, attracted a big crowd. A slight summer breeze ruffled the parts on the fourteen stands, and my kids volunteered to see that they didn't fly off. Keith MacMillan had brought a little portable recorder and caught the spatial and wayward effects. I remember this event as a unique presentation of my work; it had a quality of magic. *Taking a Stand* became part of the Canadian Brass's repertoire for several seasons: they played it on tour at the Kennedy Center in Washington and at the Edinburgh Festival, and for the 1977 "Musicanada" festival in London and Paris. The CBC broadcast their performance at the Rebecca Cohn Auditorium in Halifax and recorded it.[14] When they gave it in the New Music Concerts series in Toronto, two visiting composers on the same program, David Bedford and Sydney Hodkinson, were inspired by their playing, and maybe by the piece, to write their own brass quintets; another result, a year or so later, was Weinzweig's *Pieces of Five* (we dedicated our brass pieces to each other). With changes in personnel and growth in popularity, the Canadian Brass gradually moved away from such adventurous areas of new repertoire.

A sequel to *Taking a Stand* came into being a year later when the Junior Committee of the Toronto Symphony Orchestra asked me for a short chamber work suitable for performance in their series of school concerts. I wrote a perambular piece for string quartet and double bass, and called it *Musical Chairs: A Quintet in the Round*. "In the round" referred to the

The score of Taking a Stand (1972) was prepared for publication (Berandol) by the copyist John Fodi. As shown in this passage on page 14, a chart (lower right) indicates the players' movements.

idea that the performances would take place in school gymnasia, with the student listeners surrounding the players. Again there are entrances and exits, with an arrangement of chairs and stands serving as positions for the players to move to, sometimes while playing—and again I tried to think of the moves as being not arbitrary but motivated by the music. The bass part has a rhythmic flavour from jazz, like some of the bass lines in *Circle, with Tangents* (hearing the veteran jazz violinist Joe Venuti around this time is a vivid memory); one violin passage echoes the main theme of Rossini's Overture to *Cenerentola* (my young son was then constantly listening to the dazzling Toscanini recording). A moment of agreement among the disparate musical happenings I thought resembled a kind of drunken chorus. The season of school performances brought together for the first time a group that later called themselves the Accordes Quartet (Fujiko Imajichi, Ann Rapson, Susan Lipchak, David Hetherington), with Edward Tait, bass. With a few membership changes, this quartet has remained together for more than thirty years. *Musical Chairs* has had several revivals.

A sabbatical year, 1977–78, provided a more extended and relaxed time to concentrate on composing. The main project was Act Two of *The Shivaree*, but two instrumental commissions intervened. The first was a request from the Ottawa organist Ewen McCuaig for a work combining solo organ with a prepared tape. I had begun to dig deeper into the early hymn-tune publications in Canada[15] and thought of using some of the original tunes I liked as the basis for a series of settings somewhat akin to the chorale treatments of the German baroque, particularly those in J.S. Bach's *Orgelbüchlein*, which I knew and loved. I did five such settings and designed interludes with recorded sounds evocative of nineteenth-century Ontario (church bells, the clip-clop of carriage horses, clangs and screeches indicating the mid-century arrival of the railway and increased industrialization). Dennis Patrick helped me realize the *musique concrète* tape part. Given the unusualness of the commission, I considered the tape to be an optional enhancement of the organ part: the *Upper Canadian Hymn Preludes* should, I thought, be playable without it. Performances in both modes have taken place. The CBC recording by Patrick Wedd includes the tape part.[16] As in my later harpsichord pieces, I refrained from calling for specific registrations, since fashions in organ construction have varied over time, and organs differ even more than harpsichords. Later research has corrected my original notions about the provenance of the tunes I chose: all are from the two earliest Upper Canadian tunebooks, as I claimed, but only one was composed in what is now Canada, Mark Burnham's "Resurrection." The other four are adaptations from US and English sources.

The other commission came from the Orford String Quartet. Most composers write string quartets as part of their professional education. I had avoided this, and was some years into my active composing phase before I felt comfortable with string media. The Orfords were at a peak of their international career, and I knew them all as colleagues since they were the quartet-in-residence at the U of T. Ideas came rapidly, as if I had had a quartet inside me waiting to be written down. I devised a suitable twelve-tone set around the open-string pitches, and, drawing on my experience of collage organization, imagined various situations where contrasting kinds of string music might be heard simultaneously. Reflecting on the quartets of Béla Bartók, with their echoes of cimbaloms and zithers and their Balkan rhythms, I wondered what the equivalent string idioms would be for Canada.

I thought of the minstrel-show banjo of past generations, of my uncle's mandolin from his McGill years, of the guitar my oldest son was practising, of the fiddling traditions of central and maritime Canada. In the Quartet, as in several of my earlier works, my nostalgia (my "cultural memory"), together with my ear for regional habits of performance and

Page 1 of the manuscript score of my Quartet (1977). The first sounds
are loud "Bartók pizzicatos" on open strings. Bracketed notes
are produced by tapping on the fingerboard.

timbre, dictated a style and a form. The brief banjo imitations are done with a thick cardboard pick. The two violinists share a third instrument, tuned slightly higher than normal, and in the "fiddling" finale one of the players presents this grating element, first by itself and then in an off-unison with his partner's regularly tuned instrument. The *scordatura* third violin also allowed for a series of unusual natural harmonics, featured in the prelude and postlude of the Quartet. I was especially pleased at the way the long, slow section in the middle of the piece unfolded, with exaggerated songful phrases in the viola accompanied by muttered interjections of the other three instruments, all muted. Murray Schafer had remarked that it was no longer possible for a serious composition to end loud. I deliberately ended my finale on a *forte* unison C. Writing the Quartet proved for me why the medium has retained its popularity for well over two centuries; in texture, in range, in timbral variety, its possibilities are apparently limitless.

The Orfords presented the Quartet's premiere in a concert in Montreal in February 1978. I was spending several months of my leave in New Zealand so could not attend. I had sat in on their reading of it before I left Canada. Kathleen McMorrow, to whom I dedicated the work, travelled to Montreal for the concert and sent me her comments. The Orfords, she said, "played very carefully and cleanly." The audience was mostly French-speaking (the concert was at the Université de Montréal: "I guess McGill people don't go to U of M events") and was "attentive, & quite astounded by the banjo-playing." She mentions encountering André Prévost and at least one McGill colleague, Paul Helmer. She thought the music sounded "like you ... – intense, curious, struggling with problems." Later Marcel Saint-Cyr, cellist of the Quartet, sent me a recording of their performance, which I listened to with pleasure and played for friends in Auckland. The Orford Quartet continued to perform the piece for a few seasons. Their Toronto performance was not reviewed, the reason being (I was told) that they were considered an "over-exposed" group. Their 1979 recording, on an LP with Schafer's Second Quartet,[17] received a number of good reviews, notably from William Littler and Ken Winters. Other performers have undertaken the work; there was an exceptionally strong revival by the Accordes Quartet as part of a concert of my music given in the New Music Concerts series in 1996. The score is one of a handful to which Robin Elliott gives special analytical attention in his dissertation on the Canadian string quartet repertoire.[18]

My next instrumental ensemble project, *Keyboard Practice*, had its source in my teaching. For several years I taught a course for non-music

Page 20 of the manuscript score of Keyboard Practice *(1979). This loud phrase starts in the electronic piano (Player 4); the climactic chord in the grand piano (Player 3) is sustained in a long fadeout by the harpsichord (Player 2), clavichord (Player 1), and celeste (Player 4).*

majors at the U of T on the keyboard repertoire. It was a favourite of mine and attracted sizable enrolments. The evolution, in the fifteenth century, of a system of levers adapted to the human hand and applied to bell plates, wind pipes, plucked or hammered strings, bellows-operated reeds, and (more recently) electric impulses, is a powerful and decisive cultural breakthrough comparable to the evolution of printing. I found much satisfaction in illustrating the highlights of this history in scores, recordings, and, as often as I could, in live demonstrations on clavichord, harpsichord, or piano. It kept me in practice. A wide-open commission from New Music Concerts offered a chance to bring past and present together: I proposed a work in which four keyboardists would play a variety of historical and modern instruments. The eventual assemblage included ten: regal, clavichord, harpsichord, harmonium, grand piano, upright (honky-tonk) piano, celeste, a concert-sized electronic piano, an electric practice piano, and a dummy keyboard. I considered adding a typewriter and a carillon, but concluded their keyboards represented different species from these ten. The dummy instrument (used in earlier times by travelling virtuosos) made no pitch sounds, but produced interesting percussive clicks, as did the harmonium without bellows action, the electric keyboard without the power supply, and the harpsichord when unstopped.

Rehearsing for the premiere of Keyboard Practice, *Toronto, 1979. Performers, left to right: Douglas Bodle, Helena Bowkun, William Aide, John Beckwith. Valerie Weeks replaced Bodle for the recording.*

The piece took shape away from any keyboard. Kathleen and I took a summer cycling vacation in the Kootenays and Rockies, and, amid magnificent mountain scenery, I pondered how this keyboard orchestra might be exploited. Each evening I noted in my sketchbook charts of possibilities, interactions between this and that instrument, and started to hear the piece developing variationally, though with as yet few decisions about melody or pitch. Working later at home on my piano, I chose for each of the four players an excerpt from the historical repertoire—for the clavichord an anonymous "Alman" from the *Fitzwilliam Virginal Book*; for the harpsichord François Couperin's *Tic-Toc-Choc*, a characteristic *pièce croisée*; for the grand piano Liszt's *Au bord d'une source*; and for the honky-tonk instrument a classic rag, Charles Johnson's *Cum Bac*. The treatment was literally a collage: I pasted fragments from these numbers into my score. Each brief solo quotation would rouse the other players to free imitations, on other instruments. Characteristic cadences, and the clichés of what players call "passage work," would afford compositional comment here, as also in the variations linking the quotations. A dream-like framework evolved, in which percussive taps and clicks and tolling bells led the listener into and out of a series of crazy-mirror recollections of keyboard music old and new. The players' moves from instrument to instrument had to be calculated with care (again motivated by features of the music) and would form at certain moments a visual aspect of the work's "meaning." In one section, two of the players repeat a piano-duet stunt I had seen on television in one of Victor Borge's comedy acts. In another section, I managed to have seven different instruments going at the same time—with give-and-take of volume to allow them all to be heard.

Keyboard Practice (the title being an homage to J.S. Bach's *Clavierübung*) was an enjoyable production. The semicircular array of the instruments on the stage was startling and colourful. Gathering them, and rehearsing with them, was such an effort, and so special, that I resigned myself to thinking that the work would not be replayed often, if at all. However, there have been repeat performances in Toronto, and it has been done by groups in at least three other centres—St Catharines, Montreal, and Vancouver—and there is a good recording.[19] John Mayo has published an essay about this piece.[20]

For Instruments (2)

A commission from Arraymusic the following year, 1980, prompted me to write another collage piece with a scenario of players-in-motion. The request was for a quintet of mixed instrumentation, and I conceived a work that could be played by any five instruments—i.e., that would not be concerned with timbre or idiom but only with musical action and interaction. I excluded percussion instruments and polyphonic media such as keyboards and plucked strings; the "any five" would be single-line instruments of the conventional orchestra and band families, with no more than two instruments of the same kind. As well as perambulations, entrances, and exits, the scenario called for actions typical of live concert performance—using the clarinet pull-through, emptying the spit from the horn mouthpiece, removing hair from the bow or rosining it. I wanted to celebrate these familiar gestures by having the players draw attention to them at moments when they weren't playing. Further, the players arrive onstage with their instrument cases still unopened, and I devised percussion passages to be played on the *cases*—which therefore had to be of a hard material rather than canvas. Where *Taking a Stand* focused on stands, this work focuses on cases: the double-entendre title, suggested by Kathleen, is *Case Study*. It evolved, in music and in movement, as a satire on performing behaviour. A knotty compositional problem was how to make an interesting solo part at the beginning that could be played alternatively on many different string and wind instruments of a middle range. The practical common range proved narrow, and I had to make phrases using only the smallest intervals. Copying parts for a wide variety of conceivable transpositions was an unforeseen task in preparing the piece: depending on the ensemble chosen, the same part might be played by a viola using its distinctive clef or a horn in F with the required transposition. After the Array premiere, I organized a concert with student players at the Faculty of Music in which *Case Study* was performed three times by three different ensembles in succession—brass quintet; string quartet with flute; and saxophone quartet with double bass.

I have never been asked to compose a *solo de concours*, a test piece for an instrumental contest. The closest I have come is the Sonatina in Two Movements, which I wrote in 1981 at the request of my friend Stephen Chenette. His trumpet students at the Faculty of Music, he said, needed a fresh, new work suitable for their recital programs. The Sonatina was first played by Dan Warren at his graduation recital, with Sue Chenette as pianist. Warren has gone on to a distinguished professional solo and orchestral career. I examined my memory for associations with the trumpet and identified some of my favourites: the cornet solos of Herbert L. Clarke from the turn of the century, with their homely sentimentality and their show-off cadenzas; the conversational licks of Louis Armstrong, again largely on cornet rather than trumpet, in his early blues recordings; and the music of Herb Alpert's Tijuana Brass, in LPs which my children had worn out with many replays. Spending the previous Christmas week in Mexico City, I had enjoyed hearing the mariachi bands in the parks— the performers giving the music their all, their hands protected against the chill in gloves, with the fingers cut out so that they could play. These associations are all reflected in the Sonatina. I studied the Sonata by Peter Maxwell Davies but didn't feel I could make my work quite as demanding as his. Near the end of the second movement, the piano and trumpet play together in fast-changing rhythmic values rather in the manner of the mirror-action exercise in which two people face each other and copy each other's rapid gestures and expressions. This was demanding enough.

Apart from *All the Bees and All the Keys*,[1] it was nearly twenty years since I had written for a symphony orchestra. In fact, the flurry of 1967 centennial commissions being over, the 1970s were not a peak period for orchestral composition in Canada, and this may have been John Roberts's motive when, around 1980, as head of the Canadian Music Centre, he persuaded the Toronto Arts Council to initiate a series of orchestral commissions to Toronto composers. The first commission went to John Weinzweig for his Divertimento No. 8 for tuba and orchestra. Roberts suggested me as the second recipient. A flaw in the scheme was that the council made no commitment to arrange first performances of the commissioned pieces, and Weinzweig waited a couple of years before his Divertimento had its premiere by the University of Toronto Symphony Orchestra. I experienced a similar wait before my work, *A Concert of Myths* for flute and orchestra, was introduced in 1984 by the Calgary Philharmonic with Robert Aitken as soloist. In 2011 the work still had not been performed in Toronto.

In the '80s, Aitken used to remark repeatedly the lack of repertoire for flute and orchestra by Canadians. He performed with orchestras frequently and in many countries, and said that when asked for a Canadian work the only one he could suggest was Norma Beecroft's *Tre pezzi brevi*. If he said this to me, he evidently said it also to other colleagues, because shortly the repertoire included, besides *A Concert of Myths*, works by Talivaldis Kenins, R. Murray Schafer, Peter Paul Koprowski, and others, all written with Aitken in mind. *A Concert of Myths* is dedicated to him, and I benefited from his counsel in composing it. He accepted my prejudice against the convention-bound superficiality of much flute-virtuoso music—works in which "flute" rhymes with "cute"—and steered me to models of a more solid character such as the Concerto of Carl Nielsen, a favourite of his.

When my imagination began exploring the medium's connotations, a familiar creative starting point in such cases as the Quartet and the Sonatina for trumpet, I recalled Debussy's solo piece called *Syrinx*, and this led me to think of the Pan myth. I had for some time considered some kind of

Robert Aitken rehearsing A Concert of Myths *(1982–83) with the Hong Kong Sinfonietta (conductor, Yeh Tsung), in the Hong Kong City Hall Theatre, September 1996.*

musical representation of another powerful myth, that of Narcissus and Echo. In Jay Macpherson's book about solitude,[2] the sonorous ramifications of that myth struck me—echoes; and mirror reflections, which for musicians are aural phenomena, not just visual. The other great musical myth is the Orpheus myth, and there is a saying that every composer at some time or other writes an Orpheus piece. My plan outlined three movements, each of which would portray a classic myth about music, with the flute as the male protagonist in each.[3] The three myths shared a number of features: each concerned a male–female couple, each entailed a chase sequence, and each ended in a tragic metamorphosis—Syrinx transformed into a reed flute, Narcissus transformed into a flower, Orpheus hacked to bits by the Furies and transformed into an eternal song. Writing a piece of quasi-programmatic music was, I discovered, much like writing an opera. I identified with the stories and the characters. Program music was an outmoded genre, but I reasoned that symphony audiences might find the connection with narrative a handy key to listening, especially when derived from well-known classical sources.

So as not to overshadow the flute, I chose a modest-sized orchestra. There is no percussion, and a keyboard part acts as a foil to the soloist. The keyboardist plays alternately piano, harpsichord, and celeste. The piano provides percussive attacks and adds power to the tuttis, while the harpsichord has a double role as the lute of Orpheus and as a symbol of sinister or menacing elements in all three myths; the celeste's bell tones I associated with destiny, doom, and the supernatural. It turned out to be an ambitious venture; not many works with solo flute last as long (nearly half an hour). Among models, besides the Nielsen work mentioned, I referred to Penderecki's *Fonogrammi* and a flute-and-orchestra treatment of the Orpheus story by a fellow student of my Boulanger years, Thea Musgrave, her *Orfeo II*. Trying to outdo Penderecki in the flute's highest octave, I wrote some impossible passages which I had to ask the soloist to play on the piccolo.

The premiere of *A Concert of Myths* took place in April 1984 in Calgary. Arpad Joo, the conductor, had had the score for several months but at the first rehearsal asked me questions that indicated he had not given it much study. With the arrival of Bob Aitken, the music started to take shape, and the players began to respond more generously. The performance went smoothly, and I felt the audience was receptive. Surprise elements in the music appeared to have an effect: for example, the depiction of the pursuit of Narcissus by Echo where the solo flutist's notes are "echoed" by the orchestral flutist; or the savage scene of the Furies where the upper woodwinds become screeching birds of prey, joined by the soloist on the piccolo. However, in the hush after the sustained ending of the final "Orphic hymn," a loud male "BOO!" resounded in the hall. This mighty negative vote may be preserved on the CBC Radio recording; thank goodness, it was not broadcast. It was followed by applause and a few cheers (from listeners coming to my defence?). I was jolted by the unknown listener's public rebuke, but not really hurt: it meant the music had roused a definite reaction, not indifference. (Love me if you can, hate me if you must: just don't ignore me.) In contrast to this reception, when Aitken and I appeared together at the New Music Festival in Hong Kong in September 1996 (he played both *A Concert of Myths* and his own *Berceuse*), there was an extended ovation. He played superbly, and the performance by the Hong Kong Sinfonietta under Yeh Tsung was on a high level of musical communication. That live rendition of *A Concert of Myths* has since been released on a CD.[4]

In mid-career, I would dream of projects that would be challenging or that corresponded to particular musical interests of mine, and hoped that by mentioning them to performers or prospective commissioning groups I would eventually have a chance to work on them. In April 1983, I took part in a performance of *Keyboard Practice* for the Vancouver New Music Society and shortly afterwards was invited by the Society to write something for a future season. Two of my what-if "dreams" had been recurring. The first was a piece in collage, with a scenario of actions, for combined quintets of brasses and woodwinds—a nonet (the horn would serve in both quintets); or, an alternative way of looking at it, three differently constituted trios. I had gone as far as making a few charts of instrumental combinations and seating arrangements for this. The second was a set of études for my instrument, the piano. It was many years since I had composed anything for piano alone, and what had always fascinated me about the étude genre was the concept of deriving musical expression from the physical movements involved in playing. When I presented these two alternative ideas, the Society chose the second. (I had to wait over a decade before realizing the first, in *Eureka*.)[5]

In the piano parts of the radio collages of the 1960s, and especially in *Keyboard Practice*, I drew freely on many of the new devices such as harmonics, muting, plucked strings, and lid and soundboard attacks, as found in the piano music of composers such as Crumb. For the new work, I decided to confine myself to traditional keyboard idioms, typical of the études I had studied and admired for years, by the likes of Chopin and Debussy. In preparation, I extended my knowledge of the literature by reading earlier and later sets, by Kalkbrenner and Skryabin, among others. My set contained six Études; a further two I withdrew as being of lesser interest. In the first, I remembered William Aide telling me that the toughest demand when he played the cycle of Chopin Études as a sequence was to play the second immediately after the first; the first is based on exaggerated wide stretches of the hand encompassing the whole keyboard, and the second on squirmy motives in semitones where the hand motions are contracted. In my piece I *combine* the two kinds of hand movement; one hand does wide interval skips while the other moves in the tight six-note clusters I had used in *Circle, with Tangents*, with single notes singing out (a sound I liked in the "Night Music" movement of Bartók's *Out of Doors*—I was surprised to find a similar gesture featured in a study from the early 1800s by Kalkbrenner). Clusters are a preoccupation in the final piece in the set as well, this time played with the fists and the forearm. The third étude explores double glissandos in various intervals. Ray Dudley always played the glissando octaves at the end of the *Waldstein* Sonata with great assurance; I could never do them, but could do thirds, fifths, or sixths fairly easily (Ravel uses some of these in *Alborado del grazioso*). The danger with glissandos, I had always felt, was that they could sound banal, either a C major scale (white keys) or a pentatonic one (black); the trick was to throw in a few black keys with the white gliss, or a few white keys with the black, using the non-gliding hand (see illustration).

I was pleased that the Society could persuade Jane Coop, a player I admired, to learn the pieces for the premiere in 1984. Though not a new-music specialist, she penetrated the musical and physical demands of the Études beautifully. The performance was well received, and she later recorded them.[6] It made me happy too that they were taken up by other pianists: Charles Foreman, Mark Widner, Jane Solose, and others. Foreman astonished me by playing them *from memory*, something I wouldn't have thought possible. He played them several times on tour and included them in his remarkable series of solo concerts (1999–2001) devoted to highlights of twentieth-century piano composition. The Études display interrelated variable pitch sets (sets of twelve pitch classes arranged symmetrically with varied interval makeup). Gail Dixon, a University of Toronto graduate in music theory and professor of theory at the University of Western Ontario, wrote a detailed analytical article about them.[7] I loaned her my rough sketches because she wanted to trace the evolution of the pieces, and she pointed out a few places where I had deviated from serial order. Sometimes it was a careless mistake, which I corrected; in other cases it was a deliberate deviation dictated by my ear, which I

The third of the six Études for solo piano (1983) concentrates on glissandos, as shown in this passage from the manuscript.

preferred to leave alone. When Norma Beecroft was considering the Études for a program in the New Music Concerts series, she said to me, "They're *tough*." Well, are solo piano studies supposed to be easy? The NMC performer was the brilliant Mark Widner, who played the set at my retirement party (1990).[8]

Lawrence Cherney, with whom I had been working in the summer series at Sharon, was an active solo oboist. He was preparing for a concert at Queen's University in Kingston with William Aide, and the two of them commissioned me to write a work for their program. The project brought together a number of musical associations. Mieczyslaw Kolinski, an outstanding composer and scholar and a much-valued friend, died in 1981. One of his best-known compositions is for oboe and piano—the *Dahomey Suite*, based on traditional African melodies. This gave me the notion of writing a work in Koli's memory, based on some traditional source. What source? Beverley Diamond, one of my brightest U of T students, produced as her PhD dissertation, under Koli's supervision, a study of dance songs of the Inuit, transcribing a substantial repertoire of examples following research at Pelly Bay in the Canadian Arctic. Beverley has since become an internationally known authority in ethnomusicology. Her transcriptions broke new ground; there had been no serious study of the Inuit repertoire for several decades. I was captivated by the melodies, some of them restricted in pitch content, others surprisingly rich, their rhythms fresh and catchy. Beverley communicated with her informants to ask permission on my behalf, and there seemed to be no objection. Another association as the project grew seems quite illogical: I had often found pleasure in playing the chains of short dances by the Viennese composers of the late-eighteenth and nineteenth centuries, from Mozart to Johann Strauss, especially those of Schubert. I thought of stringing together a number of short dances from Beverley's collection, arranging them for contrast almost in the manner of Schubert (or of Ravel, who imitated Schubert in his *Valses nobles et sentimentales*). In the *Arctic Dances* that resulted, the oboe and the piano often play in an only-loosely-coordinated collage. Cherney and Aide repeated their Queen's premiere (1984) at my retirement party in Toronto in 1990. Cherney toured with the piece, and recorded it with the Montreal pianist Paul Helmer.[9] There have been a number of performances by other oboe-piano teams.

The University of Toronto Alumni Association approached me in the fall of 1984 to write a short brass number to open the installation ceremony of the University's new president, George E. Connell. They had in mind some kind of fanfare. What I produced was a four-minute brass ensemble work exploiting the acoustics of the locale, Convocation Hall. I called it *For Starters*. The available ensemble had eleven instruments, and I made a plan with four trumpets spaced across the fore-stage facing the audience, three trombones in a left balcony, three horns in a right balcony, and a tuba seated in the middle of the hall. Connell was the university's twelfth president; his initials, as musical note names, outline a downward major triad. I based my piece on a symmetrical twelve-tone set starting and ending with triads (G – E – C – C♯ – B – A♯ – G♯ – F♯ – E♭ – D – F – A). The triads could provide intervals for appropriate "calling" and fanfare-like motives, and an affirmative rouser to end with. Professor Connell told me he liked the piece. I reminded him that a nineteenth-century predecessor, the university's second president, John McCaul, was an amateur composer. "They had more time in those days," he said. *For Starters* was repeated in concert several times by the Faculty of Music brass ensemble under Stephen Chenette (conductor of the first performance), and the performance in the CBC Broadcast Centre Atrium conducted by Jukka-Pekka Saraste in 1995 has been released on a CD.[10]

In 1989, when Alex Pauk, conductor of the Esprit Orchestra, a Toronto group devoted exclusively to contemporary repertoire, offered me a commission, I found I had two recurrent "dream" projects for him to choose from. One was a dance-apotheosis akin to Ravel's *La valse* or the *Dance Suite* of Bartók, stimulated by my admiration for those works and by my participation in social dancing (specifically Scottish country dancing). The other was a concerto-like piece where the soloist would move around the stage and the audience space while playing—an "action" scheme applied to a larger ensemble situation than *Taking a Stand* or *Case Study*. Pauk liked the second idea and regarded the proposed solo role as a good opportunity for his first violist, Douglas Perry, with whom I had worked several times. I had already considered using the late-medieval psalm-tone called the *tonus peregrinus* (an allusion to its unstable, "peregrinating," modal shape) as a musical image of the soloist's "peregrinations." The title I had in mind was *Peregrine*, and the pun on Perry's name was accidental.

Perry was interested in the project and gave me valuable advice on viola idioms. To set him apart from the orchestral players, we decided to dress him in a sort of clown suit, and with his tall stature and confident stride he commanded attention. I thought the soloist should have a partner, a follower or shadow, on his travels, as if they were Don Quixote and Sancho Panza, and I chose a percussionist (at the premiere, the player was Michael Coté).[11] As another twist, I called for a second, *scordatura* viola, to be played at certain moments. At the beginning, this "mis-tuned" instrument is on a stand at centre stage. The conductor enters without the solo player, and the music starts. The solo violist is heard in a few off-stage phrases and then comes into view, repeating the same phrases. After discovering the other viola and trying a few snatches on it, he leaves the stage and the orchestra continues to play. Shortly the violist is spotlighted at a stand in the audience or in an aisle of the auditorium, with the percussion soloist in another audience position, also spotlighted. They engage in musical repartee with each other and with the orchestra and then the two of them process forward to the stage. While the percussionist resumes his orchestral position, the solo violist mounts a platform and plays looking down on the orchestra. This inaugurates a gradual departure of the orchestral players (as in Haydn's *Farewell* Symphony). In leaving the stage, the conductor toys with the strings of the abandoned *scordatura* viola. The soloist relaxes, still playing, descends to the vacant first-viola chair, and joins the remaining three players from the orchestra in some quiet quartet music.

The two phrases of the remembered psalm-tone formed an eleven-note series or matrix—a phrase of six notes (B – A – C – B – A – G) followed by another of five (A – E – G – F – E)—binding the musical sequences together like variations. To ensure the viola's audibility in its audience travels, we decided Doug Perry should use a contact microphone. In the climactic "procession" of the two soloists, reminiscent of the trombone march in *Taking a Stand*, I used a strathspey rhythm underlined by the percussionist on tambourine and flexatone. I took pains over the tambourine element, influenced by the playing of my friend George Sawa and his extraordinary collection of Middle Eastern tambourines. I wanted an instrument with more than one set of jangles, and a pattern of interplay between the skin surface and the jangles. Coté found he had to fasten the flexatone to his belt in order to use both it and the tambourine as I imagined them. Robin Elliott interpreted the quartet conclusion as an implied triumph of chamber music over orchestral music, but I had intended no such specific "meaning." The audience response to the Esprit performance was lively and warm; the CBC Radio broadcast recording gives a clear reproduction of it, despite the failure of the battery in Perry's mike. I look back on *Peregrine* as a successful work, but by 2011 there had still been no second performance.

Stephen Young, a musicologist at the University of Tennessee, had developed a specialty in Canadian music and participated in the Institute's "Hello Out There!" conference in 1986. Kathleen and I visited him in Knoxville the following year. Among his several analytical studies of Canadian repertoire is an interesting essay on *Peregrine*, as far as I know never published.[12]

Peregrine whetted my appetite for more orchestral writing. Glenn Buhr, then composer-in-residence with the Winnipeg Symphony Orchestra, had attended its premiere and wanted to suggest me for a commission. The customary procedure in Canada Council commissioning grants was competitive, but if a composer could persuade three or more Canadian orchestras to program his or her proposed new work, the peer-jury process could be bypassed and the commission would be automatic—in effect, the orchestras would be the jury.[13] I began corresponding with orchestral conductors and managers, starting with the Winnipeg and its conductor, Bramwell Tovey. He accepted my idea (perhaps Buhr had recommended me). My old friend Victor Feldbrill was then conductor of the Hamilton Philharmonic Orchestra, and he too responded cordially. I found a third supporter in my hometown, the Victoria Symphony Orchestra and its conductor, Peter McCoppin. Maybe I could now realize my dream of an orchestral dance suite.

Meanwhile other composing opportunities intruded and kept me well occupied, at a moment when I was retiring from my U of T position. Clarice Chalmers (Floyd Chalmers's daughter-in-law) commissioned me to write a work for performance at a reception honouring the Orford Quartet on their twenty-fifth anniversary as U of T quartet-in-residence. With a group of graduate students I had been engaged in research on the college songbook repertoire in Canada, and this motivated me to write a short comic piece incorporating five tunes associated with the university, presenting them in an Ives-like collage (or dream), with a sixth tune, concocted in imitation of the more banal examples, emerging as a climax. I called it *College Airs.* Then the Arraymusic group asked me to write a short work—they specified a "miniature"—for their twentieth-anniversary concert, to be scored for their resident ensemble of clarinet, trumpet, piano, percussion (two players), and double bass. My abstract score seemed to develop from the clarinet part, starting in the bass clarinet and concluding in the high E♭ instrument. It seemed to me to take on narrative qualities through its brief (four-minute) duration, so I gave it the title *Scene.* In 1995, for a Toronto Dance Theatre program, David Earle choreographed the piece under the title "Manhattan Cowboy," and the solo dancer, Andrew Giday, interpreted it effectively and wittily.

I worked on my dance-apotheosis in 1991 and '92, and the first performances in Winnipeg, Hamilton, and Victoria took place the following season, 1992–93. All three orchestras had to approve the instrumentation I proposed. The main "extra" I asked for was an alto saxophone, and this they allowed. There was no objection when I suggested a seating arrangement where the two percussion players would have a more prominent position than normal. I wanted them in some passages to play independently of the rest of the orchestra and in others to in fact *direct* parts of the orchestra, independently of the conductor. In sketching various dance types that attracted me, I remembered a review I had read in some journal in which the author cited a number of works in this genre and commented that evidently no composer had ever done such a compilation using the dance types of the "New World." The suites tended to be of pavanes or waltzes or mazurkas rather than mambos or foxtrots.[14] I decided to take up this point, and looked at a number of models, eventually choosing a *danza puertoriqueña* and a Charleston. The former is a late-nineteenth-century precursor of the tango. I found a large collection of examples for solo piano by the Puerto Rican composer Juan Campos (1857–96) and became captivated by rhythmic details and by their languorous melodic expression. My Charleston model was a piano "novelty number" from the 1920s by Zez Confrey (1895–1971), a composer best known for *Kitten on the Keys*; this one was called *Charleston Chuckles*. Of other dance types I aimed to evoke, some were traditional and some drawn from my imagination.

The suite of six movements is called *Round and Round*. It is more reliant on collage forms than any of my previous orchestral works, and in this respect relates to the orchestral music of Ives, and of his stylistic descendant Henry Brant. In the first movement three kinds of musical formation are set in motion simultaneously: six solo winds pass around a jaunty swing melody, the strings play a continuous fast dance in the background, and the other members of the orchestra (led by the percussionists) interrupt with loud outbursts at unexpected moments.

For the second movement, I took a programmatic approach, depicting almost literally a description by the behaviouralist Konrad Lorenz of the mating "dance" of the Peruvian fighting fish.[15] The pastiche *danza* forms the third movement. In the fourth, the solo saxophone and the timpani have leading roles. The Charleston imitation forms the main part of the fifth movement, and the finale is based on two rhythmic schemes, one an odd 9/8 somewhat resembling the Bulgarian rhythms of Bartók, and the other a mix of 3/4 and 4/4. The raucous ending phrases are terminated by a loud pedal note from the trombone. I strove for contrast, animation, and colour. The melodies derive from a chart of overlapping pentatonic groupings (see illustration, page 228), providing fresh harmonic textures while at the same time permitting familiar musical references—to US swing, and to dances of Scotland and (in the fighting-fish sequence) Bali.

I prefaced the full score with a selection of quotes referring to the spirit of social dancing. I wanted the suite to convey its joy and at the

Page 3 of the manuscript score of Round and Round *(1992). The wind soloists (in 4/4) are independent, and the strings are conducted in a fast 5/8, while the rest of the orchestra interrupts periodically in 2/4, cued by the percussionist.*

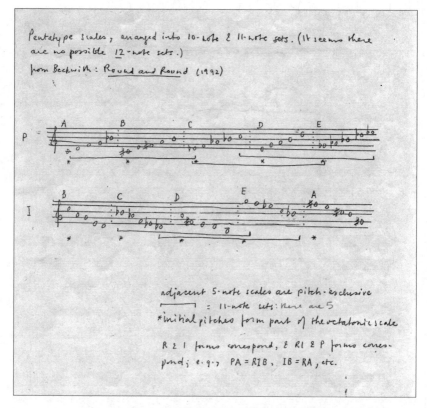

I drew up this chart of the scales used in Round and Round, *apparently for an introductory talk.*

same time its underlying or symbolic seriousness. One of these epigraphs— "Dance with your soul"—is a saying of Jean Milligan, founder of the Royal Scottish Country Dance Society, and the title of her biography.[16]

With the Winnipeg Symphony, *Round and Round* got off to a rocky start. The first rehearsal in October 1993 was scheduled for a Wednesday morning, and I planned to be there. Then it was rescheduled for the Tuesday, when I could not attend. Maestro Tovey discovered difficulties in the parts and put my piece aside to work on other repertoire. Had I been there, I could have solved the problem, but now the piece had to win back the players' confidence. Tovey was supportive and patient, and gradually under his guidance in the later rehearsals it took shape as I had intended and hoped. CBC Radio picked up the performance for a broadcast, and I was fortunate that they also picked up and broadcast (*twice*) the performance a month later by Feldbrill and the Hamilton Philharmonic.[17] In both orchestras the players, mystified at first, ended by accepting the piece and performing it with gusto. It seemed *Round and Round* had won them over despite its notational peculiarities and odd grab bag of dance allusions. In Victoria my experience was similar, but the audience was resistant. At the first of the two Victoria Symphony performances, the final trombone bla-a-at elicited an immediate and very loud BOO! from an offended audience member—was it the same boo(e)r who had greeted *A Concert of Myths* in Calgary? At the second performance, McCoppin addressed the audience before conducting the work, reminding them of Victoria's reputation for tolerance and polite behaviour. The reviewer in the *Times Colonist* evidently agreed with the protester: in his view, *Round and Round* overstayed its welcome and "should more appropriately have been titled *On and On.*"[18] Then there were the listeners who complained that you couldn't dance to this music. Well, it was not meant to be danced to, any more than are the stylized dances of Byrd, Couperin, Bach, Chopin, Ravel, or Juan Campos. It is music *of the dance*, as Guerrero had put it to me years before; much more than the early *Music for Dancing*, it is music that distills the mood of dancing, that perhaps conveys how dancing makes you feel.

I have received (so far) no further commissions for orchestral music, and my existing orchestral repertoire has been accorded only sporadic revisits by Canadian orchestras. In the 1990s my orchestral activity was more as a transcriber than as a composer. In a course called Music Literature, I had introduced graduate students to Bach's *Orgelbüchlein*, having brought back from Paris, years before, a copy of Marcel Dupré's edition, tried to reproduce on the piano the sounds I heard in the recording (on historical organs of northern Europe) by Finn Viderø, and traced in wonderment the flow of the counterpoint and the ingenuity of the musico-verbal symbolism in these miraculous little pieces. When preparing my class presentations, I often noted in my score instrumental colours I heard in the lines. Out of curiosity in spare moments after my Faculty retirement, I began developing these jottings into instrumentations of favourite chorales. My aim was to have the orchestra emulate the typical registrations of the baroque organ rather than to turn the chorales into symphonic pieces. When I had done fifteen chorales, I arranged them in a set and sent copies to a few conductors I thought might be interested. Georg Tintner, music director of Symphony Nova Scotia in Halifax, told me he wanted to program the set.

The performance in 1993 by the Halifax organization touched me deeply. The instrumentation seemed to clarify the pieces, and the players were first-class. Tintner was both agreeable to work with and intensely musical. He had a sharp intellect and authoritative musicianship, but was altogether natural and self-effacing in manner: when we were first introduced, I addressed him as "Maestro," but he protested, "Oh, don't call me 'maestro,' please, I'm not that good!" We became good friends, and with his encouragement I went on to make a second set of transcriptions from the same Bach source, dedicating one of them to him. When we spoke about the *Orgelbüchlein* setting of "O Lamm Gottes, unschuldig," he recalled that he had sung in the *St Matthew Passion* as a member of the famous boys' choir at St Stephen's in Vienna, the Wiener Knabenchor; this melody is quoted in the opening chorus of that work. He was Jewish but sang at St Stephen's? Yes, he said, if you were musical and had a good voice they wanted you. But in choosing that chorale as the one I would transcribe for him, I forgot that when he was a war refugee in New Zealand (where sheep outnumber people) his first job, as a farm worker, left him with an aversion to meat; he became a strict vegetarian. "O Lamm Gottes," indeed! He had a good laugh at my oversight. The performance of the first set was well received, and that of the second set (fourteen chorales) in 1996, again by Tintner and Symphony Nova Scotia, was also successful; both were broadcast by CBC Radio. I felt propelled to transcribe the remaining sixteen chorales of the Bach collection; in due course (February 1999) Tintner programmed this third set in his series and again led with sensitivity. He was in good spirits but, now in his early eighties, had lost some of his stamina and vigour. It was a great shock to discover later that he had been diagnosed with cancer. Later that year, rather than experience the decline of musical abilities and involvements that now seemed in store, Tintner took his own life. I am grateful for having known him and for having had the chance to work with him.

At the time of the 1999 performance of the third *Orgelbüchlein* set, I put together a talk about transcribing Bach for the orchestra, using examples by Reger, Elgar, Respighi, Schoenberg, Webern, Stravinsky, Ernest MacMillan, and Leopold Stokowski, to show different fashions and different approaches.[19] Some of the *Orgelbüchlein* chorales have attracted several transcribers; there must be a dozen of "In dir ist Freude," for example. I can't make the claim with absolute positiveness, but I may be the only musician to transcribe the entire collection (it contains forty-five chorales; Bach originally intended to do many more). Georg Tintner and I had noted that my three sets took a total of about seventy-three minutes in performance, which is approximately the limit of one compact disc. A proposal to his recording firm, Naxos, was turned down.

My transcriptions use a medium-sized orchestra but call for special extras such as alto flute, oboe d'amore, soprano and alto saxophones, Fluegelhorn, tuba, and, in a couple of numbers, a percussionist (for bells). In the titles of the sets, I refer to the pieces as "figural chorales," the term used by Peter Williams in his study of Bach's organ music, avoiding the historically inexact term "chorale-prelude" and distinguishing them from congregational chorale harmonizations.[20] Williams, with whom I corresponded when working on the chorales, is one of the dedicatees. His beautiful performance of about half of the *Orgelbüchlein* at Knox College chapel in Toronto in the mid-1990s was an extra stimulus. Another organ specialist, also a dedicatee, Lucien Poirier, told me my transcriptions had revealed the interplay of lines in Bach's music in a clearer manner than he found possible on the organ.[21] It was a nice compliment but a tribute to Bach more than to me: they're *his* lines; I just thought up ways to present them.

The 1990s and the succeeding decade brought a number of new instrumental-music projects, none of them for conventional chamber-music media. They included a series of pieces involving the harpsichord, a couple of works for percussion ensemble, and the realization of my "dream" of a wind-nonet "action piece."

At the instigation of my friend the guitarist Peter Higham, I composed a duo for guitar and cello based on the twelve-note set of Anton Webern's Opus 33 as found in the fragmentary sketches of that piece, which Webern did not live to finish. The set is exceptional in being almost a pure chromatic scale: the semitone is its most prevalent interval. I modelled my composition on Webern, and its wispy, elusive character led me to title it *After-images, After Webern*. Peter Higham and the cellist Danise Ferguson introduced it in Moncton and Sackville (they both teach at Mount Allison University); their concert in Moncton coincided exactly with the fiftieth anniversary of Webern's death, 15 September 1995. Their performance was released on a CD;[22] other duos have also done the piece.

Another commission around that time came from another Toronto new-music group, Continuum. Like Arraymusic, though more recently formed, this organization was founded by composers and performers who had studied with me, and I had for a few years served on its board. I wrote them a quintet for string trio, piano, and trumpet (or cornet). Somewhat to my surprise, the initial ideas suggested blues harmony, and the last four or five pages turned into a regular classic blues. I used the title *Blue Continuum*. In 1997 I had the pleasure of coaching a student performance of it at the University of Alberta.

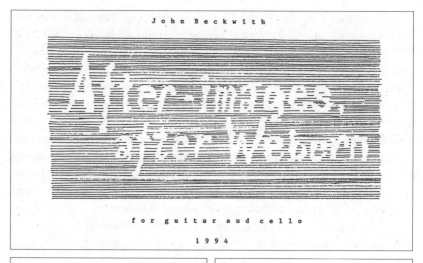

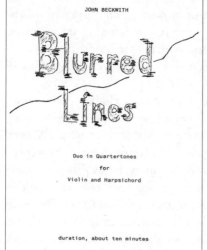

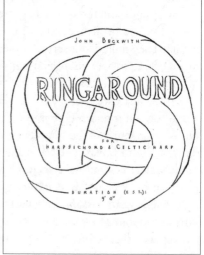

Self-designed title pages of After-images, After Webern *(1994),* Blurred Lines *(1997), and* Ringaround *(1998).*

Lawrence Cherney approached me to write a chamber work including the organ, for a concert in Roy Thomson Hall, and I produced *Echoes of Quesnel* for organ, violin, viola, and English horn. It is based on a short quotation from one of the *ariettes* in Joseph Quesnel's *Colas et Colinette*, North America's first originally composed music-theatre work (Montreal, 1790). The performance had a certain impact, but the piece has not been revived, probably owing to the unlikely instrumentation.

For a concert in Peter Hatch's Open Ears series in Kitchener the same year (1995), I composed another quotation piece, *Echoes of Thiele*, using material from a concert overture for band by the Kitchener bandmaster and composer Charles F. Thiele (1884–1954), who like Quesnel was a notable Canadian musical pioneer. The "echoes" are nostalgic and humorous variations on Thiele's score, in the manner of a crazy quilt. Other observers (Istvan Anhalt for one) had told me that my compositional habits were like quilting, and at the premiere of my work in Kitchener there happened to be an exhibition of quilts in a gallery adjoining the concert hall, so I was moved to make this comparison in an introductory talk about my piece. Choosing from the instrumentation available on the program, I wrote for an octet of oboe, two trumpets, trombone, percussion, viola, cello, and bass. The percussion part functioned as an interrupting element in the turn-of-the-century marching-band atmosphere and reflected my memories of relishing Spike Jones on the radio and on records as a kid. I read a biography of Jones around this time;[23] he seems to have had a nasty reputation, but it was illuminating to discover that he began his career as the sound-effects man in the Fibber McGee comedy series on radio. A popular gag of the series had McGee running to open the door of his untidy cupboard; the ensuing excruciating cacophonies turn out to have been percussion cadenzas by Jones. Obviously the humour in *Echoes of Thiele* veers towards slapstick.

Recalling my brass ensemble work, *For Starters*, I had from time to time thought of expanding it. To gather eleven players for this occasional piece, four minutes in duration, was impractical given its fairly complex demands. In 1994–95, I sketched two more movements with the idea of making a three-movement suite using the same spatial layout. I called these new movements "Mid-Riff" and "Wrap-up," and chose *Three Brass Rings* as an overall title. All three "rings" employ the same twelve-note series. At the time, under pressure of other projects, I was only partially satisfied and put the new scores away in a drawer, unfinished. It was not until 2008 that I looked at them again, revised and completed them, and approached performers who might be interested. Gillian MacKay conducted a first performance with players of the University of Toronto Wind Symphony in January 2009.

New Music Concerts planned a program in 1996 highlighting my music as I approached my seventieth birthday and commissioned me to compose something new for the occasion. I showed Bob Aitken the graph-paper charts and sketches I had shelved more than a decade earlier when "dreaming" about a brass and woodwind nonet. He was game to try it, so I began work on what turned out to be a major peregrination and collage exercise. There would be three clumps of chairs and stands on the stage, three in each clump (one on the level and two slightly raised), with distance between the clumps. As the piece progressed, the performers would migrate from clump to clump, forming a variety of spatially varied acoustic relationships. As in my previous works of this type—*Taking a Stand*, *Keyboard Practice*, and the rest—I would have to compose music that would suggest reasons for the moves. The lights would go up on a solo bassoon, and would fade at the end on an unlikely duo of oboe and tuba; in between, the players would have precise exits and entrances, dictated by the character of the musical moment. It was a complicated plan; I had to imagine the paths each player would follow and the successive partners with whom he or she would coordinate musically in the course of the piece. A certain amount of memorization would be called for. It was the sort of musical problem solving I greatly enjoyed. I worked with an interesting all-interval set of thirteen pitches in which each of the six interval types appears twice.

I titled the work *Eureka*—not in the sense of a surprising discovery but first simply because I liked the word and second because I had just read a strange, long poem by Edgar Allan Poe with that title, a futurist vision.[24] Aitken had arranged for a generous amount of rehearsal time, and he and I coached the players (he played the flute part; the others were almost all from the Toronto Symphony Orchestra). *Eureka* was the concluding work on a program consisting of *After-images, After Webern*, the Quartet, and a new composition by my former pupil Alice Ping-Lee Ho. The concert, held in the Glenn Gould Studio, was broadcast by the CBC. As with many first performances, this one was very good but less than definitive—and less than a full realization of what I thought the work could convey. I was therefore especially pleased when we were able to revive it in 2010 for

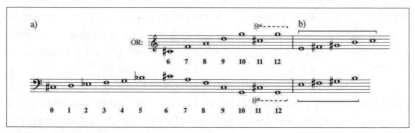

Example 5: Eureka (1996) is based on a thirteen-note set, shown (a) in its two forms, and a "corollary" (b) consisting of the remaining four or five pitches of the chromatic scale.

another New Music concert, this time in Walter Hall. The performers were a mix of Faculty of Music and TSO players (some were veterans of the premiere; for others the piece was new), and we had again the broadcast involvement of the CBC. The result was closer to the ideal I carried in my head.

In 1996 I began a correspondence with the Montreal harpsichordist Vivienne Spiteri. She was interested in Glenn Gould's recordings and writings, and, hearing that I had known Glenn, wrote me concerning my remembrances of him. Her letters were always thoughtful and detailed. I gathered that she was a musician with serious attitudes and views. We didn't always agree, but the arguments always turned out to be lively. It was a year or more before we actually met, by which time we were already on friendly terms. In one of our early exchanges she had wondered whether I would be interested in composing for her instrument. I told her of my previous attempts involving the harpsichord, among which she knew *Circle, with Tangents* through the recording. She was a harpsichordist who specialized in modern repertoire, who in fact played *only* modern repertoire; a number of composers had written pieces for her. She wanted, she said, to combine the harpsichord with another plucked-string instrument—would I consider writing a duo?

After tossing around several possible partners for her instrument, we agreed on the banjo (her first choice anyway). I loved the sound, and imagined it as a strong contrast to the harpsichord. Terry McKenna, the guitar and lute player with whom I had worked several times, steered me to the recordings of Bela Fleck and the Flecktones, as examples of banjo treatments merging with modernism, and I explored the bluegrass repertoire through recordings of Earl Scruggs and others. Craig Donovan loaned me his five-stringed banjo, and I tried out elementary patterns with the beginners' manual of Pete Seeger as a guide. My duo would have to proceed largely in dialogue if I wanted an effective acoustic relationship of the two instruments. A continuity of overlaps and interruptions, by now a habitual part of my composing, would also be appropriate. In fact, I titled the resulting work *Lines Overlapping*. A bluegrass vamping pattern characterizes the banjo in the opening and closing sections. The central part of the piece has a kind of song-and-dance shape: the banjo interrupts the harpsichord's cantilena with brief, sharp interjections ("overlapping"), after which they reverse roles; at a high-tension point, they join in a peppy dance, before the vamping fade-out.

There were problems getting this work into performance. Terry McKenna said he couldn't spare the time to learn both the instrument and the piece. Neither Vivienne nor I knew any banjo players, and when we started investigating we found that not all of the leading professionals were used to playing from conventional score notation. An experienced and well-known senior player, Don Steele, living in semi-retirement in Toronto, agreed to work on *Lines Overlapping*, coached by me. His performance with Vivienne at the Music Gallery in Toronto in 1997 was courageous and conveyed much of the essence of the piece, though under tempo and lacking in detail. Later, the versatile Kirk Elliott, who plays and composes for a vast variety of string and wind instruments, mastered the banjo part, performed it with Vivienne in both Toronto and Montreal, and eventually recorded it with her.[25]

Bruce Mather was among the composers who had written new works for Vivienne, and, in conformity with most of his later music, his solo, *Saumur*, employed microtones: in it, the two manuals of the harpsichord are tuned a quarter-tone apart. Having been attracted to, and slightly involved with, microtonal writing in *The Hector* in 1990, I took up his example and produced *On the Other Hand ...: Four Quarter-Tone Studies*. In her Music Gallery concert, Vivienne introduced both Mather's work and mine. No one had observed that while in my Studies the upper manual is a quarter-tone sharper than the lower, in the Mather the micro-tuning is the opposite; retuning in the middle of the concert was not practical, so we had to use two different instruments. The title of my work is a reference to the sometimes intricate hand positions required by the microtonal textures—for example, in passages where the two hands play on the two manuals in the same octave (the *pièce croisée* of the French *clavecinistes*, a procedure impossible to reproduce on the piano). Vivienne included my Studies in her double-disc CD album, *the door in the wall....*[26]

I had always avoided writing for the combination of piano with a solo stringed instrument. I cherished the classical violin-piano and cello-piano sonata literatures, but found in contemporary live performances that the disparity of volume between the two instruments gave an acoustically unsatisfactory result—especially when, starting in the 1990s, pianists (intent on "collaborating") opened the grand piano fully instead of using its short stick—a mistake, in my opinion. But to combine a violin with a harpsichord appealed to me. Vivienne loaned me a recording from Sweden of the "Hardanger fiddle," and I became intrigued by its nasal tone and the long, melodic phrases of its special brand of mourning music. The tuning in this nineteenth-century Scandinavian tradition is different from that of the normal concert violin. I wrote a duo with the harpsichord manuals again tuned a quarter-tone apart and the violin tuned to one of the Hardanger tunings and playing also in quarter-tones, and I called it *Blurred Lines*. The two instruments support each other's quarter-tone wailings with a contrast of perfect fifths, sustained for the violin, *tremolando* for the harpsichord. My son Lawrence, with whom I have for years played the duo sonatas of Mozart and Beethoven, performed *Blurred Lines* with Vivienne in a concert at Bishop's University in Lennoxville, and later in Toronto, and they have recorded it.[27]

Responding to Vivienne's interest and to her remarkable presence in live performances, I added another duo to this group of compositions, this time for harpsichord and Celtic harp. Performers prefer the more precise designations "lever harp" or "non-pedal harp." In my opera *Taptoo!* I had used it as a quiet contrast to all the military brass and percussion sounds, preferring it to the concert harp with pedals. With the latter, the pedals adjust the tuning of all octaves identically (at a given moment, all Cs are either flat, natural, or sharp, as are all Ds, all Es, and so on), whereas the non-pedal instrument has individual tuning tabs or levers for each string, permitting different octaves to be tuned differently (G$\sharp$ in one octave, G$\natural$ in another, for example)—a compositional advantage. My work, called *Ringaround*, is bright and jig-like, in contrast to the elegiac *Blurred Lines*. It has been performed in concert and recorded by Vivienne Spiteri with Sharlene Wallace.[28] This time Bruce Mather picked up the idea from me and wrote *Sancerre* for the same duo.

Udo Kasemets turned eighty in 1999, and I wanted to write him a piece commemorating our long friendship, which dates from his arrival from Europe in the early 1950s. I conceived a brief "domestic symphony" for an ensemble of percussionists, to be played on pot lids, wine glasses, and stainless-steel mixing bowls of various sizes, with plastic swizzle sticks and wooden spoons. The score is a coloured chart drawn on graph paper in eighty squares. I called this piece *A Game of Bowls*. As in many of Udo's own works, the duration and the coordination of parts are flexible considerations. Years before (1962), he had dedicated a game-piece to me, called *Squares*. The University of Toronto Percussion Ensemble, directed by Robin Engelman, presented my piece in one of their concerts and included it in a CD recording.[29]

Rehearsals with them, and encouragement from Engelman, started me thinking about another percussion-ensemble work. The result, in 2001, was *Workout*. The title refers to a further stimulus, my Pilates classes with Elaine Biagi Turner. I thought of a series of short percussion pieces based on the Pilates exercises. I often kidded Elaine that there should be something more musical to keep up the exercise momentum than a singsongy "one-two, one-two ..." *Workout,* dedicated jointly to Elaine and Robin Engelman, was introduced by the U of T Ensemble in December 2001.

This period brought a number of occasions for birthday tributes—to my granddaughter Alison (age one) in 1998, to Robert Aitken and Francess Halpenny (as well as to Kasemets) in 1999, and to my two sisters in 2003 and 2005 respectively. In 2001 John Weinzweig celebrated his eighty-eighth birthday. His birthdate (11 March) being two days away from mine (9 March), we sometimes celebrated together on the 10th, and he and his wife Helen joined with other friends at our house for this occasion. I played a new work I had composed for him, a suite of four short pieces for the piano—the instrument with eighty-eight keys. I called it *March, March!* An eleven-note series goes through a number of manipulations in complementary twenty-two- and forty-four-note patterns. One of the pieces, "Single File," calls for all eighty-eight keys to be struck, one at a time, with no repetitions. The final number is a rag, eighty-eight bars long, based on the earliest Canadian ragtime solo, *A Rag Time Spasm* (1899) by W.H. Hodgins.

Opportunities arose to compose for other non-standard media, besides the banjo and the Celtic harp: Would you believe Highland pipes and microtonal piano? A concert work combining the pipes with standard "indoor" orchestral instruments had been on my "dream" list for over a decade but always drew a negative response when I proposed the idea to conductors. The instrument's long and proud musical tradition and the high standing achieved by several Canadian pipers in international contests were persuasive arguments, I thought, but they failed to convince others. It rankled that Peter Maxwell Davies's *Orkney Wedding* (1985) was enjoying repeated performances—a short character piece purportedly for orchestra and solo piper, in which however the soloist appears (in costume) in the final two or three minutes only. In 2003 New Music Concerts planned a concert marking three birthdays—Weinzweig's ninetieth, Harry Freedman's eightieth, and (a year late) my seventy-fifth. The program would consist of one early work by each of us, and one brand-new work from each, commissioned for the occasion. My proposal of a work for Highland pipes, string ensemble, and percussion, was accepted. I dug out my notes from our Scottish program at Sharon in the '80s, consulted with David Waterhouse, an experienced piper and a scholar of the repertoire, read up on the instrument's history, and listened to recordings with the peculiarly notated scores in front of me. James MacGillivray, our piper at Sharon, had pointed out the distinction between the light repertoire of dance pieces and marches and the grand tradition of the *Piobaireachd* or "pibroch." The latter is the core of serious piping—an ornate variational form in slow time sometimes lasting more than half an hour. The typical pibroch is a ritual lament. Some of the examples I examined struck me as similar to Indian *ragas* in their cumulative formal design. Years before, for his graduation recital at the Faculty of Music, a percussion major, Peter Magadini, had joined a piper in a classic pibroch, and its impact had remained with me. I called my piece *A New Pibroch*. Michael Grey, one of the most prominent Canadian solo pipers, undertook to advise me and to play the solo part at the concert. He agreed, at my request, to appear in ordinary concert dress, not in his usual kilt; despite its indebtedness to a Scottish musical genre, I wanted the piece to be listened to as a piece of music, not an ethnic exhibition.

In *A New Pibroch*, the percussionist supports the pipes with a regular pulsing drumbeat, varying the tempo from variation to variation. The combination is traditional, necessitated by the lack of accent or attack in the pipes. The piper makes up for this to some extent by stressing main notes in the melody line with rapid ornamentation; but the drums are a virtually indispensable boost. Another characteristic of the instrument, compared to many others, is the absence of dynamic variety: it plays at one volume level (loud). I decided to compensate for this by having the player move offstage for one of the variations. As a contrast to the severity of the pibroch, my work incorporates brief snippets of Scottish fiddle music (fragments of a familiar reel, played first by the violins and later on the pipes). The piper's exit and re-entrance are precipitated in the music by a series of "weird" effects (temple blocks, double-bass glisses) interrupting the formality of the pibroch. The Highland pipes have a scale of only nine notes, and the tuning differs from conventional equal temperament. The "A" is more than a quarter-tone sharp compared to A=440. I chose strings for the accompaniment with the idea that they could tune their instruments to the piper's scale and match his intervals. In several passages they amplify the drone of the pipes, in different octaves but conforming in pitch. In the introduction, before the pipes are heard, there is a kind of string evocation of the pipes.

I got special musical satisfaction from this experience. Aitken conducted the ensemble, and Michael Grey and the percussionist Trevor Tureski both delivered their parts with skill and resourcefulness. Advance fears that the strings might be overpowered by the pipes proved exaggerated. *Piper and Drummer* magazine gave the new piece a rave review. The concert was broadcast by CBC Radio, but so far (2011) there is no recording. I dedicated *A New Pibroch* to the memory of Harry Somers, who died in 1999. I had always treasured both his music and his personal friendship.

Vacationing in Santa Fe in 2006, I thought of developing a phrase from an earlier work. The phrase is sung by the mezzo-soprano, Agatha, shortly after the start of *Crazy to Kill*, to Reaney's words: "Oh, silence— a silence more fearful than the loudest noise" (see example 6). I imagined it on the clarinet and sketched an elaboration for a *quartet* of clarinets. Later I added two more movements, varying the colour now and then with passages for E♭ and bass clarinets. The result was a more substantial chamber work than I had at first intended. I called it *Back to Bolivia*. Many musicians recognized this title as the spine identification on the second of the twenty volumes of *The New Grove Dictionary of Music and Musicians*. For that memorable volume, alphabetical order dictated entries on composers (Bartók, Bellini, Berg, Berlioz, Bizet, Boccherini), places (Berlin, Birmingham, Bolivia), and musical topics (bassoon, bluegrass); and—modest cough—there are even a few paragraphs on *me*. Assembling the quartet of performers took time and patience. *Back to Bolivia* was first played in 2010 in a concert of various of my wind ensemble compositions presented by New Music Concerts and the Faculty of Music.

In a visit to Bruce Mather in Montreal some time in the early 2000s, I was impressed when he played me a recording of his recent studies for the Carrillo piano. This highly original keyboard music fascinated me. Bruce had embraced microtonal composition some years before, as a result of meeting one of its pioneers, the Russian Ivan Wyschnegradsky, and in time became an exponent of Wyschnegradsky's music. Another pioneer in the early twentieth century, the Mexican Julián Carrillo, had invented microtonal keyboard instruments including a piano tuned in sixteenth tones. Rare examples of this "Carrillo piano" were starting to be cultivated by pianists in France and Germany and roused Bruce's creative and performing interests. Awarded a large cash prize in 2000, he decided

Example 6: In Back to Bolivia *(2006) I quote a line sung unaccompanied by Agatha in* Crazy to Kill.

to purchase this piano and establish it in Montreal (a firm in Germany custom-makes the instrument). With the piano available at the Conservatoire, several Montreal composers accepted his invitation to compose for it, and Bruce organized concerts to introduce their pieces. The instrument has ninety-seven keys, sixteen in each of its six whole tones, plus one to complete the octave. The strings are of almost uniform length, and are strung vertically. The closeness of pitch of the strings makes for a "roar" of mixture tones in some combinations. Ordinary scale patterns have an extraordinary rippling effect resembling, I thought, a swarm of insects, or a sigh, or a shiver. Conventional intervals demand great stretches—a whole tone covering what on the normal piano would be a major tenth. Bruce gave me a notation chart indicating the pitches produced by the keys as a pianist would be accustomed to regard them: there is no notation specific to the instrument. He encouraged me to think about composing for it.

The only restriction I found musically disadvantageous was the confinement to one octave in the middle range (the ninety-seven notes start at the normal piano's middle C and end at the C an octave higher). I conceived a chamber-music combination: the Carrillo piano together with a string quartet. Working on this project at my piano, with Bruce's chart in front of me, involved a lot of calculation, of a kind that was totally new to me. I aligned the quartet with the piano by having two of its players tune a quarter-tone higher than the others and by exploiting this difference. My score centres on repetitions of a simple melody first in whole tones, then in half-tones, one and a half tones (that is, minor thirds), and quarter-tones, each time with embellishments in the piano's smaller intervals. Scales in those smaller intervals (three-eighth-, quarter-, eighth-, and sixteenth-tones) appear as counterpoints to some of the string passages. I called my work *Fractions*. The pianist's opening and closing gestures reminded me of the standard pictographs on elevators for "open door" and "close door," although I didn't think of this when devising them: the goal of the opening scales is the C octave at the ends of the keyboard (the player's arms stretch wide), whereas the goal of the reverse-direction scales at the end is the middle note of the instrument, F♯ (the pianist's arms converge).

Another birthday! *Fractions* was first performed in Bruce Mather's Toronto concert, in the New Music Concerts series, in April 2007, shortly after I turned eighty. The performance, with my friends of the Accordes Quartet and Mather as solo pianist, brought a glow. We all sat with the audience for birthday cake afterwards. Writing in *The Globe and Mail*, Ken Winters called my piece "vintage Beckwith." In 2009, with Paul

Helmer, Bruce introduced in Montreal my *Light Work* for four-handed Carrillo piano ("many hands make *Light Work*").

What, over the years, have been my compositional habits? Starting with my first serial pieces in the 1950s, I found it productive to consider (often in formal charts) the four aspects of a given set of intervals, whether twelve or five or thirty-five. Whatever the "prime" or "original" set may be, it retains its essential identity when delivered upside-down, backwards, or upside-down *and* backwards. With students, I used to illustrate this by holding up a common object—a piece of cutlery, a file folder—from these four angles. I soon found analogous four-sided ways of treating volume and tempo: phrases could be loud getting softer, soft getting louder, soft getting louder and then softer again, or loud getting softer and then louder again; or could proceed fast getting slower, slow getting faster, slow getting faster and then slower again, or fast getting slower and then faster again. Examples occur from *Circle, with Tangents* on. In the Quartet and in *Case Study*, many phrases unfold in long note values becoming rapid ones and then long ones again. As early as the second of the Four Songs to Poems by e.e. cummings, I liked doubling a melody almost but not quite all in octaves, avoiding the obvious by varying it in one of the parts, perhaps an unconscious recollection of campfire songs or congregational hymns where not all the voices are quite together or on the exact same pitches. Again, both *Circle* and the Quartet provide instances of this, as do later works. The tips I used to pass on to composition students, as described in an article of the 1980s,[30] often apply to my own composing behaviour. They consist of basic questions to ask oneself about the treatment of pitch continuity, rhythmic values, characteristic idioms, and the shaping of phrases, and also about such fundamental considerations as communicative intentions (are you engaging in a musical argument or spinning musical patterns?).

In metrical groupings and in phrasing, I have used irregular, randomly selected groups of from two to seven or more time units. Successions of prime numbers (from two to twenty-three or more) occur in the Quartet and elsewhere, even as late as the third movement of *Back to Bolivia*. Two indispensable tools have been a metronome and a stopwatch. My indications of tempo and my timings are not infallible, but they help give my work precise shape.

Cézanne, a master of visual composition, considered a broken line to be more interesting than a continuous one. My music often proceeds as a series of interruptions; I seem to like abrupt changes of direction, the broken line leading the listener to wonder what will happen next. Parody and quotation are typical of much new music in the mid- to late-twentieth century, and this is one trend I have subscribed to.

"Avoid clichés" was one of my precepts for students, and for my own composing. You ask yourself, how can I make this piece sound new and original, rather than repeating what has already been heard over and over? On the other hand, some past modes of expression were still not exhausted, had not yet become clichés. Karel Husa, accused of "reverting" to the techniques of Schoenberg's First Chamber Symphony, op. 9, defended his choice by saying that the implications of Schoenberg's findings in that important early-twentieth-century work had been insufficiently explored. I regarded this as one of many illustrations that innovations in musical language don't erase their predecessors but rather are cumulative and remain available to composers whether dictated by fashion or not. The theorist Joseph Straus, in an article of 2008, usefully traced the "myths" surrounding twentieth-century serialism in its various US manifestations, pointing out that it remains an available technical resource for composers.[31] The same could be said for the chance operations of the Cage circle, seen in the 1960s as the obverse of serialism and then, like serialism, spurned by the fashion-mongers of the generation that came after. In a posthumously published memoir, George Rochberg describes his rejection of his early serial compositions in favour of a return to the European tradition, especially as represented in the late music of Beethoven.[32] Key works in this dramatic turnabout are his Third Quartet and the Violin Concerto written for Isaac Stern. Rochberg takes strong issue with the views of Straus in an early article by the latter.[33] Significantly, Rochberg did not destroy or disown his serially based works. As with many other issues, I came to take a middle-of-the-road position, refraining from an all-or-nothing adherence to this or that camp, and using in each compositional project the technical tools and technical approaches that seemed appropriate. For Arnold Schoenberg, twelve-tone writing was a technique or method, not a system to be followed rigidly. He often said there were still fresh tunes to be discovered in C major.

In works with words, especially in operas, my habits are not so much influenced by considerations derived from serialism and other aspects of the modern vocabulary. There are even fairly traditional tonal passages such as the finales of my first two operas. Like many composers, going back at least as far as Lully, I think of how orators and actors deliver lines; their imagined inflections and dramatic emphases occupy the centre of musical thinking more than any other technical aspects.

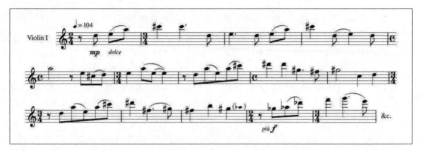

Example 7: This violin theme, from the Variations *(2011) for string orchestra, bears an unintended resemblance to my early* Montage *(see example 1, page 194).*

In managing musical form, whether the piece lasts three minutes or half an hour, I tend to distinguish between "music" and "non-music"—as in my observation have many composers of the past. The non-music is a deliberately bizarre or disjointed kind of continuity maintaining interest during a transition between one revelation of (as it were) "character" or "plot" and another, or, say, between one texture and another. There is often a slump section, a kind of musical Slough of Despond, somewhere past the halfway point, though I seldom consciously plan this; the Quartet, *Keyboard Practice*, and a late piece like *A New Pibroch* offer typical examples of many that could be mentioned.

Some habits are innate; some features "just happen." The clarinet melody of my first orchestral piece, *Montage*, has a similar contour and tempo to the theme of a much later work, the Variations for string orchestra, completed in January 2011 (see example 7, above). I can't explain that. The Variations are a reminder that many of my instrumental pieces proceed in variational form. I can't explain that either.

12

Operas

I n my early teens I became an opera buff through listening to the live
radio broadcasts every Saturday morning from the Metropolitan in
New York.[1] I subscribed to *Opera News* and, with its illustrations in
front of me, would try to visualize the performance I was hearing. Occasionally I borrowed a vocal score from the public library and followed it
while listening. Opera was a special medium, and the Met was a special
company, or so the unctuously voiced announcements told you (Milton
Cross, Edward Johnson, and those New York society women with their
upper-crust accents, Mrs August Belmont, Mrs DeWitt Peltz, and the rest).
The singing was marvellous, and the standard repertoire was a musical
storybook full of riches. Once I even wrote a fan letter to Kirsten Flagstad,
promising her I would one day compose an opera. This adolescent dream
episode came into my memory in 2007 when I heard Tan Dun confess to
an interviewer that he had often fantasized writing an opera for Plácido
Domingo—little imagining, etcetera—but here was the Met premiere of
his *The First Emperor*, starring none other than Domingo. Experience
has made me a skeptic on the star system and on the notion that opera's
specialness is associated with class.

My love of the medium was deepened through involvements in the
inaugural seasons of the Canadian Opera Company in the late 1940s,
before it assumed that name. I was a rehearsal pianist for Gluck's *Orfeo*,
Herman Geiger-Torel's first show on his appointment as stage director.
As publicity officer for the Royal Conservatory, I designed flyers and
wrote news releases and program synopses for the earliest productions
in Eaton Auditorium and the Royal Alexandra Theatre. In the early 1950s
I again served as coach and *répétiteur*, when among my assignments was

a *Così fan tutte* with Mary Morrison, Sylvia Grant, Jon Vickers, and Don Garrard.

Furthering my ambition to compose an opera, I had the great good luck to find a librettist—a writer who understood music. James Reaney shared my love of opera, and early in our friendship in student days we spoke of perhaps collaborating on an original work. In early 1953 I received from him a draft of *Night Blooming Cereus*. This one-act opera he imagined taking shape as a sort of southern Ontario miracle play. It turned out to be the first of four operatic works we produced together over succeeding decades, alongside about a dozen other words-and-music ventures that could be termed semi-operatic. This output has been a central concern of my creative life and I recognize how much I owe to Jamie for the stimulus of these pieces and for their focus on Canadian images and issues, a significant influence in other areas of my work.[2]

My decoration for the title page of the piano/vocal score of Night Blooming Cereus *(1958).*

Composing an opera, even a one-act opera, is a commitment of time. In the 1950s I was under pressure from income-producing work, and there were no opera commissions, so I worked slowly and in spare moments. Completing the first of *Night Blooming Cereus*'s three scenes, I wrote to Reaney (then living in Winnipeg) that the libretto needed trimming; it was getting too long. I also asked him for more metrical variety. He obliged with revisions, and I plowed ahead with the second scene, again working at it only when time permitted. On turning thirty, I complained in a letter to Marvin Duchow of how long the opera was taking: "I didn't expect it to become a 'life's work,'" is how I remember expressing my frustration. In 1958 I decided to risk taking the whole summer off. With my young family I went to Victoria for a couple of months and concentrated on composing the remaining (longer) scene and writing out the orchestration. Pamela and I played and sang the whole score to a group of friends just before we left to return to Toronto.

Night Blooming Cereus calls for eight singers and an instrumental ensemble of fourteen players, and lasts about sixty minutes. The dimensions, scaled down from the requirements of the grand opera stage, resembled those of the operas Benjamin Britten was then composing for his English Opera Group. The image of the flower that blooms once a year—or by poetic licence once a century—stands for human hope and renewal. The central character is an aging and lonely widow, and the central scene a fifteen-minute cycle of songs depicting aspects of her domestic routine. On the face of it, these are unpromising features for operatic potential.[3] When Herman Geiger-Torel read the libretto he said of Mrs Brown's solo scene, "I can't stage it." My readings of the score for other possible producers received polite comments but no offers of performance, until one day the music supervisor of CBC Radio, Geoffrey Waddington, expressed interest in "commissioning" the work *ex post facto*. It was written for stage performance, but the chance to assemble singers and players for a studio broadcast was irresistible. With the commission money I bought my family's first automatic washing machine.

The broadcast, in April 1959, received a good response from listeners[4] and critics, and Waddington decided to repeat it the following year, with more or less the same cast of singers.[5] This suggested that we could venture on a stage production, counting on the radio rehearsals to save us time and money. "We" refers to a group of interested friends who formed a support committee and volunteered to help with management, publicity, props, and lighting. Among its members were my old piano teacher Ogreta McNeill, Gordon Jocelyn, William Toye, Mollie Thom, Wallace Russell, and Margaret Gayfer. The conductor (Ettore Mazzoleni), singers, orchestra members, and stage crew would be under professional contract. The Canada Council approved one of its first opera production grants, and I chipped in my accumulated earnings as *Toronto Daily Star* columnist and reviewer. We hired Hart House Theatre for two evenings. The program would need augmenting, so we decided to use my Five Pieces for Brass Trio as a kind of opening fanfare, and Jamie would come from Winnipeg to perform his own *One-Man Masque*. Pamela undertook to direct the opera. For its costume and set designs, we approached the young painter Louis de Niverville, whose fantasy figures and landscapes had features in common with Reaney's literary style and indeed with Reaney's own paintings and drawings. Niverville welcomed the challenge, although it was his first experience of theatre; like the rest of the team, he didn't seem to mind working for no fee. Toye designed an elegant flyer to advertise the event, now titled *An Evening with James Reaney and John Beckwith*, using motives from Niverville's sketches.

The two performances almost sold out, but not quite. The audiences were an interesting mix of theatrical, musical, and literary publics. Jamie's relatives from Stratford brought their baby, and Mavor Moore, reviewing the production for the *Evening Telegram*, escorted the English film star Joan Greenwood, visiting Toronto for a television appearance. The reviews were also a mix: the *Star* sent both Udo Kasemets for music and Robert Fulford for theatre, the former being enthusiastic and the latter curious and culturally engaged; Moore was also enthusiastic; however, John Kraglund's piece in *The Globe and Mail* was not only negative but venomous (a letter to the editor a few days later found malice in it). Geiger-Torel was generous in his backstage congratulations to Pamela; indeed, as devised by her and sung and played by Patricia Rideout, the second-scene solo, which he had declared impossible, was transfixing. Jamie's stage direction at the end of the "Dishwashing Song" had proved unhelpful: "the dishwater is somehow disposed of"; but, as Rideout slowly drained real water into the little stage sink, gesture, text, and music conveyed a draining of her heart. Kraglund ridiculed the blooming of the cereus: Louis de Niverville had designed the plywood cactus with an invisible hook, and at the climactic moment the singers crowded round, hiding the plant from the audience's view, while one of them hung a glowing white bloom on it, also obviously made of plywood.[6] It was in keeping with the homespun quality of the show and was greeted with laughter—*friendly* laughter; it's always obvious in the theatre when laughter is *un*friendly.

My music for *Night Blooming Cereus* was mostly based on the rhythms I heard in speaking Jamie's words out loud. In the several revivals of the opera, audiences have often remarked that most of the text comes across clearly. It is an approach I have tried to maintain in subsequent operas. The pace and accent of spoken English, with appropriate dramatic emphasis, are not, in my experience, any barrier to musical expression.[7] I tried to distinguish the various characters by musical traits—long melody lines, touched with sentiment, for Alice and Mrs Brown; jerky, uneven lines for Mrs Wool and the two Girls and young Ben. I tried to bear in mind that they were rural Canadian types rather than courtesans or potentates. When Mr Orchard agrees to join in the singing of a hymn, his vocal line for "Yes, we'll sing it now the train is out of town" echoes the familiar song "She'll be coming round the mountain when she comes." (It was only later, on reading Milton Wilson's review, that this character's possible supernatural stature dawned on me: from the locale of his nursery, "Sunfish Lake," Wilson figured Mr Orchard was God.) I omitted the horn from the wind-instrument complement of the small orchestra, despite its time-honoured use for operatic accompaniment by Verdi and others, in favour of a single, snarly trombone. The trombone and the lone trumpet supply a third and a fifth respectively to the unison of all the other instruments in the opera's concluding major triad. At the start there is no overture, only a one-bar instrumental outburst, identified in Pamela's production as the giggling of the Girls. The two hymns—one sung as a solo to her own harmonium accompaniment by Mrs Brown, and the other by the assembled characters gathered beside the cereus, "to encourage it to blossom"—presented a challenge, and I can recall rewriting both of them several times to get the appropriate North American evangelical tone. Some years later I made a choral arrangement of Mrs Brown's "Houses in Heaven,"[8] which has had a fair number of performances.

Peddling the score to various prospective producers in 1959, I had imagined it might interest the University of Toronto opera school, but the response was that it was too difficult for any college workshop. In succeeding years it has been mounted with student casts at McGill, the University of Western Ontario, and the University of Victoria. Mrs Brown's solo scene has occasionally been given in concert—sometimes with the title "A Domestic Song Cycle," conferred on it by Milton Wilson when he published the text in the *Canadian Forum*.[9]

Jamie wrote his own account of our "Evening,"[10] of which his remarkable performance of *One-Man Masque* was such a unique component.

Returning to Winnipeg after the performances in Toronto, he wrote to Pamela and me:

> I remember thinking as I watched [*Night Blooming Cereus*] on Wednesday pm and trying to be detached—how very unusual all this is—I've never heard anything quite like this before. I must somehow get enough money together to buy all of the farm & build a little theatre for opera etc. on it & have a Bayreuth. That would really be something to look forward to say when we're all about 80 of course. I also go back to the day I got going on the libretto & think how brave you were to take the challenge up.[11]

The novelty of *Cereus*, I think, is its combination of homely, mystical, and humorous elements. It exhibits the shortcomings of a first opera: an overlong and over-careful exposition; a static plot where most of the action is retrospective. My music tries to delineate character, and offers variety, but has too many reflective pauses. If we decide to embark on another opera, I said to Jamie, let's make it a fast comedy with a pratfall every minute. He responded with a draft scenario for *The Shivaree*. This concept struck me then, and still does now, as a fresh and original story, veering between black comedy and farce, and ideal for operatic treatment. I feel extremely fortunate to have been able to compose for it.

Jamie prefaced his draft by explaining the term "shivaree":

> *Punch* spells it Charivari but it's an old Ontario custom—from Quebec evidently—that on bridal night bridal pair are serenaded by local rustic buffoons with musical buzz-saws, rattles, clappers, tin cans, lids, horns and drums until the husband gives them enough money to go away and leave him alone. The money is used to buy beer and the whole affair smacks of ancient rites. My mother and father were so serenaded and one of my earliest memories is the hired man in 1929 (fall) asking me for my toy drum for a shivaree night. I very reluctantly gave it to him and have never seen it since.[12]

The custom dates back to medieval France: the historian Barbara W. Tuchman cites a *charivari* at the French court in 1393 which turned from highjinks into tragedy.[13] A similar dark outcome marked a shivaree in nineteenth-century Upper Canada at a racially mixed marriage (young Irish bride, black groom).[14] A shivaree in early Toronto was reported in the *Globe* in these terms:

A CHARIVARI—Yesterday afternoon, a man who has seen over forty winters, joined himself in the holy bonds of wedlock to a girl of about sixteen summers ... A number of youngsters having heard of the affair, thought fit last night to disturb the happiness of the loving pair by congregating around their newly made home, and with pots, pans, whistles, and various other instruments of discordant sound, created a din, noise, and confusion that Stanley street itself, with all its powers, could not surpass. It was continued for a length of time, and was only stopped by the bridegroom distributing some of his small change amongst the party, when they departed and he was left in peace.[15]

This description underlines the frequent association of shivaree practices with unpopular marital unions, as was also the case, we learn, in early Quebec:

When a young man married a widow, or a widower a young girl, their neighbors in the district gathered together, and, armed with ram's-horns, soup kettles, toy trumpets, and other musical instruments or weapons of a similar stridency, they headed for the honeymooners' house, and demanded payment of a forfeit, according to an old custom ... If one did not pay right away, the house was barricaded and exposed for several hours to a continual barrage of scandalous noise.[16]

Reaney's story, designed as a full evening in two acts, interweaves this tradition with the Proserpine myth and the fable of Duke Bluebeard. Daisy, tired of waiting for her lackadaisical boyfriend Jonathan to propose, goes through a marriage ceremony with a middle-aged widower, the wealthy farmer and storekeeper William Quartz. On the wedding night, Jonathan is galvanized into action, joins the shivaree band, and abducts her literally from the balcony of the nuptial bedroom. The *dea ex machina*—the local schoolteacher, Miss Beech—discovers a flaw in the marriage certificate: with his poor memory, Quartz has written an earlier spouse's name. The shivareers cheerfully team him up with an aging tomboy of the district, Aunt Annie, and all ends happily.

When I showed the scenario to Herman Geiger-Torel, he objected to it on moral grounds—surprisingly for one who had produced several *Madam Butterflys*. He found Daisy's submission to Quartz implausible ("Why the hell did she marry him?") and thought when the shivareers distract Quartz by threatening to burn his barn that we were proposing an actual onstage fire. In his view, the opera could only succeed if the

*Still photos from the Toronto production of
The Shivaree (1982): Caralyn Tomlin as
Daisy, Avo Kittask as Quartz; Patricia Rideout
as Henrietta (courtesy of University of
Toronto Music Library).*

story built to "several big climaxes."[17] When I sent Jamie a copy of his letter, he wrote in the margin alongside this remark, "Oh my god!"

As noted above regarding *Cereus*, operas take time to compose. Reaney and I developed the libretto by correspondence while pursuing many other activities. I started to sketch some parts of the music, but could concentrate on it only by making it one of my priority projects for my Faculty of Music study leave in 1965–66. At that time I managed to complete and orchestrate Act One. I enjoyed the challenge of identifying the characters musically—the volatile and wide-ranging bass-baritone of Quartz, the folksiness of the half-witted hired man Ned (to Reaney he was "a kind of Tyl Eulenspiegel"), Miss Beech on her bicycle, the more sophisticated and reserved lovers (Daisy lost and frightened, Jonathan a reader of, in another Reaney phrase, "difficult books under easy haystacks"). The instrumentation called for eighteen players, including two percussionists (indispensable) and, for soft contrast, a guitar (Jamie's script portrays Jonathan with this instrument, evoking Orpheus with his lute). I recall performing the finished act at the piano, singing all the parts, for Jamie and Colleen at their home in London, Ontario, and later for the CBC producer Carl Little, and receiving encouraging feedback. But a further long stretch of free time was impossible for me, and during the next decade *The Shivaree* sat incomplete in a drawer. I was only able to sketch a few passages for Act Two—among them the lovers' duet and the introductory moonlight gathering of the shivareers (suggested by the "night music" strain in Bartók). My postdecanal leave, in 1977–78, afforded me a chance to concentrate on the

Fabric hangings by Kathleen McMorrow for the 1979 workshop of The Shivaree. *The three hangings define the newlyweds' buggy, the road (with Jonathan's guitar), and Quartz's farmhouse/general store).*

remainder of the opera. By mid-1978 the work was finally complete and ready to be "marketed." The two acts last around sixty minutes each.

Opera productions on television were becoming more frequent; we had designed our work once again with stage performance in mind, but adapting it for television was a possibility, and with its relatively slender forces (a chamber-sized orchestra, no chorus) it could be done on a smaller budget than most standard-repertoire works. I met with two potential producers, Lotfi Mansouri of the Canadian Opera Company and John Barnes of CBC Television, and played/sang the score for them. Both made pleasant congratulatory comments. In separate conversations later, Mansouri said he thought the work would be ideal for television, while Barnes, who might have been expected to say the COC should do it, promised to suggest it to some of his producers, but warned that under a new policy the corporation no longer undertook opera telecasts of such length. (Within a couple of months there was a three-hour telecast of *The Barber of Seville* from the National Arts Centre.) We heard nothing further from the CBC. The first positive response came from Michael Bawtree of the then-new company called Comus Music Theatre, who in 1979 organized a workshop production of the opera. A devotee of Reaney's theatrical work, Bawtree himself directed and William Shookhoff prepared the singers and played the orchestral part on the piano. Despite the limited stage action, illusion was sharpened by Kathleen's fabric hangings representing the three playing areas—the newlyweds' buggy, the highway, and Quartz's farmhouse/store. The shivareers handled an assortment of noisemakers in their assaults on the imaginary bedroom balcony. The invited audience responded warmly, but we received no immediate offers of a full staging. A year or so later, the Comus group decided to take a chance on mounting one. It was performed for four nights (3–6 April 1982) in the St Lawrence Centre's Town Hall (now called the Jane Mallett Theatre).

The Shivaree is a "numbers opera," in keeping with the libretto's basis in classical myth. Classical operatic parallels in fact abound in the script: Miss Beech is a benevolent version of the Queen of the Night, and I cast her accordingly as a coloratura; Annie and Ned are both cross-dressing sprites akin to Despina or Cherubino; Quartz's eleventh-hour pleading with the shivareers, and their defiant "No's," may recall the scene of Orpheus and the Furies in Gluck. Alongside Daisy's aria, I persuaded Jamie to enlarge the roles of Quartz, Beech, and Annie by including full arias for each of them. There are two love duets, and further duets for Quartz with Daisy, with his henpecking sister Henrietta, and with Ned. For formal ensembles there are the quartet and quintet of Act One and the three "Shivaree Musics" of Act Two, each of the three being variations on the same vamping harmonies (see example 8). When the lovers are finally united, the shivareers carry them off in the buggy to music resembling in texture "The Surrey with the Fringe on Top" from Oklahoma! The opera concludes with a "Jubilation Finale." More than in Night Blooming Cereus, I linked various scenes by reusing musical motives. Where in Cereus the rather Stravinskian piano progression associated with the cereus plant itself is virtually the only such link, in The Shivaree there are several, among them Beech's bicycle music, the barbershop-quartet-like phrases of dialogue by the shivaree band, and the three shivaree outbursts with Quartz's ensuing responses (each on a higher pitch).

For the Comus premiere, Billie Bridgman was the producer, Paula Sperdakos the stage director, and Howard Cable the conductor. The performers, both vocal and instrumental, were uniformly first class. I was pleased and excited by the preparations. In the course of rehearsals I made several alterations affecting the timing of the stage action and also several adjustments to the orchestral score (Cable, a renowned orchestrator, advised against bongo drums in one passage, which he rightly said sounded like voodoo). We equipped the six shivareers with an outsize frying pan and wooden spoon, a Harpo Marx auto horn, bells off a horse-driven sleigh, a tin drum, an enormous New Year's Eve ratchet, and other objects for their moments of "joyous racket." Jamie attended several of the rehearsals and became swept up by the realization of his imagined story.

Example 8: The same popular melodic phrase appears in different forms,
each time getting faster and higher, in the successive loud songs—a, b,
and c—of the shivareers in Act Two of The Shivaree.

When the angry Quartz tells Daisy in Act One, "You will never come out of that door again!" he observed, "And, you know, she *never does*": in Act Two, Daisy makes her escape not through the door but by jumping off the balcony. The set and costume designs for the opera, by a bright young designer, Geoffrey Dinwiddie, were more expertly done than Niverville's for *Cereus*, though in my view intrusive and not as appropriate to the story or its characters. I can recall many effective stage moments from this production, among them the mid-aria cartwheel of Aunt Annie (Susan Gudgeon) and the appearance of a defiant Ned (Henry Ingram) with a sickle in one hand and a large pig in the other.

Audiences for the performances were good, and they and the critics treated us well. The CBC picked up the opera for a radio broadcast. I believe the venture lost money, but I have never heard how much. There was financial support from a few foundations. I had applied to the Canada Council for help with the expense of preparing the full score and parts, but was turned down; I went into debt by assuming this substantial cost (in five figures) myself. The Council's rules allowed for copying grants only to *commissioned* works. There were performance royalties to Jamie and me, which compensated somewhat.

That fall, when Opera America held its annual conference in Toronto, Billie Bridgman gathered members of the cast and presented a ten-minute excerpt for delegates, as part of a "showcase" program. She chose one of the shivaree episodes from Act Two.

Later in 1982 Michael Bawtree directed a second full production of *The Shivaree* at the Banff Centre, conducted by Steve McNeff, and Jamie and I attended. The orchestra shared the large, open stage with the set and action, and this arrangement worked well. The emphasis was different than in Sperdakos's version: for example, Aunt Annie became the town tramp, contrary to the original idea of her character. Bawtree felt the work needed an introductory scene that gave an earlier hint of the shivaree band than in the original, where they appear first only at the start of Act Two. Accordingly, Jamie wrote a five-minute prologue with parts for Ned and Henrietta (both of whom had turned out to be interesting characters and merited larger roles) and for the shivareers' leader, Bo, which I set using fragments of their existing music. I am of two minds about this addition: I like it and I think it holds attention, but at the same time would not miss it if the work were given in its original version. The work has *not* been given on stage again, in either version, though I continue to hope it may be revived. In 2000, the Opera in Concert company in Toronto included a concert performance of it in their season. More about that later.

The two decades between the stage premieres of *Night Blooming Cereus* and *The Shivaree* saw a number of other Reaney–Beckwith collaborations. In 1960, the year of our Hart House *Cereus* show and the year of the first draft of the *Shivaree* libretto, I put together a background score for his play *The Killdeer*. "Put together" is the right term: following Pamela's directorial suggestions, I improvised musical cues at the piano, as she and I devised various muting devices after the model of John Cage's "prepared piano." The introductory music is a gospel hymn, "Blessed Be the Name of the Lord," from a volume which Jamie had loaned me,[18] and the remaining dozen and a half cues are variations on it. The surviving score is little more than a cue sheet. A dubbing of the recorded tape is now part of a collection of prepared-piano works gathered by Richard Bunger in California.[19] The recording has been used in later productions of the play. Working on it had a liberating effect for me, of significance in various words-and-music projects of the later 1960s. For Franz Kraemer's 1961 television production of *The Killdeer* I composed (and directed) a different set of cues for a small chamber ensemble; Kraemer found the hymn-tune variations unsuitable.

It was also in 1960 that I was asked by Robert Weaver to concoct a musical score for a CBC Radio broadcast reading of Reaney's poem-cycle *A Message to Winnipeg*. The producer, James Kent, was open to a mildly experimental approach. Jamie and I had often discussed what music does to words. W.B. Yeats is said to have objected to speaking or reciting against a musical background: in his view, the two species of rhythm tended to interfere with each other. I found this a valid point but also thought a certain give-and-take might be attained. Moreover in music it was a period when aleatoric forms and free coordination of parts were much in the air. I treated the assignment as a collage of spoken words and fragments of music, calling for three reciters and four instrumentalists (violin, clarinet, piano, percussion). This turned out to be the first of a series of six similar radio commissions which Jamie and I completed between 1960 and 1967. Television may have drawn away the big public audience, but radio was then in a higher state of technical development than in any previous era. Almost all broadcasts were still live-to-air: pre-taping and delays may have been a fresh concept, and multi-track recording and synthesizers as yet only vague dreams, but FM and sophisticated stereo miking afforded nuances that were attractive and novel. There were further advantages in sympathetic producers like Kent, a good level of budgetary support, and a talent pool of excellent performers. The collages after *A Message to Winnipeg* were: *Twelve Letters to a Small Town* (1961), Reaney's tribute to his birthplace, Stratford; *Wednesday's Child* (1962), celebrating the fifteenth anniversary of the "culture" series *CBC Wednesday Night*; and the trilogy *Canada Dash, Canada Dot* (1965–67), an "entertainment" for the centennial of Confederation.[20] The three parts of the trilogy were subtitled "The Line Across," "The Line Up and Down," and "Canada Dot." For the Winnipeg cycle, I worked to an already-completed text, but the other collages were all developed collaboratively with Reaney. *Twelve Letters*, like *A Message to Winnipeg*, uses reciters and a small instrumental group, but *Wednesday's Child* and the component pieces in the trilogy all use both singers and reciters. The *Canada Dash, Canada Dot* pieces call for somewhat larger instrumental forces. Both *Twelve Letters* and "The Line Across" have been repeated in concert; the premiere of the trilogy was in fact broadcast from Walter Hall before a live audience.

Some parts of *Twelve Letters to a Small Town* are versions of earlier poems, just as Reaney's later play, *Colours in the Dark*, closely reflecting his Stratford upbringing, includes a number of self-quotations. Our musical consultations affected the Orange Day Parade of the Third Letter, the wallpaper and bicycle images of the Sixth and Twelfth Letters, and especially the Eighth Letter, "The Music Lesson." This central set piece was first suggested by Jamie's memories of his lessons with a high-profile piano teacher in Stratford, the dynamic Cora B. Ahrens. We managed to incorporate in it scales and arpeggios (to a metronome) as well as a little pianistic tone poem ("The Storm") and a two-part invention, all infused with spoken poetic lines. The invention is rehearsed by left hand and right hand and then both hands combined, the recited lines being superimposed in tempo. The music here is mainly for solo piano, although there are interruptions for two wind instruments (to suggest a passing local train).

In *Wednesday's Child*, the speakers personify days of the week—Wednesday (Douglas Rain) articulate and cultivated, Saturday (Paul Kligman) a gum-chewing hockey fan. The big musical set number is a ten-minute "history of music," parodying a *CBC Wednesday Night* feature in which Leslie Bell had presented a potted survey of Western music history. In this, the singers took my program theme through a series of brief variations representing in turn a Gregorian chant, a medieval motet, a mock Caccini aria, a Vivaldi concerto, a Schubert *Lied*, and a piano prelude à la Debussy, with a deliberately incongruous percussion background adding to the collage texture.

Jamie outlined the centennial trilogy to me initially in geometric and Morse-code terms: there would be a long horizontal line representing an east-to-west trans-Canada journey; then a shorter vertical line representing a journey into the past, specifically from present-day Toronto north to the nineteenth-century settlement of the Children of Peace at Sharon; and then a series of short vivid images ("dots") associated with Canada and with Canadian life, like miscellaneous objects that might be found in that Reaney favourite, a child's play box. I came up with suggestions for musical models and even quotations: "The Line Across" sets a recitation of the counties in Quebec to the music of Calixa Lavallée's "War Fever Galop" (1861), incorporating the composer's name and phrases from his most famous work, "O Canada," while the "Portrait of Ancestors Newlywed" in "Canada Dot" is accompanied by a baritone singing "A Souvenir of Love," a ballad by Edwin Gledhill (1886). "The Line Up and Down" quotes several hymn verses by the leader of the Children of Peace, David Willson, and I set some of them to an original tune (varied throughout this part of the trilogy) and others to examples from period tune books. The two singers here were a contralto hymn singer (Patricia Rideout) and a male pop singer (Jack Van Evera), the latter performing the jailhouse lyric "Traveler." There were a number of memorable moments, as when the soprano, Mary Morrison, in the "Riddle" section of "The Line Across" personifies a Newfoundland iceberg with several high Cs, or when the whole cast joins in the finale of "Canada Dot," evoking a broadcast of a hockey game.[21]

The collage principle of musical organization—a flexible assemblage, whether of singing, reciting, and instrumental sounds, or of instruments only—became a compositional habit with me. I only occasionally left pitches or patterns to be improvised by the performers, but designed simultaneous parts in different tempos and often even different styles. I followed examples of the time by composers such as Lutoslawski, and others as far back as Ives, who sometimes evoked the memory of hearing several different kinds of music going on at the same moment, perhaps in adjacent rooms or neighbouring streets. Many of my instrumental works after the 1967 *Circle, with Tangents* are laid out with the parts in contrasting metres and tempos, requiring that all players read from a copy of the full score rather than just their own part. There are collage-like textures in passages of larger works such as *A Concert of Myths* and *Round and Round*. Further words-and-music collages include my score for the radio reading of *The Journals of Susannah Moodie* by Margaret Atwood (1972) and *In the Middle of Ordinary Noise*, the "auditory masque" Reaney and I prepared for the 1992 Northrop Frye symposium at the University of Toronto. The *Moodie* score consisted of instrumental collages for percussion and various keyboards (in the performance, I had a brilliant collaborator, John Wyre), interpersed between, rather than played simultaneously with, the pre-recorded poems read by Mia Anderson. There are numerous short quotations from Canadian music of Mrs Moodie's period, pasted into the score in true collage fashion. About the *Ordinary Noise* masque, more later.

In 1972–73, in response to a commission from the Women's Committee of the Toronto Symphony Orchestra, Jamie and I worked together on a children's tale for narrator and orchestra. He drew on his store of local ideas: beekeeping and town bands were topics waiting to be explored. The unlikely result was *All the Bees and All the Keys*, a fantasy of small-town Ontario in which magical bees teach music to members of a kids' wind ensemble. Jamie imagined twelve hives, one for each of the keys in classical tonality; when I reminded him there were actually twenty-four keys, not just twelve, he doubled the number of hives. He also imagined the young players having a more advanced skill to transpose at sight than most professionals, but the script was not a realistic documentary and I was entranced by it, so made no objections. (In his play *The Killdeer*, years before, lawyers in the audience had complained that the trial scene bore little relation to actual legal procedures; but it wasn't intended to, any more than the trial scene in *Alice in Wonderland*.) The audition sequence was an opportunity for members of the orchestra to play various toy instruments, and the climax of the work was an ersatz Sousa march.

Victor Feldbrill conducted the premiere, with Max Ferguson as the narrator. Ferguson indicated poetic fantasy wasn't his favourite medium and developed laryngitis before the dress rehearsal, but came through with a virtuoso multi-voiced performance nevertheless. In revivals, the narrator's part has been divided between male and female actors. In 1987, for Lawrence Cherney's "Musical Mondays" series, I made a reduced version of the orchestral score, for just ten players. Press Porcépic produced *All the Bees and All the Keys* as a children's book, with appropriate illustrations.[22] I had fancied the musical cues, arranged for piano, could be played while the tale was being read aloud, but the rigid page layout prevented this. The Women's Committee had undertaken the commission because they thought there should be an alternative to the much-played *Peter and the Wolf* on children's concerts. Indeed I often wonder at the immense popularity of the Prokofiev work. The music is charming and catchy, but the story is slight even for a young audience (has its supposed political symbolism ever been verified?). But every year almost, yet another movie star, television personality, or retired politician appears as narrator with this or that orchestra in yet another new concert production or recording.

When Billie Bridgman was appointed as Nicholas Goldschmidt's successor at the Guelph Spring Festival (1986), she wanted to emphasize new operas. While preparing her first such venture, Syd Hodkinson's operatic adaptation of Michel Tremblay's *Saint Carmen of the Main*, she approached Jamie and me to see if we would be interested in a commission. Jamie came up rapidly with two alternative possibilities—one a story based on Willson and the early history of Sharon, and the other an adaptation of a Canadian mystery novel (a "detective opera"). I had already composed several works using the literary and musical background of Sharon, so leaned more to the second idea, which seemed to me quite distinct in tone from either *Cereus* or *Shivaree*.[23] Bridgman agreed, so we began work on our first commissioned opera. Where our previous two works were original fiction, this one would be adapted from an existing source—as are most standard operas. *Crazy to Kill* is a detective novel published in 1941 in New York by Ann Cardwell (a pseudonym), an author who lived in Stratford—which is why Jamie knew of it.[24] The commission was for a chamber opera of modest size: the original suggestion was two singers and a piano, but eventually we persuaded the festival to let us have three singers, two actors, and two instrumentalists (a pianist and a percussionist). Jamie's notion was to represent the rest of the twenty-two-member cast by puppets, to be operated by the singers and actors. *Saint Carmen* was a public success but went considerably over budget, causing controversy. Early in the next season, 1988–89, Bridgman resigned and Louis Applebaum took over as acting director of the festival. There were further unforeseen complications: Allan Monk was announced to play the baritone part of Detective Fry, but shortly after the press party he withdrew, pleading "other commitments." He had agreed without looking at either the libretto or the score, and when he did see them asked for changes that we were not prepared to make. Paul Massel, with whom we had worked in *The Shivaree*, was available and willing, and made an ideal Fry. The Banff Centre proposed to do a workshop of the opera in October 1988, which gave us a deadline. But partway through the preparation of the work in mid-1988 Jamie became ill, and communication was stalled for several months. In our previous collaborations, I depended on our being able to make joint decisions about details of the text and the music, consulting by mail or by phone. I had taken a half-year's leave from my Faculty of Music duties in order to concentrate on the opera, but was pressured to send portions of it for rehearsal in Banff as I finished them, rather than wait until the whole piece was complete. Added to these deadline anxieties, I developed a growing empathy with the characters and with the grisly goings-on of the story—and for a few days felt paralyzed with "composer's block." At length I managed to regain my grip on the piece and whatever creative train of thought I was on, and Jamie recuperated in time for us both to attend the Banff pre-production.

Crazy to Kill, we had thought, might be the world's first "detective opera" ("don't reveal the ending to your friends!"), but someone in the US had beaten us to it by about half a year. The original novel borrows a device from Agatha Christie's *The Murder of Roger Ackroyd*: it is written in the first person and—big surprise!—the narrator turns out to be the murderer. Jamie devised a style of presentation that kept challenging the viewers' idea of reality, mixing live characters with puppets (some leading figures in the story appear as both) and blurring gender and sanity. The time is the 1930s and the setting for the serial killings is a private home for mental patients. As in *Night Blooming Cereus*, the main character is a woman in her sixties: Agatha Lawson is a "trusty" patient soon to be discharged who, in Jamie's ingenious invention, makes doll puppets as a hobby. His treatment could be called Pirandellian.

For the Banff Centre production—with Richard Ashman as stage director and David Boothroyd as musical director—students in the visual arts program created puppets out of found materials large and small, ranging from an intravenous pole to a pair of hand-held carnival masks. These objects took on uncanny human resemblances in the course of the show. For Guelph, an experienced puppet maker, Anna Wagner-Ott, designed a series of three-quarters-life-size puppets, with rods in the back to be

With James Reaney watching the dress rehearsal of Crazy to Kill, *Banff, October 1988.*

operated by the live performers. Again, the puppet characters took on personalities of equal force to the live ones: in one scene the singer playing Agatha, carrying the doll puppet of the head nurse, slaps her own face. The use of mechanical characters helped create distance for the audience, underlining the sense of a dramatic enactment rather than a fake reality. Given the intensity of the story, we decided the opera should have no intermission; it lasts about ninety minutes.

Opera productions at the Guelph Spring Festival during Goldschmidt's tenure were almost always mounted in the uncomfortable surroundings of Ross Hall, a high-school auditorium. One of Billie Bridgman's innovations was to stage *Saint Carmen of the Main* in the local armouries, but for *Crazy to Kill* we were back in Ross Hall. (It was almost a decade before the opening of the fine Riverrun Centre, whose main theatre is ideal for opera, but ironically by this time the festival's diminished resources together with greatly increased costs precluded such ventures.) We were fortunate to have Sue LePage as our designer. Her set was more elaborate than Jamie had imagined, but its intricate winding shapes and odd levels gave a creepy sense of madness and evil doings.

Still photo from the Guelph Spring Festival production of Crazy to Kill, *1989:
Paul Massel as Detective Fry, Jean Stilwell as Agatha, with four
of Anna Wagner-Ott's doll puppets.*

We were also fortunate in our director. Jerry Franken had known
Jamie for years and had played William Donnelly in the trilogy *The
Donnellys* in the 1970s. He had not worked in musical theatre before
but responded sensitively to the score; his invaluable asset was his close
understanding of the idiom and flavour of the work. Jean Stilwell, our
Agatha, required to be on stage almost the whole time, created a wonderful portrayal with many extraordinary vocal highlights—despite
being half the character's age. Mark Widner and Marc Duggan, the two
instrumentalists, seemed to enjoy their expanded assignments, including hospital intern coats, spoken phrases, and various stage manoeuvres.
What emerged was a smooth and effective presentation of the piece.
On opening night, after about the first half hour, I whispered to Kathleen, "When is something going to go wrong?" But there were no fluffs
and no mini-disasters. Murdo MacKinnon, a veteran GSF board member, told me that none of their previous operas had received such good
press notices.

These were gratifying, indeed, but MacKinnon's remark may have been intended to compensate for the downer of less-than-capacity houses on the production's three nights. Guelph is barely an hour's drive from Toronto, but our audiences were made up mainly of local arts patrons, with only a small Toronto contingent. Applebaum had mentioned the opera to the CBC for consideration as a television feature, but no one from CBC Television came to see it.[25] We were promised a video of the show, but somehow none was produced. Robert Everett-Green's rave review in *The Globe and Mail* had predicted a "lineup for future performances" by other producers, and in later weeks Applebaum discussed it with the National Arts Centre in Ottawa, and there was talk of bringing it to the Faculty of Music's MacMillan Theatre in Toronto. These attempts were sabotaged when a GSF staff member ordered LePage's set to be scrapped, on the grounds that the festival organization could not afford storage space for it. Our complaints to the board of directors came too late to save it. A year or so later, the Wagner-Ott doll puppets were to be offered to bidders at the festival's annual fundraising auction and would have been dispersed except that Jamie and I stepped in and bought them. We stored them in boxes in my basement, against the day when someone would undertake a revival of the opera. (This hope was to be realized in November 2011 at the Enwave Theatre, Harbourfront, with a production by the Toronto Masque Theatre, directed by another *Donnellys* alumnus, David Ferry.)

Crazy to Kill was an unanticipated project. After the 1982 mountings of *The Shivaree*, Reaney and I had been keen to work on another opera. He was immersed in a study of the adolescent writings of the Brontës and conceived a musical drama based on Charlotte, Branwell, Emily, and Anne, their lives growing up together in isolation in the Haworth parsonage, and the stories they invented as early exercises for their extraordinary imaginations. Written in minuscule script in a series of tiny notebooks (some at that time still unpublished), the tales describe wild adventures in a fictional African state, with larger-than-life romantic characters resembling prominent figures of the day, for example the Duke of Wellington. Jamie's proposed libretto would portray the four children telling these adventures in a series of flashbacks and, in a Pirandellian mood of tragic foreboding, becoming involved in them. He spent an extended time during a sabbatical from his UWO position researching the manuscripts in the parsonage museum at Haworth, and when I was living in Edinburgh in 1985 I took a spring cycling tour with Kathleen in the Yorkshire Dales and stopped in Haworth for a couple of days to view both the literary materials and the musical part of the Brontë archives: there were hand-written copies of flute and keyboard pieces from which Branwell had studied (some have been published in facsimile) and piano-duet arrangements of Weber overtures and the like with pencilled annotations indicating Emily and Anne had once played them. Juliet Barker, then the curator, had been Jamie's interested consultant, and my conversations with her were stimulating. She has since published an authoritative and wonderfully readable composite biography of the Brontë family.[26]

Jamie outlined a sketch of this ambitious operatic piece, tentatively titled *The House by the Churchyard*. We both had been deeply affected by the atmosphere of the historic parsonage in Haworth, situated at the end of the steep, grey High Street, and approached through a graveyard with immense stone markers and a constant cawing of crows overhead; beyond the door one could see the broad stretch of the moors, including in the distance the house which had inspired *Wuthering Heights*. Jamie incorporated suggestions for music, among them an elaborate scene depicting a performance of an imaginary, long-lost oratorio by Handel (with, if I remember, Branwell at the organ). Our correspondence grew as I received, and commented on, several further drafts, filing them in a folder labelled "Opera 3." The episodes became more and more complex, and the cast expanded (close to a hundred named parts at one point); Jamie said he thought the work might turn out to be a trilogy, like *The Donnellys*. Part of the developing libretto was published as a "work in progress" in *Books in Canada*.[27] My difficulty was in finding the proper *operatic* approach to this rich material. It was certainly "operatic" in its exaggerated emotionality and powerful characters, but what was the appropriate musical tone? I had had no such feelings of unease with either of our two previous operas, and was to have none with *Crazy to Kill*. Finally I told Jamie that I thought the work was a play, not an opera, and that I would love to do an incidental-music score if and when he had it ready for production. This reaction brought no show of resentment from him. He went on to shape the drama under a new title, *Zamorna*, and it received a brilliant production in 1999 by students in the drama program at George Brown College in Toronto under David Ferry's direction. It is in my opinion one of Jamie's strongest plays and deserves to be better known.[28]

One of my "Music at Sharon" enterprises in the 1980s was a program of excerpts from musical theatre works of early Canada. Dorith Cooper was preparing, for our *Canadian Musical Heritage* series, an anthology gathered from nineteenth- and early-twentieth-century operettas and other stage pieces with music—revealing a larger body of such works than had previously been widely known. I was familiar with Joseph Quesnel's *Colas et Colinette* through Ridout's restoration but had never investigated the only other known Quesnel score, *Lucas et Cécile*. Kallmann had perused the manuscript, in the Archives du Séminaire in Quebec City, and written of it in his history. It seemed no one else had ever examined it closely. Where *Colas et Colinette* survived only in a libretto and parts for voices and for second violin, the sources for this second work were even scantier, namely a score indicating the voice parts and song lyrics only—no orchestral parts and no full libretto. Nevertheless, for this "comédie mêlée d'ariettes," to give it its generic name, the manuscript showed words and music for all the "ariettes," from which one gained a clear outline of the action and the characters. Moreover the music had, to me, a good deal of charm and individuality, and in 1988 I restored four of the songs for our performance at Sharon. Restoration meant deriving harmonies from the implications of Quesnel's voice parts. This was easiest in the ensembles (of which there are five) but even in the solo songs not especially hard. In spare moments over the next couple of years, I restored the remaining numbers and made an orchestration for an orchestra such as Quesnel might have had available (a flute, a bassoon, pairs of oboes and horns, and strings). For the earlier comedy, there is contemporary documentation of the 1790 premiere in Montreal, but no evidence has survived that *Lucas* was ever produced. A performance was advertised in Quebec City in 1808–9 but seems never to have taken place, perhaps owing to Quesnel's death in April 1809. In 1994, when my restoration of the music was given in concert form in Toronto by the Tafelmusik Baroque Orchestra and a group of solo singers, we had good reason to assume it was the first time the work had ever been heard.

In order to mount a full production of *Lucas et Cécile*, someone would have to write a libretto, since like its predecessor and other works of this French genre it was a spoken play with interspersed sung numbers. The main features of the slight plot could be gathered from the succession of song lyrics; the only missing factor was the precise reason for the defeat of the unwanted suitor in the little amorous intrigue. Following the handsome publication of the vocal score of my restored version,[29] there were two different stage productions, one in Montreal and one in Toronto. In Montreal, the literary scholar Pierre Turcotte devised a script using comic elements from Molière. The production in 2000 by Turcotte's company L'Opéra du Château, used a historic setting, a salon in the eighteenth-century Château Ramezay in Old Montreal, with just a harpsichord for accompaniment.[30] The Toronto production in 2001 by Opera Anonymous and the Aradia

Ensemble used a fuller instrumentation, and Brad Walton and Alex Wiebe wrote new dialogue and new lyrics, in English, inventing a different climactic twist. Tamara Bernstein wrote approvingly in *The Globe and Mail*, but for Claude Gingras, the long-time reviewer of *La Presse* in Montreal, the work was devoid of historical interest. Surprise was expressed in an article in *L'Actualité* that a non-Quebecker would undertake its restoration: "La musique québécoise: *We like it!*" was the headline. The adjective "québécois" was unknown in Joseph Quesnel's day. The music of both of his comedies was known in manuscript for many years during which no Quebec researcher was moved to consider its potential for study or performance. Godfrey Ridout once thanked me for having been in part responsible for his work on *Colas et Colinette*. I was glad to have belatedly been able to work on the companion piece, *Lucas et Cécile*.

The Northrop Frye Centre at Victoria University in Toronto, through Alvin Lee, asked Reaney and me to prepare some kind of words-and-music piece to be performed as part of the Frye Symposium in 1992. Lee was a long-time friend and avid promoter of Jamie's work. Frye had been Jamie's thesis supervisor, and we had both had friendly contacts with him over the years. Jamie was invited to give a paper at the symposium. For the proposed performance number he suggested a literary/musical miscellany in the form of a "mandala." With musical suggestions from me, this evolved into *In the Middle of Ordinary Noise: An Auditory Masque*, a collage for a narrator (personifying Frye), two singers, three instrumentalists, and pre-recorded sound. It reminded me of a skit which Jamie had produced, directing a group of fellow grad students, towards the end of his doctoral studies in the 1950s, a zany illustrated overview of English literature from the Middle Ages to *Finnegans Wake*.[31] Here the script's concurrent lines of thought represented Frye's considerable musical experience and the theory of genres in his *Anatomy of Criticism* (comedy, romance, satire, tragedy) by means of a string of quotations both literary and musical. In the spirit of our earlier collaborations, some of the musical quotes were suggested by Jamie, and some of the literary ones by me. The premiere was well received by the symposium audience, but I was unhappy with the acoustics of the venue, the Victoria College chapel. In 2005 there was an opportunity to revisit this occasional piece when it was included by the Toronto Masque Theatre in their program entitled *Masques for a Reaney Day* (alongside Jamie's *One-Man Masque*); I had been dubious about reviving it, but this time the performance, in the upper space of the Tarragon Theatre, came across with proper clarity. The text of *Ordinary Noise* is included in the published proceedings of the Frye Symposium.[32]

It was also in 1992 (or perhaps early in 1993) that John Miller asked if I would be interested in composing another opera to a libretto by Jamie. For *Serinette*, Jamie's Sharon opera, a collaboration with Harry Somers, Miller's company, Cultural Support Services, had mounted a spectacularly successful production in 1990 at the Sharon Temple. Miller was keen to develop further operatic treatments of topics from local history, and Jamie had already written an extensive draft of a sort of "prequel" to the *Serinette* story: where *Serinette* took place in York and Sharon during the 1830s, the new piece would deal with the founding of York by John Graves Simcoe in 1793 and would cover a period of some thirty years, from the American War of Independence to just before the War of 1812. Miller envisioned an eventual trilogy—three historical librettos by Reaney, each set by a different composer. Where the Somers work had been given in the special surroundings of the Temple, the Simcoe opera could be mounted at Fort York; a third piece was vaguely planned in which the central figure would be William Lyon Mackenzie. It seems two other composers had read the new draft and declined the commission. I read it and was immediately captivated. It was a large and sprawling libretto, somewhat disorganized (a trait I recognized from previous Reaney drafts), but overflowing with original and engaging ideas, and in particular full of musical possibilities. I had various other things on my plate but decided right away that I wanted to do it.

Taptoo! as this work was called, is a historical pageant or saga in Reaneyesque terms, where real-life characters mingle with invented ones and where simple stage devices depict key events often with a tinge of satire. Its topic, as Jamie succinctly put it, is why Canadians are not Americans. As in *Crazy to Kill*, the cast members assume a variety of roles, changing age or gender rapidly, functioning for one scene in a solo role and in the next as part of a crowd; again, the orchestral players are sometimes required to join the stage action. Another Reaney characteristic: the story is told as if through the eyes and ears of a child, the drummer boy Seth Harple in Act One, and his son Seth Junior in Act Two. Jamie had visited the Fort York archives and researched the musical background, indicating contemporaneous tunes that could be quoted in the opera. The title he chose itself has musical relevance: it refers to a military ritual, the last bugle and drum signal of the day, calling troops back to barracks from their tavern visits and other evening revels.[33] By the late eighteenth century it had developed into a drawn-out series of calls, interspersed with bits of song-and-dance entertainment—the prototype of the "military tattoo" of later times.

TAPTOO!

An opera by John Beckwith and James Reaney
UNIVERSITY OF TORONTO FACULTY OF MUSIC OPERA DIVISION

For the poster and flyer of Taptoo! *the University of Toronto opera division used my pencilled lettering of the title and a photo Kathleen and I took at Fort George in Niagara-on-the-Lake, with a soldier in eighteenth-century uniform on guard.*

I was greatly attracted by *Taptoo!* but initially not keen on quoting period music in my score, even though Jamie's script, in telling the story, used many quotations from public documents, the diaries of Simcoe and his wife, and other period writings. He envisioned "Yankee Doodle" in the prologue to Act One, and "Rule, Britannia!" at the declaration of the founding of York in Act Two, along with many other musical cues. I was resistant, but (under no pressure from him) gradually changed my view. Two period productions of early music theatre affected me around this time. John Gay's *The Beggar's Opera* and Thomas Arne's *Love in a Village* were respectively the most often performed and the second most often performed ballad operas of eighteenth-century England. Spirited and informed revivals of both pieces had an immediate influence on me.[34] I had never especially admired *The Beggar's Opera* in any of the versions I had seen and heard, but the Toronto production and a recording of Jeremy Barlow's more recent London production together gave a different idea of its earthiness and its quick in-and-out occurrences of little pop melodies. It struck me that what we were working on was the modern equivalent of a ballad opera, in which scraps of familiar songs and dances would now and then drift into the musical score. I ended by including about twenty such musical references—hymn tunes, popular sentimental or patriotic songs, dances, marches, and of course period military music.

Some of the tunes were well known, others more obscure.[35] When asked to define the genre of *Taptoo!* I called it a "documentary ballad opera." A discovery in my musical researches for the work won me over to "Yankee Doodle." This British spoof of American ways seemed to me inappropriate, until I found an arrangement of it by an English-born US composer of the early nineteenth century, James Hewitt, with distinctive harmonic and rhythmic touches. With "Rule, Britannia!" I hit on a fresh but still recognizable way of treating it, by presenting Arne's five phrases (to Jamie's text) in a scrambled order. A less familiar theme called "The Rogue's March," traditionally associated with the ceremony of "drumming out," appears in scenes of "running the gauntlet" in both acts, once in an English version and once in a different US version. For the scene called "How to Play the Drum," Jamie took the title and parts of the dialogue from an early nineteenth-century manual used at Fort York in earliest times, from which I in turn drew the prescribed wind and drum figures. Ken Purvis of the staff at Historic Fort York became an invaluable adviser. A knowledgeable and adept expert on military music, he was one of the percussionists in our 1994 workshop reading.

The quotations have their effect but take up only a small portion of the opera's two and a half hours of music. The multiple roles call for a minimum of fifteen singers including three children, and the orchestration requires eighteen players. Miller kept pressuring me to reduce the instrumental score, but even with due regard for current economies I thought the length and scope of the topic justified an orchestra this size. Though "big" in relation to a new opera's budget, it was half the size normally called for by Puccini. The military scenes demanded percussion and brass (two of the woodwind players double on fife), and for contrast in more intimate moments I called for harp and accordion. The accordion had not yet been invented in the period of the story, but I reasoned that it could evoke suitably nostalgic reed-organ colours as well as reinforcing harmonies (I figured an orchestral piano would be too sophisticated). Rather than a concert harp, I decided on the smaller and more flexible "non-pedal harp" (sometimes called the Celtic harp) and consulted with an experienced player and teacher, Marie Lorcini. In the score there are a number of identifying themes, as in the earlier operas, among them the motive associated with the image of Seth's toy battleships and another sung to the words of the Queen's Rangers' motto, "Draw your swords, Rangers: the rebels are coming!" It seemed fitting to use a complicated modern chord—one containing all twelve pitch classes of the chromatic scale—in the finale of Act Two, which Jamie had imagined being played against projections of the skyline of twenty-first-century Toronto.

Miller's vision of a performance at Historic Fort York proved impossible because of the massive noise interference in that part of the city. An alternative, the grounds of Spadina House, a historic mansion beside Casa Loma on the escarpment overlooking the downtown area, was under active discussion after an encouraging reading of the opera, with piano and drums, at the Glenn Gould Studio in 1994. But the mid-90s were a much more difficult period for fundraising than the late '80s had been. Our "commission" for *Taptoo!* was a kind of gentleman's agreement, under whose terms there would be no payment until a production was contracted. Meanwhile I footed the considerable bill for the preparation of the three-hundred-page orchestral score and the parts. Eventually we made a friendly severance of the connection with Cultural Support Services and there was no more talk of a third opera for the projected trilogy. We began a campaign to raise the funds ourselves, but after a year of trying, having had responses adding up to only about one-third of what we thought we needed, we had to give up and return the donations and pledges, with due thanks. It was deeply discouraging. Agencies such as the Toronto Heritage Foundation and the Ontario Arts Council gave us sympathetic hearings, but the money to accomplish the task was not forthcoming.

One day in 1998 I had a call from Brenda Anderson, a stage director then working with the opera program at McGill University in Montreal. She was acquainted with Jamie's work, and a friend had told her about *Taptoo!* Would we "permit" her to suggest mounting it with the students at McGill? It would not be a full-scale production, but at least a staging—one step closer to full realization than our workshop reading. I conferred with Jamie, and of course neither of us considered withholding "permission." The production went ahead. Brenda put a great deal into it and proved to have a good grasp of the style it implied, as did the young music director, James Higgins. The students covered the multiple roles well, and there were some excellent voices. I sat in on several rehearsal sessions. One of the cast members asked why, if the story was about the founding of Toronto, were we doing the first production in Montreal? It happened that I had just been for a walk in Old Montreal and had seen a plaque marking the spot in the Place d'Armes where a statue of George III was destroyed by US troops during the occupation of Montreal in 1773. Here, I pointed out, was evidence that the events of the Revolutionary years had repercussions in other parts of Canada besides Toronto. As a tryout, the opera played one performance for delegates to a symposium of voice teachers at SUNY Potsdam in northern New York State, a short distance south of Montreal. Several participants took note of the irony that what could be called an anti-US opera was getting its first exposure before a US audience. The Montreal performances took place in the Black Box Theatre, a compact space in the basement of FACE, the arts high school just around the corner from the McGill music faculty on Sherbrooke Street West. Audiences were good, and Arthur Kaptainis wrote a thoughtful and positive account of the show for the *Gazette* and *Opera Canada*. On the last night, everyone seemed ready to pack up, and when Jamie asked about a cast party it seemed no one had arranged one, so he invited us all to a nearby restaurant for a proper celebration.

Peddling the opera to further producers was reminiscent of our earliest ventures—slow and dispiriting. But a new avenue suggested itself: the opera division of the University of Toronto Faculty of Music, in whose infant years (when it was the Royal Conservatory opera school and COC forerunner) I served briefly as a *répétiteur*, had up till then performed hardly any Canadian-composed operas but in 2000 commissioned and produced Gary Kulesha's *The Last Duel*. I asked the division head, Stephen Ralls, whether they would be interested in either producing *Taptoo!* or commissioning a new Beckwith–Reaney work. The scenario of a proposed new libretto did not whet his appetite, but after reviewing the score of *Taptoo!* he said he liked it and found it suited their abilities and their program. Important pluses in this prospect were Ralls's known enthusiasm for early Canadian cultural topics and the director Michael Albano's appreciation of Reaney's theatrical writings. The U of T *Taptoo!* was performed for four nights in the MacMillan Theatre, 7, 8, 14, and 15 March 2003.

Where the McGill production had a cast of fifteen, the resources at Toronto meant we could use twice that number, so that some of the ensembles could take on choral dimensions. The set devised by Fred Perruzza used period projections and Albano's direction made imaginative use of the big stage. Alison Grant contributed vital choreography for the "drumming out" scenes, the taptoo scenes, and the ball scene of Act Two. The production attracted a good deal of notice. Caryl Clark and Linda Hutcheon organized a well-attended one-day symposium about *Taptoo!* as part of the "humanities initiative" at the University's Munk Centre for International Studies. Scholars from a variety of disciplines commented on aspects of the opera, and Jamie and I both spoke.[36] The final night was promoted as a special event for U of T alumni, and I was invited to give an introductory talk before the show.

Performances improved, and audiences grew, during the opera's four-night run, so that final night had the sort of impact I had hoped for. All in all, though, the production's success was only partial. Ken Winters, who had greeted several previous Reaney–Beckwith ventures warmly, wrote for *The Globe and Mail* a review that stressed the shortcomings of the student cast while tossing in a few compliments on the work itself—ignoring, however, the contemporary relevance of its theme, Canadian–US relations. I have weathered many unfavourable notices, but on this occasion I was sufficiently upset to write Ken a personal protest. My own evaluation of the production, however, might have been just as critical. Both at McGill and here again at Toronto, I was disappointed not to have children's voices for the child characters. We had three exceptionally good boy sopranos in the original workshop, but I had to accept that in a college production you must give opportunities to as many students as possible, which meant young women of slight stature portraying boys. The women were excellent, but the illusion, I felt, was wrong. The main problem throughout the rehearsal period at the U of T was the student orchestra. Sandra Horst, an experienced and resourceful coach and choral director, was conducting her first full opera and evidently from at least some players did not receive the respect she deserved. Moreover, instead of sharing the stage with the story action (as Jamie and I had intended), the orchestra was in the pit, and this created awkwardness when individual players had to take stage roles—in the drumming-lesson scene and the ball scene, for example. There was simply not enough time to solve these difficulties, and the result was less than ideal. *Taptoo!* is a complicated opera, and I was starting to despair of further chances to prove its potential when a revival was proposed by Guillermo Silva-Marin for the Toronto Operetta Theatre company. The plan was to include the work in the company's 2011–12 season as part of Toronto's observance of the bicentenary of the War of 1812. That event is nervously anticipated at the end of the *Taptoo!* story.

Revivals, though wonderful, are unexpected and rare. In considering why this is so, I reflect on how opera composition and opera production have changed over the last half-century. A detail in the University of Victoria production of *Night Blooming Cereus* (January 1992) may have been symptomatic of one trend: the director decided that the telephone operator, Mrs Wool, had romantic yearnings for the nurseryman, Mr Orchard—a notion for which the script gives not the slightest hint. In production after production in late decades, such "concepts" have been added to operas, often in contradiction of their authors' intentions.

Sometimes the "concept" is enlightening, but more often it interferes.[37] New operas now evolve in two models—gargantuan and impossibly expensive, or else cheap and short. Among professional companies, the big ones mount spectacles costing millions, while the small "experimental" ones resist anything as ambitious as even the Britten chamber operas we used for the scale of *Cereus*. In that second category, ten or fifteen minutes, two or three characters, and a saxophone sums up approximately what your budget will stand. The opera audience, unlike the classical-concert audience, has expanded enormously; opera is a thriving enterprise, and new operas proliferate astonishingly. The pieces I produced with Jamie don't fit either of the prevailing patterns.

During its earlier years, the popular Toronto series Opera in Concert ignored the Canadian repertoire, but under Silva-Marin in the late 1990s it had begun to include some works in its programs. There was a revival of *The Shivaree* in 2000 with perhaps the best all-round cast of singers Jamie and I had ever worked with, and in 2003 the company did *Night Blooming Cereus* on a double bill with Harry Somers's *The Fool*, again with exceptionally fine singing. The OIC's *Shivaree* met with a critical drubbing from Urjo Kareda in *The Globe and Mail*. Kareda had been one of Jamie's most ardent supporters for *The Donnellys* and I found his reaction unaccountable except as a sign that we were out of the trend loop. I recalled that when we were shopping *The Shivaree*, around 1980, Kareda, as dramatic adviser to the Stratford Festival, rejected it as "early Reaney," the later Reaney of the *Donnellys* plays being at that time the new style criterion. His about-face angered me and I cooled off by writing a line-by-line rebuttal of his nasty notice, which I however refrained from sending to him or his editor. A telling detail: the young hero's name, Jonathan, is repeated several dozen times in the libretto by various characters, but Kareda referred to him as "Joseph"— this in a comedy which hinges on the villain's inability to get names straight.

One day in the fall of 2000 Kathleen announced she was going to Guelph to take part in an all-day gathering of the Centre for Scottish Studies at the University of Guelph: Would I like to come along? It was a pleasant day and the outing appealed to me. If the papers at the colloquium were not interesting, I could find other attractions in Guelph, a town I knew and liked. A member of the Centre, the historian Scott Moir, presented a case history from seventeenth-century Peebles entitled "The Minister and the Unwed Mother." About a quarter of the way through his presentation, I murmured to Kathleen, "This is an *opera*!" I spoke to

Moir afterwards, and he agreed to send me a copy of his paper. On reading it, I felt even more strongly that it could be the basis for an opera libretto, and also that it could well be Jamie's cup of tea. The situation, documented in records of the ecclesiastical courts, concerned a vagabond woman accused of murdering her illegitimate child. Her accuser, the local minister, was suspected of being the child's father; alternatively, rumours pointed to the local laird. The story had elements of conflict between classes and between church and lay authorities that I found strongly dramatic, and the central figure of Issobel Grey came across powerfully— the documentation from her trial included some of her actual words. I shared the material with Jamie and found my prediction was accurate: he became hooked. We discussed the size and shape that the opera might take and noted the musical implications—music from the early Scottish psalters, ballads, period dances. Jamie produced a scenario in seven scenes, one for each day of the week, which made a promising outline. His working title was *No Dancing on Sunday*; I leaned more toward something like *The Vagabond Mother*. I began looking at Scottish musical sources, some of which I already knew quite well.

We agreed that we did not want to embark fully on this new project without a commission or some prospect of a production. Reception of the draft scenario, when I showed it to various producers, was cool. Times had changed, and it was going to be a difficult sell. It fitted neither the lavish spectacle style nor the pocket-opera style.

Then Jamie's health worsened, and my hopes of our going ahead with this work faded. It remains as a dream of what might have been.

What *is* the style of our operas? They are different enough to belong seemingly to different genres, but they have traits in common. I remember remarking to Jamie once—I think it was during our work on *Taptoo!*—that things were perhaps becoming too complicated. "But," he countered, "we have to give them something for their money." On another occasion, in response to an interviewer who wanted to know what he aimed for in writing a stage piece, he said that his first object was "to tell a story." The scripts aim to engage audiences with standard values (plot, character), rather than setting out to change the world. The scores aim to put the words across clearly and to heighten their expression with melody and timbre. Without articulating our objectives further, I believe we wanted to affect our listeners/viewers in two ways—to move them and to cheer them.

When Jamie died (London, Ontario, 11 June 2008) there was a memorial, in characteristic Reaneyesque mode, with a series of skits, readings, and performances. Students from a London high school played a scene from *Listen to the Wind*, and Leslie Fagan sang the Bird-Girl aria from *Serinette*. My daughter Robin, my son Lawrence, and I put together a short sampling of "Favourite Libretto Passages" and read it aloud.

13

Choirs

Stanley Bulley, in whose choirs in Victoria I developed a love of classical choral literature, moved east in 1945 to work on a University of Toronto doctorate while holding a position as organist and choirmaster. At his invitation, for my first two undergraduate years I sang tenor (or baritone, as needed) in his choir at St Clement's Anglican Church, often in exchange for a Sunday lunch at his home. I had a mediocre voice, but he appreciated that I was a secure sight-reader. For my part, I continued to enjoy participating in choral music rather than just listening to it. But in those years when I was starting to act on my composing ambitions, the idea of composing for chorus was not high on my priority list. In my time in Europe and during the busy teaching and writing years which followed, I certainly heard, studied, and taught a wide variety of choral pieces but felt no urge to explore the medium creatively.

A striking new feature of Toronto's musical life in the 1950s was the emergence of a professional chamber choir, the Festival Singers, under the direction of Elmer Iseler. They adopted this name following their inaugural concerts at the Stratford Festival, and were first called the Festival Singers of Toronto; after a number of successful seasons they changed this to Festival Singers of Canada (a possessive and grandiose Torontonian gesture that rubbed British Columbians like me the wrong way). Iseler had been a student in the Faculty of Music a few years after me. He showed remarkable charisma and drive in his early work as a choral leader and attracted an outstanding team of young professional singers.

In 1963, Iseler asked if I would be interested in composing a work for the Singers. He had in mind an a-cappella piece of maybe ten minutes' length. I found the opportunity touched a number of latent strands of thought. Another bright young talent, the baritone James Milligan, had made several impressive solo appearances (he was an electrifying Mephistopheles in *The Damnation of Faust* with the Toronto Symphony and came across vividly in a number of Verdi roles with the Canadian Opera Company). Milligan said he would welcome some new songs by me, and I toyed with the idea of setting the lamentation of Jonah from the "belly of Sheol" (i.e., hell). The prospect was cut short when Milligan suddenly died of a heart attack while preparing for a major international debut as Wotan at Bayreuth—a tragic loss; he was in his mid-thirties. I was not bent on biblical or religious sources, and Iseler made no suggestions as to a theme, but the Jonah text coincided with some of my personal anxieties in those difficult years. I looked at the Book of Jonah more closely. One of the shortest books of the Old Testament, it consists of only four chapters. It now seemed to me a possible basis for a cantata for choir and soloists. Jay Macpherson kindly offered editorial suggestions on my adaptation of the biblical narrative. When I said I thought there should be some contemporary interpretive verses for the choir, she agreed to provide them. The result, instead of the modest a-cappella number Iseler had requested, turned out to be a work for soloists, choir, and chamber orchestra, whose six movements lasted more than half an hour. Unfazed, he programmed *Jonah* in one of his concerts, and the CBC gave it a broadcast. Alexander Gray sang the title part with an intensity reminiscent of Milligan, and Patricia Rideout delivered the substantial alto-voice narrator's part beautifully. In a scheme of musical symbolism, in addition to strings I chose three solo instruments to represent key images of the story: the clarinet as the worm, the horn as the gourd, and the timpani as the "big fish." Some members of the audience at the premiere interpreted the timpani's outbursts as an early-sixties reference to The Bomb, an implication reinforced when the people of Nineveh cry on God for mercy—"that we perish not."

My approach to the text was more personal than either social or religious. It was, as I saw it, a parable about forgiveness. Its God was more like the Christian deity than the vengeful Jehovah of so many earlier Old Testament passages. The musical references were varied. The chorale of the opening and closing movements linked to the Bach cantatas and also to the early Protestant tune books, specifically a Huguenot psalm-melody that I recalled from a recording, sung first in unison and then in harmony, which I imitated rather than quoting it directly. In Jonah's solo lament, accompanied by solo strings and a rumble of muted timpani, I tried to suggest Hebrew cantillation as I had occasionally heard it in synagogue

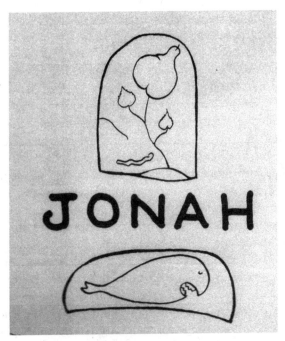

*My title-page illustration for Jonah (1963), depicting the three elements
of the biblical story (big fish, gourd, worm), was reproduced
on the cover of the published score (BMI Canada).*

visits. The outer movements, with Jay's clever verses, were based on the
phrases of the invented "psalm tune," while movements 2 through 5 (corresponding to the biblical chapters) employed a symmetrical twelve-tone
set consisting of a perfect fifth, a scale, and another perfect fifth. Shortly
after the premiere I wrote an essay about the piece for Reaney's little magazine *Alphabet.*[1]

The spurt of energy stimulated by writing my first choral piece surprised
me, and its reception was gratifying. Ready to tackle something more, I
was fortunate to receive a commission from the CBC. They were preparing a series of broadcasts marking the four hundredth anniversary of
Shakespeare's birth and approached several composers for new Shakespeare settings. I asked if I could contribute something on a text *about*
Shakespeare rather than *by* him, and was told this was okay. Obviously
there were already many, many musical settings of the lyrics from the
plays; moreover, from a student attempt I had gained a sense that the
verses were quite idiosyncratic in their treatment of rhythm and metre, and
therefore resistant to musical interference.[2] How about a choral work on

the subject of the Canadian experience of Shakespeare? Jay Macpherson approved of this suggestion but said she did not feel ready to script such a piece. She mentioned a graduate student, Margaret Atwood, already known as a talented young poet (her first novel was still some years away). I had made her acquaintance when she played a role in Jonson's *Epicœne* under Pamela's direction a year or two earlier (she also designed the poster for that production). Her text, compiled in a few weeks, struck me as brilliant, weaving an array of quotations, familiar and obscure, into a cycle of reflections on the bard in Canadian education, the authorship question, and especially the cultural phenomenon of the Canadian Stratford, then scarcely a decade old. Among several titles we considered, the favourite was *The Trumpets of Summer*, referring to the fanfares by Louis Applebaum which summon audiences into the Stratford Festival Theatre. This half-hour "choral suite," for narrator, four soloists, double choir, and a "consort" of six instruments, was several notches more complex than *Jonah*. The first performance took place in Montreal by the Montreal Bach Choir under George Little's direction. Powys Thomas was the narrator, and the soloists were the members of Little's "Petit ensemble vocal." Iseler conducted a Toronto performance for Ten Centuries Concerts and later recorded the work; this time Harold Burke took the narrator's role with Mary Morrison, Patricia Rideout, Don Bartle, and Alex Gray as the four solo singers.[3] Both collaborations were happy ones for me.

In *The Trumpets of Summer* the music is again based, in five of the six movements, on a twelve-tone set with both tonal and modal implications in its scale patterns. The exceptional second movement serializes its initial phrase, akin to a children's nursery jingle. The reviews of the Montreal and Toronto performances, by Eric McLean and Ken Winters respectively, were excellent. Iseler's recording has survived two re-releases and remains listenable. The topic of *Trumpets* is oddly special. When Iseler proposed it for one of his appearances at the Stratford Festival, where it would have had particular relevance, the management turned it down. In my memory the score was a lot of fun to put together, but it remains one of my most difficult; few choirs in later times have been inclined to tackle it.

From time to time I have tried to persuade Peggy Atwood to publish her witty and inventive libretto, but her response is that she regards it as ephemeral. For the Toronto performance of *The Trumpets of Summer*, there was a mimeographed audience handout with the full Atwood text, contributed by BMI Canada. Atwood researchers came to regard this "unpublished" item as a rarity. Robin Elliott relates that he sold his copy to an antiquarian book dealer for "a tidy sum." In 1989 I learned that a dealer in Vancouver, William Hoffer, was advertising a copy at six hundred dollars, and wrote to ask how he acquired it, since I seemed to have lost my only copy. Hoffer, a notorious crank, took offence and replied angrily; a "lively correspondence" ensued between us. He showed his opinion of my original letter by offering it in his next catalogue for two dollars. His description of the libretto had neglected to mention the clearly named publisher. I phoned Berandol (the successor firm to BMI Canada) and they told me there were eighty-two copies of this "rarity" taking up space on their shelves; did I want them? I said I did, and they remain a conceivable nest egg for my heirs. Apart from the BMI gem, Atwood's text is available in booklets accompanying the LP recording and the subsquent CD reissue. According to Elliott, the LP booklet has been advertised in a dealer's catalogue for $1,200 (US).[4]

In the mid-1960s I became interested in the nineteenth-century Children of Peace sect, their leader David Willson, and their Temple at the village of Sharon, about sixty kilometres north of Toronto. James Reaney had written about Willson and regarded him as a major figure in Canadian philosophy; Helmut Kallmann, in his music history, had published research about the musical life of the sect; and Keith MacMillan had produced a CBC Radio documentary on the subject, illustrated by recordings of the Temple's historic barrel organ. This instrument, homemade on-site by the English bandmaster Richard Coates in the early 1800s, intrigued me on visits to the Temple, sometimes with groups of my history-of-music students. In 1966 Walter Kemp, a former student who was then dean of music at Waterloo Lutheran (later Wilfrid Laurier) University in Waterloo, Ontario, and director of the student choir there, proposed a commission, and I put together passages from various of Willson's prose and verse writings to use as a text. I took a long time over this compilation but completed the music in less than a week. The musical setting is based on two tunes found on the Temple barrel organ, "Wells" and "Armley"; both are of English eighteenth-century origin and were widely sung in their day. *Sharon Fragments* approaches the level of difficulty of *The Trumpets of Summer*, and it therefore surprises me that it has become my best known and most often performed choral work. Its compactness together with its textural interest (roughly an alternation of recitatives in prose and hymns in verse) may explain this; in addition, the two quoted tunes do emerge now and then in clear tonal form as a focus for listeners. The words of Willson which I selected touch on his search for religious meaning and on the beliefs of the sect; the sincerity and simple imagery of the hymn verses appealed to me, and I found there was much I could relate to from my own "life struggle." I am always touched when I am introduced to someone and they immediately sing me a phrase they recall from having participated in a performance of this work. Such moments may be similar to the communal feeling choristers often cite as "what choral music is all about."

I had greeted Elmer Iseler's 1964 appointment as conductor of the Toronto Mendelssohn Choir as a case of "the right person at the right time."[5] When that historic large choir pondered what to do with a commission for the Canadian Centennial in 1967, he suggested my name. This was a major challenge. Where to find a suitable text? As usual, my thoughts ran to a newly written libretto. The choir agreed to let me share my commission with a librettist. When I consulted with some of my writer friends, the name of Dennis Lee came up. Like Margaret Atwood, he had been part of Pamela's Victoria College cast for *Epicœne* and was becoming known as a poet: his *Civil Elegies*, then about to be published, had pertinence to the modern city, and Toronto in particular; the children's collection *Alligator Pie*, for which he was later renowned, was still several years in the future. Lee and I discussed some ideas about living in contemporary Canada and specifically in Toronto, and he developed a text calling for chorus and three soloists (speaker, Heldentenor, and blues singer). His first idea for a title was *Civitas*, but I thought that was too high-toned, so we settled on *Place of Meeting*, which some historians claim is the meaning of the Aboriginal word "Toronto" ("the [Toronto] meeting-place" and "the carrying-place" are terms found in historical accounts). The text depicts the commercial sleaze of the modern city ("this shambles") and wonders how human dignity can survive in such surroundings. The blues singer laments, "This country ain't my country, and this city ain't my home." When the speaker climaxes a diatribe by shouting, "There is no Canada; there is NO Canada!" the chorus overlaps his sustained "NO" with the beginning of "O Canada." The tenor part represents a more optimistic and hopeful view, overriding the critical/editorial elements with penetrating high Bs and Cs. We took our commission seriously and ambitiously. Northrop Frye said of the Centennial that what we were all celebrating was the Canada we had yet to create;[6] that was, I thought in retrospect, what Lee and I had tried to convey in *Place of Meeting*.

Place of Meeting was my largest composition project to date. Starting to work on it amid other commitments in the summer of 1966, I planned to produce it in stages, the score for chorus and soloists (with rehearsal cues) first, reserving completion of the orchestra's score and the instrumental parts for later (I was promised the full Toronto Symphony Orchestra, the largest instrumental group I had yet worked with—six horns!). Elements in the work would, I figured, coexist on different planes of dynamics and speed, as in my radio collages—and with these multiple forces it would be necessary to have two conductors. When I checked out these ideas with Iseler he was supportive, indeed gung-ho. The vocal score was ready for the choir in the spring of 1967; it had timings (twenty seconds here, forty-five seconds there) for the orchestral passages I had yet to write. The soloists were booked: the speaker would be the musically sensitive actor Colin Fox; the tenor would be Jacob Barkin, one of the musical Barkins of Toronto, then a cantor in a synagogue in the US, and a singer with a powerful, ringing high register; Al Harris, well known from many CBC broadcasts, would play the guitar accompaniment for the blues singer Phil Maude.

The second conductor position was as yet unfilled. This was still the situation at the start of choral rehearsals in the early fall. With some hesitation, I said to Iseler that if necessary, since I knew the score, I could be the second conductor. He found this an acceptable solution and even asked me to take one or two of the rehearsals, which I did. This experience revealed to me a mood of unrest among the choir members: some were tremendously keyed up about the project, while others were doubtful or even hostile. The piece was turning out to be not just new but controversial. At that point in its history, the Mendelssohn Choir had, I think, never attempted any more advanced contemporary repertoire than Walton's *Belshazzar's Feast*, so *Place of Meeting* seemed to many of the singers further off the choral-music norm than it actually was. Moreover, if the musical content was unfamiliar, Lee's text was, to some, pretty strong stuff. In one passage the choir shouts a miscellany of advertising slogans then seen on billboards or heard in radio jingles, among them a particularly blatant one from a subway placard, "Shrink Hemorrhoids Now!" For some of the more squeamish sopranos, that exceeded the bounds of good taste. It certainly wasn't the B Minor Mass.

Iseler and I divided the conducting chores; for sections in simultaneous but conflicting metres (a large portion of the work), the choir was directed to watch him and the orchestra was directed to watch me. I was nervous for my rehearsals with the orchestra but felt I had good support from the players, some of whom I knew well. Audiences gave Massey Hall a superior rating for acoustics, but those who performed there regularly had a different opinion of the acoustics onstage. I understood this when I corrected the tuba on a wrong entry, only to be told that what I was hearing was the bassoon from the other side of the stage; the echoes

Co-conducting a rehearsal for the premiere of Place of Meeting in Massey Hall with
Elmer Iseler, the Toronto Mendelssohn Choir, and the Toronto Symphony
Orchestra, November 1967 (photo by Robert C. Ragsdale, courtesy
of Faculty of Music Library, University of Toronto).

played tricks. The speaker and the blues combo were positioned in a balcony overlooking the choir, and we asked for them to be miked. It turned out that the hall had no regular sound system in place (its transformation into a rock concert palace was still some years off). A part-time technician would come in when required and set up what amounted to a public address system intended for travel lectures or political meetings. There was delay and distress before this was prepared more or less adequately (it proved *in*adequate in the performance). Our dress rehearsal made *everyone* nervous, especially Elmer Iseler. He told me when it was over that he thought the performance would have to be cancelled. He was a veteran professional performer and I was making my first appearance leading a professional orchestra, but I found *I* was the one who had to rally *his* spirits. Somehow I must have managed to, because we went ahead with the show.

The night of the concert, the work came off more smoothly than in the dress rehearsal. As so often happens, the performers rose to the occasion and gave it their best. There were moments of audience reaction where it seemed our intentions got across. Fox's voice commanded attention despite the erratic miking, and in the ironic final fade-out Harris's blues guitar created a hush. I was told by two orchestra players afterwards (Gene Rittich and Bob Aitken) that my beat was clear; they had advised me as a novice that what most players want from a conductor is a strong *up*beat, and I tried to remember that. There were however some bad, uncertain moments. The passage where the choir suddenly launches into "O Canada" was to be capped by the tenor soloist's most exultant phrases, but Iseler hit "O Canada" at a faster tempo than he ever had in rehearsal—so much faster that Barkin found it impossible to sing his lines, so the effect was ruined. Dennis Lee and I were called to the stage for several bows with the conductor and soloists. It seemed *something* of the work had connected with our audience, but there were to be no more performances.

The next day's newspapers carried poor reviews; *Place of Meeting* is recorded for posterity as a failure,[7] and in many ways it *was* a failure, a case of overreaching ambition. There was no professional recording; I can't recall whether a CBC broadcast had been considered, but if so it didn't happen. Keith MacMillan, who strongly supported the project and always said he liked the work, sneaked a small portable recorder into the hall and picked up the performance from his seat in the balcony. The result gives only a rough idea of a brave but uncertain premiere. Iseler listened to a copy of it a month or so later and phoned to say he thought the piece was wonderful and we should do it again—but the opportunity has never arisen. The schism in the choir resonated after the performance. One of the tenors, Ray Pierce, a friend from student days, wrote me that participating in the work had been a memorable experience for him. On the other hand, a prominent member of the choir's board of directors, Brian McCool, resigned his position out of protest to the inclusion of such trash in the season's program. The score had some successful compositional ideas, in my evaluation, and years later I salvaged one meditative passage for *divisi* strings in the final section of *A Concert of Myths*.

Another prominent choral conductor, Lloyd Bradshaw, approached me in 1968 with a commission for choir and organ for the inauguration of a new organ in St George's United Church in North Toronto. A few years before, I had not anticipated composing for choir, and I was still resistant to the idea of composing a work specifically for church performance. I transformed the commission into a reflection on the association of music with worship in three different cultures. For a libretto, I interleaved passages from the long poem *Jubilate Agno* by the eighteenth-century English mystic Christopher Smart, from a translated Chinese poem of the Confucian era called *The Blind Musicians*, and from an anthropologist's account of a Cree sun-dance ceremony. The main choir would sing invented syllables while a narrator spoke the Smart verses, a youth choir delivered the Chinese text in a sort of speech-song manner, and six solo voices sang the sun-dance invocation. *The Sun Dance* was in fact the title I chose. The youth-choir members were positioned around the church balconies, and some of them played percussion instruments such as bells, clappers, and gongs. The organ began with some *campanella* notes, moving to other registers only after the vocal and percussion elements were established, and the music progressed in complexity from a few pitches in the bells to pentatonic phrases for the "Cree" soloists to twelve-tone harmonies in the organ. At one point the main adult choir sings what Smart called "the melody of God"—a tall compositional order. For this I formulated a simple tune from an overheard vocal improvisation by my five-year-old son Lawrence. In April 1976 I conducted a performance of *The Sun Dance* with student performers of the Faculty of Music, in collaboration with Charles Heffernan (he prepared the choirs and I coached the soloists); the narrator, my executive assistant David Keeling, declaimed the wonderful phrases of Christopher Smart in an incisive, slightly mad style.

In my observation, choral programmers too often regard their repertoire as mainly religious. While there is a vast amount of music written for divine service or using scriptural or devotional texts, there is an equal or larger amount on secular themes. When asked to write for a choir, my thoughts would not immediately run to yet another setting of the *Te Deum* or the *Stabat Mater*, even if I were a churchgoer. My choice of the Book of Jonah for my first choral work had personal reasons: I could identify with the story; I had a sense of what the "belly of hell" was like. Working on *Sharon Fragments*, I thought I knew what David Willson felt in his philosophical searching. Similarly, in the deliberately ecumenical mixture of texts for *The Sun Dance* I found many features I could endorse from experience—musical ecstasy, the assembling of an array of instruments, the excitement of performance, the association of singing with remembrance of ancestors and hopes of human well-being.

Gas! (1969), for twenty speaking voices, memorializes my harrowing adventures around that time in learning to drive. My instructor had developed his skills with the Hungarian army; when I slowed down trying to figure out what to do next he would yell "Gas!"– meaning "Step on it!" I knew the famous *Geographical Fugue* for speaking chorus by Ernst Toch, and, thinking of a similar treatment, concocted a text made up of the various commands which loomed on traffic signs (Yield; No Left Turn; Maximum 45 mph; Right Lane Must Exit; Watch for Children;

No Parking Any Time; and so forth). My idea was to counterpoint these with noises such as kids make when playing with cars. A tryout with twenty students proved hilarious, and on publication the four- or five-minute work had a number of concert performances. But when, in the Trudeau era, kilometres per hour replaced miles per hour my "found" text became immediately dated. In concept, *Gas!* probably foreshadows two larger works, *Mating Time* and *Derailed*. Istvan Anhalt analyzes *Gas!* in his study *Alternative Voices*.[8] He sees the chorally pronounced traffic commands as "an allegory for the dos and don'ts of society" and speculates that it "might pertain to childhood, perhaps to the composer's own."

In 1973, I received a last-minute call to replace Elmer Iseler, who was indisposed. The concert by his *other* choir, the Festival Singers, in the Great Hall of Hart House, had a program of works by three Canadian composers: Derek Healey, Charles Wilson, and me. We were called on to conduct our own pieces, with less than forty-eight hours to prepare, and with only one rehearsal. I remember this as an inspiring musical experience. The Singers at the time were in peak form, and their response in rehearsal was amazingly precise. Conducting them was what I imagine driving a Rolls must be like. They moved ahead with me instead of lingering, as was Iseler's habit, at certain moments in *Sharon Fragments*. The program included what I believe turned out to be their only performance of my setting of Dennis Lee's *1838*.

I had many collaborations with Elmer Iseler in the 1980s, sometimes even as co-conductor again, in the summer concerts at the Sharon Temple. For the first "Music at Sharon" series, in 1981, marking the Temple's 150th anniversary, I was commissioned to compose a new work for his Elmer Iseler Singers,[9] and the result was *Three Motets on Swan's 'China'*— a kind of sequel to *Sharon Fragments*. "China," by the late-eighteenth-century "tunesmith" Timothy Swan, was one of twenty tunes preserved on the historic Coates barrel organ in the Temple, the only one of US origin. It is an odd, tonally skewed melody, and I had become fond of it and often taught it in my "Music of North America" classes. The "motets" are based on three different sets of words: the first is a passage suggested to me by Jay Macpherson, from the Book of Esdras (in the Apocrypha) about a woman who laments her lost son; the second is a compilation I put together consisting of various hymn verses, some by Isaac Watts and some by David Willson; the third is my juxtaposition of various scriptural verses relating to the biblical community of Sharon. From a mood of bereavement,[10] the texts progress to thoughts of renewal and cultivation of the land. In the second motet, I conceived of the Upper Canadian nineteenth-century words by Willson as a choral foreground with the English eighteenth-century words by Watts as a background for a few solo voices—the soloists accompanying the chorus instead of vice versa, and the two being distinguished by not only different sound levels and texts but also different metres. The premiere by the Singers, and their subsequent recording,[11] were deeply satisfying to me. In both, we included the Swan tune, played on the barrel organ, as an introduction.

The following year I received a commission for the events marking the opening of Toronto's new concert venue, Roy Thomson Hall. I had served on the planning committee for the hall's organ, along with Hugh McLean, Andrew Davis, and others, at the invitation of its chairman, John Lawson. It was Lawson who persuaded the Royal Canadian College of Organists to commission a new work for the inaugural concert on the Gabriel Kney organ, and perhaps it was he who proposed my name. Performers on the program were McLean as organ soloist, the Elmer Iseler Singers, the Canadian Brass, and the Toronto Consort. It was suggested that my work include parts for all these groups, but I thought that was not only potential overload for ten minutes' worth of music but a practical restriction on future performances. I scored *A Little Organ Concert* for choir, solo organ, and brass quintet. I thought of "concert" in my title as implying a "concerted effort," and as if spelled in the old way, "consort," meaning "concerto": the organ was the soloist and the chorus and brasses were the quasi-orchestra, the *ripieno*. So the chorus sings no words, only made-up syllables and noises.[12] In one passage there is a kind of gender trade when the tenors and basses sing falsetto and the sopranos and altos answer in their baritone register (some of the women said they didn't have one, and when I referred them to the recordings of Bessie Smith they asked "Bessie who?"). I enacted the various freaky vocal sounds at rehearsals to help rid the singers of their inhibitions, and I had several lively coaching sessions with the Canadian Brass. Andrew (later Sir Andrew) Davis, who co-conducted the program with Iseler, had kindly advised me when I was writing the organ part and gave a generous spoken introduction at the premiere. The performance went well and was well received. I retain a recording from the CBC broadcast. In 2011 *A Little Organ Concert* still awaited its second performance.

Earlier in 1982 I had collaborated on yet another project with Iseler and his Singers. This was a Valentine's Day commission from the CBC in which I enlisted bpNichol as my literary partner. Working on this piece was a thoroughly enjoyable time. Nichol and I had become friends since

Kathleen introduced us a few years previously. His performances with the sound-poetry quartet the Four Horsemen, were among the most original and stimulating events on the Toronto arts scene. The connection with St Valentine's Day reminded me of the reference in a Chaucer text to that feast day as the day when the birds choose their mates for the season,[13] and I wondered if we could incorporate mating cries of birds and animals (imitated by the chorus). Nichol picked this up immediately and pointed out that popular crooning, in Tin Pan Alley style, was a human equivalent to mating cries. The Gershwin and Rodgers and Hart repertoires we both knew and cherished. We figured we needed to do some research, and in the university's science library we found not only treatises describing the sounds various species produce when roused but also a few recordings. I tried to reproduce the recording of the rhinoceros but always broke up. We were astonished to learn that barnacles clack their shells when under the urge. For several weeks we howled or squealed our findings to each other over the phone. These cries would be the spice of the piece, a series of interludes separating the more thoughtful sections. Nichol had already written a poem entitled "Heart," more or less a mini-anthology of puns using that word, which seemed appropriate to open with. His readings on various Valentine traditions revealed that there were two saints of this name, so he wrote a poem reflecting what is known of their characters and their careers. A third poem, "Love," was an apotheosis of 1930s pop. I had observed that a choral ensemble voicing intimate love sentiments on a public stage was hard to make convincing. Performances of the *Liebeslieder Waltzes* of Johannes Brahms had often struck me as slightly absurd—first-person endearments by mature ladies in evening gowns and gentlemen in tuxes. For this problem Nichol proposed two ingenious solutions: one, have the choir sing "I Love You" *in quotation marks* ("We are saying 'I Love You'"); and two, since we had already decided to position the choir members around the stage and the auditorium alternating male and female singers, have each individual in turn say (or sing or shout) "Sweetheart!" to the person next to them, in the spirit of "pass it on."

The piece gradually took shape; there would be an electronic piano, and I once again assigned percussion instruments to some of the choir members. A special sound effect that I found appropriate had been suggested to me when I called for one of my children at a birthday party. The kids had all been given as favours those little metal "frogs" that make a loud click, and I was astonished at the penetrating sound of twenty of them played simultaneously. In a toy store, I found frogs of two different sizes, small and large, respectively high and low in pitch; we issued small

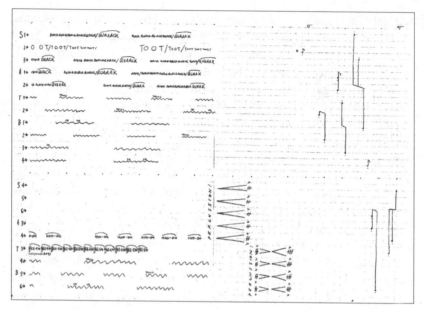

Page 21 of the manuscript score of Mating Time *(1982). The twenty individual voices deliver the various noises called for; the staffless notes are produced on metal "clackers."*

ones to the women choristers and large ones to the men. At key moments in the music there was punctuation by these resonant clicks, and at a couple of points I asked for a round-the-hall *circle* of clicks, as if they were chasing each other. To evoke the amorous barnacles, the choristers clacked their teeth.

The mating-cry interludes in fact called for *many* evocative sounds: teeth clacks were only the start, as the following note (from our introduction to the score) indicates:

The animal signals are derived from a selection of over forty words used by naturalists to describe communicative sounds observed during courtship and mating in various species ... Particular dialogue, ensemble, and chorus patterns existing in nature are imitated ... including a chorus of frog trios, dialogues and trios of various birds, a rhinoceros dialogue, a mosquito dialogue, and a characteristic solo-chorus exchange between a reigning queen bee and her rivals. The "boat-whistle" is the powerful call of the toad-fish ... The "cricketing" patterns are partly based on actual naturalists' observations. Bears, stags, tigers, elephants, whales, prairie dogs, mink, beaver, seals, geckos, alligators, chimpanzees, and kookaburras ("baby talk") are among others to whose audible behavior these sections are indebted. The choral representation … [offers] a brief and vivid collage of animal mating noise ranging from a shy murmur to what one astonished nineteenth-century scientific writer called a "deafening epithalamium."

Mating Time was successfully done a couple of times by the Iselers that season, and the work has had occasional revivals, notably by a choir under Wayne Strongman's direction for New Music Concerts in 1992. This was a spot-on live performance, but the recording of it by CBC Radio was never broadcast. The premiere back in February 1982 had been effectively recorded, conveying the spatial qualities as heard by the live audience. For Strongman's performance, however, the producer and the technician judged that the spatial placement of the choir could not be miked, so they recorded the piece in advance, with the choir all in one location. I protested in vain that part of the idea of the wider positioning was to clarify the often complex goings-on in the music; with the singers bunched together it became much harder to follow, as I knew from the example of Henry Brant and from my own spatial pieces such as *Taking a Stand*. I have often regretted that I wasn't more insistent.

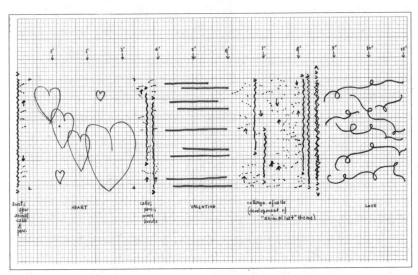

I have often charted texture and form of a composition on graph paper either during or after its creation. This chart depicts the choral work Mating Time *(1982), developed with bpNichol.*

The early '80s had produced a succession of three choral pieces: the *Three Motets, Mating Time,* and *A Little Organ Concert*—hardly a "trilogy," since they were all so different. The mid-80s were a period of concentration on my work for the hymn-tune volume of the *The Canadian Musical Heritage.* Kathleen and I spent the first half of 1985 in Edinburgh, where I added to my research in some of that city's wonderful libraries, finished planning the volume's contents, and wrote the introduction and notes. As a related side occupation, I composed an a-cappella choral work, a cycle of psalm settings, *Harp of David.* In late 1984, I had been invited by my old friend Ronald Shepherd to contribute some music to his installation as bishop of British Columbia in the Cathedral in Victoria where I was once a boy chorister. I produced a setting of Psalm 65, basing it on the tune "London New" from the Scottish Psalter of 1635. In Edinburgh I began further settings of various Psalms, using tunes from various other Protestant traditions. In a few months I found I had a suite of six; the title was suggested by the many and varied North American tune books from the nineteenth century that I had run across in my research—*Sacred Harp, Lute of Zion,* and the like. The Psalm texts I chose represented expressions and sentiments I felt I understood and could identify with; I avoided the more belligerent ones that called for the crushing of my enemies. I used an engraving of the royal harpist from a seventeenth-century Scottish source for my title page. In order, the six settings drew on Scottish, Lutheran, Huguenot, English Methodist, US Evangelical, and early Canadian Methodist tune repertoires. I chose versions from the 1552 *Book of Common Prayer,* but in one ambiguous case added a phrase or two from the translation in the *New English Bible.* Alongside the quoted tunes themselves, in five of the six settings I also incorporated parts of verse-paraphrases associated with them, in the original languages—and, in the second setting, the familiar Latin of the opening phrase, "De profundis clamavi, Domine." The choir is therefore required to sing in English, French, German, and Latin. Half an hour is a risky length for an unaccompanied work, but I recalled Iseler's gripping performance years earlier of Monteverdi's *Lagrime d'amante* with the Festival Singers as proof that it was possible.

The treatment varies from one setting to another; no two are alike. Psalm 65 uses a device like the second of the *Three Motets* where soloists in effect accompany the choir instead of the more usual reverse situation. Psalm 130 (the "De Profundis") is based on the Lutheran chorale "Aus tiefer Not" ("Out of the Depths"—or, literally, "Out of Deep Need"), with its memorable "deep" interval descent on "tief-." Here individual voices now and then interrupt the chorale phrases with anguished spoken cries, and the opening and closing sections intoned in Latin are overlapped with groans of (English) choral speech. For Psalm 1, I recycled the procedure I had used years before at the beginning of *Jonah*, inspired once again by memories of the Huguenot melody as recorded first in unison and then in Goudimel's polyphonic setting. The six-part harmonies in this movement are slithery, almost like Gershwin. Psalm 80 is a complaining prayer, along the lines of "Why *me*?" The recurrent phrase "Turn again, O Lord" seemed perfectly complemented by the slow, upward-twisting Methodist melody "Foundery" (its name refers to one of the Wesleys' early meeting places in London). Watts's versification employs a particularly bold octosyllabic line: "Return, Almighty God, return!" Psalm 148, by contrast, is one of the late "praise the Lord" celebrations, the one where all the creatures of the universe join in. On Scottish television I had seen a rock and roll rendition of the similar Psalm 150 (the one with all the musical instruments), and hated it, while appreciating its appropriateness and sincerity. My setting drew on "Shall we gather at the river?" the favourite of, among millions, my grandmother, and I used only its three basic harmonies (tonic, dominant, and subdominant) plus the chromatic inflections that join them. The piece ends on a subdominant chord, as did many rock tunes at that period—or so it seemed to my ears. In the double setting of the closely linked Psalms 87 and 122, about the holy city of Zion (Jerusalem), the basic melody is taken from the earliest Canadian tune book, Stephen Humbert's *Union Harmony*. I found special contemporary poignancy in the phrase "O pray for the peace of Jerusalem" and turned this into a quiet phrase for the altos alone.

In 1983 the World Council of Churches, scheduled to meet in Vancouver the next year, had asked me to consider a commission for a choral work on the conference theme, "Jesus Christ, the Life of the World." I declined, pointing out that as a non-Christian I was probably not the ideal person for the task. It was a curious coincidence, coming at a time when I was immersed in the hymnody research which led to *Harp of David*. Regarding my research, in another chapter[14] I have examined my responses to the question about my motives, "Why hymns?" My selection of texts for the *Harp of David* cycle might raise another question, "Why Psalms?" In my thinking, Psalm-singing represents a long Judeo-Christian community tradition, an expression of group emotion essentially separate from ritual or liturgy.

Harp of David grew in response to my own creative urges; there was no commission and no envisioned performance. I circulated the score to

Page 44 of the manuscript score of Harp of David *(1985). For this five-part passage, I copied the lines of Humbert's three-part tune "Remembrance" exactly in the soprano and alto, and composed added parts for the tenor and bass, using only the diatonic pitches, in a deliberately imprecise rhythm.*

several conductors, and Jon Washburn said he wanted to present it with his Vancouver Chamber Choir. They gave it a fine premiere in Vancouver in November 1986, later made a recording[15] and also took the work on tour. I recall with special pleasure their wonderful performance of it at the Toronto International Choral Festival in 1989. Elmer Iseler's remark to me on hearing of the Vancouver performance was, "I hear you're sleeping with someone else now." The Iseler Singers performed one or two of the Psalms under his direction but never, as far as I know, the complete score. The publication of *Harp of David* (by the short-lived firm of Jaymar) drew a full and enthusiastic review in the *Choral Journal* in the US.[16]

A year or two later, I formed the idea of trying to probe my own creative processes, and as an example wrote down what I could remember of the evolution of *Harp of David*. When Alan Lessem asked me for a contribution to the *Canadian University Music Review*, of which he was then editor, I showed these notes to him and he published them.[17] That was my first extended commentary on any of my choral compositions since the article on *Jonah*.

As noted above, Iseler and I worked together a great deal during the 1980s. The annual summer "Music at Sharon" festivals, under Lawrence Cherney's direction, regularly included a "heritage program," for which I would research, arrange, and sometimes assist in performing (as keyboardist or conductor) musical repertoire associated with early Canada, early Ontario, or specifically early Sharon—to be performed by the Elmer Iseler Singers and whatever instrumental ensemble seemed suitable (or affordable). We exploited the special acoustics of the Temple by sometimes positioning singers or instrumentalists in the balcony; we were fortunate to be able to use not only the barrel organ but the chamber organ (also built by Richard Coates and dating from the Temple's early years); both instruments had been painstakingly restored by Geoffrey Payzant. In the series' inaugural year, 1981, my *Three Motets* were introduced in a program of secular and sacred pieces associated with the Children of Peace; we recorded most of this program on an LP entitled *Music at Sharon*.[18] A major item, not on the disc, was a group of excerpts from Handel's *Judas Maccabeus*, a work for which there was evidence of a performance in the region in the mid-nineteenth century; I arranged the instrumental score for the sort of hodgepodge of locally available instruments indicated in early reports—a clarinet; a euphonium instead of a bassoon; and so on. Coinciding with my hymn-tune researches, one summer we presented a cross-section of tunes from nineteenth- and early-twentieth-century

Canadian collections; we recreated the program of an 1851 concert in Toronto's St Lawrence Hall by the sensational Jenny Lind, with Rosemarie Landry and assisting artists; reflecting perhaps my time in Edinburgh, another program centred on historical compositions from Scotland and by Scots-Canadian composers, for which of course we conscripted a solo piper.[19]

Cherney was always an encouraging supporter of these efforts. Through his contacts, in 1984 there came an opportunity to contribute a "heritage program" to the musical presentations planned at Roy Thomson Hall marking the sesquicentennial of the incorporation of the city of Toronto. The program featured the Singers and a small orchestra with two soloists we had worked with at Sharon, Rosemarie Landry and Mark Dubois. Cherney, Iseler, and I chose (and I arranged whatever needed arranging) from a repertoire covering pieces, popular and serious, sacred and secular, written in Toronto and/or associated with the city, from the mid-nineteenth century (Henry Schallehn's *Ontario Quick March*) to the mid-twentieth (Harry Somers's *Kuyas*). Iseler and I shared conducting duties. I suggested we call the event a "concert party," the term given to the variety programs put on for troops in wartime. The program was recorded prior to the concert under the title *Musical Toronto, a Concert Party* and released on an LP by Marquis Records.[20] There are some lively numbers on the disc, but I regret there was not enough room to include Dubois's performance of "I'm a Daddy!" one of two excerpts from a First World War *Dumbells* revue and a showstopper in the concert.

Iseler occasionally called on me for other arranging assignments: for example, a group of excerpts from *Moore's Irish Melodies*, the famous early-nineteenth-century collection, for a St Patrick's Day concert. Among other anniversaries, 1984 was the two hundredth year since the founding of the province of New Brunswick, and he and his Singers were invited to lead a choral music weekend in Moncton, a gathering of choirs from across the province—three hundred voices strong. I was asked to prepare something appropriate for the main concert program and came up with *Earlier Voices*, a collection of composed and traditional vocal music from New Brunswick sources, in both official languages. I travelled to Moncton with the Singers and attended the dress rehearsal and concert. The rehearsal was a revelation of Iseler's gifts as a musical communicator. He virtually mesmerized the large group of amateur choristers with his vocal and physical energy, cajoling, and mimicry. This, I thought, is sheer spontaneous inspiration and charisma; you couldn't imitate it or teach it, but when it works it is a marvel.

In my observation in many other rehearsal circumstances, Iseler was a demanding musical leader. He had attracted professionally aware singers and achieved the means to pay them decently for their services, and he insisted that they arrive for rehearsal having studied their parts. He would stop in the middle of a phrase, frown, and shake his head at what he had just heard, and say, "I don't want that," and then start again, without articulating what it was he *did* want: the singers were expected to *know*. At an uncertain entry he would comment, "tenors: you have to get your note from *somewhere*." They would scramble to find a solution, without his help. He could be difficult. There were often moments of considerable tension, although he could also exhibit a strong sense of humour.

Iseler dominated the choral scene in Toronto and beyond for more than thirty years. Apart from my personal debt to him for encouragement, commissions, and collaborations, I have memories of his outstanding performances of Monteverdi, Purcell, Bach, and many contemporary works, as well as, now and then, erratic or reckless ones. In the 1990s the standard of his work evidently began to slip, perhaps because he was venturing into hazardous chorus and orchestra repertoire such as Bruckner. In his mid-career, in 1978, the board of the Festival Singers had declined to renew his contract, and he had not only made the dismissal a public issue but effectively wiped that ensemble off the map and started his own choir. Now, in 1996, the Toronto Mendelssohn Choir asked for his resignation, and again he reacted in loudly public terms, claiming that it was a stab in the back. The choir had proposed an emeritus designation and various other tributes, and these went forward despite his expressions of betrayal. Though close to seventy, he had in fact made no retirement plans. Further complicating the situation, he was already undergoing treatment for the brain tumour from which he was to die scarcely a year later.

In the fall of 1997 Iseler conducted his last full recording session for a disc of Canadian-composed Christmas music for the Canadian Musical Heritage Society, and Clifford Ford and I attended on the Society's behalf. He was in good spirits and top form for most of the session but became agitated when technical problems arose in the final half-hour or so. I had seen him under anxiety and pressure before, and felt badly that this was to be our parting scene. Life doesn't allow you to plan your farewells.

It happened that I had received a commission in 1990 from the Elora Festival Singers, whose conductor, Noel Edison, later became Iseler's successor as musical director of the Toronto Mendelssohn Choir. Edison was one of half a dozen bright talents among the younger choral conductors of that period, and his chamber choir at Elora had attracted a following and much favourable comment. The concert for which I was asked to provide a new work would have as soloists the husband-and-wife team of Anna Tamm and Gary Relyea. I had recently worked with them at Sharon. Gary had in fact been in one of my classes as an undergraduate and later gave several performances of my e.e. cummings cycle for baritone, including a fine one at my Faculty of Music retirement concert in the spring of 1990. The Elora commission afforded an opportunity to pay tribute to bpNichol, who had died suddenly and tragically in 1988 in his mid-forties. He was a dear friend and one of the most powerfully creative personalities I have ever known. For a text I wanted to avoid elegiac or memorial writings and instead looked for typical expressions (lyrical, abstract, "concrete," funky) in a number of bp's publications, as suitable for various combinations of solo and choral voices. There was a lot to choose from; he was a prolific writer. His friend and colleague Paul Dutton showed me some unpublished poems, one of which I added to the selection. To my eventual group of nine short settings I gave the title *beep*, which is how bp (or Barry) sometimes signed letters and cards. The music reflects the almost minimalist quality of some of the texts. For one poem, "Extreme positions,1 (tree/moon)," which in published form has a great deal of space between words, the soloists first give out with a form of "tumbling strain,"[21] derived from North American Aboriginal singing, starting in full voice on a high pitch and descending continuously as long as their breath lasts. The choir sections then sing the words in a hesitant, almost pointillistic manner, against a continuous *sotto voce* murmur by the two soloists. A deadpan parody of a blues lyric, "green lady grocer early morning song" allowed me to write a realistic piece for the baritone soloist in classic blues form. The final piece, "why," is based on a delicate verse with only five words—why, not, and, but, how—set with only five note names in the music. In *beep*, as in other scores, I punctuate the sung parts with percussion and with onomatopoeic noises, both delivered by individuals in the choir. The soloists accompany themselves on claves in two of the movements. CBC Radio picked up the concert but for some reason has never broadcast it. A revival in Vancouver under Jon Washburn's direction was as far as I know not broadcast.

Another commission, in 1997, brought new and intriguing possibilities. I'm not sure how or why it came about. The Guelph Spring Festival wanted a work for amalgamated children's and youth choirs—a large group, nearly two hundred voices—with the collaboration of the Kitchener-Waterloo Symphony Orchestra. Linda Beaupré would prepare two of the choirs, situated in Toronto and Guelph, and Eileen Baldwin would prepare a third choir, from St Marys, near Stratford. Lydia Adams would conduct the concert.

Questions surrounding the development of musical awareness in infants and young children had often interested me, and I had begun to observe the responses of my grandchild, Alison Beckwith, born in June 1997. The simple melodies children make up during play: Where do they come from? and to what extent are they cross-cultural? What are the basic forms, in bodily gesture (rhythm) and vocal behaviour (melody) that direct human beings in their earliest years towards musical expression? I conceived a piece that would trace an imaginary musical evolution using first simple materials and then advancing to fuller means, as if the young choristers were learning the musical basics. I decided to call it *Basic Music*. As in *A Little Organ Concert*, I wrote abstract lines for the singers and afterwards attached whatever syllabic sounds seemed appropriate—a sustained open vowel here, sharp consonants for attack there. The vocables were mostly without conceptual meaning (I always hoped I wasn't accidentally spelling some obscenity in a language I didn't know), but at a few points they indicated the choir's reaction to features in the musical continuity ("Eh?" "Oh!"). Further voiced reactions included laughter and conversational babble. The work opens with a single child's voice singing a tune on just three pitches against a vaguely primordial orchestral background. The tune spreads to the children's choir, whose members in effect "teach it" to the older and stronger singers in the youth choir. Gradually together they attempt more complicated formations with a larger pitch vocabulary. At the end the choirs combine in a cheery major-key song in which I hoped they could convey the joy of musical performance.

While developing *Basic Music*, I visited rehearsals and talked to the young choir members, trying to get a sense of their musical views, attitudes, and tastes. Children in a choir with auditions and high musical standards and discipline are not exactly a cross-section of humanity. I asked one youngster what he thought of the Spice Girls, then ragingly popular. "I *hate* the Spice Girls," he said. There were delays in getting copies into the hands of the choirs and their conductors (although I had delivered my score some months in advance), and panic threatened as the concert in May drew closer. On the day of the dress rehearsal, the bus carrying one of the choirs to Guelph broke down, causing unfortunate loss of time. I was impressed with Lydia Adams's cool, efficient management of the proceedings, and with her sensitive musicianship. We had worked together a few times under Iseler, whose assistant she was.

In some respects the actual premiere was like a replay of *Place of Meeting* thirty years earlier: large forces, nervous and somewhat under-prepared; unforeseen difficulties in the dress rehearsal; lack of CBC broadcast involvement and therefore of a proper recording. This time I was the one who had moments of thinking we would have to cancel. Lydia Adams had made a sensible decision at the last moment to cut one passage that seemed too difficult to bring off. The orchestra was solid and supportive. In the event, the moments of unsteadiness were very few, the child who sang the opening phrase was magical, the moments of onomatopoeia had evident surprise value and the ending an upbeat exuberance. There was a good audience response, and the reviews were positive. As so often happens, all this didn't translate into a string of further performances; but I keep hoping—because I greatly enjoyed working on *Basic Music*, and I think it represents much of what I know and feel about music.[22] I later adapted the orchestral portion of the score for two pianos and percussion as a more accessible version.

From time to time there have been occasions for shorter choral compositions. In 1995 I was asked by Teri Dunn and my son Lawrence to write a piece to be sung at their wedding. I devised a "secular motet" based on two texts from Book Five of bpNichol's *Martyrology* poetry cycle. The title is *All at Once*. I have sometimes used my sketch of this two-minute number as an illustration of my working procedures in talks to students.

Most commissions have specific demands and turn out to have unique musical qualities. I had a truly unusual request in 2000 from a friend, Linda Corman, head librarian of the John Graham Library at Trinity College in the University of Toronto. The library was moving into new and enlarged quarters, and she thought it would be appropriate to have some music at the dedication ceremony. Over the circulation desk at the old library was a motto from Ecclesiastes: "Of making books there is no end, and much study is a weariness of the flesh." Why this downer was considered inspirational to librarians and students was a mystery, but Linda wanted it set to music and the College choir would be on hand to perform. I told her the phrase, sung and perhaps stretched out with a few melismas or held notes, would take thirty seconds—forty, maximum. We agreed that I might amplify it with other texts reflective of reading and learning. The result was a four- or five-minute a-cappella composition to which I gave the title *Lady Wisdom*. Some of the words I added ("Happy is the man that findeth wisdom; she is more precious than rubies") are from the Book of Proverbs. Jack Miles, in *God, a Biography*, argues that the author of Proverbs was a woman, and he calls her "Lady Wisdom."[23]

In 2002 another friend, Frances Donovan, asked me to compose a piece to be performed by her large kindergarten-age choir at Withrow Public School, and the result was *Snow Is Falling*, a "Canadian urban kids' winter song" with an accompaniment for flute (or violin) and guitar (or piano). I compiled the lyrics from cold-weather preoccupations of preschoolers as I had observed them. The title was suggested by Alison Beckwith, then five years old. The piece has been picked up by other choirs.

Around the time of my eightieth birthday, in 2007, I received a commission from the Mississauga Choral Society, a sixty-voice ensemble in the community just west of Toronto. I had friends among its members, had attended several of its concerts, and formed a good impression of its quality and spirit. When the question of a suitable text arose, I again looked for something with local relevance. The incorporation of the city of Mississauga dated only from the late 1970s, although component communities like Streetsville existed since the late eighteenth century, and the Aboriginal Mississauga tribe had roots much further back. Accounts of local history invariably draw attention to one famous recent event, the train derailment and evacuation of November 1979. I tried out on some of the Society's directors the idea of a "choral documentary" based on this event and received an encouraging go-ahead. I read several historical accounts and two post-disaster reports, one from a government inquiry and the other from a group of environmentalists. I looked up newspaper articles of the week of the accident, and CBC Archives provided me with radio and television recordings and video footage. I sent a memo to the choir members asking those who were living in Mississauga in 1979 to send me any special recollections. From all this, I developed a "found text" of quotations, to use in my imagined documentary. I believe my approach was influenced by James Reaney's local-history plays such as *The Dismissal*, *King Whistle*, and *I, the Parade*, and also by the quasi-operas of Istvan Anhalt, especially *Winthrop*.[24] The piece emerged as a score for speaking choir (including twenty solo voices), singing choir, and a percussionist. The Society received a generous grant from the Koerner Foundation for the commission. I chose the one-word title *Derailed*.

I found in the accounts a stirring example of human cooperation. A few minutes before midnight on Saturday 10 November 1979, a train carrying dangerous chemicals derailed close to a major intersection in Mississauga. A series of massive explosions, followed by escaping gases, led the authorities to order evacuation of the entire city of over 250,000. The cleanup lasted almost a week. The "Mississauga miracle" is a disaster story with a happy ending: despite considerable property loss, there were no major human casualties—astonishing in an evacuation of this magnitude. Indeed, it counts as the largest such evacuation in North America before the New Orleans hurricane of 2005. That it occurred at night and on a holiday weekend prevented the sort of loss that might have ensued in the middle of a working day. My score attempts to depict a succession of feelings, from the engineers in the malfunctioning train to worried residents ordered out of their homes, and difficulties, whether of teams repairing lethal gas leaks or officials charged with maintaining control.

Mark Duggan, with whom I had worked on *Crazy to Kill*, contributed many ideas for the percussion part, which he agreed to play at the premiere. A loud train bell opens and closes the piece, and there is a siren. A large accumulation of metal percussion suggests an out-of-synch clanging in counterpoint with the regular wheel-turning of the train, corresponding to descriptions of the warnings before the crash. The speaking choir uses choral speech to deliver the fragments of the story, and there are various noises, such as group breathing, crowd talk, and, at the conclusion, a round of applause. The singing choir provides melodic interest, to made-up syllables.

January and February of 2008 were exceptionally severe winter months. The weekly rehearsals were on Tuesday evenings, and almost every Tuesday there was a blizzard. I attended nearly all of the rehearsals, having offered to work with the speaking choir; but the three-quarter-hour drive to Mississauga sometimes became a more-than-two-hours crawl, and attendance by the choir members understandably suffered. We were unable to interest the CBC in a broadcast of the work. A further complication: Chrys Bentley, the conductor with whom I had my preliminary discussions about *Derailed*, resigned and was replaced by Mervin Fick. The individual solo voices include two children, and by the week of the dress rehearsal these parts had still not been cast. I rejected the proposal that two adult members would "imitate" children's voices: as part of the portrayal of a community in disaster mode, I argued there had to be *real* children. In the event, the parts were played by my granddaughters, Alison and Juliet, on less than twenty-four hours' notice, coached by me and by their mother, Teri Dunn, an experienced choral director.

The performance in Hammerson Hall, the main auditorium of the Living Arts Centre in Mississauga, was shaky but roused a good response. Mayor Hazel McCallion attended and gave an enthusiastic speech afterwards saying she thought the piece should be done again.[25] A number of audience members were moved to share their memories of the evacuation week. My "found text" for *Derailed* was published in the November 2009 issue of the *Literary Review of Canada,* marking the thirtieth anniversary of the event.

I am not a choral music director or specialist-composer. Each of my choral works has a separate layout and intention. While some compositional habits and predilections recur, no two works are alike. They do not fit publishers' marketing concepts. I feel fortunate that almost all have been commissioned—that is, written because someone thought I could fill a need. Working with choirs now and then has been a deeply rewarding part of my professional life for over forty years. However, from being heard, the pieces, with only a few exceptions, become soon unheard of, and then unheard. Why are my ideas so often so "difficult"?

11

For Voice(s)

The four e.e. cummings songs for soprano and piano are student works of 1950. The six e.e. cummings songs for baritone and piano were composed between 1980 and 1982—that is, thirty years later. During those thirty years I had many contacts with first-class singers but evidently no interest in adding to the song repertoire. The only examples from that period are an album of songs for children and the *Chaucer Suite* (both 1962) and two sets of arrangements from Canadian traditional-music sources (Four Love Songs for baritone and piano, 1969, and Five Songs for contralto and piano, 1971). I had continuing interest in problems of English-language prosody, and I discussed them with my students. Rhythm, pitch contours, punctuation, accent—these were constant concerns in my choral and operatic writing. But it was a period when, like many composers, I wondered whether setting extant poetry to be sung was still a valid exercise, the so-called "art song" (in French, *mélodie*; in German, *Lied*) still a valid medium. Were voice-and-piano partnerings like those of Mahler, Wolf, Debussy, and Duparc still possible? If setting extant poems or prose texts, *what* texts? My restart, signifying that my answer to the first question was "yes," began when I decided to write out the music which for years had been going through my head for cummings's burlesque lyric, "Jimmie's got a goil." One thing led to another, and in leisure moments I returned to his poetry and at length found I had another cycle. Performances by Mark Pedrotti, Gary Relyea, Doug Mac-Naughton, and other singers have been reassuring. William Aide has been an invaluable champion. The experience was for me a prelude to further solo-voice ventures.

A unique project was the set of *Ten English Rhymes* of 1962. Several teachers had told me of a need for short solo songs for very young pupils. My own children loved the beautifully illustrated collection of traditional nursery rhymes called *Lavender's Blue*.[1] Many of the rhymes went with traditional tunes, but for some that didn't I decided to make up tunes with simple piano accompaniments. A few I designed with alternative versions to be sung collectively in two parts or as rounds. Published with drawings by Mary Lou Payzant,[2] they have had a fair circulation in school classrooms and vocal studios.

My brief association with the poetry of Chaucer was spontaneous, not a response to a request or a commission. The Suite consists of four settings, the first and fourth for three solo voices (contralto, tenor, baritone), the second for two voices (tenor, baritone), and the third for just one voice (tenor). It was an odd project, and I regard it as a study based on my attraction to Stravinsky's early serial works of the 1950s. Finding ways to

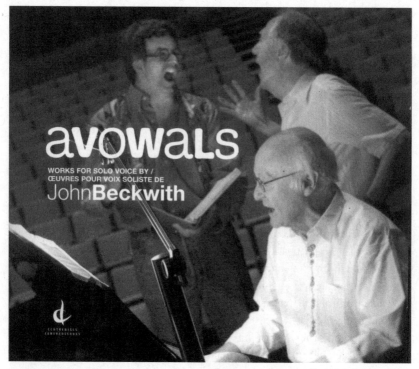

The photographer André Leduc caught Doug MacNaughton, William Aide, and me clowning during a break in the recording session of the Six Songs to Poems by e.e. cummings, 2007. The photo appears on the cover of the CD Avowals.

deal with earlier forms of English lent the task a special aspect. I have felt at times that there should be an instrumental accompaniment to the three soloists but have never been able to decide exactly what would be appropriate (certainly not piano). There have been a few performances, and I have sometimes used the Suite in demonstrating serial procedure with students.

The sets of arrangements were commissioned by the CBC for Donald Bell and Maureen Forrester, respectively, and were recorded by them.[3] The radio producer John Roberts was making efforts to develop a repertoire of concert transcriptions of Canadian "folk music," after several decades when arranging had evidently lost the appeal it formerly had for composers. I conceived groups of songs drawn from several different ethnic cultures beyond the obvious English and French sources. The baritone set includes songs in Gaelic and Tsimshian, and the contralto set has examples in Lithuanian and Ukrainian. Kenneth Peacock provided transcriptions from unpublished collections he had researched, and I was encouraged by his words of approval on my approach to the voice-and-piano settings. Mieczyslaw Kolinski had allowed me to audit his graduate seminar in ethnomusicology, and I found his method of melodic analysis helped me focus on suitable treatments for the Canadian source tunes. There was much general discussion at the time of the dangers of "cultural appropriation," and Donald Bell at first declined to perform or record the Tsimshian song on the grounds that my arranging it for concert use represented an intrusion (some years later he relented and did perform it). I was ready to plead guilty to the charge of intrusion but felt that the process of turning music from an anonymous aural tradition into a concert format had continuing positive value in making beautiful pieces of music more widely known: in my view all the songs I chose were beautiful in one way or another. The success of these two sets of arrangements made me think that I should make companion sets for the other two standard voice types, soprano and tenor, but it was not until the late 1990s that I managed to do this. Again the approach is multicultural and multilingual: to English- and French-language songs, the tenor set (entitled *Young Man from Canada*, 1998) adds songs in Gaelic and Hungarian, and the soprano set (*I Love to Dance*, 1999) songs in Russian (Doukhobor) and German (Mennonite).[4]

Shortly after the baritone songs with e.e. cummings texts, in 1985, a commission for Ruth Morawetz's "Classical Cabaret" series in Toronto called for a work for solo tenor and keyboard with a popular-music slant. I consulted with bpNichol and he came up with an original text, a ten-minute monodrama called *Avowals*. The soloist personifies a pop singer who is unable to detach his own love pangs from the lyrics he is performing onstage. Besides three fragments in a realistic crooning style, the inventive script offers vocalizing stretches on plain vowels, some with double meanings and some without. For the most extended of the three crooning sections I developed a version of a thirty-two-bar pop song chorus. For the keyboard part I decided to borrow from some of my collage experiences and called for a single player operating three instruments—piano, celeste, and harpsichord. Henry Ingram gave a striking premiere with Ruth and later repeated his performance with me. Benjamin Butterfield and William Aide have since made a fine recording.[5]

Two chamber works with solo-voice parts occupied me in the late 1980s, both commissioned by early music ensembles. From involvement in Ten Centuries Concerts twenty years before, I had retained an interest

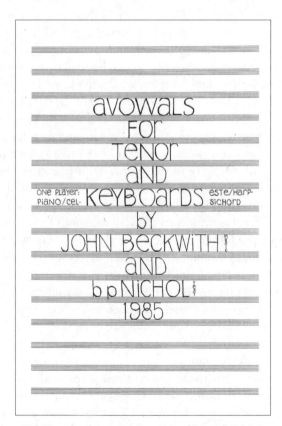

Title page for the manuscript score of Avowals *(1985).*

in the growing early music performance movement in Toronto, and regularly attended concerts by the Toronto Consort and other groups. When, in 1986, David Fallis asked me to write something for the Consort's December concert, I was unenthusiastic about writing a Christmas piece (lucrative though that might have been!). I preferred, I said, to compose something about winter—Canadian winter. It occurred to me that the instruments available (lute, recorder, viol, harpsichord) were known to at least some of the earliest European settlers in what is now Canada. Quoting from accounts of the earliest French settlements in Saint-Croix and Port Royal (1604–7), I formed a narrative text, in French, to which I gave the name *Les premiers hivernements* (i.e., *First Winterings*). It was a story with both tragic and heartening aspects. I chose passages from the diaries of Samuel de Champlain and from the writings of Marc Lescarbot, to be performed by soprano and tenor soloists with a mixed instrumental ensemble of four or five players. In the Consort's premiere the singers doubled on instruments.

A second venture, along similar lines, in 1990, was *The Hector*, a commission from Alison Melville and Colin Savage and their ensemble Musick Fyne. I again leaned towards a Canadian topic and tried to relate the instrumentation (this time period flutes and clarinets, mandolin, guitar, harpsichord), to some pioneer period in Canadian history. The players would introduce the piece in a tour of Maritime Canada, so the subject of eighteenth-century immigration to that region seemed a natural one. The sailing ship the *Hector* brought the first settlers from Ullapool in Scotland to Pictou in Nova Scotia in 1773. My piece was developed from historical accounts of the harrowing eleven-week voyage and also from both Scottish and early Nova Scotian musical sources. The score calls for a soprano soloist who besides singing also delivers the spoken narration. The instruments customarily were tuned to two different pitch standards, almost exactly a quarter-tone apart, and I decided to mix them instead of selecting one or the other. I reasoned that in the descriptive accompaniment of the storms encountered by the vessel the uncertain pitch and resulting microtonal passages had specific musical value, even if this created difficulties for the solo singer. Quotations in the music include "The Children's Lament," a classic pibroch (several children were among the casualties from outbreaks of disease during the voyage), and what to me is one of the most touching Scottish songs of the period, "Farewell to Lochaber." Pipes were not available, so I had to content myself with an "indoor" imitation of the sound. According to historical records, passengers insisted there should be a piper aboard, and he was the first to land in Pictou.

Two performers with whom I worked at Sharon, the soprano Rosemarie Landry and the clarinetist James Campbell, commissioned me to write something for a tour they planned with the pianist André Laplante. While turning over various possible texts in my mind, I found myself starting to sketch possible combinations and contrasts for the trio of voice, clarinet, and piano. One of these was a trio without the piano, the three parts being high clarinet, mid-range soprano, and low clarinet. Out of that evolved another sequence with high soprano, mid-range clarinet, and the soprano in her low chest tones, to which I added some percussion noises from the pianist. Without meaning to, I found I had the beginnings of a piece in which the voice part would be textless. As with some of my works for chorus, I invented a syllabic continuity, avoiding the monotony of a limited number of vowel sounds (as found in many classical vocalises). It was a synthetic approach to composing, and I gave the finished work the title *Synthetic Trios*. The three participants are each assigned some passages of percussion. When I played the seven short trios for Rosemarie, she said she thought the sequence resembled a life-to-death cycle. The parts for voice and for clarinet are dramatic and showy (I was well acquainted with the performers' abilities), the piano part somewhat less so. As it turned out, Laplante was unavailable for the tour and it never took

Performing Synthetic Trios *(1986) in Walter Hall, 19 September 2010. Left to right: Peter Stoll, John Beckwith, Vivienne Spiteri (page turner), Teri Dunn. Photo by André Leduc.*

place. The first performance of *Synthetic Trios* was by Carolyn Hart, Paul Bendzsa, and Edmund Dawe at a conference in Quebec City. This group, from St John's, performed the work several times, and it was repeated by Teresa Costes, Connie Gitlin, and Delores Kay-Hee at the Canadian League of Composers annual meeting in Winnipeg in 1991[6] and by Barbara Hannigan, Ameene Shishakly, and Stephen Clarke at the Faculty of Music in Toronto in 1993. These were all exceptionally communicative performances. I used the recording from Winnipeg as an illustration for talks about my work during a visit to several university music departments in Australia in 1992. I enjoyed undertaking the piano part in a performance with Teri Dunn and Peter Stoll in 2010.

My vocal music was featured several times in the Toronto series The Aldeburgh Connection, and in 1997 the directors of the series, Bruce Ubukata and Stephen Ralls, asked me to compose a new work for a concert in memory of Lois Marshall, who had died in February of that year. My association with Lois went back to student days, and I had wonderful recollections of her performances, including some of my own works. I thought the text should be something by a Canadian woman writer. My son Symon wondered if instead of poetry I should be considering prose sources: he suggested I reread Margaret Laurence's novel *The Fire-Dwellers*. In it, the central character, Stacey MacAindra, a married woman with four children, feels life has her trapped. Her imaginary dialogues with God challenge received concepts of Christian doctrine, including the figure of a male god. The novel also has musical points of reference—a Victorian hymn tune, some dance music by Tommy Dorsey. It was the tenth anniversary of Margaret Laurence's death—another link. I knew her writings fairly well and had a few personal contacts with her. Was Stacey an auto-portrait? The period and the locale, North Vancouver, hinted that she might be. I recognized that many of the pressures of her character—the horrible reports of the Vietnam war, the trials of maintaining a marriage and bringing up a family in the new social scene of the sixties—were those of Laurence's generation, which was also mine. *Stacey*, the eventual "sung monologue" or one-character mini-opera, was introduced by Monica Whicher and Stephen Ralls in 1998. Whicher projected the character of Stacey with remarkable vividness; she has performed the piece several times and recorded it twice. Among others who have brought it to life successfully is the team of Teri Dunn and William Aide; they have also recorded it.[7]

Adrienne Clarkson's installation as Governor General of Canada in Ottawa in 1999 was, I imagine at her request, a long and lavish ceremony and celebration. The impresario Nicholas Goldschmidt, a personal friend of hers, was pressed into service and signed up an impressive array of performing talent for the occasion. Niki called me one day, ostensibly to ask my advice. The program needed something to represent Newfoundland: What was the name of that lovely arrangement by Harry Somers? And did I think I could adapt it for a couple of marvellous Canadian singers, Donna Brown and Catherine Robbin? The choral arrangement he remembered was "She's Like the Swallow," and after looking at it I said no, I didn't think it was adaptable for two solo singers. Well, he jumped in, would I like to do a *new* arrangement? As usual, there was a small fee and he would have to have it by next week. I loved the tune. Okay, I said; but did I *have* to use a piano for the accompaniment? There were other instrumentalists on the schedule, so he agreed to let me have a flute (for the bird images) and a viola (for something like a bass line). The singers, both of whom I knew, were indeed exceptional, and I thought the arrangement made a good effect when performed by them with Robert Cram and Doug McNabney in the Senate Chamber. Prime Minister Chrétien is said to have whispered to Cram that he thought it was the best thing in the program.

From various arranging assignments (including those for the CBC and for the Music at Sharon concerts), I found I had developed a technical approach to traditional songs and dances. I avoided imposing standard harmonies on the original tunes, but relied instead on first observing the original, and then developing supporting lines and counter-melodies from it—that is, from its interior harmonic implications, its range and repertoire of pitches, its characteristic intervals. Often the process was like converting an unaccompanied source melody into a self-accompanied format.

For a contribution to the Aldeburgh Connection's "Toronto Song Book" by various local composers in 2000, I made a setting of a poem by Miriam Waddington, another writer whom I had known slightly and whose work I admired. The title was "A Man and His Flute," and I believe (though unable to verify this) that it was inspired by a concert performance by Robert Aitken. The flute has to be imagined in the piano part, and the ending, an atmospheric line about the scent of lemons, proved a real challenge (the singer hums a monotone). The first performance, again by Monica and Stephen, stimulated me to further settings of Waddington's poetry, in response to an expressed need in 2003. Kathryn Domoney was preparing a solo concert to be given at Queen's University in Kingston and wanted some new songs to include in her program. I added to "A Man and His Flute" settings of Waddington's poems entitled "Old Chair

Song" and "The Snow Tramp." In the latter, the main figure says she "feels like a gypsy," a reference which I picked up by imitating a Brahms Hungarian Dance in the piano part. Kathy and William Aide have recorded these songs.[8] Kathy approached me again in 2005 for a new piece to be performed in a duo recital with Maria Soulis. I discovered the remarkable poetry of the US hermit-activist Thomas Merton (author of *The Seven Story Mountain*). I couldn't appreciate the more mystical poems, but those reflecting his monk's life, his studies of oriental religions, and his participation in the civil rights campaign in the US south all had a strong impact when I read them, as did his extraordinary biography. My *Merton Duets* are based on three poems from these three areas of his work. Again resisting the conventional accompaniment of piano, I decided to write for soprano, mezzo, and a solo violin. Domoney and Soulis were joined by Marie Bérard in the Toronto premiere of this work.

Another literary discovery, in 2008, was the poetry of Samuel Beckett. I was in the middle of reading and rereading Beckett (via a biography and several plays I didn't previously know) when I recalled that Doug MacNaughton had asked me for some songs he might perform to his own guitar accompaniment. I decided to look at Beckett's small but impeccable output of poetry and chose three short and characteristic examples that I figured would be suitable; the titles are "Roundelay," "Thither," and "Something There." I intended the guitar part to be easy, but, not being a guitarist, I had a struggle to keep it that way. Doug was an indispensible adviser and gave a first-class premiere for an audience at the Arts and Letters Club. The *Beckett Songs* were also performed at Mount Allison by Peter Groom and Peter Higham. (Once more thinking of MacNaughton's enthusiasm and fine voice, in 2011 I produced *Singing Synge*, a cycle of three character studies (for baritone and piano) based on texts from the plays of the Irish writer whose work I had always greatly admired.)

Also in 2008, as a birthday gift for my grandchild Juliet Beckwith, a member of the Toronto Children's Chorus and a budding cellist, turning nine that September, I composed a little suite called *Play and Sing* for her to perform by herself. It consists of short cello pieces, an unaccompanied wordless song, and a couple of duets for voice and cello.

Like many composers, I'm asked from time to time to respond to questionnaires about my work. Over the years I've often quoted the one (from a high-school student) which included a two-part question. Part A inquired, "Do you feel your music is well-enough known?" I pondered whether to say "yes" or "no": some of my works are ignored or forgotten, but others have received repeat presentations by excellent performers. Trying to decide how to answer, I glanced at Part B. It demanded, "What do you propose to do about this?"

Another questionnaire came in 2001 from Bernard Andrews, a professor in the Faculty of Education at the University of Ottawa and a U of T music graduate, part of a survey entitled "An Investigation of the Generative Processes of Musical Composition." I have preserved my answers, and perhaps they say something of my "processes." *Why do I compose?* There's an intellectual factor which ties in with my love of music and my curiosity about music, and also a game-playing factor, more emotive or instinctual, which links to fantasy, or what the transactional-analysis people call The Child. *What starts me off?* A commission; something I've read or listened to; a travel experience; some appeal from my work in teaching or research; a favourite musical model. *Does my gender affect my music?* I don't think so. If dealing (in an opera or a programmatic piece) with human characters, I believe I can depict male and female individuals equally convincingly. *Does aging affect it?* There are more periods of wondering "what's the point?" and feeling others are less interested than they used to be: this could be either conventional paranoia or just the general decline of classical-music consumption in my time. *What are the stages of composing a new work?* Initial "research"; calculations and charting, often on graph paper, to figure the development potential of the initial musical idea (what Schoenberg called the *Grund-gestalt*), whether imagined, improvised, or borrowed; deciding the details; editing and copying, usually within reach of a metronome and a stopwatch (this stage also entails an expenditure of creative energy, i.e., isn't purely mechanical). *Is the succession of stages linear or spiral?* It depends on the size of the project. Most pieces longer than two or three minutes develop spirally or in a zigzag succession of stages, as in making a quilt. Sometimes a work grows in the form of several components for which an appropriate order is decided later. *My emotional state for composing? its fluctuations at different stages?* Concentration is more essential than a relaxed emotional mood. I like a calm, quiet stretch of at least three or four hours, free of other concerns; creative work after all is still *work*. As to my emotional attitude to what I'm working on, this can swing widely between love and hate: This is the best thing I've ever done / Why did I ever start this? / God, I wish it was *finished. Environmental conditions for composing?* Calm and quiet surroundings; access to a piano (desirable though not always essential); access to advice from performers. *The impact of my musical education?* My classical background, my keyboard studies, my CanMus researches, all have had a noticeable influence on my creative work, as well as the advice I've had from teachers and from working with performers. *What obstacles do I encounter? how do I surmount them?* They're unpredictable; by *work*.

By 1978, after composing for approximately thirty years, I had accumulated many recordings (private tapes, broadcast airchecks, a few LPs) of performances of my music. Returning from my New Zealand sojourn that year, I imagined listening to them all in one uninterrupted session. Steve Chenette liked to organize listening marathons—all the Mahler symphonies in sequence, for example—and this may have been my inspiration. Ruth Pincoe, then on the CMC staff, helped me prepare the material, and I sent out invitations to friends I thought might be interested. In a large room in the Faculty of Music building, we played almost everything from the *Five Lyrics* (1947) to the Quartet (1977), starting around noon and ending shortly before midnight. A schedule attached to the invitation indicated hour by hour what pieces would be heard; copies of the scores were on hand for those who wanted to follow; people dropped in for an hour or stayed for a whole afternoon or evening stretch; Kathleen arranged some light refreshments. It was a successful undertaking, and I wondered why no fellow composers picked up the idea. A similar marathon, of works composed in the thirty years since then, would take up considerably more than twelve hours.

LIFE, PART 2

15

Full Length

I am a man. I am an artist. I am a failure.
—e.e. cummings (Him)
Marriage: a couple of young people stoop to pick a flower and
bring down an avalanche on their heads.
—Bernard Shaw

This chapter of the tale is more like apologies and confessions. There's nothing very juicy in it. Having begun by depicting my parents, it seemed appropriate for a full-length self-portrait (now that the account nears *its* full length) to write of people and happenings in my adult life that have had comparable influence. My assorted career doings did not occur in separate compartments, although I have chosen to group them in separate chapters under separate headings; all were interwoven with experiences and situations of my home life. If full-length, the portrait cannot be literally a full one, obviously: as with any memoir writer, there are things that, consciously or (mostly) unconsciously, I'm bound to leave out. But those closest to me, and the ups and downs we have shared, form part of the story. The filtered result is "all that I would have you see / Of my brief immortality."[1]

"Doings"—it sounds like a fairly modern word. But in fact it appears in a tribal call of anglophones from the sixteenth century that I have known almost my entire life:

O Lord, who hast safely brought us to the beginning of this day, defend us in the same with thy mighty power, and grant that this day we fall into

319

no sin, neither run into any kind of danger, but that all our doings may be ordered by thy governance to do always that is righteous in thy sight.[2]

"Neither" for "nor," and "that is" for "what is" or "that which is" are obsolete usages, as is also "governance" for "set of rules"; alongside them, the phrase "all our doings" doesn't sound antiquated at all. Here is a very human morning wish—to start the day right, avoid bad scrapes, make good decisions, and do the right thing.

When Pamela and I as high-school sweethearts compared our experiences of childhood, I realized how lucky mine had been. She had lived in seven or eight different BC towns and attended many different schools. For a few years when both her parents were seriously ill she and her younger brother were cared for by their paternal grandmother and an aunt. Her father, Kingsley ("King") Terry, had lied about his age and headed overseas in the last years of the First World War to serve as a dispatch rider with the Canadian Army. Returning, he studied medicine at McGill and fell in love with the beautiful, auburn-haired Muriel Braden. Headstrong and temperamentally unsuited, they led a strained married life, with the added burden of long treatments for tuberculosis, from which he recovered but she did not.

When Muriel died, in late 1948, King remarried within less than a month and immediately left Canada to take a position as medical officer with the Canadian Immigration Service in England, in effect turning his back on his family. It was a distressing period for Pamela, and I asked my parents whether they could invite her to stay with them. They welcomed the idea, and she said the early months of 1949 represented her first experience of a stable and happy household.

Finishing high school a year before I did, she had spent a year as a clerk in a record shop, where she expanded her already impressive knowledge of performers and repertoire. While I was attending college, she took the one-year normal-school course to qualify as an elementary-school teacher, and for the next three years was in charge of grade 1 classes in the Victoria public-school system. She continued to perform as a pianist, and we participated as a duo in concerts in the summer of 1947. With a group of friends, she helped organize the Victoria Gilbert and Sullivan Society[3] and played piano accompaniments and also acted and sang in several of its productions. For the season 1948–49, she dropped teaching and enrolled in the first year of the college's arts and science course. After she moved to Toronto in the fall of 1949 her options appeared to be continuation of her post-secondary program or qualification for teaching in

Ontario. The announcement about the Canadian Theatre School, newly founded under Sterndale Bennett's direction, presented a third and more agreeable prospect, and she decided that was what she wanted. She and her brother Robin, a talented actor, had become increasingly interested in drama and had read widely in dramatic literature and the history of theatre. Just as I had revelled in being able to do music full-time, she responded eagerly and actively to immersion in theatrical studies. We led busy and exciting lives, independent but with a close sharing of experiences. At Christmas 1949 we began to talk of marriage. Maybe it was high time, but we were still young to be considering such a serious move.

Neither of us knew anything about sex. In my growing-up years, I had neither an aging *cocotte* to coach me in the basics (Colette, *Chéri*) nor kindly uncles to introduce me at the neighbourhood bordello (Bellow, *The Adventures of Augie March*). Adolescent romantic attachment remained just that until you married—such was the absurd principle of our upbringing and of our social milieu. I have often asked myself why we two didn't rebel, but we didn't. A prolonged chaste relationship— often with extended exploration of our bodies but always within strict limits—broken by long periods of separation when we communicated only in writing, was not as uncommon then as it came to be fifteen or twenty years afterwards. We idealized each other. She said that after seeing me in a high-school play she decided I was the guy she would some day marry. I placed her on a pedestal and cast myself as the knight in shining armour who would rescue her from a confused home environment. Uncommendable and unrealistic motives, for sure—we were naive but we were honest.

Pamela had definite conditions by which she would "dwindle into a wife." She wouldn't have a church ceremony, not that I was pressing for one. Civil marriages had only just been introduced in Toronto, and we were either the first or the second couple to apply for a licence. The official in charge told us the ceremony would be performed by the well-known judge Sam Factor, adding offensively, "He's Jewish: that doesn't bother you, does it?" Because of the novelty, there were short news items in the local papers about the event. Earlier, the redoubtable Pearl McCarthy, in a *Globe and Mail* report on my scholarship award, had mentioned our approaching wedding; Pamela thought it was none of her business. We told everyone we didn't want presents. Among the few we did receive, one was from my great-aunt Grace—a copy of one of her novels, written for teenaged girls, inscribed to me, with no mention of my bride. Our families didn't like the civil ceremony idea but remained supportive nonetheless. Mother and

Dad came east for the occasion and were our only witnesses. I told Pamela I would call for her in a cab in time for the eleven o'clock appointment, but she said that because she lived further away from City Hall *she* would pick *me* up. Independence; economy: I assented. At 10:45 as I waited for her to arrive I had a disturbing fantasy that she had changed her mind. It appeared that she was delayed at the bank. Dad was meanwhile doing his best to soothe and reassure the judge. We were twenty minutes late. After the ceremony was over, we all went to Irene and Arthur Rogers's home (Dad's cousins) for a lunch she kindly prepared. A photo taken in their garden shows a couple of awkward youngsters. That evening the Bennetts and their students gave us an informal party (no cake, toasts, or speeches) and accompanied us to the night train for New York, *un*kindly dousing us with confetti as a surprise sendoff (we were still trying to get rid of it two weeks later).

Our European studies and travels in 1950–52 are outlined in another chapter.[4] We shared many happy adventures and discoveries. A few issues clouded the horizon. In the first in a series of gender-based obstacles she had to endure, her passport was made out in her maiden name, and we both thought she should keep it that way (she would use "Pamela Terry" in all her stage credits); but officials at the Canadian Embassy in France insisted she should have a new one as "Beckwith." She was living with me, and the marriage certificate wasn't enough proof we were married. There were times when her attitudes or motives confused me, and she declined to explain. I had a first performance of one of my student compositions and of course wanted her to be there, but she said she wouldn't attend the concert—without saying why. Decades later, on checking this date in her diary, I find she notes it as her late mother's birthday; whatever that meant to her she kept to herself. The break with her father was a concern; she wanted to make contact with him, so we dropped in at his London office. She staged the visit as a surprise. He was happy to see her, and their estrangement ended. We learned a certain give and take. When we disagreed over the merits of a play Pamela auditioned for in Paris she gave way to my view, while in the uncertainties of our contract with the US Army in Germany (mentioned earlier) I gave way to her. As marriages go, we were evidently in pretty good shape. As we boarded the *Queen Elizabeth* to return to Canada in July 1952, she told me she was pregnant.

Parenthood made a huge change in our lives and gave us thrills and deep satisfaction over the years, as well as the usual worries—perhaps *more* than usual, since our four children passed their teens during the social upheavals of the 1960s and '70s. These four unprecedented human

The Beckwith family, Toronto, 1957. Left to right: Jonathan; Pamela, holding Symon; John; Robin.

beings are Robin, born 18 April 1953; Jonathan, born 25 November 1954; Symon (the change of spelling from the original "Simon" was his idea), born 4 August 1956; and Lawrence, born 2 December 1962.

Amid child-care responsibilities and closely recurrent pregnancies, Pamela was extremely busy in the theatre. She joined the University Alumnae Dramatic Club, a serious-minded amateur society with a strong reputation, with which over the years a long list of noted male professionals had cut their dramatic teeth—John Colicos, Donald Sutherland, William Hutt, and others.[5] Club membership was open to women with university degrees; Pamela was admitted in view of her non-resident Conservatory diploma. Members auditioned for roles and assumed backstage duties (props, stage management, lighting); the directors were all men. Pamela played Perpetua in Fry's *Venus Observed* for Sterndale Bennett and Sonia in Chekhov's *Uncle Vanya* for Herbert Whittaker; among other roles, she was the maid in Whittaker's production of Ionesco's *The Bald Soprano*. We made many friends in the Club circle, and the annual end-of-season parties were always tremendously enjoyable. I had ended my stage activities in 1950,[6] and had no great desire to resume them, but sometimes participated in skits at these celebrations.

Pamela and I kept up with theatre events in Toronto and made one or two short visits to New York to see new plays. When James Reaney produced his poetry cycle *A Suit of Nettles*, Pamela was moved by the dialogue form of some of the poems to suggest that the Club do a reading and ended by organizing and directing it herself. This, her first informal venture in directing, turned out so successfully that the next year she made a bid to direct a full production. She had been powerfully impressed on reading Samuel Beckett's *Waiting for Godot* and followed the growing literature about its recent premieres in Paris and London. It was fresh and much talked-about. A woman director was a rarity for the Club; moreover, the play had an all-male cast, no parts for women. But her proposal was accepted, and the production in the fall of 1957 was part of the inaugural season in the Club's new home, a former coach house on Huntley Street with an audience capacity of about fifty. The first week or two of rehearsals took place in our living room. I got to know the play intimately. It still strikes me as a unique masterpiece, and I can call to mind many long passages. The roles of the two tramps were taken by Fred Euringer and Kenneth Wickes. Both went on to major professional careers in theatre. Wickes once said working with Pamela on *Godot* is what turned him seriously into an actor. The production was received as a significant and far-out event in the Toronto theatre scene: no professional company anywhere in Canada had yet attempted Beckett.[7] It had both champions and detractors. When it played in the Dominion Drama Festival the following spring in Toronto and Halifax, it was judged the best production and Pamela the best director.

Reaney was becoming more and more interested in writing for the theatre. After the *Suit of Nettles* reading, he sent Pamela the script of his play *The Killdeer*, and she persuaded the UADC to produce it under her direction (1959). Southwest-Ontario Grand Guignol struck just as controversial a new note as had the minimalist images of *Godot* the year before. Nathan Cohen gave *The Killdeer* a devastating review,[8] while Mavor Moore hailed Reaney as a bright new voice among Canadian playwrights. That year's DDF adjudicator, Betty Mitchell, a theatre personality from

Pamela Terry, the director, circa 1960.

Calgary, referred to "this god-awful play," but nevertheless named it the best production and Pamela again the best director.

Pamela's directing talent blossomed, and she began to receive invitations to direct student groups in the university. When she undertook a UADC production of Jonson's *The Alchemist*, its success led to productions of *Epicœne, or The Silent Woman* for the Victoria College Drama Club and of *Volpone* for an independent company at the Ryerson Theatre[9]—amounting to a mini-cycle of Jonson, seldom (if ever) seen in Toronto. After her work on *The Killdeer* and *Night Blooming Cereus*, Reaney dedicated *The Easter Egg* to her, and she directed it for the UADC and another of his plays, *The Sun and the Moon*, for a summer theatre group in London, Ontario. *Daily News from the Whole World*, a bold avant-garde script by another London writer, Rae Davis, elicited bewildered comments from the adjudicator, Robertson Davies, although he praised Pamela's direction. In a quite different vein, she collaborated with the producer Susan Rubes and the writers Dodi Robb and Pat Patterson in two musical plays for children, and took on short-order productions for summer stock companies in Lindsay and Port Carling: one of her biggest challenges was to mount Alan Ayckbourn's complex farce *How the Other Half Loves* with only seven days of rehearsal. For a couple of summers she was an instructor for a University of Toronto summer school course in acting. All in all, the decade 1958–68 was a period of constant theatrical activity for her. She gained a reputation as a versatile director with imagination and drive, and as a stickler for discipline. Her work was regarded as professional in the sense of highly competent, though her fees were usually minimal. When looking for better pay and higher status through opportunities with the bigger companies, she experienced real prejudice as a woman in a field almost exclusively run by men. At this period there were virtually no female stage or film directors in the country.[10] Managers extended a condescending pat on the back but no contracts. The Club gave her strong support and an outlet for her ideas, and among her later shows under its auspices notable highlights were Shaw's *Major Barbara* and the first Canadian production of Peter Handke's *Kaspar*.

Her family enjoyed being on the fringes of the theatrical world. A neighbour, Betty Endicott, remarked one day what a great experience we were giving our children. Pamela loved reading to the kids as they were growing up, and they all in turn played children's roles in theatre productions. She found after the early *Killdeer* experience that taking directing seriously was a heavy strain. Her late-night preparations would conclude with a drink or two, and this became a habit. Her childhood insecurity would return, and halfway through a show she would decide she couldn't go on, wanted to quit; it was my duty to gradually persuade her that everyone was rooting for her and that indeed she *could* go on. This pattern repeated itself frequently, and she was advised to seek psychoanalysis. In the summer of 1961 I managed the children while she spent a couple of months in hospital. It was a band-aid solution, giving her a better and more secure outlook, but only temporarily before the same problems set in again. In 1963, after Lawrence's birth, she applied for and was awarded a Canada Council "B" grant to study directing at the National Theatre School in Montreal. This was a *genuine* pat on the back, an avenue to further professional status that had only come into existence a few years before.[11] Reactions from friends and relatives were mixed, to put it mildly: pleased for her, they wondered how she could combine new motherhood and career building—a question that would be much less likely to arise if we were in the 1980s; but we were in the mid-1960s. At the time of her application, we had projected ways she could cope with dividing her time between her family and the course. We were used to relying on student help and a sitters' agency, and my schedule allowed me to be at home more regularly than most fathers. At this point her insecurity feelings took over, the channels of communication closed down, and she suddenly announced that she had returned the award and decided not to go to Montreal: that was it; no discussion. In lieu of Montreal, the Council supported her in an informal appointment at Stratford as observer of Michael Langham's rehearsals for *King Lear*—a fine production with Colicos in the title role, Hugh Webster as the Fool, and Douglas Rain as Edgar. Langham was a kind mentor and seemed truly interested in her development.

As her activities continued to flourish, her problems did not diminish. The alcoholic bouts increased. Various advisers tried helping her with chemical treatments or, then a very new idea, sleep therapy, each of which worked for a limited time only. She relied on my support, and I was often commended as a liberal-minded spouse, but at the same time she resented the dependency and resented my being commended. We argued much of the time, and the household took on an air of tension. The discipline she had learned as a teacher of small children worked well when our four were small but was impossible to maintain as they became teenagers; moreover, it was the period of Timothy Leary and Woodstock. Our daughter developed an eating disorder; one of our sons got into trouble with the police; there were truancies both from the school and from the home. We had given them in their early life an unusual up-close exposure to the arts but often confused them with mixed messages and the example of our own increasingly poor communication. To use a term then just coming into fashion, ours had become a dysfunctional family.

One psychiatrist told me in my position he would leave, but I couldn't: I thought it would be irresponsible. A couple of years later, when I *did* start a plan to move out and take the two older children with me, another psychiatrist predicted dangerous consequences and advised against it. Alcohol became for me a focus of the problem. We had learned to enjoy wine with our meals in France (usually *vin ordinaire* in student days). In our early married life in Toronto we served cocktails to our friends and drank socially on occasions like the UADC parties. By the late 1960s there were bottles cached in locked cupboards around the house, like a scene from *Lost Weekend*, and I never knew on returning from my day at the Faculty of Music whether I would find Pamela in a sober state. She was always steady for rehearsals, so few of her professional colleagues were aware of this inner demon. I tried to propose ways of combatting it: we would both swear off liquor entirely, or we would agree on a limit (one drink, two drinks), or we would serve drinks to our friends but not join them. To each proposal she would mutter her agreement, but on the next occasion when the temptation arose there was always some excuse for giving in—she had misunderstood what we agreed, she thought I meant something else, and so on.

At this point I fell off the marital wagon. I wasn't a womanizer, though in my work at the university there was inevitably the attraction of younger women, and in our spats Pamela frequently taunted me by saying I "needed someone younger." Beyond a few mild flirtations, I kept clear of such involvements but found that I was developing fondness and gratitude to one bright former student who had been a sitter to the children and also assisted me in some of my writing. The physical desire came suddenly and I found myself in an affair that was to last intermittently (and aimlessly) for several years. In my lost mental state I thought of it not as a means to hurt Pamela but as a way to maintain my own stability—though of course it was both. The relationship while it lasted was a source of both strength and comfort, though I disliked the secrecy and the lying. It terminated amicably.

Meanwhile the tensions at home became intolerable, and there were physical fights. When you think things can't get any worse, sure enough they do. Pamela made several suicide attempts or enactments—swallowing a quantity of aspirins rather than sleeping pills, slashing the back of her hand rather than her wrist, and falling down a flight of stairs rather than out a window or off a bridge. Even when feeling, as she said, "lower than a snake's belly," she wasn't intending to end her life. Her load of hurt was immense but, unable to either keep it to herself or express it, she used her acting talents to signal it to others. I became less and less able to cope or extend sympathy or help, and my main aim was to try and protect the children. In the middle of straightening one of the messes, the real shock was to find myself saying "*I—don't—care.*"

Pamela and I had married on Friday the thirteenth, and on St Valentine's Day 1975 we separated. Her description of this always was that I kicked her out. Our ability to come to agreements had deteriorated and by this time was almost non-existent, so I suppose I did. I thought I was pointing out the obvious, that we couldn't go on living together: we were destroying each other; in the previous three weeks she had been alcoholically uncommunicative for all but two or three evenings, and whatever help she expected from me either I couldn't give or she couldn't accept. I said one or other of us should move out, and she immediately left and rented a cheap room in the Annex. A few days later the children and I helped her move into a decent apartment. For the next few years, I maintained the home with my three sons (Robin, my daughter, was by this time on her own), while we worked out with lawyers a separation agreement and eventually divorce papers. Negotiations were bitter and took an unnaturally long time (when there is no longer anything else to fight about, you fight about *money*), but the divorce finally came through in 1980.

On her own, Pamela tried Alcoholics Anonymous briefly but eventually learned to handle her drinking problem in her own fashion. She began a close friendship with an older man, but this lasted only a few years before he died. She continued her theatre work with directing assignments for the UADC, including another innovation, the first Canadian production of *Largo Desolato* by Vaclav Havel. She advertised as a drama coach and had several stage and television actors as clients. We had rare contacts but participated together in family events when our grandchildren started to arrive. Shortly after she turned eighty, in 2006, she withdrew from commitments, became reclusive for a few weeks, and died in her sleep. Characteristically, if she was seriously ill, she kept it to herself to the end. She used to quote Estragon's line from *Waiting for Godot*, "I can't go on," adding "but he does." And she did. The collapse of our relationship is a sad story, and I come out of it looking considerably less than heroic. The children established an annual award in the Drama Centre of the University of Toronto commemorating her remarkable achievement in acting and especially in directing.

I loved the children, and loved being a father, but handled the role mostly by instinct, referring to Spock in moments of crisis. Fond memories include taking Robin, aged not quite five, to her first opera, *Hansel and Gretel*, and Lawrence, aged about ten, to his first *Messiah*. With Jonathan and Symon a big event was the time *they* took *me* to Massey Hall for a soul-music concert by Wilson Pickett; my ears were still ringing a week later. The boys learned to play hockey, and I learned to appreciate it as a spectator at their games, as well as via television and the occasional live professional game. On a short visit to Chicago with Symon and Lawrence, they were impressed that we were able to buy tickets for a Black Hawks game, while the Chicago Symphony was sold out. When Robin was ill with the flu, she and I read together the whole of *Pride and Prejudice*. Family tensions eased on the annual summer vacations, usually by some Ontario lake; further excursions were to the west and east coasts, once including a foggy Bastille Day in St Pierre, the French island off Newfoundland. Theatre, music, literature, a sense of Canadian geography: the positive experiences we were able to give them of course scarcely compensated for the unpredictability of the home scene. We had no church affiliation, but it seemed to me important that they have some knowledge of the Judeo-Christian tradition, so for a couple of years when they were small I took the eldest three every week to Sunday school at St Paul's on Bloor Street. After delivering the children to the classroom, the parents were expected to attend morning service, picking them up afterwards. After the first few Sundays, I found the service hard to endure, especially the loud, draggy music; so after depositing the kids I would spend the hour in a neighbourhood café copying music or marking papers. But the school proved uninspiring and we eventually gave it up.

As children our four were distinct personalities and they have handled adult life and independence in distinct ways.

Robin's high-school years were especially turbulent. What stood out was a marked talent for the stage: she had a fine ear for dialect and the cadences of poetry. Her playing of the pathetic consumptive Mouser in O'Casey's *The Plough and the Stars* gained her much praise. In between high school and university, she experienced something of the publishing world as a reader for Harlequin Romances, and also acted with a few professional companies in Toronto, one of which took a production to Britain. She decided the theatre world was not the working milieu she wanted. After graduating from York University in English, she married and accompanied her US-born husband, Jim Goodale, to Houston, where he was engaged in a business-consulting partnership. To our surprise, Robin took an MBA (i.e., not an MA) and used her writing skills in a succession of jobs in business, revealing also a flair for photography. In a position with a large oil firm, she was sent on international interviewing and filming assignments to Scotland, the Middle East, northern Alberta, and elsewhere. She was active in an association of professional media people and took a turn as its president. At the start of the new millennium she faced a series of upsets. She and Jim divorced, evidently amicably. Her adviser and close friend, the psychiatrist Elizabeth Brody, died after a protracted illness. Robin had helped her write her memoirs of growing up Jewish in wartime Hungary. She underwent conversion and joined the reform Congregation Emanu-El. In the collapse of several major Texas enterprises, she lost her job, and set up as a freelance writer, photographer, and video artist. In 2004 she married Brody's widower, Tom Philbrook. When he developed a serious illness, she became a full-time caregiver. After more than two years of this confining life, she fell a victim to depression, and there was another divorce.[12] Robin gave herself

Robin Beckwith, circa 1980.

over to intense creative writing and experimental photography. Visiting us during our stay in Paris in the summer of 2009, she had a serious breakdown and spent three weeks in the Hôpital Esquirol before we could arrange her passage back to Houston. Helped by medications, family, and a few loyal friends, she regained her balance, acted in a couple of plays, and gradually resumed her professional life, landing a demanding full-time position in 2010.

Jonathan was a rebellious teen on the late-60s hippie model. From basic piano studies he had acquired facility in improvisation, at school he played violin, clarinet, and saxophone, and on his own learned the guitar. He had the hippie wanderlust, but fortunately no strong interest in drugs; his favourite pop mode was reggae. After spending most of the '70s hitchhiking—in British Columbia principally but also elsewhere around the continent—and, when there were no musical gigs, taking odd jobs such as fruit picking and tree planting, he married. The ceremony took place in a small church at Pioneer Village north of Toronto, and Geoffrey Payzant played wedding music on the small harmonium. Jonathan and Kyla had one child, Fawn (in alternative-lifestyle fashion, they had chosen the name Laughing Wind, but after weighing reactions from relatives decided on Fawn Salal). The marriage was rocky and soon ended. Fawn's mother remarried and gave her a steady upbringing. Jonathan settled in my hometown, Victoria, as a local reggae specialist (he grew dreadlocks, wrote his own songs, made a couple of CDs), guitar teacher, and occasional radical spokesperson (on issues such as clear-cut logging). As musical opportunities began to dry up, around 2000, he took a short course at the University of Victoria in teaching ESL (English as a Second Language). In the fall of 2001 he went to China and began a new career in the city of Jingmen in Hubei Province. As a teacher in school or in private coaching of children or adults, he proved versatile; students appreciated that he could use songs and instrumental music as an aid in communication. His always outgoing and friendly nature was also an asset. In the next few years he moved to Wuhan, Shenzhen, and eventually Shanghai, where he signed with a private agency for coaching and taught classes two or three days a week at a large private school in Pudong, whose pupils, a thousand or more, were children of Japanese businesspeople working in China. We visited him and his Chinese companion, Xu Zhen-Hua (Imogene, to use

Jonathan Beckwith, 2002.

her Western name), during our cycling tour in 2008; they have since parted company. Jonathan left the Japanese school for a Korean one of similar interests. His life in Shanghai is a mixture of struggle and excitement, and he shows no signs of wanting to leave. Fawn married in her early twenties and has two children, Venice and Cadence, my great-granddaughters, born in Victoria in 2005 and 2007 respectively.

If Jonathan was outgoing and often outspoken, Symon's personality was inward-looking and cautious. Like his siblings he could shine on stage, and as early as grade 1 was cast as Santa Claus in the school Christmas play for his vocal projection (Pamela had taught all of the kids to speak out clearly). He showed exceptional talent for percussion, and when the high-school orchestra did the *Egmont* Overture (or *Egghead* as he and his buddies called it) he played the timpani part with rare concentration.

Symon was some years into adulthood before anyone recognized the symptoms of clinical depression. At forty-six he took his own life.

There had been three previous attempts at suicide, the first in 1989 and the others in the later '90s. A three-year period of regular sessions in Toronto with a psychiatrist, whom he liked and trusted, stabilized him considerably, but early in 2003 the disease took hold again. In late June, Kathleen and I were away for our annual biking holiday and returned to discover him in our house—a terrible, terrible shock.

Symon was a man of fierce courage. At sixteen he spent a summer working on a turkey farm near Kamloops. At twenty he spent a winter working for an asbestos company in Cassiar, BC, near the Alaska border (the town no longer exists). During a summer at a camp for disabled teenagers near Gimli, Manitoba, he learned the deaf alphabet and other techniques, and used his musical skills (keyboard, voice, drums) with the children. The camp managers liked him and hired him for a regular position in Winnipeg; he later did similar work in Vancouver, Victoria, and Toronto, altogether for over ten years. Finding that the work with disabled people was "getting to him," he gave it up and joined a garden centre supply firm, travelling round Ontario on behalf of their products. When they "downsized" him in 2002, he was without a job for several months, and this added to his troubled condition. All the jobs he undertook had as their purpose self-maintenance allowing time for his writing, which he always thought of as his real vocation. Symon was an alumnus of four universities (York, UBC, Winnipeg, Toronto) but a graduate of none; midway in his course he would always find the intellectual discoveries too compelling; exploring them became more important than completing the degree. He was continually writing and reading. The range of

Symon Beckwith, 1993 (photo courtesy Cameron Kilgour).

his reading always astonished us. Late in 2002 he finally produced a small book—there was a lot of darkness and violence in it, but also much careful observation and much humour—and sent copies to various literary friends; the feedback was encouraging, and it seemed he was heading to a new and more creative plateau.

He had a lot of personal charm, but distrusted intimacy. A serious love affair when he was twenty and another, equally serious and more prolonged, when he was thirty, left him wary of women. He had a small circle of long-time male friends with whom he regularly played hockey and drank beer. He had a warm relationship with his two little nieces, Alison and Juliet.

On Saturday afternoon, 5 July, we held a memorial gathering under the tall maples of Craigleigh Gardens in Rosedale, an environment Symon was fond of. We expected a dozen people; about fifty came—friends of ours and friends of his. His friend Cam Kilgour introduced the short program.

His sister Robin came from Texas, and both she and his younger brother Lawrence spoke movingly; his older brother Jonathan (by now teaching in China) was represented by a song from one of his CDs. Pamela brought a scrapbook of mementoes and a lovely selection of photos. Lawrence and his wife Teri and their girls attend St Thomas's Anglican Church; for a time Lawrence taught in their church school. On Sunday afternoon, 6 July, Father Mark Andrews agreed at their request to read a brief committal for Symon. It was a beautiful ceremony, with just a handful of family and friends. At the end, the church organist, John Tuttle, played the most magnificent of Bach's chorales, the six-part "Aus tiefer Not" ("Out of the depths"). I am not a churchgoer and neither was Symon, but this was a case where, to me, the music said it all. With the help of friends (people are extraordinary) we all slowly found ways to deal with the hurt. Kathleen, more experienced with bereavement than I, was amazingly sensitive. Symon always had good respect for her, and they were sharp intellectual sparring partners.

At home, our youngest always answered to "Lawrence" (he was named for the river), and that's how by habit I still address him, although his siblings and his buddies at school used "Lar" or "the Laird" or, most often, "Larry," the name he goes by regularly now. We are especially close, I think, for two reasons: one, we were constantly together when he was in his teens and I was his "single parent," the other children having grown and dispersed; and two, he showed an early passion for music that indicated the sort of life he wanted to follow. He was an average student (he spent half of grade 10 in a high school in Auckland, during my post-decanal leave there) but a leader in music; his chosen instrument was the violin. On entering the Faculty of Music at Toronto, he was thrilled to find he could immerse himself in music full-time (I recognized the feeling). Admitted as a performance major, he continued to play but switched to the musicology program and went on to an MA in that discipline. He discovered he had a good tenor voice and joined several choirs. With two fellow students, he formed an ensemble (violin, gamba, harpsichord), the Arbor Oak Trio—its name a three-way pun on the university's motto ("Velut Arbor Aevo") and the oak in its coat of arms; the repertoire, baroque music; and the impecunious state of the performers. The series lasted for more than a decade. The inclusion of occasional stage works in their programs led in 2004 to a more ambitious venture, the Toronto Masque Theatre (TMT), of which Lawrence is artistic director. People used to ask if he was my son; nowadays they ask if I'm his father.

With Lawrence (Larry) Beckwith, circa *1995.*

Lawrence married young, and after a few shaky years realized the marriage wasn't working. After his divorce, he met and married a gifted young singer from Ottawa, Teri Dunn. With their two daughters, theirs is a household full of music. After a period as a junior music producer with CBC Radio, he became manager of the Ontario Choral Federation (later called Choirs Ontario). Then, finding arts administration frustrating, he resigned, took an education degree, and began teaching music at a high school for the arts, continuing to sing and play professionally with the Elora Festival, Tafelmusik, and other organizations, in addition to directing the TMT. Teri Dunn is an active choral director and assistant conductor of the Toronto Children's Chorus, on top of her varied solo singing engagements (for example, Varèse and Crumb with New Music Concerts, Lully with Aradia, Purcell and Monteverdi with the TMT).

The pressure of the deanship and the breakup of the family, in the middle 1970s, took a toll on my usually reliable health. I developed severe back and leg pains, no doubt brought on by stress.[13] Carol Birtch and her husband George were among several friends who helped me keep going.

George, a United Church minister, had weathered a difficult divorce, and Carol's first husband, Rowly Pack, had died of Hodgkin's disease when not yet forty. For the first while, George predicted, I wouldn't know myself, and this turned out to be true. I kept up with the busy routine of the Faculty, and tried at the same time to give the three boys the care they needed. Jonathan was uncertain about his future (in different ways, so was I); Symon's work in grade 12 was disrupted by a prolonged teachers' strike, stalling his progress; Lawrence was just preparing to enter high school. We shared domestic duties. I learned to be a cook and a discerning food shopper. In December we put on a party for a large group of friends, featuring a jambalaya that proved a big hit.

My social life was limited. I longed for female companionship but found when escorting friends of my own generation that they seemed happy in their own life patterns, perhaps set in their ways, while younger women, former students, obviously regarded me as a father figure. In late 1976, I invited the Faculty librarian, Kathleen McMorrow, to dinner and a play. At dinner I talked so much we were late for the play (it was Reaney's *Baldoon*). She was an attractive and capable woman in her early thirties; we had many interests in common, and worked in the same environment. Over the next few months I found myself deeply smitten, as we continued to enjoy music and theatre in each other's company. We became lovers—it was the start of a partnership that has had a more positive and sustained effect in my life than anything else.

Kathleen's background is Scottish. She was born in Edinburgh. Her father, from a large Catholic family in Fife, brought his wife and two children to Canada under the Ontario postwar program for UK immigrants— he "Flew with Drew," as the slogan was,[14] and they followed by ship. She was raised in Toronto's Catholic school system and took an honours degree in English and philosophy at St Michael's College, followed by a year in the Faculty of Library Science, where one of her professors was Ann Schabas. When Ann received a phone message that the Faculty of Music library had a professional opening, Kathleen happened to be in her office, a recent graduate inquiring about work. With Ann's high recommendation, she got the job and six years later succeeded Jean Lavender as head. She had become a strong devotee of the arts, especially literature and music, and her brother David became a versatile professional keyboardist. In her first years with the library, she says Harvey Olnick coached her in music, while she coached him in bibliography and library discipline.

Her appointment as head was an unanticipated result of my plans for reform in the library. The central administration advised me to post the position and invite applications: Jean declined to apply (she remained as reference librarian), and the appointments committee favoured Kathleen's over two or three external applications on the short list. In working with her I came to admire her clear and sensible grasp of her responsibilities and to appreciate her sense of humour, without attaching any personal meaning to these observations.

During her college years, Kathleen drew away from organized religion, as I had done. She joined the co-op movement Therafields, whose young-adult members included many former Catholics. The arts were well represented—musicians (Mike Malone), painters, writers (Philip Marchand, bpNichol). Members shared group houses in the Annex area of Toronto and often spent weekend retreats at the organization's farm near Mono Mills. She said the experience of kitchen duty preparing ground beef for twenty people turned her off meat. Two members of the Therafields community, Frances (Rowell) and Craig Donovan, have remained among our closest friends.

Our bond strengthened with time. Jay Macpherson sent me a Victorian verse: "What lasting joys the man attend / Who has a polished female friend."[15] Kathleen's parents were welcoming; her father, John McMorrow, quoted to me Higgins's line from *My Fair Lady*: "Let a woman in your life." But as he clearly knew, I *wanted* a woman in my life. At forty I had felt confined by my domestic situation and wondered, "Is that *all*?" Now at fifty it seemed change and renewal were possible. I bought a bicycle so as to join Kathleen on long-distance tours. Our first, in the summer of 1978, was a great success, even though my vehicle was not top of the line and, to her amusement, I protected my hands with gardening mitts instead of proper cycling gloves. In 1979, I had surgery on my thyroid, and Kathleen's concern and daily care during my hospitalization I could only describe as loving devotion. Dr Waters said a cycle tour would be good exercise for my recovery, and this time, for a more ambitious trip in the Rocky Mountains, I acquired the right equipment, including a good French ten-speed with toe clips. These were the first of a grand series of cycling expeditions, to be described in more detail shortly.

In mid-1980, when my divorce became final, Kathleen moved in with us in the Riverdale home I had bought in '78. Her Therafields home-ownership drills had included electric wiring and drywalling; she proved more of a do-it-yourselfer than I ever was. It didn't seem unduly disturbing to friends and family that we didn't go before a priest or a judge. By then I already had the feeling we were more "married" than most couples. I wondered whether the difference in our ages was going to spell trouble,

With Kathleen McMorrow, cycling tour, Gaspé Peninsula, 1984.

but referring to a couple then in the limelight she said, "You're younger than Pierre, and I'm older than Margaret."

Kathleen was a member of a Scottish country dancing group at Trinity College, directed by a professor of the college, John Hurd. I was a spectator at a few of their sessions and became fascinated to discover yet another complicated artistic mystique and to observe her obvious accomplishment and grace. She persuaded me to attempt some of the steps. I was a clumsy dancer at high school and had shied away from later "invitations to the dance," but found it was not hard to reach at least a basic competence. Hurd was an excellent teacher. We have remained in this weekly winter gathering ever since. If Kathleen's influence (cycling, dancing) brought me much more regular exercise than formerly, it also helped me towards a better diet (let a woman in your life ...). Her main principle was to use fresh ingredients, seldom packaged or prepared food. Our vegetarian meals at home we varied occasionally with seafood. I found I gradually lost my taste for meat and became, like her, a "fish vegetarian." This happened during our 1985 leave in Edinburgh, a city noted for its many fine vegetarian restaurants and, with its seacoast situation, an abundance of fresh fish. *Mens sana in corpore sano*: I found her resourcefulness as a researcher and bibliographer was a further influence. She

Kathleen McMorrow, photo by André Leduc, circa 2000.

has excellent critical and editorial judgment, as seen in her decade of service as editor of the *CAML Newsletter*.[16] Looking back, I could make a sizable list of librarians who have influenced me, starting when I was six with Hazel King at the Victoria Public Library. The profession brings out kindness as a human trait. Librarians are quiet, wise people—well, not so quiet in groups of fellow professionals, but still wise. If they don't know the answer to your question, they can always tell you where to find it.

Our shared life has the steadiness I had been hoping for. Kathleen's manner is on the surface one of shyness and reticence; the deeper traits are soft-spokenness, clear-headedness, deliberateness, and—yes—wisdom. We seem to handle the challenges and the very occasional disagreements peacefully. Early on, a birthday gift from her was the then-new English translation of Arnold Schoenberg's *Theory of Harmony*.[17] In it, she wrote, "For John: Happy Birthday 1980—after 3 years of the *practice* of harmony. Love, Kathleen."

The Riverdale house was solid and comfortable. We entertained visitors to the Faculty: Nicholas Temperley, Mervin McLean, Joji Yuasa, Milton Babbitt. We liked to host after-concert receptions, but with more than a dozen or so guests the rooms proved small and strained. Time away had accustomed us to having workspaces at home, and for this too the house started to seem cramped. In 1986, returning from Edinburgh, we started to look for something more suitable. On a sunny, cold January day we inspected a newly renovated three-storey house in the Annex, dating from 1904, fell in love with it right away, and in mid-April moved in. We rapidly made it, people said, a reflection of ourselves; we continue to cherish it. Over the years we have accumulated an eclectic small collection of art objects; among them are several original fabric hangings by Kathleen, my favourite being based on the colours and shapes of Haida art. In 2001 we commissioned a stained-glass front door, this time based on the designs of Charles Rennie Macintosh, whose work we came to know in Scotland, and on a scene from our 1998 cycle tour of northern Spain. (The collection includes three paintings by Michael ["Frank"] Forster, inherited from Pola[18] at her passing in the mid-1970s. In 2002 it was a surprise to read an obituary of the artist; he died in England, aged ninety-five. It mentioned other relationships in a colourful career but not his marriage to Pola. He is cited as a pioneer abstractionist and a notable Canadian war artist in the Second World War.[19] There was a solo exhibition of his work at a Toronto gallery, and the veteran art critic Paul Duval, who had known Forster, came to our house to photograph the pictures for a biography he planned to write.)

In the early 1990s both Nora and John McMorrow started to show signs of memory loss. It was a trying period for Kathleen as gradually she had to take responsibility for their affairs and for their physical care. For several years we had shared summer outings at their cottage on Lake Scugog, family Christmas gatherings, and other celebrations; the decline in their lively spirits was hard to accept. John's career had taken him from the coal pits of Fife to a position in real estate assessment in the Toronto financial world; Nora's experience included the Dundee publishing scene— a Canadian raised in Scotland, she once toured Britain solo on a motorcycle. They moved into a seniors' home together. He developed Alzheimer's disease and died in 1996; she lived on in a state of gradual dementia and died in 2000. Kathleen read a psalm at her father's funeral and spoke a touching eulogy at her mother's, quoting some of Nora's letters.

Reflecting on our temporary living spaces away from Toronto, I conjure the view from our fourth-storey flat on Marchmont Road in

Edinburgh—the Castle beyond the Meadows from the parlour window, and Arthur's Seat from the kitchen window to the east. Then there was our patio in Santa Fe, giving a three-way vista, and vivid sunsets, with the city at our feet, the Jemez Mountains on our left and the Sangre de Cristo Mountains on our right. In Paris our balcony overlooked the Place de la République, the scene in 2009 of many political demonstrations, with huge crowds; remarkably, their noise hardly penetrated the apartment. These were inspiring surroundings. Kathleen's project in Edinburgh concerned the history of dance. From records in the Registry House, the National Library of Scotland, and elsewhere, she found evidence of dancing masters (mainly French) active in the seventeenth century, a period when dancing was thought to be forbidden. I worked on my *CMH* hymn-tune anthology and its compositional offshoot, *Harp of David*. In Santa Fe I concentrated on my biography of Guerrero while Kathleen prepared the first Canadian volume in the *RIPM*[20] series of international indexes of historic music periodicals, using microfilm readers at the New Mexico State Library, just down the street from our *casita*. In Paris she completed another volume for *RIPM*, this time dealing with a Montreal French-language periodical, while I tapped out these memories.

Working in three of the world's most beautiful cities, we took advantage of the many local attractions and events, getting round almost invariably by bicycle. Edinburgh offered a seascape, craggy hills, and formal streetscapes with Adam-designed public buildings and, for contrast, narrow fennels and closes. Santa Fe had its central plaza, Museum Hill, the galleries of Canyon Road, and a series of connecting cycle routes following the (mainly bone-dry) arroyos, amid low-lying sand-and-turquoise adobe homes. In Paris there was much more acceptance of cycle traffic than when I was a student there; many boulevards had separate cycling lanes. We were delighted to discover what a compact metropolis it is: cycling from our apartment in the eleventh arrondissement to the boulevard Raspail in the sixth took you past incomparable sights along the Seine in less than half an hour. In Toronto we have become used to doing our errands day or night, summer or winter (when it isn't snowing) on our bikes, so it was no different when we lived elsewhere.

Early each year, we have a tendency to start yearning for travel. Our more than thirty cycle tours have covered many different kinds of terrain and each one has been a special adventure. Until 2005, we designed our own itineraries and travelled on our own vehicles, taking them with us by train, car, or plane to the starting point. We spend a January or February planning period consulting maps and travel guides. On our return from our first trip, around Georgian Bay, in 1978, I drew for Kathleen a souvenir map of our route, and every year since I have commemorated our expeditions in the same way. On our earliest trips we carried a small tent and along the way would either camp out or put up in motels, depending on the weather and our state of fatigue. We rarely reserved ahead and were seldom caught in a town where there was absolutely no accommodation. Riquewihr, in Alsace, was one of the exceptions, and we had to push on (after seven on a Saturday evening) a half-dozen kilometres to the next town, Hunawihr, where we found a rudimentary bed and breakfast and dined, exhausted, in a totally marvellous local restaurant. Another seemingly full-up town was Falkland in the Okanagan, but the local RCMP helped us secure the last motel unit instead of having to cycle (again late on Saturday) to the next centre, this time more like twenty kilometres distant. We gradually gave up tenting, and starting in 2005 we also gave up transporting our own bikes. The strain of partly dismantling them for transport had become tiresome, and we had a few experiences of damage to our bikes. The alternative was to sign up for organized cycling tours. Our first, in western Ireland, was a success, and several more have followed.

The routes seem to lead us up or, more often, down river systems (the Dordogne, the Loire, the Ohio, the Ottawa, the Skeena, the Fraser) or over mountain ranges (the Vosges, the Great Smokies, the Apennines, the Avant-Pyrénées, the Kootenays, the Cabot Trail, the Cotswolds). The tenspeeds proved inadequate to some of these terrains, so in 1988 we updated our vehicles, replacing the Merciers with twenty-four-speed Miyatas. Wine-growing areas—Burgundy, Rioja, Penedès, Tuscany, the Finger Lakes, Champagne—have had special attractiveness. The tough climbs, twists, and turns of Smugglers' Notch in Vermont, the Navacerrada Pass near Madrid, the Peak District near Manchester, and the Bobcat Pass in New Mexico have provided excitement and a sense of accomplishment at the summit. We learned to cope rapidly with mechanical glitches such as the occasional flat tire. Real accidents were few. A downhill tumble landed Kathleen in hospital in Palafrugell, north of Barcelona; in a similar fall I took my weight on my left pinkie, ending in an emergency ward in the Gaspé; another time, a doctor in Chipping Campden treated a flare-up of a chronic circulation problem in my left leg. In all cases we were able to continue the trip after a day's rest. A more severe leg infection interrupted our Italian tour in 1992: I spent a whole week in the Ospedale Civile in Venice, overlooking (prophetically?) the cemetery of San Michele across the water, with splendid care and meals that included a choice of wines—while

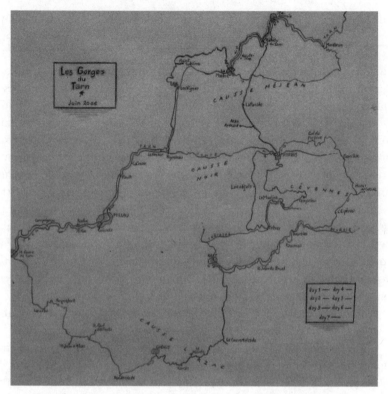

One of my homemade cycling tour maps: Gorges du Tarn, France, 2006.

Kathleen visited by herself the galleries we had planned to visit together. I was released on a pair of *canadesi* (Italian for "crutches").[21] Our wettest experience was in the Gulf Islands and Olympic Peninsula in 1990. Having enjoyed the view of the mountains from Victoria in my early years, I wanted to see them up close, but the State of Washington had its rainiest June in a century and visibility was close to zero; we were in our rainsuits for practically the whole trip. The tours brought us many scenic, artistic, and historic riches, from the Aran Islands, the Bamboo Forest and Karst Mountains in China, and the native mounds of the Lake of the Woods area (the navel of North America), to the inspiring Roman and Greek ruins of Orange, Arles, Nîmes, Tarragona, and Agrigento, and the startling twenty-first-century viaduct across the Tarn at Millau.

Such adventures offer a chance to both renew our sense of sharing and togetherness and satisfy our curiosity about the world. The name "tourist" is often used pejoratively, and Kathleen and I may at times be smug about the greater detail we supposedly take in, travelling by bike,

André Leduc took this snap of Kathleen and me at a reception in 2010 and entitled it "moment volé."

compared to others who travel more rapidly and cursorily, and perhaps more luxuriously; but we recognize that tourists are what we are. We always enjoy encountering other cycle-tourists. They are a friendly and companionable species—like musicians.

It surprises me how often in these pages the words "luck" and "lucky" appear. I seem to have inherited a sunny disposition, offsetting the suffering and reverses that have arisen. I have only limited talent as a planner, and many of the favourable circumstances in my life have arrived through sheer good luck. Largely through good fortune, I found an aptitude for music, and many opportunities to work in music came my way. At various times I have attempted to articulate a definition of music,[22] concluding that it is not only an elusive human phenomenon but also one that changes from generation to generation. The changes in my lifetime have been massive. The industrialization of music has transformed it into a commodity, turning original large-scale expressions such as quartets and symphonies into disposable objects like Kleenex. Kathleen wondered the other day whether Music—that is, music of the Western classical tradition—was on its way to becoming an obsolete university specialization like

Classics. There have been marked changes in music education, to the point where instead of "music" we have come to speak of "music studies"[23]—indicating that instead of practising it or getting inside it we walk around it or examine it with tweezers. Paul Steenhuisen described himself in 2009 as "a composer of art music for acoustic and electro-acoustic media."[24] Thirty or forty years ago there was no need for such a narrowly precise characterization; you were just a composer. The fanciful notational practices of the 1960s and '70s have undergone retraction in view of the limitations of computer notation programs, and this has affected the sound of the music produced—at least in my observation as an older composer still committed to pencil and lined paper. But despite all these changes there remains a steady, small audience for new works, and it appears that music has lost none of its ability to hold its listeners and communicate feeling.

In 1989 everyone marvelled at the collapse of the Soviet empire, signalling, or so it seemed at the time, an era of true world peace. One of the last holdouts was Czechoslovakia, and I remember Morawetz, from his knowledge of his homeland, telling me "they will never let go." But "they" did, and there was that moving scene on television of a crowd of tens of thousands gathered in the great square of Prague. The people listened to their new president, Vaclav Havel, and then spontaneously all *sang* their national song. It was a stunning moment: music said what words alone could not. In 1992, the year of the Charlottetown Accord, the media kept telling us Canadians were disturbed and upset at the prospect of the breakup of their country. I happened to be especially busy that year, and my travels took me to seven of the ten provinces. I found among my musical associates no great signs of anxiety; on the contrary, everyone seemed to me to be working vigorously and purposefully. I asked Lucien Poirier at Laval if his students seemed agitated by the alleged crisis, and he said no; in his view, the agitation was an invention of the politicians and the Montreal media. It was a badly handled, perhaps manufactured, crisis, with seemingly little effect on at least the musical sector of the populace. Was that because of our good luck in having chosen music as our vocation? Even more illustrative of the real nature of Canadian society were cycling holidays in Quebec in 1984 (Gaspésie), 1986 (Ottawa Valley), and 1995 (Saguenay–Lac Saint-Jean). In the Gaspé, Nouvelle was an anglophone community, while New Carleton was francophone: you couldn't tell from the names. Crossing from Quebec to Ontario several times, you used English as often as French, no matter on which side of the river/border, and sometimes you heard both at the same restaurant table. The francophone blueberry growers around Lac Saint-Jean seemed more resentful of the powers-that-be in Quebec City than of those in faraway Ottawa. Maybe the positive get-on-with-it attitude I encountered among fellow musicians extended generally, and bilingually. These findings were a heartening antidote to the decline in appreciation and support of the arts by public agencies throughout Canada, as observed more and more in my post-retirement years. I was especially lucky that my most productive period coincided with an upsurge of public emphasis on the arts seen in the formation of bodies like the Canada Council and with the "golden years" of the CBC. The draconian cuts to the latter by successive governments have removed the last vestiges of its role in arts promotion: few in the seats of power can now recall what it once meant.

These are mixed critical comments of a Canadian composer. I feel I've been lucky, although I deplore some of the changes I've lived through. I should reword that: even while deploring some of the changes, I've been lucky. The honours I've received have come about spontaneously rather than through lobbying. Every so often, starting around 1990, there have been live presentations of my music that have struck me as fortunate happenings, special ventures organized by the Faculty of Music (1990, 2007) or the New Music Concerts organization (1996, 2003) or sometimes through my own efforts with the cooperation of these agencies and the performers (1999, 2010). The audiences filling (or almost filling) a modest-sized concert hall on these occasions have shown genuine interest, comparable to the appreciative feedback from the modest readership of *Music Papers* in 1997 and my book on Guerrero in 2006. Unheard of? Maybe I exaggerate.

Notes

NOTES TO CHAPTER 1

1 *Dictionary of Canadian Biography*, vol. 5 (Toronto and Quebec City, 1983).

2 Obituary, *Messenger and Visitor*, Saint John, NB, 25 May 1898. Photos and documentation kindly supplied by the MacDonald Museum, Middleton, NS.

3 See Gordon Hartt Rogers, *Kindred Spirits: A New World History of the Families of Henry Wyckoff Rogers and Grace Dean McLeod* (Renfrew, ON: General Store Publishing, n.d. [2005]).

4 Arthur was secretary to the Canadian Bankers' Association, Norman a member of Parliament and defence minister under Mackenzie King, Dean an executive in the pulp industry, and David editor of the *Regina Leader-Post*.

5 I inherited his Waltham gold pocket watch and wore it for years, until it disappeared during a break-in in my house in 1986. It was engraved with the initials "JLB."

6 The cause of Uncle Fred's death was "a severe attack of pneumonia of a virulent type such as has been common during the influenza epidemic," according to the surgeon general of the hospital (letter, ? August 1918). He "was employed as medical officer on the *Oriole*, and ... contracted pneumonia, ... while doing duty in this capacity" (obituary, *The Colonist*, n.d.). He "was buried with full naval honours, and a large number of officers and men attended [his funeral]" (letter from the officiating Baptist minister, 16 August 1918). An official at Buckingham Palace sent a message of condolence to his parents on behalf of the king and queen (27 August 1918). I thank Gordon Rogers for providing this documentation.

7 Interview, 15 September 1999.

8 Peter L. Smith, *Come Give a Cheer! One Hundred Years of Victoria High School, 1876–1976* (Victoria: Victoria High School Centennial Celebration Committee, 1976), 47. "The clever acting of Miss Driver and Beckwith in

the garden scene brought down the house." *The Camosun* (school newspaper), June 1906.

9 Peter L. Smith, *A Multitude of the Wise: UVic Remembered* (Victoria: Alumni Association, University of Victoria, 1993), 43.

10 Among his instructors was John King, father of the future prime minister, W.L.M. King.

11 Interview with Susan Lewthwaite, archivist, Law Society of Upper Canada, 19 March 2001.

12 Gyro International is a service club of professional and business men, especially active on the west coast of Canada and the United States.

13 About this organization, see chapter 2, note 8.

14 For his letter to me on this topic, see pp. 70–71. It perfectly exemplifies his rational and positive views.

15 Max Spicker, ed., *Operatic Anthology*, vol. 4 (baritone) (New York: G. Schirmer, 1899).

16 H.A.B. = Harold Arthur Beckwith; M.A.D. = Margaret Alice Dunn.

17 Dale McIntosh, *History of Music in British Columbia* (Victoria: Sono Nis Press, 1989), 80 (illustration 5).

NOTES TO CHAPTER 2

1 A letter from George I. Dunn to his sister, dated "Manitoba Club, Winnipeg, 5 April 1894," gives details. The child died on 6 February, aged nine months. Thanks to Robert Dunn, Nelson, BC, for sharing this information.

2 Her piano teacher was Arthur Longfield. A 1911 certificate of the Victoria College of Music, London, Inc., indicates she received a "Primary" exam grade of 80 percent.

3 See interview, "Her Life Has Centred on Schools," in the weekly *Star*, Victoria, 23 September 1954.

4 *Star*, 6 February 1991.

5 Information from article by R.M. Duke concerning the school's seventy-fifth anniversary, *Star*, 13 March 1985.

6 See p. 17.

7 *Daily Colonist*, 4 August 1922. They travelled in Grandad Beckwith's Buick.

8 The Native Sons of B.C. was formed in 1899 as a "fraternal organization [aiming] to collect and preserve information and relics related to the early history and subsequent development" of the province. Membership was open to males eighteen years of age and over, born in BC. The affiliated Native Daughters society started in 1918. "Native" implied "post-colonial native," but there were Aboriginal members. The society exhibited an ugly tinge of racism in its between-wars opposition to Asian immigration, although it evidently had no policy barring non-whites or non-Protestants from membership. I find it hard to believe its alleged "secret" rituals appealed to my parents. The

chapters were called "posts" and the chairpersons "factors," recalling the early Hudson's Bay Co. trading forts. Among the organization's unspoken aims was "to make sure that the native born got at least an even break in competition for civic and provincial jobs with the new arrivals from Eastern Canada and the British Isles." See Forrest D. Pass, "The Wondrous Story and Traditions of the Country: The Native Sons of British Columbia and the Role of Myth in the Formation of an Urban Middle Class," *BC Studies* 151 (Autumn 2006): 3–38, 119.

9 Such locutions used to be common. Similar expressions ("Will do," "Long time no see") are still used, but without reference to their offensive origins.

10 See Robert Dale McIntosh, *A Documentary History of Music in Victoria*, vol. 2 (Victoria: Beach Holme Publishers, 1994), 82.

11 When she wrote to us, "Dad" meant *our* Dad, not hers. "Bess" refers to her late sister.

NOTES TO CHAPTER 3

1 James Reaney, *Poems*, ed. Germaine Warkentin (Toronto: New Press, 1972), 275.

2 Northrop Frye, "Haunted by Lack of Ghosts," in David Staines, ed., *The Canadian Imagination* (Cambridge, MA: Harvard University Press, 1977), 27: "The Canadian problem of identity [is] ... less a matter of 'Who am I?' than of 'Where is here?'"

3 e.e. cummings. *i: six non-lectures* (New York: Atheneum, 1967), 5.

4 The tension in this juxtaposition is exactly captured in a print by the New Zealand artist Kate Coolihan called *Victoria in the Pacific*, which now hangs in my home in Toronto.

5 Davies was a local celebrity in the 1930s. See *Hundreds and Thousands: The Journals of Emily Carr* (Toronto: Clarke, Irwin, 1966), 157, 162, 167–8. Carr was a fan of his Empire Theatre rallies and radio talks.

6 Did the musical part of the event remain in my unconscious? My hymn-tune researches included the history of this famous number; in my teaching I often compared the two different adaptations of it by Ives and Copland; in 1985 I made my own setting, the fifth of six choral psalms entitled *Harp of David* (see p. 293).

7 After the first or second year of my studies with her, she moved to Toronto, and we had many later contacts when she became the head music librarian of the Toronto Public Library and the first president of the Canadian Music Library Association.

8 The initials stood for George Henry Ebenezer. Besides being a tall and commanding school administrator, he played solo trumpet in one of the military bands and in the annual *Messiah* performances conducted by Stanley Bulley.

9 See p. 16.

10 A foretaste of my journalism and letters-to-the-editor involvements in later life—or a literary outlet for my perpetual showing off? A later and more extended example was "The Black Cat," *Colonist*, 30 May 1937.

11 Reaney, *Poems*, 229.

12 Reaney's poem "The Royal Visit," from *The Red Heart* (*Poems*, 53), captures the mood perfectly and has become a Canadian classic. He reworked elements of it in *All the Bees and All the Keys*, on which we collaborated in 1973, for a sequence depicting the visit of the Governor General to a small Ontario town. See pp. 259–60.

13 Victoria offered restricted scope to Gwen's talents. She decided in her mid-thirties to go back to university, completed a couple of degrees in Seattle, and took a position at Spokane, where she made a distinguished contribution as a performer and scholar. Retired, in her mid-eighties she still taught a few private pupils. We kept in touch, and a card around that time ended with a typical phrase: "Keep up the good work." She died in 1997, aged eighty-nine. See Marilyn Lewis, "Gwendoline Harper: An Oral Biography," 2 vols. (unpublished MA dissertation, Eastern Washington University, 1982).

14 I still have a bound volume of the Mendelssohn, given to me by Gwen Harper as a prize in 1939.

15 Robert Dale McIntosh, ed., *A Documentary History of Music in Victoria*, 2 vols. (Victoria: Beach Home Publishers, 1994), 2: 89–93.

16 I later saw a good deal of Stanley Bulley in my Toronto student days (see p. 277), and we corresponded regularly after he took a university post in Virginia. He died in 1998, aged ninety-five. His wife Joan told me he always regarded his Victoria years as the happiest of his career; at his request his ashes rest in Christ Church Cathedral.

17 In the late 1940s, Peggy Walton Packard left to study in the States but returned to spend a long and productive career as a performer, artist, and teacher in Victoria. Our warm friendship endured, and I often dropped in at "the Barn," her studio on Lansdowne Road, on my visits to Victoria. She died in 2010, aged ninety-six.

18 Portions of this account are adapted from my convocation address at the University of Victoria, 27 November 1999, entitled "Lucky Star."

19 We said "maths": the US abbreviation "math" didn't come into use until twenty years later, and I have never been comfortable with it, a probable retention from my "British" schooling.

20 The initials stood for Dunmail Horatio.

21 Later, as Patricia Adams, she had a professional career as a violinist in Vancouver and Toronto.

22 Letter to Bob Peers, 23 May 1994.

23 Pierre Berton, *Starting Out, 1920–1947* (Toronto: McClelland and Stewart, 1987), 77–78, 95, 119.

24 Letter from Myra Hess, 15 August 1943.

25 E.G. Biaggini, *The Reading and Writing of English* (London: Hutchinson, 1936).
26 E.G. Biaggini, *English in Australia* (Melbourne: Melbourne University Press, 1933).
27 I also maintained a friendly contact with Harry Hickman. When the University of Victoria was created (1963) from an expansion of the College and the Normal School, he served as its first interim president. Ruth Humphrey joined the University of British Columbia English department the year after my studies with her. Her correspondence with Emily Carr in the 1930s reveals that she was responsible for encouraging Carr to develop her writing talent. See W.F. Blissett, ed., "Letters from Emily Carr," *University of Toronto Quarterly*, 41, no. 2 (Spring 1972): 93–150 (forty-four letters from Carr to Ruth Humphrey, 1937–44).
28 At college, I was a partly lapsed Anglican and he was a United Church of Canada adherent. Surprisingly, after college, he went to UBC and entered the Anglican divinity school, and after studies in Britain and ordination had a full and wide-ranging career in many parts of Canada, culminating in a term as bishop of British Columbia. See p. 292.

NOTES TO CHAPTER 4

1 More about this interesting short street off Yonge later.
2 The location is now the headquarters of the Toronto Police Service.
3 It was called the Hazel Ireland Eaton Scholarship.
4 See p. 60.
5 See my review of Pearl McCarthy's *Leo Smith: A Biographical Sketch*, *University of Toronto Quarterly* 26, no. 3 (April 1957), quoted in *Music at Toronto, a Personal Account* (Toronto: Institute for Canadian Music, 1995), 19. This description has often been quoted by other commentators.
6 See *Music at Toronto*, 6.
7 See "Glenn Gould, the Early Years: Addenda and Corrigenda," *GlennGould* 2, no. 2 (Fall 1996): 56–65.
8 I came to know Bob and Margaret Fleming some years later.
9 Brock McElheran, *V-Bombs and Weathermaps: Reminiscences of World War II* (Montreal: McGill-Queen's University Press, 1995).
10 Margaret Sheppard (later Margaret Privitello) left Toronto to study in New York and established herself there in piano teaching and then in computer art. Many years later, at the time of the Guerrero commemoration in 1990, we renewed our friendship by correspondence. Her reminiscences were enormously helpful in the writing of my *In Search of Alberto Guerrero* (Waterloo, ON: Wilfrid Laurier University Press, 2006).
11 Now home to the University of Toronto Bookstore.
12 I had sent him as a Christmas present a book about the Quebec painter Clarence Gagnon, with reproductions of some of his work.

13 A relative of the Norrises, family friends in Victoria.

14 Evidently a recording I had sent of my playing. I can't recall the repertoire.

15 These were the first of a series of eight or ten short piano pieces written during 1945–48. The one called "Frolic," which I dedicated to Ron Shepherd, was imitative of Poulenc. I'm not able to identify precisely the other two in the group Dad mentions.

16 See pp. 87–88.

17 The reasoning could not be challenged, but was, I thought, faulty: those covering other fields also had their free perks, and we all had to work at the task of reporting/reviewing/writing. I soon came to the view that free tickets were a mistaken idea: reviewers should expect to pay admission like everyone else. But of course the practice continues.

18 Colin Sabiston, "Beckwith Piano Recital Unique in Originality," *Globe and Mail*, 4 December 1947.

19 See *In Search of Alberto Guerrero*, 91ff.

20 For more about later Forster findings, see p. 341.

21 Pearl McCarthy, "Beckwith Offers Night with Bach in Unique Recital," *Globe and Mail*, 22 March 1950.

22 See Mária Kresz and Péter Király, *Géza de Kresz and Norah Drewett: Their Life and Music on Two Continents* (Toronto: Canadian Stage and Arts Publication, 1989), 170, 173–75.

NOTES TO CHAPTER 5

1 The quotation, from *Musicanada* 6 (November 1967), appears in John Robert Colombo, ed., *Colombo's Canadian Quotations* (Edmonton: Hurtig, 1974), 41, 555, and in Peter Such, *Soundprints* (Toronto: Clarke, Irwin, 1972), 60.

2 I sent copies to Pamela, and she performed them for my parents. See the quoted comments of my father, chapter 4, pp. 70–71.

3 The Canadian firm used initials only ("BMI Canada"), not the full New York name.

4 Two are long-playing discs and two are compact discs: Pierrette Alarie, sop., John Newmark, pf., CBC-ACM 26 (2B); Barbara Fei, sop., Nancy Loo, pf., Phillips 6514 157 [nos. 3, 4, 5 only]; Jon Vickers, ten., Richard Woitach, pf., Centrediscs CMC CD 6398; Albert Greer, ten., Karen Rymal, pf., Cedar Island C101 CD 96.

5 In a letter around this time, I refer to a sixth, but it must have been abandoned; I cannot recall more than five.

6 James Reaney, *The Red Heart and Other Poems* (Toronto: McClelland & Stewart, 1949).

7 Chester Duncan, "A Note on John Beckwith," *Northern Review* 3, no. 3 (1950): 47.

8 The CAHA had been persuaded to devote surplus funds to annual scholarships in music, drama, and art, administered through an Ottawa office called the Canada Foundation. Offered for a few years only, 1949–52, the awards were a modest foretaste of the Canada Council grants inaugurated in 1957.

9 In student days in Toronto I participated in no sports or exercise activities, despite living for three years at the Central YMCA. Tennis and swimming were summer holiday occupations.

NOTES TO CHAPTER 6

1 The Hôtel Raspail, at the corner of boulevard Raspail and boulevard du Montparnasse, was still in operation in 2011, as were the local brasseries, Le Dôme, Le Sélect, La Coupole, and La Rotonde, gathering places of the Hemingway crowd and subsequent generations of American-Parisians.

2 Another similarity is to the foreground succession of fourths in Schoenberg's Chamber Symphony, op. 9, but I didn't become acquainted with that work until later.

3 Phone communication was complicated; we didn't have one, so had to borrow the concierge's. More usually, we sent and received messages by *pneumatique*—an efficient and rapid cross-Paris system which went out of use with the advent of email.

4 An English journalist, reporting the occasion, said Mademoiselle Boulanger "conducted with the poise of a caryatid"—an evocative description. *New Statesman and Nation*, June 1951.

5 *Nadia Boulanger, Mademoiselle: A Film by Bruno Monsaingeon*, NTSC, DVD5DM41 (2007); see also Monsaingeon's book *Mademoiselle: Conversations with Nadia Boulanger*, trans. Robyn Marsack (Boston: Northeastern University Press, 1988).

6 See Vivian Perlis and Libby Van Cleve, eds., *Composers' Voices from Ives to Ellington* (New Haven, CT: Yale University Press, 2005), 256–57, 268–69, and Carol Oja, "Composer with a Conscience: Elie Siegmeister," *American Music* 6, no. 2 (Summer 1988): 159.

7 See Léonie Rosenstiel: *Nadia Boulanger: A Life in Music* (New York: Norton, 1982). The intersection near Mademoiselle's apartment building now appears on maps as the Square Lili Boulanger. A plaque on the building identifies it as their home, but clearly Mademoiselle insisted the square be a tribute not to her but to her sister, the gifted but far less renowned Lili.

8 The young officer was later regarded as a hero, and still is.

9 See Rosenstiel, *Nadia Boulanger*, 95–96.

10 Aaron Copland and Vivian Perlis, *Copland since 1941* (New York: St Martin's Press, 1989), 146–47.

11 We directed people to the building by the sign of the street-floor dry cleaner: "Pressing Mozart." The French word for a dry-cleaning establishment is *le pressing*. In 2009 this one was still in operation.

12 *The Music Room* is the title of a short piano piece I composed in the summer of 1951. We both practised on this instrument pretty regularly. Constant use, combined with the fluctuations of temperature on the sixth floor, led to frequent broken strings. When the tuner called for the second or third time to make repairs, his advice to prevent this was, "Tapper moins fort, monsieur."

13 In his *Memoir* (New York: Vantage Press, 1995), Gene Gash, a black performer from Denver, describes his European sojourn in the '50s and the racial barriers he encountered on his return to the US. He performed both Somers's Fourth Sonata and my *Novelette* in Paris.

14 The Jackmans—Nancy, Edward, and their brother Hal—have all had prominent public careers, and on occasion I have enjoyed reminding Reverend Edward of this episode.

15 Pamela Terry's journal of our stay in Paris is now held by Larry Beckwith, who kindly loaned it to me to check details and dates.

16 See Mátyás Seiber's largely unfavourable review of the festival in *The Score* 7 (December 1952): 61–62.

17 Years later, critics compared the work of Scandinavian artists in Munch's generation to the contemporaneous art scene in Canada: was that part of his attraction for me? I still have a print bought in Zurich of *Girls on a Bridge*, a topic he returned to often, and *The Dance of Life* has always seemed to me to carry a lot of emotional power.

NOTES TO CHAPTER 7

1 Smith had assumed the post on his retirement from the Faculty of Music in 1950. Sabiston wrote on 16 April 1952: "Leo Smith will have died by the time you receive this. He is very low tonight, but fortunately is not suffering any pain." Smith died on 18 April.

2 The first position in music at Saskatoon, it was filled with distinction for many years by Murray Adaskin.

3 A newspaper critic complained, "All they did was talk." We didn't know what to make of that. In the announcement in the *CBC Times* for the second series, someone had evidently taken down the title "Roadshow in Germany" over the phone; it came out as "Groucho in Germany."

4 Already mentioned as a teacher and choral conductor in Victoria. See pp. 26–27, 31.

5 See p. 148.

6 "Composers in Toronto and Montreal," *University of Toronto Quarterly* 26, no. 1(October 1956): 47–69. The composers whose music I chose to write

about were Weinzweig, Freedman, Somers, Kasemets, Joachim, Anhalt, Charpentier, and Papineau-Couture.

7 Ernest MacMillan, ed., *Music in Canada* (Toronto: University of Toronto Press, 1955).

8 Julian Park, ed., *The Culture of Contemporary Canada* (Ithaca, NY: Cornell University Press, 1957).

9 This conference took place in 1959. Events included a concert of music by French composers, by the Cleveland Orchestra under George Szell.

10 Malcolm Ross, ed., *The Arts in Canada* (Toronto: Macmillan, 1958).

11 "Jean Papineau-Couture," *Canadian Music Journal* 3, no. 2 (Winter 1959): 4–20; "A Stravinsky Triptych," *Canadian Music Journal* 6, no. 4 (Summer 1962): 5–22.

12 See pp. 247–48.

13 I contributed to the *Star* from 1959 to 1962 and again from 1963 to 1965. Udo Kasemets was a fellow reviewer for part of that period, and soon after I resigned William Littler came from Vancouver to take on the job full-time, remaining for the succeeding four decades.

14 Partch's recordings were obtainable only by mail order from the composer. In correspondence with him, I asked his permission to include excerpts in my broadcast and managed to persuade him that my intention was not to ridicule the music, which he said had happened in the past. This broadcast, and R. Murray Schafer's review of some of the recordings in the *Canadian Music Journal*, constituted, I think, the first exposure of Partch's work in Canada.

15 See Arthur Hedley, *Chopin*, revised by Maurice J.E. Brown (London: J.M. Dent, 1974), 60.

16 *Musicanada* 21(July-August 1969): 12.

17 *Encyclopedia of Music in Canada* (Toronto: University of Toronto Press, 1981); *Encyclopédie de la musique au Canada* (Montreal: Fides, 1983).

18 Keith MacMillan and John Beckwith, eds., *Contemporary Canadian Composers* (Toronto: Oxford University Press, 1975).

19 The term "studies" was adopted in early planning stages as an alternative to "monographs."

20 Brian Cherney, *Harry Somers*, Canadian Composers 1 (Toronto: University of Toronto Press, 1975).

21 Udo Kasemets papers, Faculty of Music Library, University of Toronto.

22 Marie-Thérèse Lefebvre, *Serge Garant et la révolution musicale au Québec* (Montreal: L. Courteau, 1986).

23 Louise Laplante, dir., *Compositeurs canadiens contemporains* (Montreal: Les Presses de l'Université du Québec, 1977).

24 Pierre Mercure's life and work formed the topic of one of the first volumes in the series of pamphlets, *Compositeurs du Québec*, begun in the late '70s under the editorship of the CMC's Quebec director, Louise Laplante, but

there was still in 2011 no book-length study. Louise rejected my suggestion that we explore translating these attractive pamphlets into English (an easier task than translating the studies). She considered her series a Quebec project and saw no publicity value in making them available to anglophone readers.

25 Sheila Eastman and Timothy J. McGee, *Barbara Pentland*, Canadian Composers 3 (Toronto: University of Toronto Press, 1983); Stephen Adams, *R. Murray Schafer*, Canadian Composers 4 (Toronto: University of Toronto Press, 1983); Louise Bail-Milot, *Jean Papineau-Couture: la vie, la carrière et l'œuvre*, Canadian Composers 2 (Montreal: Hurtubise, 1986).

26 George Proctor, "Notes on Violet Archer," in John Beckwith and Frederick A. Hall, eds., *Musical Canada: Words and Music Honouring Helmut Kallmann* (Toronto: University of Toronto Press, 1988), 188–202.

27 Elaine Keillor, *John Weinzweig and His Music: The Radical Romantic of Canada* (Metuchen, NJ: Scarecrow Press, 1994).

28 "Shattering a Few Myths," in John McGreevy, ed., *Glenn Gould Variations* (New York and Toronto: Doubleday, 1983), 65–74.

29 Geoffrey Payzant, *Glenn Gould, Music and Mind* (Scarborough, ON: Van Nostrand Reinhold, 1978). The book had several later revisions and was translated into five or six languages.

30 Clifford Ford, *Canada's Music* (Agincourt, ON: GLC, 1982).

31 The editorial reports are preserved in the Society's Fonds at Library and Archives Canada.

32 The preface to volume 5 served as the basis of my article "Canadian Tunebooks and Hymnals, 1801–1939," *American Music* 6, no. 1 (Spring 1988): 193–233, for which the Music Library Association awarded me its Richard S. Hill Prize. Offshoots of volume 18 were two other articles: "Choral Music in Montreal ca. 1900: Three Composers," *University of Toronto Quarterly* 43, no. 4 (Summer 1994): 504–17, repr. in *Anacrusis* 15, no. 4 (Summer 1996): 5–11; and "Ernest MacMillan and *England*," *Canadian University Music Review* 19, no. 1 (1998): 34–49.

33 Starting in the mid-1990s publishing technology made it possible for the Society to offer off-print copies of individual works. These continued (in 2011) to be available through the website of Clifford Ford Publications.

34 Marie-Thérèse Lefebvre (Université de Montréal) joined the editorial board as a replacement for Lucien Poirier on the latter's untimely death in 1997.

35 Thurston Dox, review of *The Canadian Musical Heritage, vol. 9*, *American Music* 7, no. 2 (Summer 1989): 216–18.

36 Richard Crawford, editor-in-chief, *Music of the United States of America* (Madison, WI: A-R Editions, 1993–).

37 *Historical Anthology of Canadian Music*, 2 vols. (Ottawa: Canadian Musical Heritage Society, 1998). "HACM" is distributed by Clifford Ford Publications.

38 *Le souvenir*, Centrediscs CMC-CD 5696; *Noël*, Marquis 77471-81227-2-8.

39 *Encyclopedia of Music in Canada*, 2nd ed. (Toronto: University of Toronto Press, 1992); *Encyclopédie de la musique au Canada*, 2nd ed. (Montreal: Fides, 1993).

40 "Glenn Gould, the Early Years: Addenda and Corrigenda," *GlennGould* 2, no. 2 (Fall 1996): 51–65.

41 "Master Glen Gold," *GlennGould* 3, no. 1 (Spring 1997): 14–16.

42 Kathleen McMorrow, my life partner.

43 See *Psalmody in British North America: Humbert, Daulé, Jenkins, Burnham* (Toronto: Institute for Canadian Music, 2002); and "Mark Burnham and Upper Canada's Earliest Tunebook, *Colonial Harmonist*," *University of Toronto Quarterly* 71, no. 2 (Spring 2002): 623–50.

44 *Music at Toronto: A Personal Account* (Toronto: Institute for Canadian Music, 1995).

45 "'Ruptures': qu'en aurait pensé Garant?" *Cahiers de la SQRM* 1, nos. 1–2 (1997): 59–64; "New Music and the Public: Serge Garant and Quebec's 'Ruptures' Debate," *Musicworks* 68 (Summer 1997): 36–40. See also Raymond Daveluy et al., *Pour l'amour de la musique: les mélodistes indépendants* (Roxboro, PQ: Éditions Essentiels, 1996).

46 "Un manuscrit québécois du XIXᵉ siècle: *Annales musicales du Petit-Cap*," *Cahiers de la SQRM* 7, nos. 1–2 (2003): 9–22; "Thomas-Étienne Hamel and His *Annales musicales du Petit-Cap*: A Manuscript Song Collection of Nineteenth-Century Quebec," *Canadian Journal for Traditional Music* 29 (2002): 1–18.

47 "Father of Romance, Vagabond of Glory: Two Canadian Composers as Stage Heroes," in Robin Elliott and Gordon E. Smith, eds., *Music Traditions, Cultures and Contexts* (Waterloo, ON: Wilfrid Laurier University Press, 2010), 227–59.

48 "The Present State of Unpopular Music," *CAML Review* 35, no. 2 (August 2007): 11–23, reprinted in *Intersections* 27, no. 2 (2007): 8–18.

49 I included my 1983 biographical sketch of Weinzweig, "John Weinzweig at Seventy," commissioned by New Music Concerts, in *Music Papers* (Ottawa: Golden Dog, 1997), with an introductory suggestion that "some day" I might add to it.

50 *Weinzweig: Essays on His Life and Music* (Waterloo, ON: Wilfrid Laurier University Press, 2011).

51 Professor of music at McGill University for many years, Brian Cherney is the older brother of the Toronto oboist and impresario Lawrence Cherney.

NOTES TO CHAPTER 8

1 The recalled quotation appears in slightly different forms several times in Frye's many writings, for example: "We cannot have education without incessant repetition and drill, and going over the same things over and over until

they become automatic responses." Jean O'Grady and Goldwin French, eds., *Northrop Frye's Writings on Education,* Collected Works 7 (Toronto: University of Toronto Press, 2000), 331. Thanks to John Robert Colombo for providing this information.

2 See p. 104.

3 Gilbert Highet, *The Art of Teaching* (New York: Knopf, 1950).

4 Gustave Reese, *Music in the Middle Ages* (New York: Norton, 1940); *Music in the Renaissance* (New York: Norton, 1954); Archibald T. Davison and Willi Apel, eds., *Historical Anthology of Music,* 2 vols. (Cambridge, MA: Harvard University Press, 1946–50).

5 See p. 75.

6 Teaching loads in the '50s were decided by the director or the department head rather than by departmental consensus, as later became the norm.

7 Part of this description derives from a talk, "Composers and Musicologists," delivered to the Music Students' Graduate Association at the U of T in 2008.

8 Northrop Frye, "The Primary Necessities of Existence," in Jean O'Grady ed., *Interviews with Northrop Frye,* Collected Works 24 (Toronto: University of Toronto Press, 2008), 744–51 at 749.

9 The two talks were published as *Music at Toronto: A Personal Account* (Toronto: Institute for Canadian Music, 1995).

10 The proposal originated with John Weinzweig, who had wanted a course in "Music of Canada" but calculated that "Music of North America" had a better chance of acceptance by his musicologist colleagues. Interview, Canadian Composers Portraits series, Centrediscs CMC CD 9102.

11 Ibid.

12 See "CUMS Remembered / Souvenirs de la SMUC," *Canadian University Music Review* 20, no. 1 (1999): 1–4.

13 A group photo from this conference appears in the entry "Ethnomusicology," *Encyclopedia of Music in Canada,* 2nd ed. (Toronto: University of Toronto Press, 1992), 423.

14 *CanMus Documents* (Toronto: Institute for Canadian Music, 1987–91): 1, *Sing Out the Glad News: Hymn Tunes in Canada*; 2, *Hello Out There! Canada's New Music in the World, 1950–85*; 3, *Three Studies* (Songbooks, Toronto Conservatory, Arraymusic); 5, *Ethnomusicology in Canada*; 6, *The Fifth Stream*.

15 "Notes on *Harp of David,*" *Canadian University Music Review* 11, no. 2 (1991): 122–35.

16 Around the time I was working on the *Canadian Musical Heritage* hymn-tune volume, I developed these observations into two papers: "Chorale and Hymn-Tune References: How? Why?" (Toronto: American Society of University Composers, 1986); and "Composing with Chorales and Hymn-Tunes" (Ottawa: Carleton University, 1987). Both are unpublished.

17 McGee edited a book of essays in my honour under the title *Taking a Stand* (Toronto: University of Toronto Press, 1995). Aide (a former student, in the same remarkable graduating class as Pierrette LePage and Teresa Stratas) is the pianist most closely associated with my music (Concerto Fantasy, *Keyboard Practice*, *Arctic Dances*, most of the solo vocal works). He initiated the CD *Avowals* and performed *March, March!* at my eightieth-birthday concert.

NOTES TO CHAPTER 9

1 I describe my association with these two musical organizations in "Memories, and a Few Red-Neck Opinions," *Music Papers* (Ottawa: Golden Dog, 1997), 197–203, and "Ten Centuries in Five Seasons: The Music Comes First," Women's Musical Club of Toronto, *News and Notes* 33 (January 2006): 3–5.

2 McPeek (1934–81), a former student and a versatile musician, had a highly successful career as a composer of film music and commercial jingles.

3 *The Modern Composer and His [sic] World* (Toronto: University of Toronto Press, 1961).

4 See "Golden Memories: The Canadian Music Centre at 50," *Notations* (newsletter of the CMC's Ontario region) 15, no. 1 (Winter 2009): 1, 30.

5 See p. 134.

6 From the original draft of my remarks in "Golden Memories."

7 Letter to Allan Bell, 2 January 1988.

8 Edward A. Suderman, CMC board president, memorandum to associate composers, 12 December 1994.

9 "The Present State of Unpopular Music," Université de Montréal, 12 May 2007; talk reproduced in *Intersections* 27, no. 2 (2007): 8–18.

10 Ibid., 9.

11 At a special meeting of the board with a group of Montreal composers, Schwartz responded to the composers' statements of their artistic ideals by saying music was a business and had nothing to do with culture. I rebutted, with the support of Jean Papineau-Couture and others, pointing out that SOCAN was a *non-profit* "business," whose product was indeed cultural, and that it was a *society* of professionals working for their mutual interests, not a company. The "weaning" comments in *The Record* (November 1993), afterwards quoted in the Canadian League of Composers *Newsletter* (Spring 1994), evoked letters to Mark Altman, SOCAN president, from me (27 April 1994) and from Schwartz (24 May 1994).

12 "The Present State of Unpopular Music," 9, note 4.

13 I later learned that the two nominations came from a staff member, Anton Kuerti, and a group of students, among them Timothy Maloney and Clifford Ford.

14 Letter from Claude Bissell, 22 December 1969.

15 On Faculty–Conservatory relations, see my *Music at Toronto: A Personal Account* (Toronto: Institute for Canadian Music, 1995), 45–50.

16 See pp. 152–54.

17 Faculty of Music, *Alumni Directory* (Toronto, 1990), 22–29.

18 Kathleen calls it my Lady Macbeth complex.

19 His unpublished memoir, "A Schöneberg Family in the 1930s," describes movingly and in detail their life under the Nazis. See also Dawn L. Keer, "Helmut Kallmann: An Account of His Contributions to Music Librarianship and Scholarship in Canada" (master's dissertation, University of Alberta, 1991).

20 Helmut Kallmann, "The Matter of Identity," *Outlook: Canada's Progressive Jewish Magazine* 39, no. 4 (July/August 2001): 15–16.

21 IA on JB: *Encyclopedia of Music in Canada*, 1st ed. (Toronto: University of Toronto Press, 1981), 70–72; *Alternative Voices* (Toronto: University of Toronto Press, 1984), 206, 244–47. JB on IA: "Composers in Toronto and Montreal," *University of Toronto Quarterly* 26, no. 1 (October 1956): 61–64; "Recent Orchestral Works by Champagne, Morel, and Anhalt," *Canadian Music Journal* 4, no. 4 (Summer 1960): 44–48; "Orchestral Works," in Robin Elliott and Gordon E. Smith, eds., *Istvan Anhalt: Pathways and Memory* (Montreal and Kingston: McGill-Queen's University Press, 2001), 111–31; "Istvan Anhalt: A Character Sketch," in Friedemann Sallis, Robin Elliott, and Kenneth DeLong, eds., *Centre and Periphery, Roots and Exile: Interpreting the Music of István Anhalt, György Kurtág, and Sándor Veress* (Waterloo, ON: Wilfrid Laurier University Press, 2011), 29–35.

NOTES TO CHAPTER 10

1 See pp. 246–50.

2 I discussed the Schoenberg Concerto, op. 42, with Gould when he was first learning it. There was at the time only one LP recording. A few years later I contributed an illustrated analysis of it to a new-music radio series produced in Vancouver by Peter Garvie.

3 The Concerto Fantasy is dedicated to Guerrero.

4 Henry Leland Clarke, "The Abuse of the Semitone in Twelve-Tone Music," *The Musical Quarterly* 45, no. 3 (July 1959): 295–301.

5 In November 1988 the work was revived by the CJRT Orchestra under Paul Robinson. The soloist, William Aide, made a number of useful suggestions, clarifying and intensifying the solo piano part.

6 Letter from Hans Gruber, 2 September 1960.

7 Van Perry, "Canadian Composers Score Hit at 'Pops,'" *Vancouver Daily Province*, 15 March 1950.

8 Pam Chambers, *Sixty Years of Music Making: The Vancouver Youth Symphony Orchestra* (Vancouver, n.d.), 25.

9 See pp. 256–57.

10 I never discovered the reason for the lateness of the request. Two possibilities have occurred to me: someone suddenly decided there should be a new work marking the country's centennial, or another composer was approached and turned down the offer.

11 CBC Records SMCD 5168; reissued, CBC Records PSCD 2028-5.

12 The trombonist could of course be "she."

14 *Taking a Stand* was not composed with a program or a conceptual "meaning" in mind. This interpretation occurred to me only when I heard the piece in performance.

14 Centrediscs CMC CD 9102.

15 See pp. 161–62.

16 Centrediscs, CMC CD 5897.

17 Re-released on CD, Centrediscs CMC CD 5897.

18 Robin Elliott, "The String Quartet in Canada" (unpublished PhD dissertation, University of Toronto, 1990).

19 Centrediscs, CMC CD 5897. In this recording, the delicate regal (medieval reed organ) used at the premiere was replaced by a small chamber organ.

20 John Mayo, "Coming to Terms with the Past: Beckwith's *Keyboard Practice*," in Timothy J. McGee, ed., *Taking a Stand: Essays in Honour of John Beckwith* (Toronto: University of Toronto Press, 1995), 94–109.

NOTES TO CHAPTER 11

1 See pp. 259–60.

2 Jay Macpherson, *The Spirit of Solitude: Conventions and Continuities in Late Romance* (New Haven, CT: Yale University Press, 1982).

3 By this casting I did not mean to preclude performance of the solo part by a female flutist. I was thinking of the instrument, not the player. In cultural history, flutes are male and guitars are female.

4 CBC Records, PSCD 2028-5.

5 See pp. 233–35.

6 Centrediscs, CMC CD 5897.

7 Gail Dixon, "Symmetry and Synthesis in Beckwith's *Etudes* (1983)," in Timothy J. McGee, ed., *Taking a Stand: Essays in Honour of John Beckwith* (Toronto: University of Toronto Press, 1995), 70–93.

8 Both Foreman and Widner are former students of mine.

9 McGill Records 85026 (LP).

10 CBC Records PSCD 2028-5.

11 The idea of a solo player being shadowed or partnered seems to be one of my composing habits: the celeste alongside the piano in the Concerto Fantasy, the viola with the harpsichord in *Circle, with Tangents*, the multiple-keyboardist with the flute in *A Concert of Myths*.

12 See Faculty of Music Library, University of Toronto, special collections, 10, B.11.78.

13 The Council later abandoned this alternative commissioning program.

14 I have not been able to trace this review.

15 Konrad Lorenz, *King Solomon's Ring: New Light on Animal Ways*, trans. Marjorie Kerr Wilson (London: Methuen, 1952), chapter 4.

16 Alastair MacFadyen and Florence H. Adams, *Dance with Your Soul: A Biography of Jean Callander Milligan* (Edinburgh: Royal Scottish Country Dance Society, 1983).

17 A CD of the live performance by the Hamilton Philharmonic is available on CBC Records, PSCD 2028-5.

18 Review by Deryk Barker, *Victoria Times Colonist*, 11 January 1993.

19 I gave this paper, called "Hyphenating Bach," at both Dalhousie University and the University of Toronto in 1999.

20 See Peter Williams, *The Organ Music of J.S. Bach*, 3 vols. (Cambridge: Cambridge University Press, 1984), 1: 338; 3: 83. The titles of my three sets of transcriptions are *Fifteen Figural Chorales, Fourteen Figural Chorales (Second Set)*, and *Sixteen Figural Chorales (Third Set)*.

21 The letter is quoted in "Lucien Poirier: Souvenirs," *Les Cahiers de la SQRM* 2, no. 2 (November 1998): 46.

22 Musicworks 68.

23 Jordan R. Young, *Spike Jones and His City Slickers: An Illustrated Biography* (Beverley Hills, CA: Disharmony Books, ca. 1984).

24 On holiday, Kathleen and I happened to pass through the town of Eureka, California, around the time I was planning this composition.

25 *Jalsaghar*, Centrediscs CMCCD 16410 (2010).

26 *the door in the wall … instrumentS d'illusion?* Isidorart (1999).

27 *Jalsaghar*, Centrediscs CMCCD 16410 (2010).

28 Ibid.

29 *Rondino*, University of Toronto Percussion Ensemble (2001).

30 "Composing in the Eighties," in *Music Papers* (Ottawa: Golden Dog, 1997), 208–9.

31 Joseph N. Straus, "A Revisionist History of Twelve-Tone Serialism in American Music," *Journal of the Society for American Music* 2, no. 3 (August 2008): 208–9. See also his *Twelve-Tone Music in America* (Cambridge University Press, 2009).

32 George Rochberg, *Five Lines, Four Spaces: The World of My Music* (Urbana and Chicago: University of Illinois Press, 2009).

33 Ibid., 104–6. The Straus article is "The Myth of Serial 'Tyranny' in the 1950s and 1960s," *Musical Quarterly* 83, no. 3 (Fall 1999), 301–43. For Rochberg, serialism had an "aesthetic death-grip" on US composers of the 1950s and '60s (*Five Lines*, 104); for Straus, serialism was "a viable compositional alternative in this period, but only one among many" (quoted in *Five Lines*, 105).

NOTES TO CHAPTER 12

1 Victoria is in the Pacific time zone, so we heard the 2 p.m. New York matinee broadcasts starting at 11 a.m.

2 I have written elsewhere about our partnership and in 2004 was editor for a collected volume of the librettos. See "My Collaborations with James Reaney," in *Music Papers* (Ottawa: Golden Dog, 1997), 217–25; James Reaney, *Scripts: Librettos for Operas and Other Musical Works*, edited, with an introduction, by John Beckwith (Toronto: Coach House Books, 2004).

3 Reaney recognized this. As he put it in a retrospective article some years later: "The people who wanted to dress up and drag their husbands in tuxedos to an opera were certainly not going to accept an aria about washing dishes." Gloria Dent and Leonard Conolly, eds., *Guelph and Its Spring Festival* (Guelph, ON: Edward Johnson Music Foundation, 1992), 72.

4 In a letter of 9 June 1959, Hugh Le Caine, the pioneer of electronic music, "particularly liked the dishwashing scene where permutations of the names of utensils were accompanied by permutations of rhythmic and pitch patterns."

5 The 1960 cast had one or two changes. Both presentations were "live" broadcasts.

6 Dorothy Cameron, Louis de Niverville's agent, acquired the bloom "to suspend from the ceiling of my office" at her art gallery (letter, 30 April 1960). I don't know what happened to it later.

7 The sources cited in note 2, above, contain facsimiles of some libretto pages with my jottings of word rhythms.

8 *Houses in Heaven* (Toronto: Gordon V. Thompson Music, 1987).

9 James Reaney, "A Domestic Song Cycle," *Canadian Forum* 39, no. 463 (August 1959): 114–16.

10 James Reaney, "An Evening with Babble and Doodle: Presentations of Poetry," *Canadian Literature* 12 (1963): 37–43.

11 James Reaney, letter to Pamela Terry and John Beckwith, 18 April 1960. "The farm" refers to the property just east of Stratford where Reaney was born and raised.

12 James Reaney, ms. draft for *The Shivaree*, n.d. [1960?].

13 Barbara W. Tuchman, *A Distant Mirror* (New York: Knopf, 1973), 503.

14 See Susannah Moodie: *Roughing It in the Bush* (London: Richard Bentley, 1852; reprinted Toronto: McClelland and Stewart, 1962), chapter 11.

15 "City News," *The Globe*, 11 October 1864. This item was kindly relayed to me by Dorith Cooper.

16 *Le Charivari*, text accompanying a pen-and-ink illustration by Edmond-Joseph Massicotte (1875–1929), *L'almanach du peuple* (Montreal: Beauchemin, 1928), 351 (trans., J.B.). Again it was Dorith Cooper who brought this to my attention. We reproduced the illustration on the cover of the published libretto of *The Shivaree* (Toronto: self-published, 1982).

17 The date on Geiger-Torel's letter, 2 March 1960, suggests this scenario preceded the *Cereus* stage premiere.

18 The tune, "Blessed Name," is by Ralph E. Hudson (1843–1901). Reaney recalled loaning me a version in one of the gospel publications of Homer A. Rodeheaver, but I may also have encountered it in the *Baptist Hymnal* (Nashville: Convention Press, 1956), no. 140.

19 Richard Bunger, a pianist specializing in new music, organized an "Extended Piano Resources Project" at the California State University, Dominguez Hills, including a "collection of music that features muted piano" (letter, 19 May 1981).

20 "Entertainment" was the word used by John Roberts, the CBC executive who commissioned us. The three segments were written and produced in three consecutive seasons, 1965–67, for budgetary reasons. The full trilogy was broadcast in November 1967.

21 Ken Winters's *Evening Telegram* review praised Reaney's text but panned my score, calling it "background music with ideas beyond its station."

22 James Reaney, *All the Bees and All the Keys* (Erin, ON: Press Porcépic, 1973).

23 Reaney's concept of a Sharon opera eventually became *Serinette*, with libretto by him and music by Harry Somers.

24 It was out of print at the time, but in 1989 Nightwood Editions in London, Ontario, reissued it with an introduction by Reaney.

25 There was a broadcast by CBC Radio, but many listeners found it confusing that each of the voices depicted several characters.

26 Juliet Barker, *The Brontës* (London: Weidenfeld and Nicolson, 1994).

27 James Reaney, "The House by the Churchyard: A Play with Music" (work in progress), *Books in Canada* 17, no. 2 (March 1988): 14–16. The excerpt is illustrated by Greg Curnoe.

28 The text of *Zamorna* was first published in *Reaney Days in the West Room*, an anthology edited by David Ferry (Toronto: Playwrights Canada Press, 2009).

29 Joseph Quesnel, *Lucas et Cécile* (Quebec City: Doberman/Yppan, 1992).

30 My review of this production appeared in *Opera Canada* 48, no. 2 (Summer 1999): 25, 27.

31 The title of this piece was *From Beowulf to Virginia Woolf*.

32 Robert D. Denham and Alvin Lee, eds., *The Legacy of Northrop Frye* (Toronto: University of Toronto Press, 1994), 261–75.

33 At the signal, the original Dutch word indicated, the tavern-keepers would "put the taps to"—that is, close down—the supply of drink.

34 *Love in a Village* was produced at the Glen Morris Theatre in April 1993 and *The Beggar's Opera* at the Bathurst Street Theatre in May 1995, both by the Arbor Oak Trio and associates.

35 I later wrote an account of this aspect of the work in "Musical Quotations in *Taptoo!*" *Sonneck Society Bulletin* 21, no. 3 (Fall 1995): 5–7.

36 Speakers were Eric Domville, John Mayo, Ken Purvis, Robin Elliott, Ramsay Cook, and Cecilia Morgan. Cook's talk has been published: "*Taptoo!* Telling Tales and Making It Up in Canada," *Journal of Canadian Studies* 38, no. 2 (Spring 2004): 172–78. The papers are all available online at http://www.utoronto.ca/mcis/hi/taptoo_papers.htm.

37 I once wrote a short critical piece on this phenomenon for the *Globe and Mail* ("Samurai Warriors? Oh, That Must Be *Macbeth*," 23 November 1993).

NOTES TO CHAPTER 13

1 "Notes on *Jonah*," *Alphabet* 8 (January 1964).

2 See above, p. 86.

3 Re-release, Centrediscs CMC CD 9102.

4 For more details of this bizarre story see Robin Elliott, "Margaret Atwood and Music," *University of Toronto Quarterly* 75, no. 3 (2006): 826–28.

5 "Music in Toronto 64–65," *Canadian Forum* 45, no. 534 (July 1965): 83–85.

6 Northrop Frye, *The Modern Century: The Whidden Lectures, 1967* (Toronto: Oxford University Press, 1967), 122–23.

7 John Kraglund's review appeared beneath a heading five columns wide, "Beckwith's Place of Meeting Fails in Its Purpose," and contained the phrases "mishmash of borrowed tunes" and "essentially characterless" (*Globe and Mail*, 16 November 1967).

8 Istvan Anhalt, *Alternative Voices: Essays on Contemporary Vocal and Choral Composition* (Toronto: University of Toronto Press, 1984), 244–47.

9 The Elmer Iseler Singers was a new chamber choir formed after the collapse of the Festival Singers of Canada in the late 1970s.

10 The text commonly associated with "China" is Watts's funeral hymn "Why Should We Mourn Departed Friends?"

11 Melbourne MSLP 4041 and CBC ACM 26.

12 Abstract vocables also occurred in previous works such as *Sharon Fragments* and *The Sun Dance*, and apparently by this time had become part of my choral-composing vocabulary.

13 "Now welcome, somer" is the first setting in *A Chaucer Suite* (1962).

14 See pp. 161–62.

15 Centrediscs, CMC CD 3790.

16 Review by D. Royce Boyer, *Choral Journal* 34, no. 5 (December 1993): 66–67. Boyer called the work "wildly eclectic." The published score is now distributed by Counterpoint Music Services.

17 "Notes on *Harp of David*," *Canadian University Music Review* 11, no. 2 (1991): 122–35. The published version contains a few small errors, as one of my graduate students pointed out.

18 Melbourne MSLP 4041.

19 In May 1990 at the University of Victoria, I gave a talk, "Canadiana Realizations for 'Music at Sharon,' 1981–9," describing these and other programs in greater detail.

20 Marquis MAR 104.

21 "Tumbling strain" is a term used by the ethnomusicologist Curt Sachs. See his *The Wellsprings of Music*, ed. Jaap Kunst (The Hague: Martinus Nijhoff, 1962), 49–59.

22 There exists a live recording of *Basic Music* from this first performance, but, in view of its unprofessional quality and the excisions, it does not represent the score adequately.

23 Jack Miles, *God: A Biography* (New York: Knopf, 1995), 290ff.

24 In a radio interview with Anhalt, Glenn Gould referred to *Foci*, *La Tourangelle*, and *Winthrop* as "documentaries."

25 In her mid-eighties, she had been mayor continuously since the incorporation of the city; she told me the derailment crisis was her "first real test."

NOTES TO CHAPTER 14

1 Kathleen Lines, compiler, *Lavender's Blue: A Book of Nursery Rhymes* (London: Oxford University Press, 1954).

2 *Ten English Rhymes* (Toronto: Berandol Music, 1964).

3 *Four Love Songs*, CBC SM 111 (nos. 1, 3, 4); CIS ACM 26 (all); Unical UC CD 9101 (all); publication, Berandol. *Five Songs from Canadian Folk Collections*, CBC SM 77 and CIS ACM 26; publication, Waterloo.

4 Excerpts from these two sets: Centrediscs CMC CD 12907. They were published in 2011 by the Avondale Press.

5 See Paul Dutton, "bpNichol and the Past-Present of a Future Music," *Musicworks* 44 (Autumn 1989): 4–16.

6 A recording of this performance exists: Centrediscs CMC CD 9102.

7 Whicher/Ralls: Centrediscs CMC CD 9102 and Marquis 81381. Dunn/Aide: Centrediscs CMC CD 12907.

8 Centrediscs CMC CD 12907.

NOTES TO CHAPTER 15

1 From the poetic caption by Bernard Shaw on M. Pikov's frontispiece portrait in his *Sixteen Self-Sketches* (London: Constable, 1949).

2 *Book of Common Prayer*, 1552.

3 In 2011 the Society was still in existence.

4 See pp. 105ff.

5 See "University Alumnae Dramatic Club" in Eugene Benson and L.W. Conolly, eds., *Oxford Companion to Canadian Theatre* (Toronto: Oxford University Press, 1989).

6 That is, apart from being briefly called back into service in Germany in early 1952.

7 An amateur production of *Waiting for Godot* in Vancouver had preceded Pamela's by only a few months.

8 The ominous headline was "Mr Reaney Writes a Play."

9 The title role was played by Timothy Findley.

10 By contrast, of eleven productions in the 2009 season at the Shaw Festival in Niagara-on-the-Lake, Ontario, seven were directed by women.

11 The Canada Council was inaugurated in 1957, the National Theatre School in 1960.

12 Tom Philbrook died in September 2009.

13 My worried frown from those years is preserved in an oil portrait by Barker Fairley, dated 1974. Fairley, a good friend, was always looking for sitters, for what he called "heads" rather than portraits. My wife and two of the children also sat for him around this time.

14 The program was introduced by the then-premier of Ontario, George Drew.

15 Attributed to the Rev. Cornelius Whur (1782–1853).

16 The newsletter of the Canadian Association of Music Libraries, later renamed the *CAML Review*. Tim McGee had waggishly suggested an alternative name, *CAML Droppings*.

17 Arnold Schoenberg, *Theory of Harmony*, trans. Roy E. Carter (Berkeley: University of California Press, 1978).

18 See p. 78.

19 Brian Vallee, "War Artist Brought 'Order Out of Chaos,'" *Globe and Mail*, 27 July 2002.

20 *Repertoire international de la presse musicale / Retrospective Index to Periodicals in Music*.

21 The doctor commented: "Forse in Canada sono italiani."

22 In essays of 1970, 1981, and 1992; see *Music Papers* (Ottawa: Golden Dog, 1997), 3–8, 90–91, 205–7.

23 See Peter Williams, "Centre Forward: Whither 'Music Studies'?" *Musical Times* 150, no. 1908 (Autumn 2009): 7–15.

24 On the dust jacket of a book he edited: *Sonic Mosaics: Conversations with Composers* (Edmonton: University of Alberta Press, 2009).

Acknowledgements

This written-down story of my life started in the late 1990s with memories and researches about my parents and with an attempt to recall my initial composing adventures—the eventual chapters 1, 2, and 5. Sketches and results of further archival digging were added now and then over the following years. Planning, shaping, and writing were a main occupation during my stay in Paris in the first half of 2009, and the draft manuscript was completed in Toronto that fall. The sequence of chapters is unconventional but seemed to grow as I wrote: family background, childhood, and youth; a short reminiscence of my beginnings in composition; European studies; then, in succession, accounts of my activities as a writer, critic, and researcher, as a teacher and scholar, and as an administrator and musico-political activist; then, chapters outlining my musical output chronologically genre by genre (instrumental music, opera, choral music, music for solo voice); and finally, some notes on my personal and family life.

A few facsimile pages will give a visual impression of various composing ventures. Dan Foley has copied the music examples. Family members, the Faculty of Music Library, the Canadian Music Centre, Rick MacMillan of SOCAN, and others have helped me locate appropriate illustration materials.

With the written text, I have had assistance and advice from many quarters—family, friends, and friends of friends. Musical friends—William Aide, Robin Elliott, Vivienne Spiteri—as well as my daughter Robin and my sisters Sheila Gould and Jean Vantreight have all read portions and offered criticisms and corrections. Judith Williams, a professional editor, and two professional writers, Jay Macpherson and David Helwig, have kindly read the complete manuscript and supplied me with helpful suggestions, as has my son Larry. My life partner Kathleen McMorrow has endured my out-loud readings of several chapters in early versions, read the whole with an especially critical eye, and volunteered her expertise as an indexer.

The publisher's two anonymous peer reviewers gave encouraging assessments and many detailed suggestions. It has been a pleasure to work once again with Lisa Quinn, Rob Kohlmeier, and the other resourceful and devoted staffers of the Wilfrid Laurier University Press. Finally, the publication would not have been possible without generous grants from the SOCAN Foundation and from the University of Toronto's Institute for Canadian Music.

I am enormously grateful to them all. If the book still contains wrong facts and doubtful opinions, the fault is mine, not theirs.

—J.B., Toronto, 2011

Recordings and Scores

The Canadian Music Centre is the principal source for scores and recordings of my works. Most scores are available for loan or purchase, or for perusal in the libraries of Centre locations in Toronto, Montreal, Vancouver, Calgary, and Sackville. Over 150 recorded performances can be listened to on the "Centrestreams" program on the CMC's website (www.musiccentre.ca). In the Centre's catalogue of composers' works, the prefix MI or MV indicates an instrumental or vocal score, CD indicates a commercial recording (not "streamed"), and AR or ND indicates an archival "streamed" recording.

The notes to chapters 5, 10, 11, 12, 13, and 14 of this book give label numbers of recordings. Thirty-nine works, some in multiple performances, were available on commercially released recordings in 2011.

—J.B.

Index

Page numbers in italics indicate illustrations or musical examples.

Books in the Life Writing Series
Published by Wilfrid Laurier University Press

Haven't Any News: Ruby's Letters from the Fifties edited by Edna Staebler with an Afterword by Marlene Kadar • 1995 / x + 165 pp. / ISBN 0-88920-248-6

"I Want to Join Your Club": Letters from Rural Children, 1900–1920 edited by Norah L. Lewis with a Preface by Neil Sutherland • 1996 / xii + 250 pp. (30 b&w photos) / ISBN 0-88920-260-5

And Peace Never Came by Elisabeth M. Raab with Historical Notes by Marlene Kadar • 1996 / x + 196 pp. (12 b&w photos, map) / ISBN 0-88920-281-8

Dear Editor and Friends: Letters from Rural Women of the North-West, 1900–1920 edited by Norah L. Lewis • 1998 / xvi + 166 pp. (20 b&w photos) / ISBN 0-88920-287-7

The Surprise of My Life: An Autobiography by Claire Drainie Taylor with a Foreword by Marlene Kadar • 1998 / xii + 268 pp. (8 colour photos and 92 b&w photos) / ISBN 0-88920-302-4

Memoirs from Away: A New Found Land Girlhood by Helen M. Buss / Margaret Clarke • 1998 / xvi + 153 pp. / ISBN 0-88920-350-4

The Life and Letters of Annie Leake Tuttle: Working for the Best by Marilyn Färdig Whiteley • 1999 / xviii + 150 pp. / ISBN 0-88920-330-x

Marian Engel's Notebooks: "Ah, mon cahier, écoute" edited by Christl Verduyn • 1999 / viii + 576 pp. / ISBN 0-88920-333-4 cloth / ISBN 0-88920-349-0 paper

Be Good Sweet Maid: The Trials of Dorothy Joudrie by Audrey Andrews • 1999 / vi + 276 pp. / ISBN 0-88920-334-2

Working in Women's Archives: Researching Women's Private Literature and Archival Documents edited by Helen M. Buss and Marlene Kadar • 2001 / vi + 120 pp. / ISBN 0-88920-341-5

Repossessing the World: Reading Memoirs by Contemporary Women by Helen M. Buss • 2002 / xxvi + 206 pp. / ISBN 0-88920-408-x cloth / ISBN 0-88920-410-1 paper

Chasing the Comet: A Scottish-Canadian Life by Patricia Koretchuk • 2002 / xx + 244 pp. / ISBN 0-88920-407-1

The Queen of Peace Room by Magie Dominic • 2002 / xii + 115 pp. / ISBN 0-88920-417-9

China Diary: The Life of Mary Austin Endicott by Shirley Jane Endicott • 2002 / xvi + 251 pp. / ISBN 0-88920-412-8

The Curtain: Witness and Memory in Wartime Holland by Henry G. Schogt • 2003 / xii + 132 pp. / ISBN 0-88920-396-2

Teaching Places by Audrey J. Whitson • 2003 / xiii + 178 pp. / ISBN 0-88920-425-X

Through the Hitler Line by Laurence F. Wilmot, M.C. • 2003 / xvi + 152 pp. / ISBN 0-88920-448-9

Where I Come From by Vijay Agnew • 2003 / xiv + 298 pp. / ISBN 0-88920-414-4

The Water Lily Pond by Han Z. Li • 2004 / x + 254 pp. / ISBN 0-88920-431-4

The Life Writings of Mary Baker McQuesten: Victorian Matriarch edited by Mary J. Anderson • 2004 / xxii + 338 pp. / ISBN 0-88920-437-3

Seven Eggs Today: The Diaries of Mary Armstrong, 1859 and 1869 edited by Jackson W. Armstrong • 2004 / xvi + 228 pp. / ISBN 0-88920-440-3

Love and War in London: A Woman's Diary 1939–1942 by Olivia Cockett; edited by Robert W. Malcolmson • 2005 / xvi + 208 pp. / ISBN 0-88920-458-6

Incorrigible by Velma Demerson • 2004 / vi + 178 pp. / ISBN 0-88920-444-6

Auto/biography in Canada: Critical Directions edited by Julie Rak • 2005 / viii + 264 pp. / ISBN 0-88920-478-0

Tracing the Autobiographical edited by Marlene Kadar, Linda Warley, Jeanne Perreault, and Susanna Egan • 2005 / viii + 280 pp. / ISBN 0-88920-476-4

Must Write: Edna Staebler's Diaries edited by Christl Verduyn • 2005 / viii + 304 pp. / ISBN 0-88920-481-0

Food That Really Schmecks by Edna Staebler • 2007 / xxiv + 334 pp. / ISBN 978-0-88920-521-5

163256: A Memoir of Resistance by Michael Englishman • 2007 / xvi + 112 pp. (14 b&w photos) / ISBN 978-1-55458-009-5

The Wartime Letters of Leslie and Cecil Frost, 1915–1919 edited by R.B. Fleming • 2007 / xxxvi + 384 pp. (49 b&w photos, 5 maps) / ISBN 978-1-55458-000-2

Johanna Krause Twice Persecuted: Surviving in Nazi Germany and Communist East Germany by Carolyn Gammon and Christiane Hemker • 2007 / x + 170 pp. (58 b&w photos, 2 maps) / ISBN 978-1-55458-006-4

Watermelon Syrup: A Novel by Annie Jacobsen with Jane Finlay-Young and Di Brandt • 2007 / x + 268 pp. / ISBN 978-1-55458-005-7

Broad Is the Way: Stories from Mayerthorpe by Margaret Norquay • 2008 / x + 106 pp. (6 b&w photos) / ISBN 978-1-55458-020-0

Becoming My Mother's Daughter: A Story of Survival and Renewal by Erika Gottlieb • 2008 / x + 178 pp. (36 b&w illus., 17 colour) / ISBN 978-1-55458-030-9

Leaving Fundamentalism: Personal Stories edited by G. Elijah Dann • 2008 / xii + 234 pp. / ISBN 978-1-55458-026-2

Bearing Witness: Living with Ovarian Cancer edited by Kathryn Carter and Lauri Elit • 2009 / viii + 94 pp. / ISBN 978-1-55458-055-2

Dead Woman Pickney: A Memoir of Childhood in Jamaica by Yvonne Shorter Brown • 2010 / viii + 202 pp. / ISBN 978-1-55458-189-4

I Have a Story to Tell You by Seemah C. Berson • 2010 / xx + 288 pp. (24 b&w photos) / ISBN 978-1-55458-219-8

We All Giggled: A Bourgeois Family Memoir by Thomas O. Hueglin • 2010 / xiv + 232 pp. (20 b&w photos) / ISBN 978-1-55458-262-4

Just a Larger Family: Letters of Marie Williamson from the Canadian Home Front, 1940–1944 edited by Mary F. Williamson and Tom Sharp • 2011 / xxiv + 378 pp. (16 b&w photos) / ISBN 978-1-55458-323-2

Burdens of Proof: Faith, Doubt, and Identity in Autobiography by Susanna Egan • 2011 / x + 200 pp. / ISBN 978-1-55458-333-1

Accident of Fate: A Personal Account 1938–1945 by Imre Rochlitz with Joseph Rochlitz • 2011 / xiv + 226 pp. (50 b&w photos, 5 maps) / ISBN 978-1-55458-267-9

The Green Sofa by Natascha Würzbach, translated by Raleigh Whitinger • 2012 / xiv + 240 pp. (8 b&w photos) / ISBN 978-1-55458-334-8

Unheard Of: Memoirs of a Canadian Composer by John Beckwith • 2012 / x + 391 pp. (74 illus., 8 musical examples) / ISBN 978-1-55458-358-4

Borrowed Tongues: Life Writing, Migration, and Translation by Eva C. Karpinski • forthcoming 2012 / 260 pp. / ISBN 978-1-55458-357-7

Basements and Attics, Closets and Cyberspace: Explorations in Canadian Women's Archives edited by Linda M. Morra and Jessica Schagerl • forthcoming 2012 / 355 pp. / ISBN 978-1-55458-632-5

Not the Whole Story: Challenging the Single Mother Narrative edited by Lea Caragata and Judit Alcalde • forthcoming 2012 / 176 pp. / ISBN 978-1-55458-624-0